John & Louise —

A solid paperweight!
why I had to study so
(to write chapter 22!) Thanks for the
inspiration and history lessons when we visit!
Happy Reading! (I haven't even read this yet —
but wanted you to at least
~~have~~ a copy ♥)

Much Love,
Erica

POWER UP

POWER UP

Leadership, Character, and Conflict Beyond
the Superhero Multiverse

Edited by

STEVEN LEONARD, JONATHAN KLUG,
KELSEY CIPOLLA AND JON NICCUM

CASEMATE
Philadelphia & Oxford

Published in the United States of America and Great Britain in 2023 by
CASEMATE PUBLISHERS
1950 Lawrence Road, Havertown, PA 19083, USA
and
The Old Music Hall, 106–108 Cowley Road, Oxford OX4 1JE, UK

Copyright 2023 © Casemate Publishers

Hardback Edition: ISBN 978-1-63624-339-9
Digital Edition: ISBN 978-1-63624-340-5

A CIP record for this book is available from the British Library

Printed and bound in the United Kingdom by CPI Group (UK) Ltd, Croydon, CR0 4YY.

Typeset in India by Lapiz Digital Services, Chennai.

For a complete list of Casemate titles, please contact:

CASEMATE PUBLISHERS (US)
Telephone (610) 853-9131
Fax (610) 853-9146
Email: casemate@casematepublishers.com
www.casematepublishers.com

CASEMATE PUBLISHERS (UK)
Telephone (0)1226 734350
Email: casemate-uk@casematepublishers.co.uk
www.casematepublishers.co.uk

Contents

Foreword   viii
    Jon Niccum
Introduction   x

PART I: GREAT RESPONSIBILITY

1	Boys Will Be Boys *Kayla Hodges*	3
2	Call it, Captain *Cory S. Hollon*	11
3	The Rise of a Reluctant Leader *Mick Ryan*	19
4	The Unexpected Hero *Kari McEwen*	27
5	The Command of Masks *Ronald J. Granieri*	35
6	Ethical Excellence Through Decisive Dimness *Jeff Drake*	41

PART II: AVENGERS ASSEMBLE!

7	Blood in the Inkwell *Geoff Harkness*	49
8	We Could Be (Super)Heroes *Heather S. Gregg*	56
9	When Being a Superhero Ain't So Super *Mathew Klickstein*	65
10	Lumberjanes and Team Building the Hardcore Lady-Type Way *Julie M. Still*	73
11	There Was an Idea *Amelia Cohen-Levy*	81

12   The Ordinary, Everyday Superhero   88
Mike Burke

PART III: GREEN LANTERN'S LIGHT!

13   The River of Truth   99
Matt Lancaster

14   They Only Lack the Light to Show the Way   107
Eric Muirhead

15   Could the Sokovia Accords Save the (Real) World?   115
Theresa Hitchens

16   A Fitting End for His Kind   121
Jo Brick

17   Injustice for All   129
James Groves

18   It's Not Just Black and White   136
Alyssa Jones

19   Black Vibranium in the Hour of Chaos   143
Aaron Rahsaan Thomas

PART IV: IT'S CLOBBERIN' TIME!

20   Who Runs the World? Squirrels!   151
Kelsey Cipolla

21   Your Cape and Cowl, Mr. Bond?   158
Mitch Brian

22   Trick or Deceit   165
Erica Iverson

23   Unbeatable   173
Dan Ward

24   The Veidt Method   179
Ian Boley

PART V: TO THE BATCAVE!

25   I've Come to Save the World   189
Kera Rolsen

26   Your Ancestors Called It Magic, But You Call It Science   196
Jonathan Klug

27   Where Does He Get All Those Wonderful Toys?   203
Candice E. Frost

28   To the Warrior, Their Arms   211
      Mick Cook
29   We Need to Be Put in Check   219
      Clara Engle

PART VI: KNEEL BEFORE ZOD!

30   The Caped Crusader and the Road to Radicalism   229
      Max Brooks
31   Where Monsters Dwell   234
      Steven Leonard
32   Marvel Zombies   241
      Jon Niccum
33   Strip Mining the Superhero Archetype   249
      Janeen Webb
34   The New Gods   257
      Patrick Sullivan
35   ХАЙЛЬ ГИДРА!   265
      Joshua C. Huminski

Contributors   273
Index   283

Foreword

Jon Niccum

We are all living in a shared universe.

Whether Marvel or DC, Dark Horse or Image, the heroes (and villains) spawned from the pages of comic books now represent a unifying pop-culture force across the globe. In many respects, this has mutated into modern society's version of epic mythology, with swords and shields replaced by repulsor rays and robotic arms. To future generations, our costumed champions will no doubt be as renowned as the Pantheon of Greek Gods or Knights of the Round Table.

Yet these icons aren't merely muscle-bound do-gooders garbed in garish spandex. They also exemplify a collection of multifaceted personalities whose motivations often prove much deeper than surface heroism. In addition to upholding the time-honored ideals of "truth, justice, and a better tomorrow," they tackle hot-button topics ranging from racism and bigotry to substance abuse and sexism. Their ambitious stories refuse to retreat from the defining issues of our time, while repeatedly providing a soapbox for embracing social change.

Haymaker punches and heat vision yield a certain impact, but ideas make an even bigger impression.

The last few decades have expanded the reach of superheroes, further popularizing these already pervasive characters in ways previously unthinkable. Movies, television, and streaming shows are dominated by caped crusaders. Seemingly every teenager in the world knows billionaire Tony Stark is Iron Man; every grandparent knows the Joker's hair is green.

But ... why?

Why the surge in recognition? In acceptance? In dignity?

Perspective!

Comic books were originally considered lowbrow pablum. They were disposable time wasters. Kids' stuff. Trash. (In the 1950s, they actually suffered accusations of being primers for juvenile delinquency—but that's another story.)

Slowly, that changed. But it wasn't necessarily because comics changed; it was due to how society's view of their audience did.

An annoying-yet-somewhat fitting generalization was comic books got read by nerds. While these outsiders were invariably versed in obscure rock albums, horror films, computer tech, *Star Trek* conventions, and/or collectible toys, they sure loved their superheroes. Nerds answered questions with algebraic precision of whether Wonder Woman could lift Thor's hammer or the Flash ran faster than Quicksilver.

Sometime during the internet era, it was the nerds, geeks, and dorks who gained respectability. Mainstream success, even. It became OK for everyone to like the colorful creations born of comics.

These same individuals were responsible for developing the technology to make their favorite characters come to life. The shots of Superman "flying" in a 1950s black-and-white serial did not seem convincing. When Spider-Man shot "webs" on a primetime series of the 1970s, it looked, well … stupid.

A $200 million blockbuster of Dr. Strange battling foes in a mirror universe when viewed on an IMAX screen does not.

Now the collision of nerd culture and mainstream entertainment are virtually interchangeable. Superheroes aren't going away. They're not retreating back to the underground. They aren't relegated to a cardboard box in the basement of your parents' house. These fearless defenders are as crucial to the medium as talking pictures and digital sound.

So are their beliefs.

As experienced through microscopic realms or celestial reaches, the challenges our heroes confront prove legitimately significant in today's world. Philosophy, ethics, morality, accountability, and all things relating to the human condition are reflected in the works of these "metahumans."

Their universe is always expanding. And we are along for the ride.

Introduction

In July 2017, seated before a sold-out crowd at Royce Hall on the UCLA campus, the legendary Stan Lee regaled the audience with a superhero story of his own. Tasked by his publisher with creating a new hero for Marvel Comics in the early summer of 1962, Lee told the assembled faithful how he was inspired by a solitary fly crawling on a nearby wall. "Hey, if I can get a superhero that could stick to walls and crawl on them, man, that would be cool," he said. "But now I needed a name. Let's see. Fly man, mosquito man … I got down to Spider-Man."

Lowering his voice to a deep baritone range, Lee continued: "Spider-Man. It just sounded dramatic." Unlike the superheroes of the time, Lee cast his hero as a teenager. He gave his new hero personal problems. A lot of them. Then he ran into his publisher's office to share the news. "Stan, that is the worst idea I have ever heard," his publisher told him. People hate spiders. Teenagers can only be sidekicks. Superheroes do not have personal problems.

Undaunted, Lee put his new hero on the cover of the final issue of *Amazing Adult Fantasy*—shortened to *Amazing Fantasy* for its grand finale—and introduced young Peter Parker to the world. When the sales figures came in a month later, Lee's publisher raced into his office. "Stan! Stan! You remember that character we both loved so much, Spider-Man? Let's do him as a series."

Lee's message that day was one of personal faith, perseverance, and determination. He told the crowd, "If you have an idea that you genuinely think is good, don't let some idiot talk you out of it." Lee believed deeply in the heroes he was creating. There was something very special happening in Marvel Comics during those tumultuous early years, and the characters spawned by the creative trio of Stan Lee, Steve Ditko, and Jack Kirby have endured through the decades since. Beloved across generations of fans, they evolved to become the driving force behind the reawakening of the superhero genre. Individual characters such as Iron Man, the Incredible Hulk, the Mighty Thor, Ant-Man (or, occasionally, Giant Man), the Vision, and the Scarlet Witch. Incredible teams like the Fantastic Four, the X-Men, and the Avengers. And, of course, everyone's favorite friendly neighborhood web-head, the Amazing Spider-Man.

But it all began with an idea.

Just as that simple fly inspired Stan Lee in a way that fundamentally redefined the superhero genre, that idea—and the genre it awoke—is the super soldier serum empowering *Power Up*. Sixty years after Spider-Man graced the cover of *Amazing Fantasy* #15, superheroes are an integral part of our daily lives. Iron Man taught us that even a fatally flawed human being can overcome their own demons to make a difference in our world. Captain America gave us hope that values and character still matter. Batman reminded us that vengeance never sleeps. Spawn forced us all to look in the mirror and face the choices we make in life. And Thor, well … he showed us that gods are imperfect beings, after all.

Superheroes have inspired us. They have motivated us. They have captivated us. Along the way, they have served as role models, exemplars, and ideals. They have crossed racial, ethnic, and gender boundaries with impunity. They've taken us to other worlds, other galaxies, and other universes. With a spark of imagination, they have allowed us to dream about the great possibilities in life, to ponder what might have been had we been gifted with great power. And through it all, Stan Lee reminds us that with great power must also come great responsibility.

Today, the superhero genre reimagined by Lee is a form of modern mythology, a literary exploration of the nature of humanity and its place in the world we know. Like the mythology of antiquity, the genre is home to myriad metaphors that help us to learn, grow, and evolve. *Power Up* draws on the genre as inspiration to explore contemporary challenges in leadership, strategy and conflict, while focusing on the role of humanity and our interactions with one another, technology, and ourselves.

By using the superhero genre to draw out and examine modern-day lessons, *Power Up* will be an entertaining and valuable learning resource. The stories we grew up with—the tales that leapt from the pages of our comic books—provide a familiar, shared context that allow authors and readers alike to explore deeper issues within familiar settings. Established franchises such as *The Avengers* and *Captain America* are relatable and allow for a thorough exploration of leadership, strategy, and conflict. Characters such as Black Panther, Iceman, and Ms. Marvel present opportunities to delve into important societal issues. And long-running comics like *Batman* and the *Fantastic Four* have always served as a proving ground for new—and imagined—technology.

Power Up is divided into six thematic sections to explore related concepts and ideas, focusing deeply on what the superhero genre can teach us about leadership, strategy, conflict, and humanity. In true comic book fashion, each section of the book explodes from the pages with a barnstorming bullpen of brilliant writers, scintillating stories sure to surprise, and titanic topics to tantalize the mind. Rapacious readers will revel in a realm of magic and mayhem, experiencing exciting adventures in an epic superhero extravaganza. Like the comics of our youth, the authors engage their subjects with the grit and determination of Luke Cage, the strength and tenacity of Wonder Woman, and, in some cases, the unpredictable and irascible wit of Deadpool.

Part I: Great Responsibility examines the mantle of leadership: the burdens of responsibility, the consequences of decision making, and the art of leading others. In "Boys Will Be Boys," Kayla Hodges leaps into action to tackle the ethical challenges of power and leadership, viewed through the lens of the Netflix series, *The Boys.* Cory Hollon assembles the Avengers with "Call It, Captain," drawing on the military concept of mission command to address how we lead in challenging situations. Bestselling author and perennial media pundit Mick Ryan draws on the HBO series *Peacemaker* in his chapter, "The Rise of the Reluctant Leader," to show us how adversity forges the best of our leaders. In "The Unexpected Hero," Kari McEwen shines a beacon of light on the trusted sidekicks that support some of our greatest heroes, from Bruce Wayne to Winston Churchill. Next, Ronald Granieri's chapter, "The Command of Masks," offers a revealing take on secret identities and the public responsibilities of leadership. Finally, author Jeff Drake slips to the satirical side with The Tick to explore the intersection of intelligence and ethics in his chapter, "Ethical Excellence Through Decisive Dimness."

Part II: Avengers Assemble! steps into the world of high-performing teams and the art and inspiration behind their creation. Geoff Harkness stabs at the heart of superhero team building with "Blood in the Inkwell," using the comics of the rock band Kiss as a narrative metaphor. In "We Could be (Super)Heroes," Heather Gregg traverses the space continuum to *The Hunger Games* universe to explore the foundations of building an effective resistance movement. Author and ComicCon staple Mathew Klicktein journeys across the nine realms to lay bare the hidden secrets of team building in his chapter, "Why Being a Superhero Ain't So Super." In "Lumberjanes and Team Building the Hardcore Lady-Type Way," Julie Still hoists her literary axe to take a hearty swing at the role of gender in forming high-performing teams. Amelia Cohen-Levy declassifies the stunning secrets behind the Avengers Initiative to explore the art that underpins team building in her chapter, "There Was an Idea." Finally, Mike Burke closes this section with his chapter, "The Everyday, Ordinary Superhero," a study in the relatability of superheroes who really aren't all that much different from the rest of us.

Part III: Green Lantern's Light! illuminates topics of character, values, ethics, and diversity in leadership. Matt Lancaster takes a perilous plunge into the "River of Truth," an examination of character and values viewed through the lens of *Captain America: Civil War.* Eric Muirhead explodes from the corner phone booth with "They Only Lack the Light to Show the Way," a study of transformational leadership drawing on Christopher Reeve's portrayal of Superman. Theresa Hitchens returns triumphantly to the events of *Captain America: Civil War,* asking, "Could the Sokovia Accords Save the (Real) World?" Emerging ominously from the shadows of the Gotham City underworld, Jo Brick examines the nexus among law, ethics, and vigilantism in her chapter, "A Fitting End for His Kind." Jimmy Groves reaches into Earth's distant past in "Injustice for All," where he queries Thucydides on the parallel downfalls of the Justice League and the Delian League. In her chapter, "It's Not Just Black and White," Alyssa Jones returns readers to the Red Room for a revealing review of Natasha Romanoff's redemptive journey of superhero-ism. Finally, screenwriter and producer Aaron Rahsaan Thomas closes with an explosive exploration of the limitations of character with "Black Vibranium in the Hour of Chaos."

Part IV: It's Clobberin' Time! charges headlong into strategy, competition, and conflict. Kelsey Cipolla opens the section with a unique perspective on conflict resolution, peering through the furry lens of *The Unbeatable Squirrel Girl* with "Who Runs the World? Squirrels! In his chapter, "Your Cape and Cowl, Mr. Bond?" filmmaker and educator extraordinaire Mitch Brian examines the evolution of 007 from lone wolf agent of chaos to charismatic leader, drawing parallels with the *Batman* film franchise. Erica Iverson regales readers with a rare feat of literary sleight of hand in "Trick or Deceit," her exploration of deception as a tool of warfare. Dan Ward returns the faithful once again to the world of *The Unbeatable Squirrel Girl* in his exploration of how conflict can be channeled through effective alliance building. Finally, Ian Boley offers a compelling glimpse into the strategy of nuclear deterrence, cleverly drawing comparisons to Ozymandias' character from *The Watchmen*.

Part V: To the Batcave! plunges into the complex relationship between humanity and science, technology, and innovation. The first offering, Kera Rolsen's "I've Come to Save the World," tears a page from the epic tale of Ultron, examining the fundamental necessity of a human heart in artificial intelligence. Jonathan Klug opens a portal to the Sanctum Sanctorum in "Your Ancestors Called It Magic, But You Call It Science," where he lays bare the challenges of cyberwarfare. Returning to *The Hunger Games*, Candice Frost's "Where Does He Get All Those Wonderful Toys?" describes how the film trilogy serves as a fitting metaphor for technological innovation. Mick Cook channels his inner Obadiah Stane in "To the Warrior, Their Arms," focusing on the militarization of research and development, drawing on the *Iron Man* films for inspiration. Finally, Clara Engle's chapter, "We Need to Be Put in Check," journeys between the worlds of S.H.I.E.L.D. and *The Boys* to explain why new and often dangerously advanced technology must be effectively regulated by responsible and forward-thinking governments.

The final section, *Part VI: Kneel before Zod!* assesses the alluring and often captivating connection between monsters, villains, and redemption. In "The Caped Crusader and the Road to Radicalism," *New York Times* bestselling author Max Brooks blazes a trail to our not-so-distant future with Frank Miller's *The Dark Knight Returns* for a necessary lesson on the dangers of radicalization. Steven Leonard wades into the swamps of Citrusville with the Man-Thing for an eye-opening examination of redemption and rebirth in his chapter, "Where Monsters Dwell." Journalist and educator Jon Niccum takes readers deep into the dark depths of depravity with

"Marvel Zombies," a chilling chapter that explores how monsters allow us to confront issues of morality. In her chapter, "Strip Mining the Superhero Archetype," author Janeen Webb peels back the layers of our favorite comic book villains to better understand their complex motivations. Patrick Sullivan fearlessly ventures into the mysterious mind of comic legend Jack "King" Kirby to draw leadership lessons from one of his darker creations, *The New Gods*. In the final entry of this section, Joshua Huminski's "ХАЙЛЬ ГИДРА!" traces HYDRA's torment and conditioning of the Winter Soldier in a disturbing exploration of the Russian intelligence apparatus of the Cold War.

Until his death in 2018, Stan Lee continued to encourage and inspire the imaginative spirits among us. Throughout his life, he created relatable heroes, characters who shared our problems, our phobias, our challenges in life. They had special abilities and powers but were more like us than not. They were human, even when they were not. And none were more human than Lee, whose own superpower will continue to entertain us long after his memory fades. But perhaps his greatest legacy will be the words with which he closed *Amazing Fantasy* #15, his admonition about great power and great responsibility. In the spirit of Stan Lee, the thirty-five chapters that comprise *Power Up* are presented to encourage and inspire the reader to celebrate the explosion of creativity and imagination that each author brings to this book. We hope to provide an entertaining experience that helps to better understand our world and provide beneficial insight into our leaders, strategies, conflicts, and ourselves.

Excelsior!!

PART I

GREAT RESPONSIBILITY

"And a lean, silent figure slowly fades into the gathering darkness, aware at last that in this world, with great power there must also come—great responsibility!!"

—*AMAZING FANTASY* #15 (1962)

CHAPTER I

Boys Will Be Boys

Culture, Corruption, and Compound V

Kayla Hodges

"With great power comes the absolute certainty that you'll turn into a right @#$%."
—BILLY BUTCHER[1]

The Boys' Vought International represents a juxtaposition of the noble and courageous ideals we love—and the abhorrent, crooked behavior we hate. The multibillion-dollar corporation projects a public image of honor, service, and integrity centered around an elite team of all-American celebrity "supes." Known as The Seven, their mission is to save lives, protect freedom, and make the world a safer place.

But let's be honest—in reality, Vought's depravity has no bounds in pursuit of its role as America's indispensable savior. Blackmail, fraud, malfeasance, and murder are all instruments used in the pharmaceutical conglomerate's methodical manipulation of The Seven and the American public. The world has been told supes are born with their powers, but in actuality, Vought has been secretly injecting infants with Compound V—the experimental supe-making drug—for decades. Because of the deliberate disconnect between Vought's espoused values and actual values, Vought International evolves to represent a villain *we love to hate*. So much so, we don't really know whether to be disgusted or slow clap when Hughie explodes the seemingly invincible Translucent—a well-respected supe yet secret sexual predator—with an ass bomb.

When we consider the traditional superhero story, it's often occupied by optimistic portrayals of how heroes with great power behave greatly. In reality, this isn't necessarily an accurate representation of how fundamentally flawed beings engage with unrestricted power. Classic superhero characters like Wonder Woman or Captain America may experience moments of internal conflict, but they're ultimately depicted as beacons of light guiding us through an imperfect world. The plot may twist, and the characters may make mistakes or poor decisions, but fundamentally, *superheroes do what is right because they represent the best of us.*

Conversely, *The Boys* bursts this bubble by fashioning a complex landscape of characters who are not only flawed, but also plagued by vices in the worst ways. They're killers, addicts, cynics, and narcissists. The superheroes and those that control them are the true villains, and the fugitive "villain" vigilantes are the true heroes … sort of. It's crass. It's grisly. It's a devilishly dark-humored depiction of reality that seems more like a Quentin Tarantino film than a superhero series.

It may feel like a step into *The Twilight Zone*, or some sort of Bizarro world portrayal of the Avengers vs Thanos, but the truth is, *The Boys* may actually be a more realistic depiction of a world filled with supes than we'd like to acknowledge. Part of *The Boys'* notoriety comes from how "extreme" it is. But we should ask ourselves, isn't this closer to what we actually experience in everyday life? Aren't our real-life leaders and "heroes" just as human and susceptible to vices as the rest of us?

The Boys allows us to explore the depravity of humanity through the lens of unbridled power. Art imitates life—and similarly, literature provides an opportunity to examine the intricacies of the human condition and learn powerful lessons without being forced to contend with the consequences.

In each episode, *The Boys* confronts us with provocative portrayals of the interplay between unethical behavior and great power in the context of an outwardly reputable, influential organization. How does the routine abuse of power impact organizational culture and individual behavior? And ultimately, what should people do about it? It's certainly a glimpse into a dark, twisted mirror of the human condition, but maybe it's the one that we need to see.

The Dog and Pony Show

Within large organizations, the human element creates opportunities for unethical behavior. Given enough time, unethical conduct can even become incentivized for the sake of organizational or individual "success."

Vought claims it is in the business of saving lives and making the world a better place. In reality, it's a corrupt pharmaceutical company that manufactures and peddles commercialized superheroes while fixated on profits and its carefully curated public image. We've seen Vought executives cover up Homelander's murdering sprees; we watched Stan Edgar blatantly lie in a press release after Compound V was leaked to the media. We observed Madelyn Stilwell use blackmail to bully members of the U.S. Congress into militarizing The Seven. Public perception became the second-highest metric of success at Vought, only surpassed by profit.

This obsession with public perception and social media is a direct consequence of Vought leaders' tolerance of unethical conduct as acceptable behavior. Institutionally, Vought decides that perception is more important than reality. Do what it takes—whatever it takes—to meet corporate objectives. And if you can't actually meet those goals, *make it look like you are.*

Starlight experienced this nearly immediately upon induction into The Seven. She rescued a girl in a dark alley who was about to be raped, but it didn't matter. It didn't matter that Starlight attacked the perpetrators in an effort to protect the victim. It didn't matter that victim was spared and was able to escape unharmed. All that mattered is that someone had filmed Starlight physically assaulting two men in an alley and *it looked bad.* Ashley Barrett and Madelyn Stilwell, Starlight's bosses, quickly made it clear that media coverage and poll ratings take precedence over truth.

Ultimately, this fundamentally paradoxical relationship between what the company claims to be and what the company actually is represents institutionalized dishonesty. Because Vought tolerates and encourages unethical behavior that is universally unacceptable, Vought *must* publicly portray a false representation of itself.

When there's an obsession with perfection and perception, any question that implies the organization isn't performing optimally or ethically jeopardizes the methodically constructed public image. Consequently, such an institutional culture is often intensely adversarial to change, nonconformity, or questioning the status quo. Reform is nearly impossible when the existing culture and leaders refuse to entertain it. To do so would be to admit they are somehow less than their perfect public image.

While we already recognize the truth is dangerous to a corrupt corporation like Vought, the truth is also dangerous to the individual employee. Vought fostered a toxic environment where individuals were bullied into compliance with illegal and unethical conduct. Simultaneously, Vought employees were also pressured to accept the risk that they may be held personally responsible or scapegoated for that unethical conduct. This dynamic is quite convenient for Vought because it ensures employees are personally motivated to keep company secrets due to fear of reprisal and external repercussions. Unfortunately, the individual's decision to protect themselves reinforces this culture, which then validates the company's theory that success is achievable through unethical conduct.

Individuals within companies that operate in this manner personally watch this dishonesty and corruption unfold before their eyes, and the impact is cancerous. Though individual experiences vary, a corporate culture like this is a meat grinder: It chews people up and spits them out. Employees don't have intrinsic value as humans—your value is in how you contribute toward the company's metrics and image. Trust between the organization and the employee erodes; if the company is willing to be publicly dishonest with the press and the government, then what's stopping internal dishonesty toward employees? Nothing.

This atmosphere is absolutely suffocating: Employees walk on eggshells, live in fear, and become vulnerable to coercion. When people are consistently pressured into doing things that are objectively wrong, and they succumb to that pressure, it rots them from the inside out as they begin to live a lie.

Maeve reflects on this in a conversation with Starlight, explaining that she used to be *just like Starlight*: 23 years old, bright-eyed, ready to save the world. Maeve admits, "I really did want to make a difference. I really did care. I was just like you. And then, I started giving pieces of myself away and ... I guess I gave away everything."[2] Maeve had gradually compromised her personal values until she backed herself into an ethical corner: She was trapped between the trauma of her past sins and the inevitability of her future sins, slowly deteriorating into a shell of her former self.

Ultimately, systemically unethical organizations leave people in a problematic position: Do you choose to die a hero, or do you live long enough to see yourself become the villain?

Lying to Ourselves

Ethical fading and rampant rationalizations have allowed leaders to espouse lofty professional values while slogging through the mire of dishonesty and deceit. The end result is a corrosive ethical culture that few acknowledge and even fewer discuss or work to correct.[3]

Perhaps what makes *The Boys* so appealing has something to do with the relatability of the challenges characters encounter. We're living in a time when social media, quotas, checked blocks, and perception often seem to matter more than reality. Companies and individuals can discover fame or get canceled at the whim of a tweet in the court of public opinion. Yet a fixation on short-term metrics and popular opinion is at odds with communicating nuance and truth about a situation. Does any of this sound familiar?

Ashley Barrett's entire character as the Director of Talent Relations is based upon her obsession with poll ratings and social media. She's a superficial, anxious yes-man who displays complete indifference toward anything of real substance. But Ashley's individual fixation on public image is driven by Vought's executives: Stan Edgar and Madelyn Stilwell. The dishonest, superficial culture promoted by the company's leaders is accepted and perpetuated by the employees. Everyone seems to downplay and trivialize Vought's ethical deficit, but why?

> Ethical fading is a condition in a culture that allows people to act in unethical ways in order to advance their own interests, often at the expense of others, while falsely believing that they have not compromised their own moral principles. Ethical fading often starts with small, seemingly innocuous transgressions that, when left unchecked, continue to grow and compound.[4]

In other words, ethical fading was the instrument by which Maeve chipped away at her personal moral standard throughout her years on The Seven. By convincing herself that within a given situation she didn't *really* do anything wrong, or that she was forced to conform to survive, she managed to relieve her sense of guilt and personal responsibility. But as mentioned before, Maeve got to a point where she "gave away everything," forfeiting her integrity and honor only to later be tormented with intense regret.

Simon Sinek contends the source of ethical fading is "excessive amounts of pressure to hit short-term goals to the point where doing it ethically becomes more and more difficult."[5] Meeting Vought's superficial and unrealistic expectations required dishonesty and unethical behavior from employees. Ethical fading is one of the primary ways in which these behaviors became accepted and even encouraged within the organization. To maintain your own sanity as an employee in this environment, *you must detach yourself from the moral implications of your actions: a self-delusion.*

Telling ourselves "It's what you gotta do to get ahead," "It's what the boss wants," "Everyone's doing it," and "It's the system," are ways we distance ourselves from the impact of our decisions. It can be a slippery slope—you do it once and it works, so you do it a little bit more again and again, and soon you have full-blown ethical fading.[6]

Homelander does it when he uses his laser vision overseas in a rural village to kill a supe terrorist while unknowingly eviscerating a young boy standing behind him. When Ashley later confronts him, Homelander scoffs, "What? They're all starving but one of them happens to have a cell phone?" He then learns he's dropped nine approval points and there have been protestors outside Vought Tower all day, and he snaps, "Don't those ingrates realize I killed that asshole *for* them?! What do they think 'saving America' fucking means anyway?"[7] In other words, Homelander used the intention of protecting America for the "greater good" to disassociate himself from the act of killing the boy.

Do we see this occur in our own companies and institutions? Does the status or reputation of our own organization provide us with an incentive to accept ethically questionable behavior? What about more quantifiable incentives—does the assurance of pay, benefits, or family stability alleviate or assuage the objections we might have about unethical conduct? Or perhaps we simply have reservations about "rocking the boat" or challenging accepted norms because we've seen what happens when people question the status quo?

Sinek maintains that ethical fading almost always starts from the top and is usually a leadership problem. However, it's also not a singular event. It doesn't occur overnight like flipping a switch. It's more like an infection that festers over time.[8]

The bottom line for Vought has always been its share price: A short-term, quantifiable metric very much tied to public opinion. To influence public opinion, Vought leaders applied intense pressure on employees—including The Seven—exercising meticulous control over their individual speech, behavior, and personal image. Vought executives created a corporate culture that set conditions for ethical fading and pressured employees to conform. Subsequently, as enough employees were manipulated into compliance, peer pressure provided another source of affirmation and validation for ethical fading. When everyone else in the company appears to be "successful" complying with these organizational pressures, and non-compliance results in significant negative consequences, ethical fading can become the status quo.

So when we find ourselves in an organization like this, do we just go along to get along? Do we quit and leave? Do we stay and try to make a difference from the inside? While these are valid questions, as leaders, we must inevitably ask ourselves: How dirty are we willing to get to effect change?

Don't You Worry—Daddy's Home

> "See, people love that cozy feeling supes give them … but if they knew half the shit they get up to. Fuckin diabolical. But then, that's where I come in. To spank the bastards when they get out of line."
>
> —BILLY BUTCHER[9]

And now, The Boys: They'll kidnap you, blackmail your girlfriend, snort a line of cocaine, and blow you up with an ass bomb; all in a night's work. The foul-mouthed vigilante fugitives seem to be the only ones truly aware of what the supes at Vought get away with. They're perfectly content with their own moral decay yet motivated to expose a greater evil and burn Vought to the ground. Are The Boys heroes? Not by society's standards, but we still find ourselves cheering for the only ones willing to cover themselves in gore and put everything on the line just for a chance to fight back. The Boys didn't create the game, Vought did, but if you want to win, you *have* to play—at least according to Billy Butcher.

Over the course of the series, we gradually learn The Boys' mission is as much about vengeance as it is about justice. Each member of the vigilante group has experienced traumatic loss at the hands of Vought and the supes, and that reality clearly manifests itself in their approach. Explosives, theft, and the occasional homicide … nothing is off-limits for The Boys—they're criminals. Ironically, these outlaws seemed to be the only ones realistically equipped *and* willing to do what it takes to actually defeat Vought.

While Butcher and the original Boys view illegal, immoral, and unethical activity through the lens of greater good, others draw a line in the sand. Starlight and Hughie both represent goodness and morality as they display genuine restraint and object to unethical behavior. Conversely, the rest of The Seven and The Boys are much more willing to push past ethical boundaries.

We don't live in a perfect world—we all know this. Does that mean sometimes we *have* to break the rules? Or do we stick to the rules and the straight-and-narrow letter of the law and potentially fail to produce real change? And what if the rules are corrupt? When should we abandon ship altogether? According to Starlight: "If you jump ship and you let the assholes steer, you're part of the problem."[10]

As a result, she was forced to live a lie every day, sacrificing her personal ethics for the potential to bring about institutional reform for the sake of an unaware public.

Like Starlight, Maeve also chose to stay in The Seven, but for different reasons. She felt trapped, resigned to her destiny, surrendering to cynicism and hopelessness as she perpetuated the very culture she hates. "It doesn't matter what we do, nothing changes. Nothing ever changes or gets better. And I'm tired," Maeve told Starlight and Hughie when asked for her help.[11]

Part of Maeve's internal conflict had something to do with the struggle between two parts of her identity: one that was a bright-eyed, idealistic supe who cared about saving lives and one that had simply given up after being subjected to controlling, abusive relationships with Homelander and Vought. Maeve had lived long enough to see herself "become the villain" and it was tearing her apart.

Others, like Butcher, try to drive change from the outside, free from constraints. He believes that to bring about meaningful reform, good people sometimes have to do really bad things. If Vought is willing to ignore truth and rule of law by ruthlessly lying and killing to protect their interests, you must be willing to get dirty to take them down. For Butcher, his own ethical suicide is nothing in comparison to the evil of allowing Vought to continue unabated.

Despite the best efforts of Hughie and Starlight to destroy Vought "the right way" it ultimately didn't matter. Compound V was leaked to the press and the world discovered that supes aren't born, they're made in a lab—a shocking scandal. But it didn't matter that Vought's share price tanked, and its reputation was in shambles. Stan Edgar simply lied, claimed plausible deniability, and made a scapegoat out of Homelander's latest murder victim, his boss Madelyn Stillwell. This cycle repeated every time The Boys tried to beat Vought "the right way," disillusioning Hughie and leaving Butcher even more convinced of the need for extreme measures.

Sometimes, trying to effect change within the confines of what's legally and socially acceptable simply doesn't work. And when an organization is characterized by systemic corruption and dishonesty, change from within these confines becomes difficult, if not impossible. At the very least, people trying to effect change from within risk being ostracized and marginalized, and *The Boys* shows us it can become necessary for change to be forced externally.

How Low Will You Go?

The war between Vought and The Boys makes us question how we should go about reforming ethically compromised institutions. What are the appropriate channels individuals should use to seek change? How long should one continue compromising their personal values to perpetuate their existence in an unethical organization? Are we simply lying to ourselves to get by?

Perhaps some might think that if they can *just* manage to stay in the organization long enough to reach a position of leadership, then *they'll* be able to make *real* change. Others feel that staying in an unethical organization compromises their integrity. As a leader, your choices have implications beyond your own life—what about everyone else aboard the ship? Are you going to let the assholes steer or is it time for the Billy Butcher approach?

All of us are eventually forced to reckon with ethical challenges and determine how we should navigate them. Maybe your organization doesn't commit war crimes or blackmail U.S. senators, but perhaps they pencil whip paperwork for an annual report or backdate forms for an audit. Or maybe they knowingly present dishonest information to appease a client or report inaccurate readiness levels prior to a training exercise.

The Boys offers a commentary on ethical fading, the power to do whatever you want, and the behavior of a company that values public image more than truth. At first, our ethical compromises may seem like harmless white lies, but how long until they become something more? In the case of Vought, we eventually see seemingly innocuous dishonesty evolve into letting a plane of innocent people crash into the Atlantic Ocean for the sake of a PR campaign.

Where do you draw the line?

Notes

1   *The Boys*, season 3, episode 5, "The Last Time to Look on This World of Lies," directed by Nelson Cragg aired June 17, 2022, Amazon Prime Video.
2   *The Boys*, season 1, episode 8, "You Found Me," directed by Eric Kripke aired July 26, 2019, Amazon Prime Video.
3   Stephan J. Gerras and Leonard Wong, "Lying to Ourselves: Dishonesty in the Army Profession," *Strategic Studies Institute* (February 1, 2015), 33.
4   Simon Sinek, *The Infinite Game* (New York: Penguin Random House LLC, 2019), 132.
5   Ibid.
6   Ibid.
7   *The Boys*, season 2, episode 5, "We Gotta Go Now," directed by Batan Silva, aired September 18, 2020, Amazon Prime Video.
8   Sinek, 132.
9   *The Boys*, season 1, episode 2, "The Name of the Game," directed by Dan Trachtenberg, aired July 26, 2019, Amazon Prime Video.
10 *The Boys*, season 2, episode 8, "What I Know," directed by Alex Graves, aired October 9, 2020, Amazon Prime Video.
11 Ibid.

CHAPTER 2

Call it, Captain

Mission Command in *The Avengers*

Cory S. Hollon

It is nearly impossible to discuss the command and control of U.S. military units without coming across the phrase "mission command." It is almost as challenging to understand precisely what it is.[1] For example, in a single doctrinal publication, the Joint Force calls mission command a way of conducting a military operation and a philosophy of command and control. It concludes that mission command "emphasizes the human element in joint operations emphasizing trust, force of will, initiative, judgment, and creativity."[2] Leaving aside the exceedingly wretched prose, a reader of joint doctrine can distinguish seven mission command principles: competence, mutual trust, shared understanding, commander's intent, mission-type orders, disciplined initiative, and risk acceptance.

But what does this look like in practice? Confusion reigned within the Army's ranks after the first iteration of doctrine focusing on mission command, and misunderstandings still abound.[3] Fortunately, Captain America gave a perfect example of the employment of mission command elements during the Battle of New York in the 2012 Marvel Studios film, *The Avengers*.

Six superheroes put aside their differences and personal animosity to defeat an overwhelming extraterrestrial invasion. The unlikely squad formed in the span of six-and-a-half movies and faced a threat that none of them could singlehandedly defeat. As Steve Rogers, aka Captain America, noted, they had to work as a team. He transformed a haphazard street brawl with three disparate efforts into a dynamic and flexible operation by issuing mission-type orders. The ensuing battle demonstrated the seven principles of mission command and, most importantly, the importance of establishing a foundation for this leadership style well before a fight.

As the heroes gathered in the shadow of Grand Central Station, the situation appeared grim. Tony Stark, aka Iron Man, had confronted the Asgardian villain Loki, but the opening of an interdimensional portal with the Tesseract allowed Loki's mercenary army of Chitauri to stream into New York City from above. As Stark began attacking the waves of Chitauri on chariots, Rogers, Clint Barton (Hawkeye), and Natasha Romanoff (Black Widow) arrived in a Quinjet and promptly were shot out of the sky. Thor flew into the battle, pleaded with his brother Loki, and then fought his fellow Asgardian prince on the penthouse balcony of Stark Tower. A single Chitauri Leviathan descended into the conflagration, discharging scores of fighters to wreak havoc on the civilian population. While Black Widow and Hawkeye fended off the aliens, Rogers showed that parkour was actually a superpower and directed the New York Police Department to establish a roadblock and begin civilian evacuations. Thor joined Rogers, Barton, and Romanoff on the bridge south of Grand Central Station as Stark continued to distract the Leviathan. Captain America began to outline a plan, but the arrival of Dr. Bruce Banner interrupted him. Iron Man then lured the Leviathan to the group, Banner revealed his "secret," and the Avengers assembled for the first time on the big screen.

Up to that point, the Avengers at the Battle of New York were essentially in triage mode. Stark and the Quinjet crew coordinated for a moment, but the fight went poorly for the heroes because each targeted what they viewed as the priority. Stark went after the invaders, Thor attempted a decapitation strike, and Cap's group tried to protect the innocents in the crossfire. The defense of the city and the planet lacked a coherent effort to neutralize or even mitigate the threat. As two more Leviathans and hundreds of Chitauri poured through the fissure in the sky, Captain America brought order from the chaos with a simple message to the team. He took thirty-five seconds to establish a shared understanding, provide commander's intent, and deliver mission-type orders. It is important to note, though, that the other principles of mission command were equally vital to the successful defense of New York.

The individual Avengers demonstrated their competence to the audience and each other over the fourteen hours and eleven minutes of runtime preceding the battle at Grand Central. Army Doctrine Publication 6-0 asserts that "tactically and technically competent commanders, subordinates, and teams are the basis of effective mission command."[4] Tony Stark developed the Iron Man technology, escaped from Raza, defeated Obadiah Stane, synthesized a new element, and overcame Ivan Vanko. He proved his capability to Thor and Rogers in the fight in the woods and to Banner during the search for the Tesseract. Rogers had taken down Hydra, fought Loki to a draw, and emerged as the leader for the team. Thor proved himself worthy of Mjølnir and vanquished the Destroyer from Earth. Banner and his alter-ego, the Hulk, showed their aptitude for problem-solving and problem-making, respectively, in Brazil, Harlem, and the helicarrier. Romanoff infiltrated Hammer Industries headquarters to remove the command node of Vanko's iron drones, successfully interrogated Loki, survived an attack from the Hulk, and cognitively recalibrated Barton. Hawkeye had a close friendship with her, and his actions while under Loki's control evidenced his formidable skill as a fighter. Most of the team, however, took Romanoff's testimony that he was up for the task because of his recent emancipation from Loki's enslavement and their lack of first-hand knowledge of his experience.

Competence served as a baseline for the mutual trust that the team developed throughout the movie. At the first meeting for the Avengers (minus Hawkeye), Stark gave his grudging respect to "Point Break" because of his prowess during their fight. Stark also found a mutual respect for Banner based on the latter's work on the quantum-tunneling effect and "breathtaking anger management issues." And, obviously, Romanoff and Barton trusted each other dating back to their mission in Budapest despite their very different recollections of the event. Nevertheless, most of *The Avengers* was about resolving the lack of trust between the heroes. As Banner astutely observed just before Barton's attack on the helicarrier: "What are we, a team? No, no, no. We're a chemical mixture that makes chaos. We're a time bomb."[5] To effectively repel the Chitauri attack, the Avengers would have to diffuse the bomb in order to harness and direct the chaos toward their ultimate goal.

The team eventually coalesced, though, and developed trust in each other. Stark and Rogers learned to trust one another during their efforts to restore the damaged motor of the helicarrier and then bonded over the shared loss of Agent Phil Coulson. Their relationship at this point was based more on respect than personal affection, but they overcame the initial tension between their almost diametrically opposed personalities and combat styles. Stark's trust in Rogers became explicit as the entire Avengers squad gathered on the bridge and witnessed the second wave of Chitauri forces emerge from the wormhole. Iron Man acknowledges Captain America's leadership of the team with a simple yet powerful line: "Call it, Captain."

The heroes shared an understanding of the overall mission because of the tribulations they had endured to that point. Units do not usually generate shared understanding in a moment; it develops over time and through dialogue as the various team members iteratively examine, reframe, and reassess a problem. The audience gets a glimpse of this as Stark and Rogers mourned the loss of Coulson. Rogers tried to move Stark past the grief. "Right now, we've got to put that behind us and get this done. Now Loki needs a power source. If we can put together a list ..." Stark interrupted to dramatically reframe the problem as he stared at the blood stain from where Coulson died. The billionaire, genius, playboy, philanthropist realized that Loki's decision to accept capture was purposeful. "He made it personal." After a brief pushback, Cap went along with Stark's analytical exercise. Rogers sensed that Stark was on to something and encouraged the line of reasoning. The two heroes gained insight into the character of their enemy and deduced where Loki was building his portal.

As the situation changed during the battle, the Avengers also gathered and disseminated intelligence to ensure a shared appreciation of the environment.

Immediately after Thor landed on the bridge, Cap asked for a situation update. The original plan of preventing or disrupting the Tesseract seemed unfeasible because of the energy shield surrounding it. Stark confirmed Thor's assessment, and Rogers began to outline a plan for the fight. However, the arrival of Dr. Banner cut his orders short. Again, Rogers immediately shared the information about the new resource for the struggle with the team to maintain a common operating picture.

With competence, mutual trust, and shared understanding established, Cap gave a model commander's intent and mission-type order in an extremely abbreviated form. Doctrinally, mission-type orders consist of a description of the situation, the commander's intent, desired results, and required subordinate tasks. ADP 6-0 states, "mission orders are directives that emphasize to subordinates the results to be attained, not how they are to achieve them."[6] The Air Force adds sustainment and communication to the format but reaffirms the other elements.[7] However, both documents admit that the level of detail in orders and control the commander retains over subordinate units varies based on the situation. Captain America adhered to this format while employing a range of control levels with the group. He first established the operation's overall goal and immediate needs: "Until we can close that portal, our priority is containment." The opening sentence placed the two tasks in relative priority and importance. The ultimate goal was to stop the invasion, but that task was beyond their means at the moment. Instead, the team had to focus on containing the fighting and limiting the damage Loki's army could do to the city and the population. However, if there came a time when the Avengers could close the portal, the priority would shift as disrupting the Tesseract would strike at the source of Loki's power, his center of gravity.

After establishing the priority, Cap started assigning individual tasks to the team members. The first order of business was to maintain situational awareness of the battle. For that, he turned to Clint Barton. "I want you on that roof, eyes on everything, call out patterns and strays." Most importantly, Rogers entrusted Hawkeye with providing situational updates for the team. At first glance, the assignment of a particular location seems contrary to the spirit of mission command in that it dictates (at least partly) how to do a task rather than just assigning it. However, mission command requires the exercise of various levels of control. Because Captain America intended to keep the fighting focused on the area around Grand Central, it made sense for him to position Barton on a building with adequate sight lines to the battle. Mission command is more than setting a goal for subordinates; it requires tailoring the level and style of control to the followers' mission as appropriate.

Rogers then turned to Iron Man. "Stark, you've got the perimeter. Anything gets more than three blocks out, you turn it back or turn it to ash." These orders gave a clear mission, limits, and discretion to the individual responsible for executing it. They also aligned the mission with Iron Man's skills. As one of two Avengers who could fly and the most maneuverable team member, Stark was a unique asset. His firepower and intelligence-gathering skill would have been helpful in various tasks; however, because preventing the Chitauri from escaping into the broader city was the priority, Cap wisely chose Stark to perform this task. Mission command is not just about giving broad outlines of what needs to be done. Leaders have to ensure the units or people they assign to tasks are the best suited for those jobs.

Thor was best suited for slowing down the flow of enemy forces through the wormhole. Rogers told him, "Thor, you gotta try and bottleneck that portal. Slow 'em down. You've got the lightning; light the bastards up." Like with Stark, Cap chose the most effective tool for this particular job. Purists may bridle at the last line because it gave specific instructions on how to proceed, but others may contend it was a brief explanation of why Rogers chose him. Only by harnessing his power over lightning could the God of Thunder create enough destruction at the opening to slow down the invasion.

Rogers then told Romanoff that they would "stay here on the ground, keep the fighting here." He could have gone into detail about how that fit within the overall mission, but because of the initial statement of the commander's intent, such an explanation was unnecessary.

Captain America saved perhaps the best order for last. "And Hulk—smash." Again, Cap aligned the mission with the capabilities of the individual he was tasking. The Hulk was incredible[8] at creating chaos and generally disrupting an enemy's plans. Rather than focusing the brute's aggression on a single target, Rogers released it on the invasion as a whole. The wide latitude Rogers afforded the Hulk resulted in a maximum advantage for the Avengers with minimal complications for the big guy. A more complicated mission might have been beyond the comprehension of the enormous green rage monster. Rogers had seen the destruction the Hulk could wreak, but there was no indication that Banner's alter-ego could understand, much less follow detailed directions and longer-term timelines. So, Cap decided to use the raw strength and fury of the Hulk to throw the enemy forces off balance.

During the Battle of New York, the Avengers each displayed disciplined initiative and appropriate risk acceptance to accomplish the mission. As Hulk started making a mess and Thor paralyzed two Leviathans at the portal entrance, the scene shifted to Barton telling Stark, "[The Chitauri] can't bank worth a damn. Find a tight corner." Not only had Hawkeye called out the strays pursuing Iron Man, but he also provided valuable vulnerability analysis based on his observation. Stark quickly leveraged this knowledge and eliminated several of his pursuers.

As a Leviathan menacingly approached an office building, civilians nervously watched from the windows. A collision seemed imminent, but the Hulk tore through the workplace, leapt out the window, and turned the giant slug away from the bystanders. With the Chitauri everywhere in the vicinity, Hulk passed up several relatively easy targets to attack the larger flying armored troop carrier; however, he demonstrated the disciplined initiative critical to mission command. Informed by the commander's intent and mutual understanding of the situation, disciplined initiative is "the proactive application of inventiveness and creativity when existing orders no longer fit the situation or when unforeseen threats or opportunities arise."[9] For the Hulk, the benefits of charging through the office to prevent a larger disaster outweighed the cost of skipping out on smaller targets. Additionally, his actions furthered Captain America's intent of containing the fighting and keeping it focused on the Avengers.

Nearly midway through the battle, Romanoff exercised a different style of initiative. After blasting away the latest in a seemingly endless wave of Chitauri foot soldiers, she told Cap, "None of this is gonna mean a damn thing if we don't close that portal." She implicitly volunteered to execute a mission to disrupt or destroy the machine creating the gateway. Cap was receptive to the idea but confirmed her commitment before launching her into the fray. "You sure about this?," he asked. With an affirmative response, he boosted her onto a passing chariot, and she made her way to the top of Stark Tower—apparently because the elevator would have been too slow.

In the decision to support Romanoff's relocation, Rogers accepted a reasonable risk to the force to begin progressing toward the ultimate goal. Commanders and subordinates exercising mission command must weigh the consequences of potential courses of action against the potential for losing troops and failing to achieve the mission. In extremely high-stakes situations, as in the Battle of New York, commanders place the mission well ahead of force survival, but that does not mean they should direct suicide efforts on a long shot of success. Rogers understood that Romanoff's technical skill might offer a solution that the brute force of Thor, the Hulk, or Iron Man lacked. Further, because of her acrobatic and fighting skills, she had a decent chance of getting to the top of the tower via the Chitauri chariots. He also calculated that his efforts on and around the bridge would be sufficient to keep the fighting focused on the Avengers. Still, to pursue overall success, he had to accept some risk to that mission as well. A student and product of history, Rogers had developed what Carl von Clausewitz called the *coup d'oeil*, the ability of a commander to assess a situation with a mere glance and almost instinctively decide on the best course of action.[10] His risk assessment and acceptance demonstrated the mission command's final component.

The audience is then treated to one of the most fantastic long action sequences in cinema as the camera follows Black Widow and subsequently switches through the fights of Iron Man, Captain America, Hawkeye, Hulk, and Thor. Cap ran to save civilians, doing his best to mitigate the consequences of being the sole Avenger still on the ground; Romanoff discovered the means to close the portal; the Hulk annihilated the puny god after downing a Leviathan with Thor; and Stark impersonated Jonah and the whale. But the fight began to go against the heroes. Overwhelming airpower drove Barton from his rooftop vantage point and neutralized the Hulk. The World Security Council, responsible for overseeing S.H.I.E.L.D., decided to launch a nuclear weapon against the city to meet the threat and overrode Director Nick Fury's election to ignore the order. Stark raced to intercept the missile, abandoning his perimeter patrol to deal with the more significant threat.

At the battle's climax, the Avengers (primarily for narrative purposes) began to stray from mission command principles. Black Widow successfully found a way to close the portal, but the master assassin did not execute with disciplined initiative despite knowing she could achieve the commander's intent. Instead, she communicated the information to the team. Romanoff would not have been at fault for acting immediately; however, her decision to announce the new capability was reasonable. As she had been out of the fight for several minutes at least, it made sense for her to check in to see if the intent had changed. Stark, on the other hand, had no excuse.

Fury skipped the chain of command and directly called Iron Man to inform him of the incoming nuclear threat. Without waiting for permission, Stark wisely acted on that new intelligence and moved to intercept. So far, so good. However, at this point, he had time to update Rogers on his relocation and the reasons for it. Under the principles of mission command, it made sense for Stark to use his capability to mitigate the risk to both the mission and the force. He had time, though, to inform the team. He accepted the risk to the mission by leaving his patrol, but he incurred a more significant risk by playing a game of "I have a secret." When Romanoff told the Avengers that she could close the portal, Rogers immediately responded to do it. Stark quickly belayed that order to have a place to put the nuke. An immediate reaction from Romanoff would have foiled Stark's secret plan, but he would have been culpable because the team was acting with limited information.

Ultimately, though, *The Avengers* is still a movie, so it all worked out. Stark delivered the nuke and destroyed the command ship; the Chitauri went lifeless as their animating power source exploded; Romanoff closed the portal; Stark got lucky and fell back to earth just as the hole closed; and Hulk caught the falling Iron Man before he crashed. The heroes then captured Loki and adjourned for some well-earned shawarma.

Military professionals continue to refine command and control techniques to meet today's challenging operational environment. The concept of mission command offers definite benefits to a highly trained and well-organized unit; however, it is sometimes difficult to find examples for leaders new to the practice. *The Avengers* gives a great example of mission command in action and a couple of instances where the team violates the principles of mission command. Understanding the advantages and pitfalls of this type of leadership makes it possible to assemble a winning approach to the complex problems of the day.

Notes

1   See Travis Zahnow, "Can Mission Command Actually Work?" Modern War Institute at West Point,
    30 July 2020, https://mwi.usma.edu/can-mission-command-actually-work/; Air University Public
    Affairs, "Air Force rewrites basic doctrine, focuses on mission command, airpower evolution,"
    AF.mil, 22 April 2021, https://www.af.mil/News/Article-Display/Article/2581921/air-force-re-
    writes-basic-doctrine-focuses-on-mission-command-airpower-evolution/; James W. Harvard,
    "Airmen and Mission Command," *Air and Space Power Journal* 27, no. 2 (March–April 2013):
    131–146; Fred N. Tolman, "Mission Command: A Senior Enlisted Leader's Perspective," NCO
    Journal, 15 May 2020, https://www.armyupress.army.mil/Journals/NCO-Journal/Archives/2020/
    May/Mission-Command/; James D. Sharpe, Jr., and Thomas E. Creviston, "Understanding Mission
    Command," Army.mil, 30 April 2015, https://www.army.mil/article/106872/understanding_mis-
    sion_command; Sandeep Mulgund, "Evolving the Command and Control of Airpower," Wild Blue
    Yonder Online Journal, 21 April 2021, https://www.airuniversity.af.edu/Wild-Blue-Yonder/Article-
    Display/Article/2575321/evolving-the-command-and-control-of-airpower/#sdendnote3anc;
    Deployable Training Division of Joint Staff J7, "Insights and Best Practices Focus Paper, Second
    Edition: Mission Command," Joint Chiefs of Staff Insights and Best Practices, January 2020,
    https://www.jcs.mil/Doctrine/focus_papers.aspx.
2   Joint Publication 3–31, *Joint Land Operations* Change 1, 16 November 2021 (Washington, DC:
    Government Printing Office, 3 October 2019), V14-V15.
3   Lee Robinson, "Understanding Mission Command," *Military Review* 102, no. 4 (July–
    August 2022), 67–73.
4   Army Doctrine Publication (ADP) 6–0, *Mission Command: Command and Control of Army Forces*
    (Washington, DC: Department of the Army, 31 July 2019), 1–7.
5   All subsequent character quotations are from *The Avengers*, directed and written by Joss Whedon
    (2012; Burbank, CA: Walt Disney Pictures, 2022), DVD.
6   *Mission Command*, 1–11.
7   Air Force Doctrine Publication (AFDP) 1, *The Air Force* (Maxwell AFB, AL: Lemay Center for
    Doctrine Development and Education, 10 March 2021), 11–12.
8   See what I did there?
9   *The Air Force*, 13.
10 Carl von Clausewitz, *On War*, indexed ed., trans. Michael Howard and Peter Paret (Princeton:
    Princeton University Press, 1989), 141.

CHAPTER 3

The Rise of a Reluctant Leader

Emilia Harcourt and the Peacemaker

Mick Ryan

In 2021 and 2022, American filmmaker James Gunn was responsible for a film, *The Suicide Squad*, and a television series, *Peacemaker*, which introduced us to the character of Emilia Harcourt. While playing a minor role in *The Suicide Squad*, Harcourt's character is a central element of *Peacemaker*, eponymously named after the misfit anti-hero, Chris Smith, who has dedicated himself to world peace, regardless of how many men, women, and children he has had to kill. The show charts Smith's development within a team of other misfits. Harcourt (played by actress Jennifer Holland) is central to Smith's transformation from murderous thug to something resembling a superhero.

In Gunn's film, *The Suicide Squad*, the audience observes the support staff for the squad's mission that's about to begin. Operating from an undisclosed location, in a secret command center, the underlings of Amanda Waller scurry back and forth as the film's Task Force X transitions from its helicopter transports to its separate beach landing sites.

But the conduct of the support staff is not entirely professional. Just four minutes into the film, a betting syndicate emerges to wager on who among the newly comprised Suicide Squad is likely to survive. In the thick of things is a young blonde agent. She receives betting funds and places her own wagers. This is our first meeting with Agent Emilia Harcourt.

Harcourt, at least until the later stages of the film, is not a pleasant character. She demonstrates no empathy for the members of Task Force X, and little more for the other members of the support crew in the command center. It is only as Amanda Waller begins to make questionable decisions toward the end of *The Suicide Squad* that we see the hints of Emilia's character that show she can think about the ethical implications of her actions, and those around her.

Harcourt begins to assist Task Force X as they go "off mission" in Corto Maltese. She also plays a minor role in the restraint of Waller and supporting the extraction of the surviving members of Task Force X in their culminating battle with a giant, alien starfish that is seeking to enslave the human race. Despite this, she remains a reticent and dislikeable character. And her story may well have ended here if not for a follow-on television series called *Peacemaker*.[1]

Harcourt features prominently throughout the first season of the eight-part *Peacemaker*. In the first episode, she shows the same selfish characteristics and lack of empathy for others as seen in *The Suicide Squad*. But, by the end of the series, she has become the accepted leader[2] of a group of misfits who are able to successfully pre-empt an attempted takeover of the world by a group of aliens.

What explains this conversion of Harcourt, who reluctantly but gradually assumes a leadership role, and how does such a self-centered individual transform into a leader? The aim of this chapter is to explore Harcourt's leadership journey. And while a focus on Harcourt as an individual is important, it must be founded upon relevant leadership theory. For that reason, we begin with a short exploration of the concept of the reluctant leader.

The Reluctant Leader

The key to understanding Harcourt's journey is the concept of a reluctant leader. This is a sub-strand of leadership theory that concerns the examination of why people are hesitant to become leaders in different organizations. There is a small but growing body of work that explores the theory and how to nurture these reluctant yet talented potential leaders.

A recent *Harvard Business Review* article described how "it is fairly common to see someone choose *not* to lead, whether it's a capable co-worker who passes up an opportunity to guide a team project, or a manager who, when confronted with a challenging situation, simply waits for things to happen instead of taking charge."[3] It is common in business, government, miliary, or not-for-profit endeavors to see people who do not wish to step into positions of leadership.

In one study on this phenomenon explored in the *Harvard Business Review* article, the authors found that reluctant leaders were concerned with three different types of risk when it came to leadership positions. The first was interpersonal risk, where assuming the responsibilities of leadership might have a negative impact on their relationships with fellow workers. A second risk was that of personal brand or image. Prospective yet reluctant leaders were hesitant to step forward because they were afraid of what others, especially their peers, might think of them.

A third and final risk was that of "being blamed" and being held responsible for the failure of the group they lead. As the article notes, "fear of being associated with and blamed for failure is a powerful deterrent that keeps people from taking on opportunities to lead."[4] These fears are often informed by the personal experience of those who resist leadership positions.

American columnist and author David Brooks has explored reluctant leaders from a different perspective. In a 2014 article, he defined the essence of reluctant leaders as being self-divided, that they feel compelled to do things that they would rather not do. This self-division has both negative and positive impacts. An unsuccessful reluctant leader is not motivated to undertake assigned tasks. However, a reluctant leader can be successful if they are motivated by their own conscience and embrace the fact that "while this is not the destiny they would have chosen, it is their duty, and they will follow it to the end."[5]

Brooks further characterized reluctant leaders as possessing four key traits. First, that they were generally more realistic about their goals. Second, that they should be skeptical and that reluctant leaders can make wise decisions precisely because they are aware of their own limitations. A third trait is that they are dogged in pursuit of outcomes, even unpleasant tasks. And finally, reluctant leaders can be collaborative; because they don't want a task, they are often keen to share it.[6]

In Pat Williams's and Mark Atteberry's book *The Reluctant Leader*, the authors identify multiple traits exhibited by people who might possess leadership potential yet are reluctant to step into leadership roles. This reluctance to "take charge" is driven, essentially, by an overlapping set of fears. These include a reticence to delegate or take risks, a reluctance to confront others or to rock the organizational boat, and the unwillingness to fail.[7]

Perhaps the most important trait identified by Williams and Attebery is the reluctance to fail. This is a quality inherent in all humans. However, it also something that many people learn, through experience, to overcome in different ways in their personal lives. Overcoming it as a leader should be no different. As Williams and Atteberry note, leadership and failure go together:

> Anybody who steps into the leadership role that is currently beckoning you is going to produce some failures.... Any leader who steps into the role and stays for a significant amount of time is going to fail ... there's no way to guarantee that you'll never fail, but you can sure take steps to minimize failure.[8]

This fear of failure is also explored by Eva Doyle in her 2016 book on reluctant leadership.[9] She writes that "you are going to make mistakes, a lot of them, some of them embarrassing. It's not going to feel good. It's going to be bumpy." But Doyle also notes that reluctance is normal:

> True leadership is exercising power in the interests of the people you lead. If you are willing to serve and sacrifice and sweat, then you're at least ready to explore the topic.... It makes sense to ponder what price you will pay to be a leader. Approaching the role with a sense of realism is important.[10]

A recent article by Julia Cunningham, Laura Sonday, and Susan Ashford explored this phenomenon from the perspective of being afraid to identify as a leader. They found several reputational fears that can often hold back individuals from seeing themselves as leaders, and thus assuming greater responsibility within organizations.[11]

The first fear is appearing to be different. Individuals can perceive that acting as a leader can see them singled out and "receiving too much attention for being different from others." Consequently, people are concerned that in stepping into leadership roles, they will have to sacrifice their sense of belonging within their work group.[12]

A second fear is appearing to be too dominant. The authors found that many participants in their study said they did not want to be perceived as pushy or bossy. A third and final fear was that of seeming unqualified. As the authors note, "people who reported higher levels of fear around these reputational risks were less likely to see themselves as leaders. As a result, they were less likely to act as leaders, and therefore less likely to be seen as leaders by their supervisors."[13]

There are some common themes that can be drawn from this exploration of reluctant leaders. First, fear of multiple negative outcomes appears to be common across the different studies, books, and articles reviewed on the topic of reluctant leadership. Whether this is a fear of being seen as incompetent or domineering in an office environment or a fear of failure in a military environment, fear is at the heart of reluctant leadership. Or as one study of reluctant leaders in the field of education found, "the fear of increased workload, lack of support, and the wrong balance of authority versus responsibility are significant inhibitors to leaders stepping forward."[14] Fortunately, most good leadership programs have as a core element the gradual improvement in personal confidence to (mostly) overcome these fears. However, good leaders never overcome all their fears, and that is healthy. Some degree of fear must propel leaders to think harder and lead better.

Second, reluctant leaders are skeptics. This is a skepticism about their own talents or of the larger goals of the organization they are a member of. It appears to be a common characteristic in the studies that explore why individuals are reluctant to assume leadership responsibilities. As the study of reluctant leaders in the field of education found, skepticism about being managers rather than teachers is a strong inhibitor for leadership.[15] While this is a characteristic that might easily become an overwhelmingly negative one, small doses of skepticism in leaders are useful in questioning the status quo, nurturing creativity in subordinates, and reviewing multiple different options to achieve an institutional goal.

Interestingly, however, the combination of these traits can often result in reluctant leaders becoming good collaborators. There are several drivers for this including sharing risk (and addressing their personal fears) and a lack of confidence which results in leaders seeking the ideas of others. Often, because a reluctant leader may not want a particular task, they are keen to share the task with others. While this might result in blame shifting, indecision, and a lack of leadership accountability in its worst manifestations, collaboration can also result in multiple good ideas being explored to solve complex problems. It can, and does, result in buy-in from the entire group being headed by the reluctant leader.

The reticence of people to assume leadership roles is a subfield of leadership that is probably worthy of much more study. While there are many confident and ambitious leaders across all fields of human endeavor, there are probably just as many individuals who are reluctant leaders. Their motivations, and their achievements, should be considered. It is why Emilia Harcourt is a fascinating case study of reluctance in assuming the mantle of leadership.

Harcourt the Leader Emerges

This theoretical exploration is a good foundation. However, how does it apply to Harcourt's journey as reluctant leader across *The Suicide Squad* and the eight episodes of the first season[16] of *Peacemaker*?

When the audience is introduced to Harcourt in *The Suicide Squad*, and again at the commencement of the first season of *Peacemaker*, she demonstrates no discernible leadership qualities. She starts as a character disinterested in fellow team members, focused only on the mission at hand, and keen to ensure that she redeems herself in the eyes of her boss (Waller) through success in her new mission. She is also bitter and self-centered. Harcourt shows little interest in being, or potential as, a leader.

The two key traits of reluctant leaders—fear and skepticism—are obvious in Harcourt, particularly as the audience comes to know her better in the early episodes of *Peacemaker*.

As a new team is assembled, under the leadership of the mysterious Clemson Murn, Harcourt is clearly afraid of being part of another failure and the implications it might have for her personally. Being associated with the breakdown of Task Force X in *The Suicide Squad*, she is reticent to step forward into any kind of leadership responsibility. This fear of failure extends to how she associates with the other members of her team. She is disrespectful and looks upon her new colleagues with scorn.

Harcourt gives the bird to Peacemaker when they first meet and taunts new team member Leota Adebayo as "new girl" when they move into their new (secret) headquarters. Not long afterwards in an exchange with Peacemaker, she informs him that "I have no interest in you, other than your ability to kill." Harcourt drinks alone, and at surface level, displays no inclination to know the rest of the team except in the most superficial of ways.

However, her inclinations here are not just a quirk of her personality. There are very valid reasons for her initial reluctance to trust her new teammates or seek anything other than superficial bonds with them.

Her comment to Peacemaker takes place just after she has been harassed and attacked by several men. Having read into Peacemaker's background (particularly his sexist, bullying behaviors) and also been on the receiving end of his unwanted advances, Harcourt's response is fully justified. Her lived experience is part of her suspicion about the members of the new team she is a member of—especially Peacemaker—and how she treats them initially. It is an important aspect of her initial reticence to lead.

While her frequent snarky remarks are a defense mechanism due to her previous experiences. But they also indicate a level of skepticism in Harcourt. She appears to accept the mission that she is part of but is skeptical about their chances of success with the team she is part of. She is skeptical about the capabilities of her fellow team members, at one point telling John Economos that he is "too big a pussy to betray us."[17] Harcourt also constantly questions the motivations of others on her team in the early episodes. She questions Adebayo's motivations for being on the team in Episode 4. But it is also at the end of this episode that we see the early inklings of Harcourt's human side when she demonstrates empathy for The Vigilante when picking him up from jail.

The turning point for Harcourt takes place in Episode 5. In the absence of team leader Murn, Harcourt temporarily fills in as the leader for an assault on the Glan Tai facility. The site of alien food distribution, Harcourt and the team engage in combat with aliens who occupy human bodies, as well as an escaped gorilla. The mission is a success, albeit one that sees the entire team covered with gore by its end. In taking a photo of the team in the rear of their van when returning to their headquarters, we see Harcourt smile. It is evident she has taken pride in the team's achievements during the mission.[18]

From here on, the audience sees a more honest and empathetic Harcourt. She is becoming more positive in her interactions with fellow team members and more collaborative while listening to the ideas of others. She is beginning to value the others on her team.

In the final two episodes of the series, Harcourt overcomes her fears and skepticism to become the leader of this small band of misfits. In the wake of the death of Murn, the team turns to her to lead them. Understanding that they still have a final mission—to find and destroy the ultimate source of the alien's food—she emerges as a dogged-yet-consultative leader. She provides purpose and clear direction to the characters of Peacemaker, Vigilante, Adebayo, and Economos,[19] and they depart on their final mission, heartened by Harcourt's leadership.

It is in the final assault on the alien base, set in an old barn, where we see the ultimate expression of Harcourt's transformation from a reluctant to a determined leader. While some skepticism remains, especially about the capabilities of Peacemaker's pet eagle, she places aside her fears and any lingering uncertainty to lead her team in the attack on the alien base. Ultimately, she deliberately places herself in harm's way to ensure the mission is successful. This self-sacrifice, on behalf of her team and the mission, is a classic example of heroic leadership. She is reluctant no more.

Conclusion

Many reading this chapter will have had experiences with people who might be described as reluctant leaders. Whether it is friends or subordinates at work, it is common to discover people with the raw talent to become good leaders but who lack the confidence to step into leadership roles. It requires mentorship, example, and the right incentives to nurture these reluctant leaders to achieve their potential and contribute more fully to the institution they are members of.

At the end of the *Peacemaker* series, Harcourt's transition from a disinterested and bad-attitude team member to team leader is complete. She has led her small, diverse group in the conduct of a very difficult and dangerous mission, which results in both physical and emotional injuries to them all. Harcourt herself is badly wounded, and in the wake of the successful mission, requires significant physical therapy to re-learn how to walk.

Despite the success of her team, it is perhaps one of the final scenes at the end of the series that demonstrates Harcourt's transformation as a person and a leader. Lying in hospital, and severely wounded, the Peacemaker visits Harcourt. He says nothing but sits by her side and holds her hand. Harcourt begins to weep. And it is here we see her as someone who is willing to show personal vulnerability to those on her team. But more importantly, she is also now a leader who loves those same people she is leading.

Notes

1 The television series referred to here is the 2022 series, directed by James Gunn and released on HBO Max. It is not the 2003 show called *Peacemakers*.
2 In Episode 8, Harcourt's leadership is confirmed by Amanda Waller just before the team assault the aliens who are located in an old barn.
3 Chen Zhang, Jennifer D. Nahrgang, Susan (Sue) Ashford, D. Scott DeRue, "Why Capable People Are Reluctant to Lead," *Harvard Business Review* (online version, December 17, 2020), https://hbr.org/2020/12/why-capable-people-are-reluctant-to-lead.
4 Ibid.
5 David Brooks, "The Reluctant Leader," *The New York Times* (September 11, 2014).
6 Ibid.
7 Pat Williams and Mark Atteberry, *The Reluctant Leader: Overcoming the Hesitation That's Holding You Back* (Charleston: Advantage Books, 2021).
8 Ibid.
9 Eva Doyle, *The Reluctant Leader: From Technical Expert to Human Expert* (Bloomington, Archway Publishing: 2016).
10 Ibid.
11 Julia Cunningham, Laura Sonday, and Susan Ashford, "Are You Afraid to Identify as a Leader?" *Harvard Business Review* (September 5, 2022), https://hbr.org/2022/09/are-you-afraid-to-identify-as-a-leader.
12 Ibid.

13 Ibid.
14 Kirk Anderson and others, "Reluctant Leaders: Why are some capable leaders not interested in principalship?" *International Journal of Management in Education* (January 2011), 388.
15 Ibid.
16 A full synopsis of the season can be found at https://dcextendeduniverse.fandom.com/wiki/Peacemaker_(TV_series)#Season_Two.
17 *Peacemaker*, season 1, episode 2, "Best Friends, For Never," directed by James Gunn, aired January 13, 2022, HBO.
18 *Peacemaker*, season 1, episode 5, "Monkey Dory," directed by Rosemary Rodriguez, aired January 27, 2022, HBO.
19 With the death of their leader, Clemson Murn, the core team around Harcourt is Leota Adebayo, Christopher Smith (aka Peacemaker), Adrian Chase (aka Vigilante), and John Economos.

CHAPTER 4

The Unexpected Hero

Leadership and the Trusted Sidekick

Kari McEwen

"And a lean, silent figure slowly fades in the gathering darkness, aware at last that in this world, with great power there must also come—great responsibility!"[1]

In the *Spider-Man* films, Peter Parker's revered Uncle Ben is the first to utter the phrase that inspired this book, the words that set Peter on a reluctant path to becoming the friendly neighborhood Spider-Man. The phrase that closed Spider-Man's inaugural appearance in *Amazing Fantasy* #15 became *the* Marvel maxim through the years, embodying a centuries-old sentiment that nobility, heads of state, military leaders, and CEOs alike feel to their core and have lamented throughout history: "Uneasy lies the head that wears the crown."[2] Such phrases allude to the burdens of leadership and the pressures that comes with protecting—and sometimes saving—the world. They imply that while superheroes and brilliant leaders possess (super)human powers and finely tuned leadership abilities, those alone are not enough.

Pepper Potts, Alfred Pennyworth, and Uncle Ben: three otherwise unremarkable characters in the lore of the superhero genre who seemingly exist solely to serve others: an assistant, a butler, and an uncle-turned-father-figure. Remove them from the stories, and all that remains are three ordinary superheroes who lack the necessary skill, empathy, and foresight to save the world. These average sidekicks are the unsung heroes of our superhero stories.

Superheroes who were once ordinary humans are innately flawed. They overcome these flaws by relying on someone close to them to account for their deficiencies. That person may be a family member or a lover, an assistant or a butler. Regardless of their role, it is someone with whom the superhero can be vulnerable. Someone who sees them even when they can't see themselves. Someone who embodies all the traits they are lacking. Without the help of this *someone*, our superheroes would not be saving the world and in some cases might even become the very villains they loathe. Rarely though, does the credit go to those waiting in the wings, nor do those who make it all possible want the recognition.

The Assistant

A brilliant, narcissistic, arms-dealing defense contractor billionaire who undergoes a life-altering transformation into Iron Man, Tony Stark's ego often gets the best of him. If not for his personal assistant—who ultimately becomes so much more—Tony's ego and rash decision-making would be his demise.

Pepper Potts is everything Tony is not. She holds herself to a high moral standard, constantly battling to convince Tony to do the right thing. To balance Tony's mischievous and self-serving character, Pepper must be reasonable and mature, pure and good.

With his newfound superpowers, Tony struggles with choices of right and wrong. Pepper serves as his conscience, reminding him to consider the consequences of his actions and stopping him from doing irreparable damage. "Pepper Potts constantly acted as Tony Stark's moral compass. Every time he was on the fence about doing something that maybe wasn't the right thing for him, she always spoke up in favor of reason and logic. She combined her logical way of thinking with her positive morals and continually pushed Tony in the right direction."[3]

Not only is Pepper crucial to Tony's ability to choose right over wrong, she is also a capable assistant central to his existence as a superhero. In the 2008 film *Iron Man*, Pepper assists Tony in swapping out his jury-rigged Mark I arc reactor for a newer high-tech piece that will power the advanced armor technology while keeping him alive. This requires her to reach into his chest cavity to retrieve the old chest piece, a task for which she feels uniquely unprepared: "I don't think that I'm qualified to do this." Despite her misgivings and a minor faux pas that causes Tony to slip into cardiac arrest, Pepper successfully installs the new arc reactor in time for Iron Man to return to action.[4]

During the film's climactic scene in which Iron Man clashes with the Iron Monger (his mentor Obadiah Stane), Pepper finds herself in the arc reactor control room, unsure of how to shut it down. She calls Tony—in pitched battle with the villain—who offers vague instructions to "open the control panel and push the red button." Pepper opens the control panel to find it awash in red buttons. Pepper does what Pepper does best: She gets to work, reads the instruction manuals, and leverages her own superpower (her critical thinking skills) to shut down the reactor and spare the lives of millions and, effectively, save the world.

Pepper is the unsung hero of the Iron Man story arc: She becomes CEO of Stark Industries, marries Tony, becomes a mother, becomes a superhero (Rescue) and saves the world again in the battle against Thanos. She does it all.

The Butler

We know him as Bruce Wayne's butler, but for every fatal character flaw in the Caped Crusader's alter ego—and there are many—Alfred Pennyworth possesses those traits in spades and uses them to help Batman protect Gotham City. In the various versions of Batman stories, Wayne is portrayed as a standoffish, brooding, spoiled, billionaire playboy. He has very few redeeming qualities.

Though Alfred appears to be little more than a lowly household butler, his vast experience and wisdom allow him to be the perfect mentor to young Master Wayne and aid him in his superhero quest. Alfred's origin stories differ depending on which version you consume. In 2019, Epix launched a series titled Pennyworth, in which Alfred was a former British special forces soldier living in London. Yet another version portrays him as a retired combat medic following his true passion, theater. In this story arc, MI-6 recruited him to train secret agents in the art of stagecraft to enhance their abilities. He later uses the skills he honed to follow in his father's footsteps as a loyal butler to the Wayne family.[5]

It is in his role as a butler in Wayne Manor and mentor to young Bruce Wayne that Alfred's special forces background and medical and acting skills pay dividends. In the 2005 film *Batman Begins*, Alfred possesses not only the necessary medical skills to treat Batman's injuries from late-night, city-saving escapades, but also the stagecraft to shape a more favorable public narrative for the young millionaire.

The bonds of trust that Alfred shares with Bruce enable him to speak truth to power in a way others cannot. Alfred is fulfilling a promise made to the boy's parents to protect Bruce no matter what, to ensure he chooses the right path in life. "Alfred has been absolutely integral to the success of Batman. Alfred was the moral compass for Batman. With his dry wit, sarcastic comments, and genuine love for the man behind the mask, he could tell Bruce the true, unvarnished truth, whether he wanted to hear it or not."[6]

Bruce is vulnerable with Alfred in a way that he can't be with others, and he trusts Alfred to tell him the truth even when he doesn't want to hear it. In the first act of the 2008 film, *The Dark Knight*, Alfred arrives at Wayne's side as he is licking his wounds from another night of crime fighting.

> ALFRED: Know your limits, Master Wayne.
> BRUCE: Batman has no limits.
> ALFRED: Well, you do, sir.
> BRUCE: Well, can't afford to know 'em.
> ALFRED: And what happens on the day that you find out?
> BRUCE: Well, we all know how much you love to say, "I told you so."
> ALFRED: On that day, Master Wayne, even I won't want to. Probably.[7]

Later, Bruce contemplates turning himself in after the public condemns Batman's vigilantism and the Joker threatens to kill thousands of people if Batman does not reveal his identity. Alfred steadfastly reminds Bruce that revealing his identity would mean an end to Batman. An end to Batman leaves the city to fall into the hands of psychopaths and criminals. Batman must stay the course:

> BRUCE: People are dying, Alfred. What would you have me do?
> ALFRED: Endure, Master Wayne. Take it. They'll hate you for it, but that's the point of Batman, he can be the outcast. He can make the choice that no one else can make, the right choice.[8]

The Father Figure

Despite Uncle Ben's and Aunt May's best efforts to raise Peter Parker, they could not replace the hole in his heart left by the death of his parents. And when the class geek with low self-esteem gains his newfound superpowers, selfishness takes over. He puts his new abilities on display for money and is only focused on serving himself. He is ungrateful and rude to Uncle Ben and Aunt May, the two people who love him most in the world.

In the 2002 film *Spider-Man*, Uncle Ben is in the car with Peter, discussing his displeasure with the boy's suddenly changed and insolent behavior. Uncle Ben finishes the conversation, saying, "These are the years when a man changes into the man he's going to become for the rest of his life. Just be careful who you change into."[9] In the 2012 film, *The Amazing Spider-Man,* Uncle Ben tries to steer Peter's moral compass by telling him about his father. But Peter is still resentful that he grew up without a father.

> BEN: You are a lot like your father. You really are, Peter, and that's a good thing. But your father, he lived by a philosophy, a principle, really. He believed that if you could do good things for other people, you had a moral obligation to do those things! That's what's at stake here. Not choice. Responsibility.
> PETER: That's nice. That's great ... That's all well and good. So where is he?
> BEN: What?
> PETER: Where is he? Where's my dad? He didn't think it was his responsibility to be here to tell me this himself?
> BEN: Oh, come on, how dare you?
> PETER: How dare I? How dare you?[10]

Uncle Ben's sudden and violent murder, shortly after the conversation in the car, is the catalyst for Spider-Man to use his powers for good, not evil. The last words spoken to Peter by the man he loved most in life, a man who was like a father to him, becomes his mantra, "Remember, with great power comes great responsibility."[11] Were it not for the death of Uncle Ben, Peter would not have become the superhero we know today as Spider-Man. If Uncle Ben had lived, Peter might have continued to resent him and could have continued down the wrong path. Without Uncle Ben's tragic death, there might not be a Spider-Man.

Pepper, Alfred, and Uncle Ben share many of the same traits. They are level-headed, reasonable, unpretentious, considerate, and understated. They are the antithesis of their superheroes, who are arrogant, narcissistic, brooding, aloof, selfish, and greedy. Rather than allow ego to take center stage, Pepper, Alfred, and Uncle Ben—despite being just an assistant, just a butler, or just an old man—serve as the change agents for their respective charges. Through them, Iron Man, Batman, and Spider-Man develop the self-awareness and humility to overcome their shortcomings to become the heroes we need to be.

The Real-World Sidekick

It's lonely at the top. Like "uneasy lies the head that wears the crown," both are expressions of despair conveyed by rulers, business leaders, government officials, and military commanders when the burdens of leadership become too much to bear. Solutions for the challenges of the uneasy head and the loneliness of leadership range from mentors and coaches to a silent advisory board.[12] Benjamin Franklin sought comfort and advice in his Junto Club, "an informal group of men, most of whom were more or less at his level of responsibility and standing in Philadelphia. The club provided Franklin an outlet where he could develop real friendships, speak freely, seek advice, and develop ideas."[13]

Such solutions may temporarily resolve the feelings of loneliness and free a leader's mind from the complex decisions and consequences they face but are no substitute for a sidekick who possesses the key traits the leader lacks and without whom, saving the world would not be possible. The sidekick still plays an outsized role in the success of the leader and the organization but is not overly burdened by the pressure of command.

In a 2004 *Harvard Business Review* article, Michael Maccoby discusses the emergence of CEOs with larger-than-life personalities and magazine cover close-ups that accompanied the rise of the internet.[14] Historically, business leaders were content to minimize large-scale public interaction and relied on carefully scripted advice from their public relations consultants. But business success in the Internet Age required innovative leaders who could inspire people to support a different, forward-thinking vision.

Like Tony Stark and Bruce Wayne, many contemporary business leaders are classic narcissists. The negative connotations associated with the term doesn't necessarily mean they are bad leaders, however. "Narcissists are good for companies in extraordinary times, those that need people with the passion and daring to take them in new directions."[15] Maccoby goes so far as to recommend narcissists find a trusted sidekick, a person whom they trust to "point out the operational requirements of the narcissistic leader's often overly grandiose vision and keep him rooted in reality."[16] The role of the sidekick is more than just carrying out orders. The sidekick must be someone who has the standing to get the leader to accept ideas and opinions that may be contrary to their own. "To do this, he must be able to show the leader how the new ideas fit with his views and serve his interests."[17]

Winston Churchill's trusted sidekick was Professor Frederick A. Lindemann, a professor of physics at Oxford University who was every bit the prime minister's opposite. Affectionately known as "The Prof," Lindemann lived a life shaped by healthy choices and preferred to exist outside the limelight. Not one to imbibe in smoke, drink, attention, or heavy meals, he seemed an unlikely companion for Churchill, who enjoyed such things.[18] Churchill relied on Lindemann and his opinion in both his professional and personal life. "The man the family called 'the Prof' showed Churchill total loyalty," and despite possessing some undesirable traits, "his biographer said his life was driven by 'absolute loyalty and love for his friends, and sustained rancor towards his enemies.'"[19]

Lindemann had a unique ability to translate complicated scientific concepts into terms that were easy for Churchill to understand. As such, Lindemann was placed in charge of the Statistics Division, which assessed each of the ministries' performance and helped set priorities for military sustainment and logistics. "Lindemann attended meetings of the War Cabinet, accompanied the prime minister on conferences abroad, and sent him an average of one missive a day. He saw Churchill almost daily for the duration of the war and wielded more influence than any other civilian adviser."[20]

Like Pepper and Alfred, Lindemann knew Churchill trusted his judgment enough to tell the prime minister when he was wrong. "On most matters Lindemann's and Churchill's opinions converged; and when they did not, the scientist worked ceaselessly to change his friend's mind."[21] Lindemann was Churchill's Pepper Potts, the Alfred Pennyworth to his Batman. Were it not for the straightforward advice and trusted counsel of Lindemann, Churchill would have struggled to lead Britain to victory in World War II and would likely not have ascended to become one of history's greatest statesmen.

For a young Walt Disney, Ub Iwerks served in the sidekick role. Never heard of him? It's not surprising. Like Lindemann, Iwerks preferred a life away from the spotlight, eschewing the fame for relative anonymity. Walt Disney and Iwerks met in Kansas City, where they worked for a commercial art studio creating advertising copy. When both artists lost their jobs at the studio, Disney suggested they go into business together and the two moved to Hollywood, where Iwerks-Disney was born.[22]

Disney, the more charming, charismatic of the two business partners, was an engaging storyteller and natural salesman. Iwerks was quite the opposite—a quiet, efficient, technically skilled cartoonist and animator. In an interview with National Public Radio, Kansas City journalist Mackenzie Martin described the friendship between Disney and Iwerks: "When the Laugh-O-Gram Studio eventually went bankrupt, Disney took a train out to Hollywood. But not very much time had passed before he was begging Iwerks to come out too. He couldn't make his cartoons successful without him."[23] Martin—continuing the dialog with Iwerks enthusiast Butch Rigby and author Jeff Ryan—goes on to explain that Iwerks could produce more drawings in two weeks than other animators could produce in months.

> RIGBY: You know, Ub was quiet but a genius, and I mean literally a genius. And Walt recognized that.
> MARTIN: In addition to being an extremely efficient and talented animator, Iwerks was able to solve literally any technical problem that was thrown his way. Disney, on the other hand, was an incredible storyteller. His characters were charming and lovable, and he knew how to get the best out of other people.
> RYAN: And when you put Walt and Ub together, they were able to do just about anything.[24]

In Ryan's book, *A Mouse Divided*, he describes the creation of Mickey Mouse by the two friends as something that would be incomplete had they not worked in tandem.

> Walt's Mickey and Ub's Mickey were very different. Walt preferred the aw-shucks Mickey, the bashful guy you see who pinks up if Minnie gives him a peck on the cheek. Ub preferred the man of action, the Mickey you see in a park attraction taking arms against a dragon every night. Neither man realized the irony in their preferences. For in real life Walt was the brash one, while Ub was retreating and kind. Each of their Mickeys was an idealized version of their partner. Ub's half of Mickey was Walt's derring-do soul. Walt's half was Ub's golly-gee heart. Mickey is friendship personified.[25]

As friends and business partners, they breathed life into the most iconic cartoon characters ever created. Neither could do it alone. But together, they possessed the skills that made the Mouse the most recognized cartoon character in the world. Alone, Walt Disney launched to superhero stardom while his sidekick—the man behind the miracle—remained in the shadows. Although he preferred to stay out of the limelight, Iwerks was unhappy with Disney for crafting a creation story that made no mention of his contribution. The two ultimately parted ways.

For those countless government, business, and military leaders who lament their loneliness, a trusted sidekick might not only possess the traits they most require to be successful in their positions but serves as someone they trust to hold them accountable. "In the end, the story of Mickey Mouse is a good reminder that everything is a team effort. Behind every powerful mouse, there might be a Walt Disney. But behind every Walt Disney, there's probably at least one Ub Iwerks."[26] Or a Pepper, or an Alfred, or an Uncle Ben.

Notes

1   Stan Lee, *Amazing Fantasy #15*. New York: Marvel Comics, August 1962.
2   William Shakespeare, "Henry IV, Part II." *The Folger Shakespeare Library.* Edited by Paul Werstine, Michael Poston, Rebecca Niles, eds Barbara Mowat. (Washington, DC: Folger Shakespeare Library, n.d.), 1600. https://shakespeare.folger.edu/shakespeares-works/henry-iv-part-2/.

3   Stephanie Harper, "Iron Man: 10 Times Pepper Potts Was the Real Hero," *Comic Book Resources*, August 10, 2020. https://www.cbr.com/iron-man-pepper-potts-real-hero-iron-man-avengers-tony-stark/.

4   Matt Holloway, Art Marcum, Mark Fergus, and Hawk Ostby. "Iron Man," *Screenwriters Network*, 2007. https://www.cbr.com/iron-man-pepper-potts-real-hero-iron-man-avengers-tony-stark/.

5   John Wilson, "DC: 10 Things Everyone Forgets About Alfred Pennyworth," *Comic Book Resources*, April 29, 2020. https://www.cbr.com/alfred-batmans-butler-trivia-facts/.

6   Ibid.

7   *The Dark Knight*, directed by Christopher Nolan (Los Angeles CA: Warner Bros., 2008).

8   Ibid.

9   *Spider-Man*, directed by Sam Raimi (Los Angeles, CA: Columbia Pictures / Marvel Enterprises, 2002).

10 *The Amazing Spider-Man*, directed by Marc Webb (Los Angeles, CA: Columbia Pictures / Marvel Entertainment, 2012).

11 *Spider-Man*, Raimi.

12 Naz Beheshti, "Is It Truly Lonely at The Top?" *Forbes*, September 26, 2018. https://www.forbes.com/sites/nazbeheshti/2018/09/26/is-it-lonely-at-the-top/.

13 Arthur C. Brooks, "Why It's So Lonely at the Top." *The Atlantic*, August 27, 2020. https://www.theatlantic.com/family/archive/2020/08/how-make-friends-lonely-boss-workaholic/615709/.

14 Michael Maccoby, "Narcissistic Leaders: The Incredible Pros, the Inevitable Cons," *Harvard Business Review*, January 2004. https://hbr.org/2004/01/narcissistic-leaders-the-incredible-pros-the-inevitable-cons.

15 Ibid.

16 Ibid.

17 Ibid.

18 Bradley Tolppanen, "Great Contemporaries: Frederick Lindemann ('The Prof')," *The Churchill Project*, February 17, 2016. https://winstonchurchill.hillsdale.edu/frederick-lindemann/.

19 Andrew Roberts, *Churchill: Walking with Destiny* (New York City: Viking Penguin, 2018), 287.

20 Madhusree Mukerjee, "The Most Powerful Scientist Ever: Winston Churchill's Personal Technocrat," *Scientific American*, August 6, 2010. https://www.scientificamerican.com/article/the-most-powerful-scientist-ever/.

21 Ibid.

22 Mackenzie Martin, *Remembering Ub Iwerks, The Father of Mickey Mouse*, July 7, 2021. https://www.npr.org/2021/07/07/1013645653/remembering-ub-iwerks-the-father-of-mickey-mouse

23 Ibid.

24 Ibid.

25 Jeff Ryan, *A Mouse Divided: How Ub Iwerks Became Forgotten and Walt Disney Became Uncle Walt*, New York: Post Hill Press, 2018, 17.

26 Mackenzie, *Remembering Ub Iwerks*.

CHAPTER 5

The Command of Masks

Secret Identities and the Public Responsibilities of Leadership

Ronald J. Granieri

In the final scenes of Quentin Tarantino's two-part epic of balletic cinematic violence, *Kill Bill*, vengeance-seeking heroine The Bride finally confronts her lover/mentor/tormentor Bill at a secret resort for high-profile miscreants. While engaging in the eminently domestic activity of making a sandwich for their daughter (including using a ridiculously large butcher knife to cut the crusts off the bread), Bill begins a long soliloquy about superheroes and secret identities.

Intending to help The Bride see why she had been wrong to think she could escape her past as an assassin for the life of a small-town civilian, Bill explains how hard it can be to hide one's true nature. Of particular interest for Bill was the paradox of Superman. Most superheroes, the murderer-cum-professor explains, are (or at least were) normal humans who assumed a new identity when they donned their costumes and used their powers. Superman, however, was Kal-El from Krypton; for him, the process was reversed. To put it another way, mild-mannered science nerd Peter Parker had to choose to be Spider-Man after that spider bite. Kal-El, however, was born with near-divine powers. He had to choose to become Clark Kent, the nebbishy reporter for the *Daily Planet*, which was a comedown in power and status. Implying that The Bride was like Kal-El, Bill concluded that Clark Kent was Kal-El's satirical take on humanity, mocking us and indulging his own sense of superiority while play-acting at weakness. Bill considered this a flawed model; superheroes should not stoop to mere humanity.

David Carradine's assuredly cynical performance as Bill aside, this argument that Kal-El is mocking humanity by pretending to be weak is deeply flawed. Ultimately, Bill's argument makes more sense for a villain than a hero. Of course, a villain would chafe at the thought of voluntary self-restraint—a selfish desire to take whatever one wants whenever one wants is what makes a villain a villain. Heroes, however, act in part through selfless desire to serve. Superman works to save humanity because he feels humanity is worth saving, so it stands to reason he would want to live among human beings. One could even argue that Kal-El's masquerade reflected a bit of wish fulfillment. Clark Kent could theoretically enjoy a normal man's calm and ordered life (perhaps even marrying Lois Lane) without the heavy responsibilities that come with nearly limitless powers. Far from a burdensome pretense, living in his secret identity could be a welcome respite.

Beyond that philosophical objection, Bill's contempt for Kal-El's secret misses the important point of his and all secret identities: Secret identities are a crucial part of their heroism, though they also highlight the difficulty of reconciling great power with social order. Kal-El recognized that in a world made up of fallible human beings, superheroes may occasionally be necessary, but it can be very difficult to live with gods in our midst.[1] Heroes thus need to find ways to mix in the larger population until needed and to find the distance that can allow them to choose when and where to intervene in human affairs.

One of the ur-texts of the superhero genre, Baroness Marie Orczy's 1905 novel *The Scarlet Pimpernel*, lays out many tropes about secret identities that have shaped every superhero story since. In the midst of the Terror of the French Revolution, Sir Percy Blakeney, a wealthy British gentleman, secretly rescues French aristocrats from the guillotine, using a variety of disguises to thwart the fanatical French, embodied by the sinister secret policeman *Citoyen Chauvelin*. To the outward world (even to his disappointed French wife, the beautiful Marguerite, the viewpoint character in the novel), Sir Percy is a lazy, conceited fop who ignores politics and makes inane jokes about world affairs. However, his confederates know that "the Scarlet Pimpernel works in the dark, and his identity is only known under a solemn oath of secrecy to his immediate followers." The secret is essential to the Pimpernel's work. When a pretty French émigré, freshly arrived in England, asks about the name of her deliverer, one of those followers proclaims, "The Scarlet Pimpernel, Mademoiselle ... is the name of a humble English wayside flower; but it is also chosen to hide the identity of the best and bravest man in all the world, so that he may better succeed in accomplishing the noble task he has set himself to do."[2]

Heroes take on secret identities for a variety of reasons. To confuse and confound their enemies, most of all. The Scarlet Pimpernel's North American counterpart, El Zorro of California, also hid his skills as swordsman, horseman, and acrobat behind the foppish façade of Don Diego de la Vega.[3] Don Diego was harmless, even ridiculous, and thus was above suspicion in the eyes of corrupt authorities. Sir Percy and Don Diego were also both aristocrats, whose wealth and high society connections allowed them to gather intelligence and support detailed (and probably expensive) campaigns for justice. Both are spiritual ancestors of future multimillionaire superheroes such as Bruce Wayne, whose wealth allows the construction of the Batcave and all those wonderful toys in his utility belt.

Having a secret identity was also but one aspect of the hero persona. OG superheroes such as the Scarlet Pimpernel and El Zorro were generally masters of disguise, often appearing and disappearing at will, slipping past their enemies in various costumes, even cross-dressing to evade suspicion. Although he did not have an alter ego, Victorian superhero Sherlock Holmes (would anyone deny his superhuman detective skills?) also often disappeared into humble disguises, only to emerge at the crucial moment. In "His Last Bow," he thwarts a German spy on the eve of the First World War by engaging in a transatlantic masquerade as an Irish-American thief. "It has cost me two years, Watson," he tells his old friend at the climax, "but they have not been devoid of excitement. When I say I started my pilgrimage in Chicago, graduated in an Irish secret society at Buffalo, gave serious trouble to the constabulary at Skibbereen, and so eventually caught the eye of a subordinate agent of Von Bork ... you will realize that the matter was complex."[4] To triumph over evil, even the greatest hero sometimes needs to conceal himself.

Heroes also choose secret identities to protect their loved ones. Peter Parker initially cannot share his secret with his true love, Mary Jane Watson. He even initially foregoes any relationship out of a desire to protect her without telling her why. Percy Blakeney would understand, as he hides his identity as the Pimpernel from his beloved wife even as it damages their relationship. He acts aloof and disinterested because he is concerned that her revolutionary sentiments may betray them and because he wants to avoid implicating her. As she discovers the secret, Marguerite muses that "his coldness was a mask ... worn to hide the bitter wound she had dealt to his faith and his love. His passion would have overmastered him, and he would not let her see how much he still cared and how deeply he suffered."[5] With his "worldly inanities, his foppish ways, and foolish talk, he was not only wearing a mask, but was playing a deliberate and studied part ... to throw dust in everybody's eyes."[6] There is a paradox in the relationship between the superhero and intimate friends. Peter Parker, Bruce Wayne, or even Kal-El may want to avoid burdening a loved one with their secret, hoping to have a normal life. But keeping the secret makes any truly intimate relationship nearly impossible. Thus, it is not surprising how many of these stories, like that of the Pimpernel, end with the hero finally finding someone whom they can trust enough to tell—the willingness on one side to break the secret and on the other to keep it being an expression of love, the greatest secret of all.

All of which leads to the idea that a secret identity is essential for maintaining the essence of the hero as hero. To be anyone but no one, everywhere but nowhere, multiplies the hero's power, inspiring devotion in followers and terror in the enemies of justice. Superheroes are separate from the rest of humanity, so it makes sense to maintain that separation. One of the most potent scenes in Sam Raimi's *Spider-Man 2* comes after Spider-Man has saved an entire trainload of civilians after

Dr. Octopus has destroyed the elevated tracks. He collapses from the effort and is borne back onto the train by the grateful passengers. As he comes to, Parker realizes that he has lost his mask. He looks wide-eyed at the people standing over him, one of whom muses, "He's just a kid. No older than my son." But then two boys, who had found his mask, hand it back to him. Momentarily embarrassed, one of them says, "Don't worry, we won't tell nobody," as everyone nods. That moment of mutual trust maintains the special compact between hero and society.

Maintaining such secrecy may have seemed easier in pre-Freudian days when authors assumed heroes could maintain multiple personalities with minimal fuss. It says something about contemporary society, though, that beyond Spider-Man virtually every superhero story made in the last half-century portrays heroes with secret identities as tormented by their divided nature. For example, Bruce Wayne is no longer a playboy with an exciting double life; now, he is a brooding and damaged semi-psychopath, beating criminals in hopes of killing his own demons. Unable to share in the life of the community, superheroes become nearly indistinguishable from villains, having more in common with them than with the society they are allegedly trying to protect.

Considering how difficult it is to imagine a superhero with a secret identity and a healthy inner life, contemporary stories often dispense with secret identities altogether. At the conclusion of the first *Iron Man* movie, for example, Robert Downey Jr.'s Tony Stark shocks the attendees of a press conference by simply announcing, "I am Iron Man." Downey's acting in that scene shows how much Stark struggles with the secret and suggests why he decides to expose it. Hearing the throng of reporters shout questions about the suit he has built and its most famous wearer, Stark consciously decides to break with tradition. As a man with nothing to lose (his health being dependent on his inventions in any case) and a hunger for public acclaim, he ultimately neither needs nor wants anonymity. His announcement is both honest and profoundly selfish. Unlike Clark Kent, who never seems to be around when Superman does his thing, Stark does not want to share the spotlight with someone else, even if that someone else is himself.

What works for Stark, however, poses significant problems for the rest of society. It is not surprising that stories in which the heroes do not hide behind secret identities quickly raise complicated questions about how these demigods should live in the world. The entire *X-Men* comic and film franchise centers on how mutual suspicion and resentment can poison the uneasy relationship between mutants and humans. The mutants cannot really hide their powers, so they struggle with the need to hide themselves away. Brad Bird's *The Incredibles* also wrestles with the issue, suggesting that human society would rather ban superheroes than deal with the possibility that some creatures have powers beyond the rest of us. The most clear-eyed, even cynical view of how superheroes would function in the contemporary world comes in the television series *The Boys*, in which some superheroes are contemptuous of mere humans and are marketed and manipulated by wealthy and powerful corporations. Instead of serving humanity, the Seven become a menace to society, to be held in check by the titular Boys, who act as vigilante surrogates for a world that has neither the power nor will to stop them.

Both the *Justice League* and *Avengers* franchises, following the example of Tony Stark, make less effort to hide the identities of the heroes. They also explore how hard it can be for society to deal with the existence of superheroes, culminating in a literal Civil War. It is only with the emergence of extraterrestrial threats that humanity and superheroes can make their peace. Indeed, many of these heroes, alongside Superman, are either literal gods (Thor, Wonder Woman), sorcerers (Doctor Strange), altered humans (Captain Marvel), or extraterrestrials (The Guardians of the Galaxy) who spend much of their time dealing with problems in dimensions beyond the quotidian earth.

Indestructible superheroes who have no real relationship to human society and who can leave the planet at any time may initially appear to be awkward role models for ordinary human leaders. But as the other essays in this collection make clear, such heroes nonetheless offer useful insights into the challenge of relating leaders to the societies that they serve. This is where the concept of a secret identity proves especially important. For just as the Scarlet Pimpernel or El Zorro could inspire loyalty and respect in those who both needed and appreciated their work by maintaining their secrets, leaders today have to both connect with and separate themselves from the people they lead. Leaders may want to cultivate a common touch, but they cannot always be just regular folks. They have to know when to present themselves as leaders to help lift their spirits and direct common energies to a common goal. This can only happen if the leader is willing and able to take on a new persona when needed. As military historian John Keegan put it in his classic analysis of generalship, *The Mask of Command*: "The leader of men in warfare can show himself to his followers only through a mask, a mask that he must make for himself, but a mask made in such form as will mark him to men of his time and place as the leader they want and need."[7]

Keegan's work, with its biographical analysis of Alexander, Wellington, Grant, and Hitler, remains important not only for how he describes the way great generals appeared but even more for how they chose to appear to those that they led. Leadership does require making choices rather than leaving things to chance. The challenge for any leader is not only to be part of the community but also to be willing to stand outside of it. Taking on the responsibilities of leadership requires accepting a degree of loneliness. Leaders should resist the temptation to view those they lead with contempt or the thought that being like their followers would be beneath them. In other words, leaders should reject Bill's characterization of Kal-El. But leaders also need to know when it is necessary and proper to take on a persona that can inspire.

That inspiration does not require superhuman powers, just the willingness to see things clearly and make the necessary choices that responsibility demands. One example is Grant on the night of April 6, 1862, at Shiloh. After a day of fierce fighting, standing in the uncertain shelter of a tree in a drenching rain, Grant greeted Sherman, who had come to counsel a retreat. As he approached his commander, however, Sherman saw something in Grant that made him drop the idea of retreat. He could only say, "Well Grant … We've had the devil's own day, haven't we?" To which Grant, after pulling on his cigar, responded: "Yes. Lick 'em tomorrow, though."[8]

Whether Grant felt the confidence that he expressed in that moment is less important than his realization that he needed to express it. By presenting that image to Sherman, Grant put on the Mask of Command, inspiring Sherman to the exertions that would make the next day a success. Being able to see beyond the dreary moment and imagine the triumphs of tomorrow requires the leader to be willing to stand apart from others, to take on a different persona. By wearing the mask, the leader becomes who and what we want ourselves to be.

Notes

1   Christopher Knowles, *Our Gods Wear Spandex: The Secret History of Comic Book Heroes* (Newburyport, MA: Weiser Books, 2007).
2   Baroness Orczy, *The Scarlet Pimpernel*, Signet Classic Paperback (New York: Signet Classic, 2000), 31. Interested readers should also seek out the classic film version from 1934 (London Film Productions, dir. Harold Young) starring Leslie Howard and Merle Oberon.
3   The original Zorro story, "The Curse of Capistrano," published as a 1919 magazine serial by Johnston McCulley, was republished in novel form as *The Mark of Zorro* (Grosset and Dunlap, 1924, after the success of the 1920 silent film of that name, starring Douglas Fairbanks. The *Mark of Zorro* was remade in a 1940 version with Tyrone Power, then a 1950s television series starring Guy Williams and a 1974 US television film with Frank Langella, as well as a 1976 European theatrical version starting Alain Delon, all before the 1990s reboots starring Antonio Banderas.
4   Sir Arthur Conan Doyle, "His Last Bow," in *The Complete Sherlock Holmes* 2 vols (New York: Doubleday, 1930), 2: 978.
5   *Scarlet Pimpernel*, 136, 147.
6   Ibid., 152, 157.
7   John Keegan, *The Mask of Command*, New York: Penguin, 1987, 11.
8   Ibid., 168.

CHAPTER 6

Ethical Excellence Through Decisive Dimness

Why The Tick is "Better" Than Superman and Captain America

Jeff Drake

Gather any group of comic book fans together in a room, in any of the last four decades really, and ask them which superhero they think is the most "good"—not subjectively "the best" but objectively the most ethical, the hero with the most unimpeachable moral standards. Chances are comic book fans would agree on the two heroes at the top, and the answer would come quickly: on the DC side, Superman, and for Marvel, Captain America. It's hard to think of two superheroes more worthy of that lofty elevation. Both characters are so ingrained in our culture by now that we instinctively know how wholesome and good they are. Allies and enemies in their respective universes (along with readers of their comics) often paint Superman and Captain America as goody-goodies, Boy Scouts, perfect, maybe too perfect.

"Consider how Superman and Captain America are held up as moral exemplars within their respective universes," author Travis Smith writes in *Superhero Ethics*. "They are heroes even to the other heroes, like Michael Jordan is to other basketball players."[1] So certainly the choice of the ultimate "most good" superhero has to be one of those two gentlemen, right?

Consider Superman. He literally fell from the sky into the American Heartland, into wholesomeness. There he received his moral and ethical tutelage first, in person, from his adoptive Earth father, Jonathan Kent, and eventually from his Kryptonian birth father Jor-El. His most popular catchphrase serves as convenient shorthand for his ethical foundation: "fighting for truth, justice, and the American way," which dates back to an episode of the 1942 radio show. But one could also use "truth, tolerance, and justice," which was spoken by Pa Kent in the 1948 *Superman* film serial or "truth, justice, and a better tomorrow," which DC, in late 2021, announced as Superman's new, updated catchphrase.[2] In the 1978 *Superman* film directed by Richard Donner, Jor-El urges his son to find where his strength and power are needed among the people of Earth. "They can be a great people, Kal-El, they wish to be. They only lack the light to show the way," he says. "For this reason above all, their capacity for good, I have sent them you … my only son."[3]

On the Marvel side, consider Captain America. A frail and weak Steve Rogers, unable to join the Army because of his small size, volunteers to be transformed into a "super soldier." He would have gladly fought fascism as a non-super-powered soldier because it was the right thing to do. And that motivation, that basic moral fiber, is only strengthened by the serum.

"It is said that Captain America is the moral compass of the Marvel Universe, the standard against which all other heroes should be measured with respect to purity of heart and conscience," Smith writes.[4] American comic book readers' initial exposure to Captain America, penciled and inked by Joe Simon and Jack Kirby, was a cover image of him famously punching Adolf Hitler in the face, which might be the clearest moral statement ever dedicated to a four-color printing process. Though the comic bore the cover date March 1941, it actually hit the stands in December 1940, a full year before the attack on Pearl Harbor. From that dramatic introduction, Steve Rogers never wavered. With his portrayal in the Marvel movies, Chris Evans retained Cap's strait-laced nature but leavened it with a layer of self-effacing charm, which evolved the character considerably from his roots while keeping the moral compass true.

So, sure, Superman and Captain America are at the top, but they are not alone there. Next to them, possibly above them is an even more virtuous hero, the superhumanly strong, nigh-invulnerable blue do-gooder known as The Tick. And he's there, basically, because he doesn't know any better.

The Tick didn't appear on the scene punching Hitler in the jaw, and he didn't fall from the sky. He wasn't conceived to fight for American ideals or to stand as a beacon of the good we could all be. Nope. The Tick popped into existence in 1986 as a shill, a mascot in a newsletter published by New England Comics, a chain of Boston-area comic bookstores. Despite this less-than-noble beginning, something about the big blue crimefighter, created as a superhero parody by an eighteen-year-old Ben Edlund, stuck. Something clicked, something about him mattered to people, attracted them to him. And whatever that something was exactly, it elevated The Tick out of the hype-man game and into full-time superhero-ing.

"Initially, he appeared, and he was barely sentient. He was very strange and furred, and I think in his first appearance only spoke high school French," says creator Edlund in a recent interview. "He grabbed off the rack this identity of superhero and didn't really engage in any of the actual superhero stuff. He was, I guess, making fun of that whole idea of taking that identity on."[5]

So, The Tick survived his awkward birth and grew up, in a sense, to become a real superhero—complete with a battle cry that may not be as inspiring as "Avengers

Assemble!" but works pretty well for him: "Spoon!" And before too long, the parody part began to wash away, maybe in large part due to the glut of superheroes and villains that sprang into existence in the '90s and '00s. With all of those names and powers and origins clogging up our vernacular, the didn't seem so outlandish as he once did.

Despite starring in comics, an animated series, and two separate live action iterations, The Tick's actual origins remain cloudy nearly forty years later. He's either an alien or an escaped mental patient. (Who is to say he can't be both?) Not that his specific origin matters. Like Superman and Captain America, The Tick was born tilting toward goodness. Doing the right thing is a natural state for The Tick. But unlike those other two heroes, knowing right from wrong is as uncomplicated as knowing right from left. The Tick views life through a very simple moral lens, not childish, but certainly childlike. "I guess when we start to unwrap that, what are his morals?," Edlund says with a laugh. "They're not exactly 100 percent what we need or want or can withstand in our tribal group. I guess he's got the core moral right. He's got the good one. He's got the big one, which is to do unto others as he would like them to do unto him."[6]

His approach to life and crimefighting might best be explained by quoting author Robert Fulghum's 1986 book *All I Really Need to Know I Learned in Kindergarten*. In part, the list includes: "Share everything, play fair, don't hit people, put things back where you found them, clean up your own mess, don't take things that aren't yours, say you're sorry when you hurt somebody, take a nap every afternoon."[7] It's perfect, if you keep in mind that this "credo" applies not to The Tick's own behavior but to how The Tick sees the world and how good people move through it. From that perspective, the Kindergarten list comes pretty close.

"I don't see the Tick as an idiot. I don't see him as stupid. He's just simple," says voice actor Townsend Coleman in a recent phone interview.[8] Coleman voiced The Tick in the original animated series that ran on Fox from 1994–96, and as such was the first person to literally breathe life into the character. Coleman's voice performance set the standard for the succeeding live-action interpretations. You can hear echoes of Coleman's Tick in the cadence of Patrick Warburton, who was the first live-action Tick, and Peter Serafinowicz, who played him most recently. "He's not a dumb guy smashing around The City. He's a simple guy … smashing around The City. A simple guy, with a big heart." Coleman sees the character's guilelessness as "very justice oriented." He says, "I think The Tick was very black and white. You know? And there's right and there's wrong, and there's good and there's evil. And if you're evil, you shouldn't be here. I think his worldview would have been something that is very simple."

At that point, he switches into the Tick's voice and adds, laughing, "The whole point of life is to be good to each other, so be good to each other and do it good. "It's exactly this simplicity, of worldview and of purpose, that sets The Tick apart. He is as impervious to moral quandaries as he is to bullets. He is incapable of enduring a Frank Miller's *The Dark Tick* phase. There just aren't any thorny unanswered questions in The Tick's mind for such bleak contemplations to grab hold of. At the end of the day, the scales of justice, at least in the mind of The Tick, always end up in perfect balance. Being impervious to the gray areas of morality helps make him "better" than Superman or Captain America.

Like those two goody-goodies, The Tick is motivated by a higher calling, but his is named Destiny, with a capital D, and is anthropomorphized as a female presence speaking directly to him, albeit sometimes cryptically. Where other heroes are motivated by vengeance or trauma or the need for the world to have a beacon of good, The Tick is on a very personal journey.

"Destiny, I've only ever wanted to do what you asked of me," the Peter Serafinowicz version of The Tick asks. "And I know that's the right way."[9] Destiny speaks to him much as a higher power speaks to a recovering addict and urges that person to follow the path that his/her/their higher power has laid out for him/her/them. It is not for the addict to choose the path, but to follow it. "God has a plan," twelve-step programs say. And it's up to the addict to surrender to that plan and follow the path. This is exactly what The Tick does. Not to say that he is an addict—unless one can be addicted to destiny?

The Tick is only a hero because that's what he's supposed to be. Not because of some ideal like "America" or "freedom" but because a voice in his head tells him it's what he should do. When it comes to his extraordinary power, his binary choice is not whether to use it for good or evil, but to use it (to accept destiny) or not (to deny destiny). The math is dazzlingly clear: You are endowed with heroic powers, so you use them to be a hero. Who do you use them against? Bad guys. Who are the bad guys? The ones doing bad things. This isn't rocket science to The Tick, and thank goodness for that. He would have no ability to understand rocket science. There is no moral ambiguity like there is for a hero like Batman because the question of why, if that question even occurs to The Tick, is answered succinctly and predictably with, "Because." The decision is an easy one for The Tick because he gets a kick out of being a hero. As he says to accountant-turned-sidekick Arthur, when offering to put himself in harm's way in Arthur's stead: "I can explode and barely feel a thing. In fact, I enjoy it."[10] It's worth nothing that he makes that choice not out of the noble stance of the soldier who sacrifices himself for the good of the company.

It's my job to be a hero, The Tick seems to say, and I'm pretty good at being blown up, so I should be the one to get blown up. It's not self-sacrifice because he'll survive it and have fun doing it. In that way, for The Tick, it's less like exploding and more like, say, eating an ice cream cone. The Tick leaps before he looks, acts before considering the consequences. "This is true of heroic action, like you can't put much thought into it," Edlund says. "People who have been heroes in the past, I think, they have gone into a place that is larger than usually we live in. They have stepped into a place where they are operating more clearly and cleanly, likely (more) than they do necessarily at every point in life. And I think, it's not about thinking as much as it's they're giving themselves over to some larger collective."[11]

"In classical ethics, there is the idea that what is natural isn't simply what is empirically given or possible," author Smith writes, "but rather, what would be best—what something would be like if it were fully developed in accordance with its highest purposes."[12] Doing good because you are capable of doing good is deeply ingrained in The Tick's psyche. The Tick *is* that "something" that is "fully developed in accordance with its highest purposes."

And this is exactly what makes The Tick the most ethical superhero. He does good things only partially because he is capable of doing them. More importantly, he is entirely and utterly incapable of *not* doing good. His ethics are unimpeachable because he is incorruptible by any means. Opening himself up to corruption would indicate that he was being "bad" and "not being a hero" is not his destiny, as Destiny tells him repeatedly. "He is, I'd say, basically incorruptible," Edlund says. "The Tick is missing that fear, the fear that makes things turn out good. The constructive fear of like, 'Shit, we should measure this before we jump.'"[13]

But if one was in the market to corrupt The Tick, what method could one even use? Edlund adds, "That's the idea of, like, he has embraced his destiny. He is a radical convert to justice, and justice will provide. So, he has no other needs."[14]

He doesn't want power. He already marvels at the power he has and additionally doesn't seem to fully understand what he might be capable of. He cannot be affected by nostalgia. He doesn't remember enough of anything to even have nostalgia. He cannot be seduced romantically by women or men because none of that matters to him. Sure, his strongest emotional need is enthusiasm: He always wants more of it. But that's not really a thing with which he could be bribed or induced or lured astray. Also, ordinary riches that most people aspire to or dream of hold no sway over him. "Money is just paper," the Peter Serafinowicz version of The Tick tells Arthur.[15] Nothing that normally threatens to cloud the judgment of a superhero darkens the clear blue sky of The Tick's psyche. Beyond "fighting bad guys," he has no other need. He wants for nothing. Consider his sleeping arrangement. He's more than happy to sleep on a couch in Arthur's apartment.

Thus, through the uncomplicated filter of The Tick's childlike wonderment of the world and his loyalty to follow the voice in his head, The Tick rose to become a paragon. "There's something about what he is," Edlund says. "He sort of like just culls the best out of the people around him or something. He believes in them."[16] Destiny called The Tick, from his bed in an unnamed booby hatch or some distant expanse in space or who knows where, and he answered the call to fight bad guys, to administer justice. The world he sees in his uncomplicated mind may not fully resemble the one we know, but there's a lot of overlap. And if we look closely at The Tick's unwavering certainty and goodness we can perhaps see a little glimmer of doubt. Not from him, but from ourselves. Because if he's that certain, that untroubled, at how the world works, at what good and bad are, if it's all so clear in his admittedly simple brain, maybe, just maybe there's a possibility that he's right and we're the ones who are misguided. And maybe that makes him exactly the hero we really need right now.

Notes

1   Travis Smith, *Superhero Ethics: 10 Comic Book Heroes; 10 Ways to Save the World; Which One Do We Need Most Now? (Acculturated)* (West Conshohocken, PA: Templeton Press, 2018), Kindle Edition, location 112.
2   "Superman's Catchphrase Is no Longer 'Truth, Justice and the American Way,'" *The Wrap*, October 16, 2021, https://www.thewrap.com/superman-catchphrase-changed-truth-justice-better-tomorrow/.
3   *Superman*, directed by Richard Donner (Los Angeles, CA: Dovemead Films, 1978).
4   Smith, location 1283.
5   Phone interview with Ben Edlund, December 21, 2022.
6   Ibid.
7   Robert Fulghum, *All I Really Need to Know I Learned in Kindergarten: Uncommon Thoughts on Common Things: 25th Anniversary Edition* (New York: Ballantine Books, 2004), 2.
8   Phone interview with Townsend Coleman, October 27, 2022.
9   *The Tick*, season 1, episode 12, "The End of the Beginning," directed by Thor Freudenthal, aired February 23, 2018, Amazon Prime Video.
10 *The Tick*, season 1, episode 11, "The Beginning of the End," directed by Romeo Tirone, aired February 23, 2018, Amazon Prime Video.
11 Ibid.
12 Smith, location 1203.
13 Ibid.
14 Ibid.
15 *The Tick*, season 1, episode 1, "The Tick," directed by Wally Pfister, aired August 15, 2016, Amazon Prime Video.
16 Ibid.

PART II

AVENGERS ASSEMBLE!

"And there came a day, a day unlike any other, where Earth's mightiest heroes and heroines found themselves united against a common threat. On that day, the Avengers were born—to fight the foes no single superhero could withstand! Through the years, their roster has prospered, changing many times, but their glory has never been denied! Heed the call, then—for now the Avengers Assemble!"

—*THE AVENGERS* #150 (1977)

CHAPTER 7

Blood in the Inkwell

Kiss and Marvel Comics in the 1970s

Geoff Harkness

The best-selling and most expensive Marvel comic book ever produced involved Dr. Doom, the Fantastic Four, Spider-Man, a demon, a starchild, a spaceman, a cat, Stan Lee, a notary public, the Nassau Coliseum, a DC-3 prop plane, eight platform boots, and four syringes of human blood. I'll explain.

In 1977, Kiss, the hard-rocking costume-and-makeup-ed New York quartet, was at the height of its popularity, dashing off platinum albums and selling out arenas around the world. From day one, Kiss was conceived as the Avengers meet the Beatles. "We're a band that has a dual identity in that we're musicians, but we're also superheroes," guitarist and co-lead singer Paul Stanley has said.[1] The group consisted of distinctive members, each with a unique look and set of talents. Kiss's Demon, Starchild, Spaceman, and Cat were intended to be as iconic and mysterious as any member of the X-Men or the Super Friends.

By 1977, Kiss was well on its way to becoming a cartoon. The band had appeared in animated form on the cover of its latest album, *Rock and Roll Over*, drawn by renowned illustrator Michael Doret. In concert, Kiss breathed fire, spit blood, strummed smoking guitars, and flew over the heads of its youthful audiences. Songs such as "God of Thunder," "Hotter Than Hell," and "100,000 Years" evoked a larger-than-life universe of fantasy and science fiction. Putting the quartet in a comic book was a no-brainer. Doing so also fit with Kiss's expansionist credo.

The German philosopher Friedrich Nietzsche wrote of a will to power, referring to human's internal desire for strength and force. Kiss could be said to have a will to merchandise, deeply yearning to affix its image to all manner of retail gewgaw, be it trading card or lunch box, pillowcase or pinball machine. Kiss was a brand years before anyone talked about musicians as brands, and the group continually sought to increase its market share through publicity and merchandising. Comics, as it turned out, were the perfect avenue for both.

Kiss first appeared in comic book form in Marvel's *Howard the Duck* #12 and #13. The issues sold well, despite limited publicity—the quartet was not featured on the cover of either edition. Marvel approached the band about putting together its own comic book. Never one to pass up an opportunity for promotion through salable goods, Kiss immediately agreed. Soon after, Casablanca, the group's record label, devised a publicity stunt that was as ridiculous as it was ideally suited for Kiss's brand.

On February 21, 1977, Kiss had just wrapped up a photo shoot in the corridors of the Nassau Veterans Memorial Coliseum in Uniondale, New York. Out in the arena, Sammy Hagar was warming up 13,759 concertgoers, while the four members of Kiss were backstage, rolling up their sleeves and extending their arms.

In an essay titled "Blood on the Plates," author Stark Raven (reportedly Paul Stanley writing under a pseudonym) recounted the prickly process. "The doctor unveiled the gleaming needles, and one by one, with cold, professional precision, the veins were pierced and the dark red liquid extracted … A bond exists now and forevermore among Kiss, their fans, and Marvel Comics. A blood brotherhood of truth, justice, and rock 'n' roll."[2]

As a physician drew syringes of blood, the four musicians stopped to pose for pictures, needles submerged in flesh. The fluid was stored in a Kiss-themed medical kit and, according to a sworn statement signed by the band, remained "under guarded refrigeration until [May 26, 1977], when it was delivered in an armored truck to the Borden Ink Plant in Depew, New York."

In his 2001 memoir, *Kiss and Make Up*, bassist and co-lead vocalist Gene Simmons described what happened next. "We got into a DC-3, one of those big prop planes, and flew up to Buffalo to Marvel's printing plant, where they pour the ink and make comic books."[3] Along for the ride that afternoon was famed Marvel writer and publisher Stan Lee.

Adorned in their stage costumes and makeup and standing alongside Lee and a notary public to serve as witness, the four members of Kiss poured the vials of their blood into a vat of red ink. A photographer snapped away for posterity—and publicity. "Every kid or everybody who bought a Kiss comic book in some way was getting a little bit of Kiss's blood," Lee said in a 2016 interview.[4]

"I couldn't have imagined in my wildest dreams that America would allow me to actually *become* a comic book superhero," Gene Simmons wrote in his 2014 book *Me, Inc.*[5] On the plane ride home from Buffalo, Simmons regaled Stan Lee with Marvel minutiae. "He's apparently a big fan," Lee recalled, pleased. "He was telling me, 'Stan, do you remember that story you wrote in Spider-Man number twenty-three, the third panel on the fifth page?' He remembered everything!"[6]

Of the four original members of Kiss, none have a closer relationship to comic books than Gene Simmons. In 1958, the eight-year-old and his single mother, a concentration camp survivor, immigrated from Israel to New York City. At the time, Simmons was known by his birth name, Chaim Witz, and did not speak a word of English.

A year later, Simmons was still learning the culture and language when a friend introduced him to comic books. "I remember it clearly," Simmons wrote. "It was *World's Finest Comics*, and it included Superman and Batman. I was awed by the fact that these weren't just regular people. They were extraordinary people, leading extraordinary lives.... I was hooked. I devoured comic books.... That first *World's Finest* comic book launched my love affair with comics.... I can quote you psalm and verse from the Old Testament of comic books."[7]

Simmons says that comics were an essential part of his self-education, including how he learned to read English. He was struck by the distinct style and image of the protagonists. "The concept of anybody dressing up in outlandish outfits just attracted me," Simmons explained in a 1979 interview.[8] "They always looked completely different from everybody else. When Superman walked into a room, you noticed him. Nobody else dressed like that. I believe this relates very strongly to what Kiss does today."

As an adolescent, Simmons composed and drew his own comics and fanzines, which he self-published and sold to neighbors and classmates. Simmons was such a devotee that he penned a letter to Marvel and was astonished to receive a handwritten response from none other than Stan Lee. "Never give up," scrawled the Marvel publisher on a postcard, signing it with his first name. "That's it, I've made it," the young Simmons declared to himself.

"We were kindred spirits," Simmons wrote of Lee. "He had changed his name because he didn't want people to know he was Jewish, as had I."[9] Simmons became immersed in music in his late teens, and the future Kiss bassist changed his name, first to Gene Klein and then to Gene Simmons. In 1970, the 21-year-old Simmons met an 18-year-old singer and guitarist named Stanley Eisen. Eisen soon transformed himself into Paul Stanley and the pair set out to create the world's most colorful, cartoonish rock band. "Paul and I used to talk about that," Simmons wrote. "Kiss was a real concept. I kept talking about Superman and the Incredible Hulk, and that Kiss could be like that."[10]

To complete the ensemble, Stanley and Simmons recruited guitarist Ace Frehley and drummer Peter Criss. They envisioned a group with four identifiable characters, each one distinct but equal. The musicians drew from their own lives and experiences when creating their band identities. "The images all enhanced or reinforced characteristics in each of us, and in that way, they weren't just costumes," Paul Stanley wrote in his 2014 memoir, *Face the Music*. "They were outward shows of things inside of us. It made sense. And we all in some way enabled each other to find those personas."[11]

Kiss's costumes, makeup, and stage show emphasized the band's comic book personas. "We had them write their stories," recalls Joyce Bogart, who was married to Neil Bogart, the president of Casablanca Records. Joyce was part of a team dedicated to developing the Kiss personas so that each one was unique. "Who were each of these characters? What was the Cat? Where was he from? Why was Peter the Cat and Ace the Spaceman? We incorporated this into their PR kits and their interview stories in magazines. It gave them a mysterious aura—a larger than life essence—and kind of a comic-book quality."[12]

At times, the Kiss characters were influenced by comic books in specific ways. For example, Simmons says that the wings on his Demon costume were inspired by Black Bolt, a Marvel character who first appeared in a 1965 issue of Fantastic Four. Simmons further claims that his "devil horns" hand gesture was an homage to Steve Ditko's Doctor Strange. "When Ditko's other creation, Spider-Man, shot his webbing from his wrist, the same hand gesture was used, but upside down."[13]

Cartoon luminaries such as Spider-Man and Batman are regular people by day and costumed crime fighters at night. These superheroes go to great lengths to hide their true identities from the public, making them appear enigmatic and otherworldly. Similarly, Kiss contrived to be known only as their costumed alter egos; the band's "real" likenesses would be shrouded in secret. For more than a decade, at the pinnacle of their celebrity, the group members refused to be photographed or appear in public without face paint.

Kiss scored a surprise hit a few years into its career with an in-concert double LP, *Alive!* To capitalize on its growing popularity, the quartet doubled down on its comic book image for 1976's *Destroyer*. The album included Simmons's signature tune, "God of Thunder," where he refers to himself by Superman's nickname, the man of steel. *Destroyer* also featured the New York Philharmonic, a children's choir, cinematic sound effects, and "Beth," an earnest ballad that scored the band its first top ten hit. These efforts were aimed squarely at the hearts and wallets of mainstream America. "It was comic-book like," says Bob Ezrin, who produced the record. "When we took it to yet another stage of comic-bookdom, I understand that at first glance *Destroyer* could have looked to the hard-core grassroots critic like Kiss selling out, but more to the point it was Kiss reaching out."[14]

When Marvel approached in-house writer Steve Gerber with the idea of adding Kiss to an issue of Howard the Duck, he was reluctant. But Gerber said he changed his mind after learning that Kiss's "costumes were inspired by those of the Marvel superheroes."[15] Gerber went on to helm the first Kiss comic book, *A Marvel Comics Super Special* #1.

Super Special tells the story of four college-aged friends who metamorphose into the Kiss characters and are bestowed with superpowers. The Demon breathes fire while Starchild zaps villains with a laser beam that shoots from his pentagram. Spaceman warps time and distance as the Cat leaps about and claws things. The entire band can teleport, too, which comes in handy when it does battle with everyone from

Mephisto to Dr. Doom. Cameos abound—Spider-Man, the Fantastic Four, and the Avengers pop in for brief appearances.

"It was really the first comic book of its kind," recalls Gerber, who says that Gene Simmons had significant input into the finished product. "The difference in those earlier comic books is that they were all aimed at children. The Kiss comic was aimed at the real audience of the band. It was a leap for comic books at the time."[16]

Marvel's interest in Kiss was part of a larger plan to enter the lucrative rock magazine market, joining the ranks of *Rolling Stone, Creem,* and *Crawdaddy.* The Kiss edition was to be the first in a line of comics devoted to musicians. For the series debut, Marvel went all out, rendering the band's logo in silver metallic ink on the cover and enlarging the edition so it would be shelved alongside magazines. Production costs soared. The sixty-six-page issue was the most expensive piece Marvel had ever published, requiring a list price of $1.50 at a time when copies of *The Amazing Spider-Man* sold for 30 cents.[17]

"It was the first magazine size comic book done in color, and it was a real fight to get it done that way," says Gerber, who estimates that the entire project took two to three months. "It was going to be out there on the stands with all those other rock magazines. There was no reason for anyone to buy this if it didn't look as good as any of the music magazines. In that sense, it had to be something spectacular. It had to be something to just leap off the stands at you." Of course, the cover prominently declared it to be "printed in real Kiss blood."

The band and Marvel generated considerable publicity for their sanguine stunt, and the Kiss comic was a massive hit. "The fans went crazy," band publicist Carol Ross recalls.[18] *Super Special* #1 purportedly moved 500,000 units and was Marvel's best-selling single issue until the 1990 Todd McFarlane relaunch of Spider-Man.[19] Marvel went on to publish 41 *Super Specials* over the next decade, including installments dedicated to the Beatles and movies such as *Jaws* and *Raiders of the Lost Ark.*

Once Kiss got a taste of being comic book superheroes, the band never looked back. Illustrations were featured in lieu of photographs on the covers of its 1977 LP *Love Gun,* and the four simultaneously released solo albums the following year. Kiss commissioned a full-blown comic strip for the front of 1980's *Unmasked.* The band also partnered with Mego, the Japanese company known for its Marvel and DC action figures, to produce a popular set of Kiss dolls.

Like Marvel and DC, Kiss aimed to propel its characters from the illustrated page to the silver screen. The band's 1978 celluloid disasterpiece, *Kiss Meets the Phantom of the Park,* was produced by Hanna-Barbera, creators of *Tom & Jerry* and *The Flintstones. Phantom* was a critical flop and a low point. Peter Criss and Ace Frehley soon departed, but Stanley and Simmons soldiered on, retiring the Kiss characters for much of the 1980s and early 1990s.

The original foursome reunited in 1996, donning the costumes and makeup and packing stadiums around the globe. Since the 1990s, Kiss has made comic books a cornerstone of its merchandising strategy, partnering with numerous publishers, including Dark Horse Comics and Platinum Studios. From 1997–2000, the group worked with Todd McFarlane's Image Comics to produce a series based on the band's album *Psycho Circus*. In 2011, an Archie meets Kiss comic book and graphic novel series was launched. *Kiss Kids* reimagined the band's characters as children. Today, original editions of the first Kiss comic sell for thousands of dollars on eBay.

"Kiss can last forever. They are superheroes, like Superman or Spider-Man," manager Bill Aucoin once proclaimed.[20] After the band's mid-1990s reunion, Ace Frehley and Peter Criss departed Kiss a second time. Spaceman and the Cat lived on, however, with replacement musicians stepping into their platform boots. Like their Marvel and DC counterparts, those behind the Kiss masks are interchangeable. Anyone can don Ace or Peter's costume and makeup and play their role. Ageless, the Kiss characters can be reformatted and repackaged in perpetuity. "Kiss will continue in ways that even I haven't thought of," Simmons insisted during a 2022 podcast interview.[21] "The Blue Man Group and Phantom of the Opera tours around the world with different personnel." Whenever Kiss finally stops touring, Simmons envisions a TV show where unknowns compete for his spot in the band. "I have no problem with four deserving 20-year-olds sticking the makeup back on and hiding their identity."

Long after Simmons and company have retired, an officially sanctioned version of Kiss will be performing on a prop-filled stage somewhere, cranking out a note-perfect rendition of "Rock and Roll All Nite" while deploying the group's signature moves. The self-proclaimed "hottest band in the world" turned out to be the hottest *brand* in the world. Or at least the most enduring. Like that blood-tainted ink used to create its first comic book, Kiss intends to stick with us forever.

Notes

1   "Gene Simmons, Paul Stanley Talk About Comic Books," *Blabbermouth.net*, January 31, 2007. https://blabbermouth.net/news/gene-simmons-paul-stanley-talk-about-comic-books.

2   Stark Raven, "Blood on the Plates," in *Kiss: A Marvel Comics Super Special* (New York: Marvel Comics, 1977), 30–31.

3   Gene Simmons, *Kiss and Make-Up* (New York: Crown, 2001), 136.

4   Web of Stories, "Stan Lee (Writer)," 2016, https://youtu.be/V-Wpjcv-MqQ.

5   Gene Simmons, *Me, Inc.: Build an Army of One, Unleash Your Inner Rock God, Win in Life and Business* (New York: Dey Street Books, 2014), 20.

6   Web of Stories.

7   Simmons, 18–19.

8   David Leaf and Ken Sharp, *Kiss: Behind the Mask* (Grand Central Publishing, 2003), 6.

9   Simmons, 136.

10 Leaf and Sharp, 52.

11 Paul Stanley, *Face the Music: A Life Exposed* (New York: HarperOne, 2014), 109.
12 Leaf and Sharp, 138.
13 Simmons, 20.
14 Leaf and Sharp, 258.
15 Steve Gerber, "Kiss and Tell," In *Kiss: A Marvel Comics Super Special* (New York: Marvel Comics, 1977), 5.
16 Leaf and Sharp, 160.
17 Marvel University, "Kiss Want to Rock and Roll All Nite and Read Funny Books Every Day!" February 10, 2016. http://marveluniversity.blogspot.com/2016/02/september-1977-part-two-kiss-want-to.html.
18 Leaf and Sharp, 162.
19 Chris Kaye, "Kiss Used Band Members' Blood in Marvel Comic Book," *Business Insider*, March 28, 2021, https://www.businessinsider.com/kiss-used-band-members-blood-in-marvel-comic-book-2021-3.
20 David Leaf and Ken Sharp, 97.
21 Dean Delray's Let There Be Talk, "#660: Gene Simmons." September 16, 2022, https://www.iheart.com/podcast/299-dean-delrays-let-the-27979446/episode/660-gene-simmons-of-kiss-100882577/.

CHAPTER 8

We Could Be (Super)Heroes

Building a Resistance Movement in *The Hunger Games*

Heather S. Gregg

Following Russia's invasion of Ukraine in February 2022, the term "resistance" has become a buzzword in media coverage of the war. Within days of the invasion, average citizens flocked to voluntary recruitment centers where they received rapid training in military tactics, groups organized to make Molotov cocktails to slow Russian military vehicles entering cities, and small teams engaged in hit-and-run attacks on Russian convoys throughout the country, frustrating efforts to resupply forward troops.[1] Alongside these efforts to stop Russian military advances, Ukrainians and individuals allied with their cause launched a concerted effort to counter Russian misinformation and disinformation through cyber "elves" and to spread their own narrative as part of information warfare.[2]

The concept of resistance to invasion and occupation is not new. Resistance movements took hold throughout Nazi-occupied portions of Europe during World War II and were aided and supplied by allied powers, particularly Great Britain and the United States.[3] Resistance movements also sprang up in Soviet "satellite states"—states on the periphery of the Soviet Union under heavy political, economic, social, and military control during the Cold War—including failed uprisings in Hungary in 1956 and Czechoslovakia in 1968 but followed by a series of successful resistance movements in the 1980s, particularly Poland.[4] Somewhat similarly, the fictional Hunger Games trilogy depicts a resistance movement against the occupation of the Capitol, a tyrannical and exploitative dictatorship that rules the country of Panem.[5]

The Hunger Games trilogy offers an in-depth look at how to build a resistance movement in the face of an unjust and illegitimate power, especially the role symbols and information warfare play in explaining, fostering and spreading the resistance. Using military doctrine on resistance, this chapter considers *The Hunger Games'* protagonist Katniss Everdeen's early acts of defiance and how they became the seeds of a carefully crafted "resistance narrative" that spawned a mass movement and took down the Capitol. Katniss becomes a superhero through this resistance narrative.

As Will Brooker describes in "We Could Be Heroes," superheroes are "about imagining a better world and creating an alternative version of yourself—bigger, brighter, bolder that the real thing."[6] In *The Hunger Games* Katniss is transformed from an everyday human into a larger-than-life symbol of courage, action, and hope. She becomes the superhuman embodiment of the Mockingjay.

Building a Resistance Movement

Several military documents help explain what resistance is and how to build it. Joint Publication 3-05, *Special Operations,* defines resistance movements as "an organized effort by some portion of the civil population of a country to resist the legally established government or an occupying power and to disrupt civil order and stability."[7] The individuals and groups attempting to resist the government or occupying power are usually called insurgents, while the process of supporting these movements by an outside power is defined as unconventional warfare (UW). Typically, operatives and foreign militaries engage in UW on behalf of a government to support their own interests and policy goals in that country or the wider region.[8]

JP 3-05 and the Army's *UW Pocket Guide* identify four reinforcing components of a resistance movement. First, the "underground" is a "cellular organization within the resistance that has the ability to conduct operations in areas that are inaccessible to guerrillas, such as urban areas under the control of the local security forces."[9] Second, guerilla forces are "a group of irregular, predominantly indigenous personnel organized along military lines to conduct military and paramilitary operations in enemy-held, hostile, or denied territory."[10] Third, both of these elements are supported by "auxiliary forces," which "refers to that portion of the population that provides active clandestine support to the guerrilla force or the underground."[11] Finally, a resistance movement requires a "public component," which is a visible entity that provides political or material support but, unlike the auxiliary, does so overtly.[12] The resistance movement is separate from but supports a "shadow government" inside the country and possibly an exiled government outside the country, which are poised to take over governing once the occupying force or government in power is removed.[13]

In 2019, the Swedish Defense University and the U.S. Special Operations Command Europe published the *Resistance Operating Concept* (ROC), a 250-page manual that describes how to build a resistance movement.[14] The ROC defines resistance as "a nation's organized, whole of society effort, encompassing the full range of activities from nonviolent to violent ... to reestablish independence and autonomy within its sovereign territory that has been wholly or partially occupied by a foreign power."[15] Unlike JP 3-05 and the *UW Pocket Guide*, which can be used to overthrow existing governments, the ROC is designed to resist an occupying force and restore sovereignty and the legitimate government to power in a given country. Despite this difference, the ROC still refers to the same four components of a resistance movement—the underground, guerilla forces, auxiliary and public component—as the building blocks of a resistance movement.[16]

The ROC expands on several components of a resistance movement only touched upon in JP 3-05 and the *UW Pocket Guide*. Perhaps most importantly, the ROC pays considerable attention to the centrality of the general population for a successful resistance movement, arguing that "the population is the primary actor in a resistance."[17] Within its focus on the general population, the ROC also underscores the need for non-material components of a successful resistance movement. It emphasizes the importance of an information strategy, highlighting the need for a strategic narrative that clearly explains to the population what the goals of resistance are, communicates to a state's allies how to provide passive and active support, and signals to its adversaries the cost of invading and occupying the country. The ROC calls this a "resistance narrative."[18] Within the resistance narrative, the ROC identifies the utility of symbols, calling them "attention-getting devices."[19] Additionally, it notes that symbols are important for identifying who is part of the movement and who is not and for overall unity building.[20]

The ROC also includes the importance of nonviolent resistance as part of an overall strategy of frustrating and overthrowing an occupying power. It notes the importance of nonviolent resistance for raising international awareness and sympathy for citizens struggling under occupation while providing an avenue of activism for the broadest portion of the population, including children and those unwilling or unable to engage in violent resistance. Building off Gene Sharpe's manual, *From Dictator to Democracy*, the ROC argues that "a resistance [movement] can use various activities to undermine the enemy's control over territory and the population.[21] Nonviolent actions include protests, demonstrations, sit-ins, boycotts, occupation of government buildings or other locations, graffiti, symbols, media postings, and ignoring occupier orders." It also includes "formal statements, blogging, group presentations, distributing leaflets, wearing symbols, drama and music, joining Facebook protest groups, processions, honoring the dead, and public assemblies" as powerful means of nonviolent resistance.[22]

Finally, the ROC emphasizes the critical need to maintain legitimacy throughout all resistance efforts, especially with leadership and the shadow government. "The ROC attempts to demonstrate both the significance of national resilience and the criticality of maintaining legitimacy during the conduct of resistance operations during the struggle to restore and resume national sovereignty."[23] Without legitimacy, a resistance movement may become like the very occupying force it is fighting.

Building a Resistance Movement in *The Hunger Games*

The Hunger Games trilogy provides a powerful example of how to build a resistance movement in the face of corrupt and unjust leadership. The story begins roughly a hundred years after a rebellion destroyed North America. In its place, Panem "rose up out of the ashes … a shining Capitol ringed by thirteen districts, which brought peace and prosperity to its citizens."[24] However, another rebellion of the districts against Panem in the "Dark Days" forced the Capitol to violently put down the uprising, ending with the complete destruction of District 13. Every year since the Dark Days, the Hunger Games have been held in memory of the rebellion "to guarantee peace." Each of the 12 remaining districts is required to offer one boy and one girl, known as "tributes," through a lottery called the reaping, to fight to the death until only one is standing in a large arena generated by the "Gamemakers." Katniss Everdeen summarizes, "taking the kids from our districts, forcing them to kill one another while we watch—this is the Capitol's way of reminding us how totally we are at their mercy. How little chance we would stand of surviving another rebellion."[25]

The Capitol's chokehold on Panem is first challenged in the reaping for the 74th Hunger Games when Katniss' twelve-year-old sister, Primrose, is picked to be the tribute for District 12. Instinctively, Katniss volunteers to be the tribute in her place, an act that has not happened in decades.[26] This initial act of resistance to the ritual compounds as Katniss undergoes training in the Capitol. When her efforts to gain attention for her archery skills go unnoticed, she shoots an apple from a roasted boar's mouth just inches from the Gamemakers.[27] Katniss' resistance continues throughout the 74th game. She befriends Rue from District 11, the youngest tribute in the games, and defies the Capitol by providing a funeral for her death.[28] Finally, Katniss refuses to kill her fellow district tribute, Peeta Mellark, when they are the last remaining tributes, instead proposing they commit suicide by eating poisonous berries, forcing the Gamemakers to name both as victors.[29] From these initial acts of rebellion, the resistance movement begins to take hold.

Information warfare becomes a critical component of the resistance movement and includes intentionally crafted symbols and narratives. The Mockingjay became one of the most important symbols of the resistance. Katniss explains that Mockingjays were accidentally created when jabberjays, a species of bird that the Capitol genetically engineered to spy on citizens during the Dark Days, mated with mockingbirds. "A mockingjay is a creature the Capitol never intended to exist. They hadn't counted on the highly controlled jabberjay having the brains to adapt to the wild, to pass on its genetic code, to thrive in a new form. They hadn't anticipated its will to live."[30] Katniss is given a mockingjay pin by a fellow District 12 citizen to wear in the Hunger Games after volunteering to take her sister's place as the tribute. The Mockingjay then becomes a symbol of the resistance following her rebellious victory.[31] As the resistance builds, the symbol is used as graffiti to encourage rebellion and is even imprinted on bread.[32] Mockingjay pins are replicated and "all the rage" in the Capitol, prompting Katniss to ask: "Has the mockingjay on my pin become a symbol of resistance?"[33]

The three-finger salute becomes another important symbol of the fledgling resistance movement. Members of District 12 touched the three middle fingers of their left hand to their lips, and they then held them up in silent defiance following Katniss' decision to volunteer as tribute in place of her little sister Primrose. Katniss explains that it is "an old and rarely used gesture of our district, occasionally seen at funerals. It means thanks, it means admiration, it means good-bye to someone you love."[34] Members of District 11 also give the three-finger salute after Peeta promises a portion of his winnings to the district, and Katniss thanks the families of the fallen tributes, Thresh and Rue. It is in that moment that Katniss recognizes the impact of what she has done: "It was not intentional—I only meant to express my thanks—but I have elicited something dangerous. An act of dissent from the people of District 11."[35]

Like the Mockingjay symbol and three-finger salute gesture, songs play an essential role in the resistance. The four-note melody Rue teaches mockingbirds as a signal to Katniss in *The Hunger Games* is repeated as a form of protest in District 11.[36] Katniss sings a folk song to Rue as she dies during the 74th Hunger Games, a song known to citizens watching the event.[37] And Katniss sings "the hanging tree," a song about a lynching, which becomes a metaphor for the Capitol's unjust behavior and the resistance.[38]

The *sine qua non* of the resistance movement, however, is Katniss Everdeen herself. Her bravery in volunteering for the Hunger Games on behalf of her sister, her friendship with Rue, and her refusal to kill Peeta all become examples of resistance. Katniss herself realizes the inspiration of her actions when considering the threat to commit suicide with poisonous berries inside the arena at the end of the 74th Hunger Games. She considers the many reasons for refusing to kill Peeta but, ultimately, how that act became a key act of resistance. "But if I held out [the berries] to defy the Capitol, I am someone of worth ... could it be that the people in the district are right? That it was an act of rebellion, even if it was an unconscious one? ... Life in District 12 really isn't so different from life in the arena."[39] Following her defiant victory in the Hunger Games and tour through the districts with Peeta, Katniss' image is put on banners and used as a sign of rebellion in District 8, inspiring ordinary people to take to the streets and violently protest the Capitol.[40] And Katniss is transformed into the Mockingjay in a dress created by her stylist, Cinna, which is an act of defiance that gets him killed by the government.[41] Ultimately, Katniss is transformed from an average person into a superhero. She becomes a powerful tool of resistance.

These initial acts and symbols of resistance become the bedrock of a "resistance narrative" cultivated by the shadow government and underground, which is District 13. Assumed to have been obliterated in the "Dark Days" of the rebellion, District 13 was allowed to persist underground (literally) in exchange for not launching nuclear weapons it had captured during the fighting. A small team of conspirators—including fellow District 12 victor, Haymitch Abernathy, along with Finnick Odair, the tribute from District 4, and Plutarch Heavensbee, one of the Gamemakers—secretly work to keep Katniss alive. They successfully transport her to District 13 following her successful destruction of the arena in the "Quarter Quell," which is the 75th Hunger Games.

Katniss discovers that District 13 comprises a robust underground and shadow government headed by President Alma Coin and a team of military and civilian leaders. District 13 also includes thousands of citizens who have survived "due to strict sharing of resources, strenuous discipline, and constant vigilance against any further attacks from the Capitol."[42] District 13 includes not only guerilla fighters, but also a growing conventional force backed by thousands of citizens who have fled from other districts to join the resistance.

Perhaps more importantly than fighters, District 13 has created a robust capability to wage information warfare. Plutarch assembles a public relations team to build a series of newsreels focused on Katniss. He explains, "Our plan is to launch an Airtime Assault ... to make a series of what we call propos—which is short for 'propaganda spots'—featuring you and broadcasting them to the entire population of Panem."[43] Katniss learns that "they have a whole team of people to make me over, dress me, write my speeches, orchestrate my appearances ..."[44] However, she concludes, "what they want is for me to truly take on the role they designed for me. The symbol of the revolution. The Mockingjay ... I must now become the actual leader, the face, the voice, the embodiment of the revolution. The person who the districts—most of which are now openly at war with the Capitol—can count on to blaze the path to victory."[45]

Katniss and the propos team deploy to districts under attack to film "live-action" shots of the team engaging in staged guerilla attacks with "Soldier Katniss Everdeen."[46] A staged engagement in District 8 becomes real when the Capitol attacks a hospital in an aerial raid. Katniss and Gale, a fellow member of District 12, succeed in shooting down two aircraft. Knowing she is being filmed, Katniss delivers a speech to President Snow and the Capitol: "Fire is catching! And if we burn, you burn with us!"[47]

Katniss continues to participate in propos when her team of fighters and camera crew, dubbed the "Star Squad," secretly deploys to the Capitol to shoot a series of propos. Plutarch argues that this squad "is of most value on television," especially Katniss, who has become the face of the resistance.[48] Therefore, he directs them to "get to the Capitol and put on a good show!"[49] Ultimately, these propos, together with other information from the resistance, emboldened the population to rise up, surround the Capitol building, and rebel in mass protests that could be put down, even by force.

What *The Hunger Games* Teaches us about Building a Resistance Movement

The Hunger Games reinforces many concepts identified in JP 3-05, the *UW Pocket Guide*, and the ROC. First, it underscores the importance of a "resistance narrative" for successfully motivating the population to action and building a resistance movement. Within a resistance narrative, the Hunger Games emphasizes the importance of symbols for motivating and sustaining the movement, including most notably the Mockingjay, along with songs and the three-finger salute. These symbols, in turn, become powerful physical and verbal reminders of the resistance narrative, providing ordinary people with small forms of empowerment and allowing them to become active participants in the movement.

The Hunger Games also underscores the critical importance of legitimacy in resistance movements. When Gale asks Plutarch who will be in charge of the new government once the Capitol is defeated, Plutarch answers, "everyone ... we're going to form a republic where the people of each district and the Capitol can elect their own representatives to be their voice in a centralized government."[50] However, Katniss begins to doubt the legitimacy of the shadow government's leader, President Coin, following their successful capture of the Capitol, especially when speculation arises that Coin may have used cluster bombs against her own people to elicit greater outrage against the Capitol. Coin's call to use children from the Capitol for one last Hunger Games as revenge for years of suffering convinces Katniss of Coin's loss of legitimacy. Katniss assassinates Coin in the hopes of preventing a repeat of history.[51]

Finally, the Hunger Games identifies an additional element of a successful resistance movement not emphasized in the ROC or military doctrine, namely the importance of a person that embodies the resistance and inspires others to join the movement. Although reluctant, Katniss becomes the example to emulate through her acts of bravery, rebellion, and honesty. Katniss literally becomes the face of the movement and a living example of how to resist. Katniss is transformed from an average person into a superhero designed to inspire others to take courage and join the resistance. Her persona is further amplified through the creation of propos designed to spread the resistance narrative through Katniss' actions and deeds. Katniss herself realizes that "what they want is for me to truly take on the role they designed for me. The symbol of the revolution. The Mockingjay ... I must now become the actual leader, the face, the voice, the embodiment of the revolution."[52] Her critical role as superhero and the face of the resistance thus combines multiple elements of the resistance narrative and becomes the example of what to do and why.

At the time of writing this chapter, the world is watching the war in Ukraine unfold. The real-life example of President Zelenskyy may prove to be an example of an individual successfully embodying a resistance narrative, encouraging others to join the movement, and fighting for legitimacy and freedom for the oppressed. He may be transformed into a superhero.

Notes

1   Oren Liebermann, "How Ukraine is Using Resistance Warfare Developed by the US to Fight Back Against Russia, *CNN*, August 27, 2022. https://edition.cnn.com/2022/08/27/politics/russia-ukraine-resistance-warfare/index.html.

2   Adéla Klečková, "The Role of Cyber "Elves" Against Russian Information Operations," *George Marshall Foundation,* January 28, 2022. https://www.gmfus.org/news/role-cyber-elves-against-russian-information-operations.

3   Oliver Wieviorka, *The Resistance in Western Europe: 1940–1945,* translated by Jane Marie Todd (New York: Oxford University Press, 2021).

4   *Revolution and Resistance in Eastern Europe: Challenges to Communist Rule*, edited by Kevin McDermott and Matthew Stibbe (New York: Bloomsbury Publishers, 2006).

5   Suzanne Collins' prequel, *The Ballad of Songbirds and Snakes* (New York: Free Press, 2020), is not included in this discussion.

6   Will Brooker, "We Could Be Heroes," in *What is a Superhero?* ed. Robin S. Rosenberg and Peter Coogin (New York: Oxford University Press, 2013), 11-17. Quote taken from p. 11.

7   Joint Publication 3-05, *Special Operations* (Washington, D.C.: Joint Staff, 16 July 2014), xi.

8   United States Army Special Operations Command, *Unconventional Warfare Pocket Guide*, version 1.0 (Fort Bragg, NC: USASOC, 5 April 2016). This can also be done through proxy forces, third-party forces that act on behalf of a foreign government. It should be noted that this Army UW doctrinal construct has existed for decades.

9   Ibid., 6.

10   Ibid.

11   Ibid.

12   Ibid., 7.

13   Ibid., 8.

14   Otto C. Fiala, *Resistance Operating Concept* (Stockholm: Arkitektokopia, 2019).

15   Ibid., 15.

16   Ibid., 39–41.

17   Ibid., 17.

18   Ibid., 24–25; 36.

19   Ibid., 76.

20   Ibid., 99.

21   Gene Sharp, *From Dictator to Democracy: A Conceptual Framework for Liberation,* Fourth Edition (Boston, Einstein Institute, 2010).

22   Fiala, *Resistance Operating Concept*, 75 and 108.

23   Ibid., 17.

24   Suzanne Collins, *The Hunger Games* (New York: Scholastic Press, 2008), 18.

25   Ibid.

26   Ibid., 22.

27   Ibid., 189–190.

28   Ibid., 184–238.

29   Ibid., 343–345.

30 Collins, *Catching Fire*, 92.
31 In the book, it is a gift from "Madge," a privileged District 12 member; see Collins, *The Hunger Games*, 38. In the movie, Katniss buys the pin from Greasy Sae.
32 The Mockingjay appears in the movies as graffiti. For the Mockingjay's image on bread, see Susanne Collins, *Catching Fire* (New York: Scholastic Press 2009), 135.
33 Ibid., 91 and 158.
34 Collins, *The Hunger Games*, 24.
35 Collins, *Catching Fire*, 62.
36 Ibid.
37 Collins, *The Hunger Games*, 184–238.
38 Collins, *Mockingjay, 123.*
39 Collins, *Catching Fire*, 118.
40 Ibid., 88.
41 Ibid., 252.
42 Suzanne Collins, *Mockingjay* (New York: Scholastic Press, 2010), 18.
43 Ibid., 44.
44 Ibid., 18–19.
45 Ibid..
46 Ibid., 86.
47 Ibid., 100.
48 Ibid., 257.
49 Ibid.
50 Ibid., 83–84.
51 Ibid., 368–372.
52 Ibid., 18.

CHAPTER 9

When Being a Superhero Ain't So Super

Mathew Klickstein

MR. INCREDIBLE: I'm not strong enough.

ELASTIGIRL: If we work together, you won't have to be.

MR. INCREDIBLE: I don't know what will happen.

ELASTIGIRL: We're superheroes. What can happen?

—*THE INCREDIBLES* (2004)

Alone, We Suck; Together, We're Super!

"We may not be the prettiest, or the smartest, or the most powerful. But we don't exist for the beautiful people of the world! We're there for the oddball, the outcast, the rebel, the geek!"

It's the siren call of The Specials, the world's sixth or seventh very best superhero team. And what these superhuman (or, at least, slightly-better-than-human) mutants, monsters, and misfits lack in ability, they make up for in gumption, determination, and—most importantly—team spirit. Not to mention brand loyalty and messaging in an increasingly competitive market for superhero teams these days.

True, as chronicled in their eponymous, James Gunn-penned feature film/mockumentary (*The Specials*, 2000), when the Earth is under attack by villainous aliens from another galaxy, a volcano is about to erupt and decimate an entire chunk of Northwestern America, or the President's cat is being held hostage by terrorists, you're likely using the oval office's red phone to call a few of the *other* leagues of power saviors before scraping the bottom of the barrel with the Weevil, the Strobe, Ms. Indestructible, Amok, Power Chick, and their (more-or-less) mighty colleagues.

They're nevertheless a team whose members are both personally and professionally interdependent on one another, and by gum, they do their very best to save the world ... once given the chance. *And* for a far more reasonable government-sanctioned salary than the number one through five best superhero teams, at that! Saving the day *and* your tax dollars!

Though they might end up dropping the ball, The Specials are always ready to play the game. It's a formidable fortitude that's based solely on their rigorous standards of team building, communication amongst their members, and recruiting the very best … of the worst. Sure, first-class superheroes may go elsewhere when they're ready to join up with a protective collective: Justice League, The Avengers, the Craptacular B-sides (look 'em up). But the mystical, magical majesty of The Specials is that they exist, they survive, and they *endure*.

Regardless their abject failings, general geekiness, and seemingly supernumerary strangeness, they work under one triumphantly robust shield of justice to turn their liabilities into assets, to learn from their mistakes in an effort to continue evolving, and—ultimately—to valiantly make mediocrity itself into a milestone. The Specials are proof positive even the average or sub-average superhero who has the same problems and foibles as you and I can achieve greatness when united with his peers.

They are the *homme moyen sensuel* league of heroes. They are, like Festivus, the superhero team for "the rest of us." They are, as fellow traveler The Shoveler proclaims in *Mystery Men* (1999), "not your classic superheroes. We're not the favorites. We're the 'other guys.' We're the guys no one bets on."

"But I'll tell you what I think," The Shoveler resolutely proceeds to proclaim, "we're all in over our heads, and we know it. But if we take on this fight, those of us who survive it will forever after show our scars with pride, and say, 'That's right! I was there! I fought the good fight!' So whatdaya say? Do we all gather together, and go kick some [arch-nemesis villain] Casanova [Frankenstein] butt? Or *do I eat this sandwich?!*'

As with the similarly motley crew of outcasts showcased in *The Goonies* (1985) on their communal *Pilgrim's Progress* hero's journey from childhood to adulthood, and the Lambda Lambda Lambda uber-dweebs vying to defeat their strong and sexy campus rivals the Alpha Betas during their university's intramural Greek Games in *Revenge of the Nerds* (1984), the value of each individual's idiosyncratic peccadillos can be harnessed *together* for a powerful wallop as per Mystery Men member Invisible Boy's salient remark: "That's what's so cool about this team: Everyone has these different powers for different situations."

Off on their own, the gregarious Spleen and his embarrassingly *Le Pétomane*-esque "super"-power of hyper-controlled flatulence may simply *stink*. While hanging out alone at a late-night diner hitting on a lovely waitress, mercurial Mr. Furious may just be a furious *jerk*. And humble Invisible Boy himself may possess an ability that is so seemingly worthless on its own that it only works when no one (including himself) is watching. But when each Mystery Men member works in tandem together *Voltron/ Transformers/Mighty Morphin' Power Rangers/Captain Planet* style, their unique (if worthless as solo) powers combine to create a foundation so triumphant against their enemies that upon viewing their onscreen victory on that evening's news broadcast, even the group's resident mad-scientist-cum-nonviolent-weapons-designer Dr. Heller back home can remotely cheer them on from the comfort of his easy chair, raising a fist proudly: "That's *my* team!"

By themselves, the Mystery Men are a mere jumble of loose broken parts that barely fit in anywhere in our ever-changing society. Together, they are finely attuned cogs clicking together perfectly in a cosmic tumbler that can, as their Shoveler puts it after beating the baddest of the bad guys: "[strike] down evil with the mighty sword of teamwork and the hammer of not bickering."

As scruffy super-pal Weasel warns the morally ambiguous and massively burly Cable about the titular *anti*-superhero who can (despite his aversion to joining a team such as, say, the X-Men) be surprisingly, if not unwittingly, collaborative under the right circumstances in *Deadpool 2* (2018): "I wouldn't fuck with Deadpool … He's *built a team*: He's *unstoppable*."

This in a movie that *begins* with Deadpool suicidally blowing himself to smithereens. Alone, he's dead. But, regardless his faults (which include his wanting to destroy the very thing that makes him so super—his inability to *be* destroyed), Deadpool is, with the right teammates drawn to him as leader, saved.

Our Kryptonite, Ourselves

It's no accident that the prototypical superhero origin story often begins with not only a bang but an *accident*. A vital subtextual element embedded into virtually all superhero storylines is the protagonist(s)' reconciling their super-abilities with the fact they often never asked for or may not even *want* their new talents at all. It does, after all, impact their *non*-super ability to live a normal life without the hassles of "having" to be a hero, an exhausting and dangerous lifestyle to be sure. Often lonely, too.

The *wunderkind* Cleveland-based progenitors of Superman, Jerry Siegel and Joe Shuster, were so fascinated by this concept of a terra firma *Übermensch* who must still cope with the complex nuances of being a sentient humanoid of sorts, they produced their very own. Children of a devastating era of deep and widespread poverty ably complemented by profound global society tumult, Siegel's and Shuster's conjuring would be *both* a messianic "man of steel" *and* a thoughtful figure of their time, the tempestuously dystopian 1930s.

Being raised by humans on *their* home planet, Siegel's and Shuster's extraterrestrial savior would be imbued with complex and often contradictory human personality traits to keep him that much more grounded and approachably accessible for readers. It would make Superman far more compellingly *real* and thus *aspirational,* which was something Siegel and Shuster themselves craved, along with most of the rest of the country at that desperate time in history.

To level up the expanded narrative of Superman, ten years after his birth on ink-blotted parchment, Kryptonite first appeared in his canon via the 1943 broadcast of his continuing radio drama's episode "The Meteor from Krypton," written by George Lowther. It would take another six years for Kryptonite to appear in the comic book series itself: *Superman #61*, published in 1949.

Kryptonite would laser-focus Superman's palpable ability to fail to such an extent that it has today become a synonym for *any* of our fatal flaws. Which is particularly notable being that of the various remembrances and discussions of why Kryptonite was first introduced into the Superman saga to begin with, a prominent suggestion is that of historian Michael J. Hayde, who in his 2009 book *Flights of Fantasy: The Unauthorized but True Story of Radio & TV's Adventures of Superman* writes "it's likely that Lowther's primary intent was to create a means for Superman to discover his own origin."[1]

It's surely a revelation that injecting such an Achilles heel into the narrative flow of Superman is what in large part illuminated for him where it was he came from (or that, indeed, that Achilles heel *is an actual PIECE of where he came from, too).* It's a more potent sentiment when we consider Superman is, after all, the comic book character who is the second-most prominently featured superhero (13,164 appearances in comics as of March 2022) after Batman (14,358 appearances).[2]

Aside from being the most featured superheroes of comicdom, Batman and Superman have in common the experience of having been launched into their roles as superheroes through devastating loss, reborn as who they eventually became anew through the calamitous failure of their previous lives. And how profound this is in light of their superpowers being such an integral part of who they would become in these new identities.

It should be noted here that the *non*-superhuman Batman's "super"-powers could probably be best described by Kick-Ass arch nemesis The Motherfucker who bombastically declares in *Kick-Ass 2* (2013) "my superpower is being super-*rich!*." Or, as Kick-Ass' friend Marty notes in *Kick-Ass* (2010), Batman "has all the expensive shit nobody else has."

Batman has more money than you or me. More gadgets and doodads than you or me. Not to mention, in his earliest incarnation, he was known to be "the world's greatest detective" on par with the similarly superlative Sherlock Holmes (himself possessing the vulnerabilities of inveterate restlessness, crippling manic-depression, and a desperate dependence on opium).

It is worth noting that, *yet again*, Batman's "super"-powers herein catalogued stem from his "accidental" and extremely world-shattering origin story, one that he would likely reverse the course of if given the option. Indeed, as is realized in Christopher Nolan's coda to his Dark Knight film trilogy, Bruce Wayne casts aside his "superhero" life for a "normal" (or at least domestic) one, a family of his own thrown in for good measure.

The trick for a superhero then, whether he be one of the two most statistically prominent figures in comicdom or a member of the loseriest bunch like our Mystery Men and The Specials, is to not only work toward discovering how best to utilize his abilities-as-vulnerabilities in aid of achieving whatever goal he's pursuing, but also to hopefully find an appropriate group of those with unique powers that fit with his own in order to dramatically bolster chances of mission accomplishment.

The superhero in question must better understand himself, his powers, and what he can and cannot do with them. He must seek out (or allow himself to be sought out by) the right members of the right team that will ameliorate this understanding of how to best utilize said powers.

And finally, he must decide (or allow for, if unwitting) which goals—those on the side of "good" versus those one the side of "bad"—to work toward. This will in turn dictate which group he'll be joining and which leader he'll be following (or, of course, if perhaps *he* will be that leader himself, whether out of personal choice or circumstantial ineluctability totally beyond his control).

The only real difference, remember, between the superhuman mutants who fight under the aegis of Professor X as the X-Men versus those who fight under the banner of arch-rival Magneto is the type of guidance they received (in the form, for the most part, of said leaders themselves) when it comes to what to do with that burdensome thing that has *made* them alienated mutants—their strange but wondrous superpowers.

In the exact same way, The Motherfucker only becomes Kick-Ass' arch-rival because of the two's diametrically opposed "leaders" in the form of their very different fathers. The two in their normal, *earlier* personas were otherwise extremely similar in almost every way—same age, same class at high school, same DIY means of *becoming* "super" through an elaborate sort of cosplay, same lonely outcast status while wanting to do something *special* to stand out in the crowd.

In a very similar way, Buddy Pine (aka Syndrome, formerly Incrediboy) in *The Incredibles* universe wanted so badly to use his nerdy intelligence and drive to be a super-hero, but, without the attempted mentorship of his childhood hero Mr. Incredible, he later takes a different path, leading him toward life as a super-*villain* instead.

It is, as the namesake "super"-human creature of Mystery Men's Casanova Frankenstein in Mary Shelley's 1818 science fiction genre-launching novel morbidly pronounces, "I will revenge my injuries; if I cannot inspire love, I will cause fear."[3]

If only Dr. Frankenstein, the creature's father for all intents and purposes, had been that much better of a guiding force, and had better instructed his monstrous creation how to use his abilities-as-vulnerabilities ("injuries") for *good* instead of *evil*, for *creation* instead of *destruction*, for love *instead* of fear.

Being a Team Leader Can Be a Major Bummer

A prime candidate for the quintessential loser-as-superhero/superhero-as-loser paradigm that runs throughout so much of legacy comicdom is also defiantly irreverent anathema to the garden variety superhero/superhuman: DC Comics' Lou "Major Bummer" Martin.

Major Bummer is first and foremost billed on the covers of his 1997–1998 comics series as "the first inaction hero" by his mischievously contrarian co-creators John Arcudi (writer) and Doug Mahnke (artist), who earlier collaborated on establishing the Dark Horse comic series from which Jim Carrey's *The Mask* (1994) was a rather attenuated onscreen adaptation.

Conflict and action are the first hidebound foundational principle of other super-hero narratives. That's why such a vast majority take place in a major metropolitan city, as recalled during a lengthy discourse published as transcript in 2005 involving pioneering multigenerational comics godheads Will Eisner and Frank Miller. They spoke about two of our most prominent superhero friends in interviewer Charles Bernstein's *Eisner/Miller*:

> MILLER: It's hard to imagine what Superman would do in a cornfield in Kansas!
> EISNER: Yeah. If Superman or Batman had his lair in a small city in Nebraska [*laughs*], what kind of adventure would he have?[4]

Now, Major Bummer *does* live in a generic, chaotically bustling metropolis. And there's plenty of conflict and action swirling around him because of that. He's just chosen to ignore it so that he can instead focus his energies on his string of blue-collar day jobs and otherwise being a stubbornly sedentary couch potato.

Co-creator/writer Arcudi explicitly states in the initial series proposal that Major Bummer's original human identity before being accidentally imbued with his powers (as a thesis science project gone awry, courtesy of two bumbling alien college students) Lou ("Major Bummer") Martin is an "irresponsible good-for-nothing" whose "powers complicate and ruin [his] low stress, unambitious life, and much of his time is spent trying to return to that life."[5]

So much does Lou not *want* to utilize his newfound superhuman powers of super-size, super-strength, and super-smarts, that he is only ever referred to by his "superhero" name on the 15 issue covers of his series.

"Lou will try to stay on his own," Arcudi continues in the proposal, "but circumstances will occasionally force him to yield to the pleas of the other 'heroes' to team up with them, or drive him to seek *their* help to bail out his sorry lazy hide. Usually, he'll quit their ranks right after things have calmed down again. In other words, *this is not a team book*."[6]

Major Bummer *is* a joke concocted by two of the scene's most dynamic duo of comedy comic creators, and yet he remains so unavoidably attractive as a guiding force by his fellow freaky weirdo losers who were also imbued with superpowers by their alien college student overseers a la the 1961 *Twilight Zone* "Mr. Dingle, The Strong," in which the unassuming Burgess Meredith is suddenly granted superpowers by unseen aliens who are scientifically inquisitive about what he'll do after so empowered.

The entire *Major Bummer* run is strung along through the primary plotline of Lou's fellow extraterrestrially experimented-upon loser-y weirdos attempting to force him to both join their team *and* lead them as much as it's about the freaky weirdo loser super-villains who were *also* given superpowers by the same alien puppet-master manipulators.

After all, there can't be a *true* superhero team without a super*villain* team to battle them. As one alien college student explains, "Simply put, your [superpower implanted] body becomes a kind of magnet for danger ... The idea was to help form the team, as well as truly challenge our subjects."

The origin of Lou's and his potential team members' superpowers being the very thing that presents them with their greatest obstacles a la Superman's intimate connection to Kryptonite is hammered home with Lou's rejoinder to the alien explaining how all these extraordinary occurrences came to pass: "Yeah, I figured all the weird stuff happening to me was more'n coincidence."

Granted, Louis Martin's implanted super-team leader status was originally supposed to go to a completely different person (all-around good Samaritan Martin Lewis). But the aliens risk losing their grant for their experiment if they admit they made a mistake, so onward they must proceed with the hapless Lou.

Unfortunately for the experiment, Lou doesn't "wanna play Justice League of Dorks with nutwitted feebs," as he so colorfully puts it when his potential teammates continually come around to corral him in and lead them on following their implanted drive to fight evil and injustice.

When Lou's humble goal of being left alone to serve ice cream for minimum wage before going home to watch TV/play video games is massively derailed *by* the supervillains sent off as sentinels to attack their "good guy" counterparts (including himself), Lou will at last not only arise to fight back (he's made to believe the baddies have, amongst other things, stolen his long coveted VHS copy of *Abbott and Costello Meets Frankenstein: Director's Cut* ... including a blooper reel, after all!) but he'll act as the super-team's chosen leader to ensure the job gets done right ... or at least *fast*.

In the end, someone like Lou can't *not* be a leader. The most effective team leaders, after all, are those who lead by *doing* (whatever they have to do to achieve what they want to achieve, even if it's ultimately self-serving, as is the case with Lou). They don't need to call themselves the leader. They just *are* the leader, and their team members are invariably drawn to their irresistibly compelling charisma, to the fact that they *are* living exemplars of what their teammates want to be in order to achieve *their* goals ... even if they can't stand him on a personal level because he's an irritatingly sluggish layabout like Lou Martin.

Lou is such a resilient team leader that despite not wanting to *be* superhero leader (let alone a superhero in the first place), he succeeds *as* leader just by matter of doing whatever he has to do to get what he wants done. And his myrmidons follow suit not because they *want* to but because they inherently recognize his way—whether they agree with it or not—is *the* way to probable success. They may not "get" where he's going, but they *will* follow him wherever he's going to get there.

Lou, meanwhile, finds that as much as he wants to be left alone to sleep till noon on the ratty couch with an empty pizza box on his face to keep the light out, being part of a group does help make the world (particularly *his*) better.

The super-villains in his universe, on the other hand, end up destroying themselves in the final pages of *Major Bummer #3* by *not* working together, by *not* wielding that "mighty hammer of not bickering" that Mystery Men's Shoveler attributes to *their* win against *their* universe's baddies.

All but one of Lou's supervillain counterparts, in fact, later return in the series in a plea to team up with Lou and his newfound group to fend off *their* former leader who has gotten far too out-of-hand evil even for *them*. "See, that's why we gotta go together, Lou," they implore him: "… as a group, we'll be stronger, and we'll go to him. A surprise attack!"

Despite his faults, Lou does defeat the even bigger and stronger (*monstrously* so, actually) principal supervillain with both Lou's own team *and* the united force of the supervillain's quisling super-flunkies.

Which is perhaps the most extant proof positive that even the most obnoxiously, goofily unreliable of superheroes such as Deadpool, The Specials, Mystery Men, and Kick-Ass can best leverage their skills to overcome their failings *together* under the auspices of the right leadership—even in the unconventional situation when that leadership is initially unwitting or unwilling.

It is the glowing wisdom one can glom from the electrifying intersection of the Mystery Men's visionary sage The Sphinx: "The team must learn to work together, or mark my words, it will be torn apart," and the words of Kick-Ass' petite partner Hit-Girl: "Maybe that's the real meaning of being a superhero—it's taking that pain and turn it into something good, something right."

Notes

1   Michael J. Hayde, *Flights of Fantasy: The Unauthorized but True Story of Radio & TV's Adventures of Superman* (Duncan, Oklahoma: BearManor Media, 2009).

2   "Top 100 Most Popular Superheroes and Villains in Comic Books," *Ranker*, March 9, 2022. https://www.ranker.com/list/superheroes-ranked-by-most-comic-book-appearances/ranker-comics.

3   Mary Wollstonecraft Shelley, *Frankenstein, or, the Modern Prometheus* (New York, New York: Everyman's Library, 1992).

4   Charles Brownstein, *Eisner/Miller* (Milwaukie, Oregon: Dark Horse Books, 2005).

5   John Arcudi and Doug Mahnke, *The Complete Major Bummer Super Slacktacular!* (Milwaukie, Oregon: Dark Horse Books, 2011).

6   Italics added by author.

CHAPTER 10

Lumberjanes and Team Building the Hardcore Lady-Type Way

Julie M. Still

What does Miss Quinzella Thiskwin Penniquiqul Thistle Crumpet's Camp for Hardcore Lady-Types have to do with the Avengers and Seal Team Six? For those not acquainted with said camp, it is a scout-like summer camp for Lumberjanes, a fictional group similar to the Girl Scouts (though the copyright statement says any similarity to existing institutions is coincidental). All of these groups require teamwork in high-stakes situations. They fight for what they believe in; they work together to save their teammates, friends, and community. The teambuilding strategies they use are remarkably similar. The Lumberjanes motto is "Friendship to the max!!," which, really, is not that different from "Semper Fi!" Thus, the Lumberjanes have much to teach about loyalty to the team, team building, and the primacy of purpose.

The Lumberjanes were introduced in comic book form in 2014, originally planned as a series of eight issues. It followed a band of five misfits assigned to Roanoke Cabin, whose adventures include fighting velociraptors, river monsters, zombies, and others. The response was so positive that the comic went on for 75 issues, with offshoot publications, such as young adult novels. There are occasional rumors of a movie. It is often pigeonholed as a feminist title, since the group is entirely female, as was the initial creative team, and sometimes an LGBTQ-friendly title. The initial single issues have been collected into trades, four issues per volume.

This chapter will focus on the initial eight issues, as presented in the first two trades. The issues maintain their original number as chapters. The trade, Volume 1, includes chapters 1–4,[1] and the second, chapters 5–8.[2] Each chapter includes the first page of instructions for a badge relating to the events of that issue. Badge names supply comedic relief, for example, the Naval Gauging badge and the Pungeon Master badge. The mathematical badge is called Everything Under the Sum. Each volume includes an overall title page as if it were from the *Lumberjanes Field Manual for the Intermediate Program* and a "Message from the High Council."

The Lumberjanes clearly struck a cultural chord. The strong and positive response to the adventures of Mal, Ripley, April, Molly, Jo, and their circle of friends and associates went largely under the radar of mainstream media. This may be because the main characters are female, and teenagers at that. None of them have the precocious appearance of many young teens in modern popular culture. They display varying heights, sizes, hair colors, complexions, and stages of development. They have differing skills. The most feminine in appearance, April, is also the best arm wrestler. She is also the only one of the group to have the stereotypical oversized big baby eyes that so many illustrated women do (see all of the Disney princesses for examples). The smallest, Ripley, is the most ferocious and chaotic. She is, at times, launched at an opponent as the Avengers might send forth The Hulk or the X-Men Wolverine. Molly's hat is actually a raccoon named Bubbles that sometimes assists the team.

They may have slipped under the radar because they lack laser eyes, elasticity, invisibility, telepathy, or other superpowers. These are not the Powerpuff Girls; they cannot fly. The Lumberjanes use standard, ordinary skills such as knowledge of mathematical theories, anagrams, or archery. There are magical, mystical creatures and objects around them, but none belong to the Lumberjanes. Near the end of the eight-issue story arc Ripley thwarts two villains by taking on and then destroying a magical power they wanted. The Lumberjanes outwit and outmaneuver three-eyed foxes, a river monster, and assorted other supernatural beings with native intelligence, teamwork, and sometimes dumb luck.

How does this relate to superheroes and elite soldiers? A superhero does not always have superpowers. Most do, but not all. For example, the Bat Family (Batman, Robin, and Batgirl) has some snazzy gear but no superpowers. In the Marvel Universe, Iron Man, Black Widow, and Hawkeye are in the same category, high-tech tools but no extraordinary abilities.

We do not consider Chesley "Sully" Sullenberger a superhero, though he certainly did something extraordinary landing that plane in the Hudson River. We do not consider SEAL teams superheroes, though they also do extraordinary things. Medical professionals such as epidemiologists, virologists, nurses, and emergency room doctors have been heroic during the recent and ongoing pandemic, but we do not consider them superheroes. Perhaps we do not want superheroes in the real world, or maybe these folks need to wear colorful spandex, so we can recognize them more easily. Although elite athletes sometimes do and can accomplish feats that surely seem beyond human ability, we do not consider them superheroes.

Perhaps it is the power of the villains that makes the heroes who defeat them "super." Most supervillains have superpowers. Otherwise, unpowered superheroes might content themselves with fighting tax cheats and subway muggers. Unpowered humans fighting magical or superpowered foes makes them superheroes, although colorful spandex helps. In this regard, the Lumberjanes would be superheroes as they battle monsters, classical deities, and ensorcelled humans.

The lack of superpowers means the Lumberjanes must work together and leverage what advantages they have as individuals in order to survive attacks by stronger foes. While being an "Army of One" is a good recruitment slogan, in truth the military is a team-based organization. The lone hero, a staple of Westerns and cinematic quasi-military stories, like *Rambo*, is a romantic figure. Misunderstood, lonely, lovable but unloved, the follower of a personal code of honor that does not always coincide with that of the standard military, he perseveres, saves the day, and lives to fight again. Yet the military cannot function this way, because the goals are bigger than any one individual. Command structure is necessary. Some missions require individual action and sacrifice, but the team works together as one. Business successes are also often viewed as the accomplishment primarily of one person, the brilliant CEO or genius entrepreneur, who leads the company through a dangerous or difficult time, or the loner engineer or computer whiz who unleashes cultural change with mechanization or digital innovation. While it is true that often one individual leads the way, a close examination will usually reveal that there is usually a partner, support group or team behind the scenes.

Even superheroes work in teams. Those we think of as solitary will sometimes join in with a team, for example, Batman and Superman are also part of the Justice League. Here, too, though, it is easier to focus on individuals than on a group, perhaps more so in recent years than in earlier ones. For example, when Adam West played Batman in the 1960s television show, he consulted with his butler (Alfred), his sidekick (Robin), his gal pal (Batgirl), and his friends in law enforcement (Commissioner Gordon and Chief O'Hara). In more recent cinematic versions, Batman is much more alienated. His butler still tries to advise him, with mixed results, and he is more often than not at odds with law enforcement.

Superhero teams, such as the Avengers, the X-Men, and the Justice League, face near-constant infighting, often destructive on a massive scale. Egos run amuck, and at times no one is sure who will show up to fight until the thick of battle, not because they are unsure who is still left alive, but because hotheads threw a hissy fit and stomped off. That is no way to run any team, let alone an army. It is no way to run a rebellion either—note Han Solo's last-minute return to the fleet in the original *Star Wars* movie. If he had been part of the mission earlier, it might have gone more smoothly.

Forming a team is also a common cultural trope. The transformation of individual misfits into a cohesive team to fight bad guys, often through subversive means, has been a perennial theme seen in military television shows such as *McHale's Navy* (1962–1966), *F-Troop* (1965–1967), *Hogan's Heroes* (1965–1971), and *Baa Baa Black Sheep* (1976–1978). In recent years, the zany misfit theme has shifted to other settings such as the scientific community in *The Big Bang Theory* (2007–2019) and *Silicon Valley* (2014–2019). These are usually comedies or have a comedic subplot relating to the personal quirks of one or more team members. Nor is this exclusive to adults. A group of youngsters, either just below, at, or just above legal majority, finds themselves in a perilous situation and must work together to solve a problem, survive and find a way out or home. Examples here are *Stranger Things* (television), *The New Mutants* (comic books and television), and *The Hunger Games* (novels and movies).

Zany misfits with poor social skills and prone to arguing amongst themselves make for good television but not for an effective or productive team. In October 2015, the U.S. Department of the Army produced a lengthy Army Techniques Publication (ATP 6-22.6) entitled *Army Team Building*. The first sentence in the introduction states: "Army organizations rely on effective teams to complete tasks, achieve objectives, and accomplish missions."[3] In late 2018, this document was condensed to a two-page hip-pocket guide called *Stages of Army Team-Building*. This sets out effective team characteristics and the roles of team leaders and team members. The six characteristics of an effective team are listed as:

1. Trust each other and predict what each will do
2. Work together to accomplish the mission
3. Execute tasks thoroughly and quickly
4. Meet and exceed the standards
5. Adapt to demanding challenges
6. Learn from experiences and develop pride in accomplishments[4]

Historical surveys of teambuilding find similar characteristics. A review of 60 years of research on military teams found five significant themes: groups are often more effective than individuals, teams with a shared purpose and cohesive thinking are more effective, there are cycles of activity in a team, many teams working in concert are often required, and learning should take place within a relevant context.[5]

The military is not the only study population for teams. The civilian workforce also often works in groups or teams. Some are formed organically, others deliberately, either by choice or by assignment. Bradley and Aguinis reviewed research on teams for the journal *Organization Science* and came to several conclusions.[6] Among them are that teams are more successful if they can learn and adapt, if they start well (as teams that start well tend to continue doing well), and if they are working on similar projects at the same time as they can leverage what they learn on one to help solve another.

All three of these sources, the Army publication, the review of military teams' research, and Bradley and Aguinis contain similar themes: Teamwork, adaptivity, trust, and leveraging skills learned in one area into another. Teaching teamwork is more difficult than one might imagine. Telling people to trust each other (and to trust themselves) is not the same as those people actually trusting. There are internal factors (are people disposed to trust others?) and external factors (how trustworthy do they think others are?). Trustworthiness also has internal and external factors—do people view themselves as competent to do their job, and do they view others on the team as competent? Trust behaviors predict team performance.[7] A team that does not trust does not function well.

Instruction in teamwork, as in all things, is effective only if the literary or cultural contexts are shared. Saying something is rarer than hen's teeth is only meaningful if the person listening knows that hens do not have teeth. Saying something is rarer than rocking horse manure has the same meaning, but, again, the listener must have some familiarity with a rocking horse. A group purpose and an understanding of that purpose and how to achieve it is essential. Building a team is a difficult and nuanced task, as drill sergeants throughout history have learned. The Avengers, the X-Men, and other superhero teams had to deal with a lot of powerful people with big egos, but on a day-to-day level in military and strategic situations, success often depends on people who are barely more than scared kids, and you hope their training and group identity hold.

What makes a group cohesive and focused enough to continue when separated from its commander? The Lumberjanes are frequently apart from their camp counselor and yet stay together. In part this is because the girls trust themselves and each other, and also respect their camp counselor, even when she is not present. They trust that she will have their back and will not abandon them. How does a military/fighting group react when two people in that group have a close friendship? We saw that in the movies *Aliens*, *Forrest Gump*, and *Top Gun*, as well as in various comic-based superhero groups. We see it in the *Lumberjanes* as well. April and Jo have known each other for years and even have a special handshake. In later issues, Mal and Molly have a deeper friendship with each other than with the rest of the girls. Instead of these individual friendships interfering with team performance, they seem to enhance it, as the survival of all members requires an effective team. Jo knows that April's survival requires the rest of the team valuing her, and the rest of the team must trust that Jo will place as much importance on their survival as she would on April's.

How do you turn a small group of young knuckleheads into a fighting force that can defeat far more powerful opponents? The standard tear them down/build them up model does not work with everyone. A structure for learning shared language and culture is necessary, but most of the time, this structure is based upon and aimed at a male-dominated society. The most common use of a team that young adults in the developed world know is related to sports and athletics. Female participation in school or community sports shot up after Title IX was passed, but it still by no means equal to males. Sports and athletics require skill only in that area; broader skill sets are not required. It is also a competitive environment which might pit members of the team against each other as well as against another team. Thus, the

Lumberjanes stories provide another cultural context to use in discussing teams, teamwork, and teambuilding.

The Lumberjanes take their inspiration not from a competitive individuality but from collaborative work represented as scouting. While membership and participation in scouts has decreased as teens have more options for extracurricular activities it is still sufficiently part of the cultural zeitgeist for most to understand that structure, even if they have not participated themselves. The uniforms shown in some illustrations and usually worn by their camp counselor (but not by the girls themselves within the comic) are similar to the Girl Scout uniform. The Lumberjanes pledge is very similar to the Girl Scout Law. The Lumberjanes also parallel Girl Scouts with the use of badges and a field manual. Badges must be earned individually, but scouts can work on them at the same time, doing activities together, learning skills that can be transferred to other areas. The Lumberjanes are an organic group—randomly assigned to Roanoke cabin; they have to learn to trust each other and to overcome the challenges they face.

Very little analytical work has been done on the Lumberjanes, but one scholar, Rachel Dean-Rucizka notes, "The girls have to function effectively as a group in order to succeed."[8] She also draws parallels to early feminism, which was based on collective activity instead of individual action. As asinine as the saying "there is no 'I' in 'team'" can be, it is accurate. The rugged individual, the lone wolf with a personal agenda, has little place here.

The girls are quirky. The camp director, Rosie, constantly mangles the name of the girls' camp counselor, Jen. Some of the girls are cautious and thoughtful; others not nearly cautious enough, and that can change based on the circumstances. They rely on each other's talents. Like all teams, they do not always agree. They slip away from their camp counselor. They do not always follow orders. Their attempts at earning badges are seldom successful. These are all activities for which misfit crews are known. Yet, they are able to overcome obstacles and outwit their opponents.

While it is visually evident that they are a group of girls, and their language has feminine qualities, many of their activities are gender-neutral—hiking canoeing, archery, and other standard outdoor activities. The camp is a female-only space, figuratively as well as literally. Their exclamations invoke notable women, for example "oh my Bessie Coleman" and "Holy Mae Jemison." (Short biographies of these women were collected into the 2020 *Encyclopedia Lumberjanica*.) While most of the mythical or magical creatures the girls encounter are nameless, the reader observes a conversation between yetis guarding the entrance to a lighthouse where one calls another Janice. We don't often think of yetis as female, and this is an example of the Lumberjanes reminding readers that females are everywhere. A sense of female community is intrinsically woven into the narrative but never explicitly stated. There are no discussions of "girl power." The only gendered tension is between

Diana/Artemis and Apollo, sibling villains who are thwarted by the Lumberjanes. A group of Scouting Lads, the male equivalent of the Lumberjanes, have a camp nearby, and they are their camp counselor and director are ensorcelled by Apollo. They attack the Lumberjanes, but it is understood they do so only because they are zombified. The Scouting Lads make appearances in later issues and the girls in Roanoke befriend one of them. However, they are not intrinsic to the plot, other than as unwilling henchmen of Apollo.

It is from the badge outlines and the field manual that the most relevant and pithy training and teamwork instruction is found. The comic panels, with text and artwork, illustrate the principles found in that material. For example, this sentence from the Robyn Hood Badge (archery), found in vol. 1, chapter 4: "In these modern times the basic practices of what was once a right practice is seen more as a sport, but the Lumberjanes recognize the importance of not only the respect and care of their tools, but by training with their fellow Lumberjanes, they will learn to trust in not only each other, but in themselves and the skills they already possess."[9] The last part is almost parallel to the wording from the military team training research.

At times the wording of Lumberjanes material is overtly militaristic. The Jail Break Badge "is only earned on the battlefield."[10] Of the Con-Quest badge: "To obtain the Con-Quest badge, the Lumberjanes must display their knowledge in the art of war. They must be able to look at their challenge and understand what it takes to win. They must be able to understand what they are capable of and the capabilities of their fellow scouts."[11] This speaks directly to trust and teamwork.

More frequently, the wording is softer but still similar to the military and general teamwork literature. Adaptability is listed as an important team function. For example, in Chapter 5, "Friendship to the Craft," the Lumberjanes try to make friendship bracelets with varying degrees of success. However, they later capture rampaging velociraptors by creating a net from the bracelets and the materials used to make them. One of the Lumberjanes appears riding a velociraptor using a bridle made of friendship bracelets. A theme in chapters 5 and 6 is that not only should a Lumberjane know how and when to lead, she should know when to step aside and let someone else lead. They might not recognize the military/sports metaphor "next man up" but they carry it out in practice.

While the Lumberjanes do not possess extraordinary physical or mental abilities, they provide a good example of a successful team, and one that is accessible to people who might not participate in other cultural contexts where teambuilding is taught. The girls are frequently startled and frightened, but they persevere. They face challenges and enemies and overcome them, learn new skills and put them to use, and adapt to changes in circumstances and settings. They are confident in their abilities, and they trust each other. All of this enables them to survive the magical, mystical environment they find themselves in at a summer camp like no other.

Notes

1   Noelle Stevenson, Grace Ellis, Brooke Allen, and Shannon Watters, *Lumberjanes Vol. 1: Beware the Kitten Holy* (Los Angeles: Boom! Box, 2015).

2   Noelle Stevenson, Grace Ellis, Brooke Allen, and Shannon Watters. *Lumberjanes Vol. 2: Friendship to the Max* (Los Angeles: Boom! Box, 2015).

3   ATP 6-22.6, *Army Team Building* (Washington, DC: Department of the Army, 2015).

4   U.S. Government Printing Office, *Hip-Pocket Guide: Stages of Army Team-Building* (Washington, DC: Department of the Army, 2018).

5   Gerald F. Goodwin, Nikki Blacksmith, and Meredith R. Coats, "The Science of Teams in the Military: Contributions from Over 60 Years of Research," *American Psychologist* 73 #4 (2018): 329.

6   Kyle J. Bradley and Herman Aguinis. "Team Performance: Nature and Antecedents of Nonnormal Distributions," *Organization Science*, September 8, 2022, https://doi.org/10.1287/orsc.2022.1619.

7   Adrienne Y. Lee, et al. "Team Perceived Trustworthiness in a Complex military Peacekeeping Simulation," *Military Psychology* 22 (2020): 237-261.

8   Rachel Dean-Ruzicka, "'What the Junk?' Defeating the Velociraptor in the Outhouse with the *Lumberjanes*," in *Graphic Novels for Children and Young Adults: A Collection of Critical Essays*, eds. M. A. Abate and G. A. Tarbox (Jackson, Mississippi: University Press of Mississippi, 2017), 226.

9   Stevenson, *Lumberjanes Vol. 1*, 78.

10   Stevenson, *Lumberjanes Vol. 2*, 30.

11   Ibid., 102.

CHAPTER 11

There Was an Idea

Empowering Your Fellowships, Guardians, and Rag-Tag Misfits

Amelia Cohen-Levy

Many of us long to experience that inspiring moment when our people come together, united and ready to face a high-stakes mission—that unity of purpose, that sense of community, that commitment to something greater than themselves. When this inciting incident occurs, when a seemingly all-powerful force of evil tries to destroy all the everything, heroes take action.

This decision to act is all the more poignant when it happens among superheroes. From Tony Stark to Rocket Racoon, heroes give their individual selves over to something larger than themselves, their own needs, and their own agendas. They do so despite already being othered from the everyday world they are trying to protect. Whether they are literally of another realm or humans with special talents and abilities, they are fundamentally different from the world around them. They are misfits, and yet, they are willing to risk it all for a world that never fully accepts or understands them. When they commit to this path, they become superheroes. The orchestral music swells and the movie audience commits itself to an hours-long journey of viewing time (not counting sequels and extended universes).

I'm Always Angry: Recognizing Misfits' Superpowers

In life, literature, and film, the trope of a rag-tag band of misfits is seen time and again.[1] We've seen them in the timeline of Marvel's Earth-616 and within our own organizations. We recognize them as being "different." But, by recognizing the superpowers associated with being a misfit, we can then consider their value proposition, both the benefits to working with them and costs to working without, or in opposition, to them.

Misfits *know* they are misfits. Their behaviors, attitudes, and goals already set them apart. They have enough self-awareness to know that they aren't a perfect match with the larger community, even when there is overlap with common purposes, values, or beliefs. They know that they represent a challenge to the perceived norms of the world order and have faced the social trials that come with that reality.

We could argue whether misfits perfectly align with the characteristics and framework put forth by Lois Kelly and Carmen Medina in their book *Rebels at Work*[2] (though, if we did so, we'd naturally have to incorporate another science fiction franchise and would have more than enough to fill another chapter). Just as Kelly and Medina seek to quantify rebels and guide them into becoming an "untapped resource for creating more innovative, engaged corporate cultures," so too should we do so when thinking of misfits.[3]

To others, misfits may be seen as difficult to work with or someone who does not grok what the collective is trying to accomplish. When viewed through the lens of the collective, or one's own bias, they may seem unquantifiable. None of this makes them less talented, less interested in meaningful work, or less curious about finding ways they can apply themselves to multiple problem sets. In fact, these qualities might make them *more* valuable to a team or a mission. Misfits may not do it gracefully, or by following established processes, but they are just as capable of getting the job done.

Misfits carry a certain energy and have common traits. Those traits enable misfits to identify one another, and they can also be used by leaders to identify them. Of the many traits common to misfits—their passion, their courage (or recklessness), and their creativity—it is the most challenging to look beyond their tendency toward disruption.

Some individuals sacrifice their sense of self in order to be homogenous contributors and trade some of their own personal quirks so that they can feel like they belong. Misfits aren't inclined to do so. Over the course of their lives, misfits have experienced moments where they faced the choice to fit in or to stand out. Likely, they have tried both.

Misfits often have more reason to fear speaking truth to the collective because they have spent years being ignored, mocked, or shamed for sharing their ideas. However, by living on the periphery of that collective, they have had more time to observe it, see how it functions, and assess its capabilities. In doing so, if they see a different way, they will likely share it, even if only because they feel their purpose in life is to be the One with The Crazy Idea.

If everyone already expects them to say all the things, to raise their hand and ask the tough questions, the risks are often lessened. What's the worst that can happen—they become *more* set apart from the collective? They assess the risks, prepare for the blowback, and make their decision. They may be afraid, and they do it anyway.

When misfits speak, it's rarely without cause. To be fair, sometimes it's a social experiment, just to shake things up and see what happens. More often than not, when a misfit speaks up, they have observed that others share the same concern, but are too afraid to speak up for themselves. When a misfit speaks up, it reframes the problem. Their distinctive approach might benefit the mission or the team, but it can also inspire others. Once someone spends time with a misfit and gains an appreciation for their imaginative approaches, they may be motivated to try it on their own. In this way, misfits use their creativity and their disruption to spark innovation.

Stay Who You Are: The Challenge of Belonging

Nick Fury spent years cultivating relationships and his vast, varied network served him well. He knew that getting to know different people was time well spent. He knew that the benefits of inclusion and diverse participation usually outweighed the risks, so he either met, or sent his trusted Agent Coulson, to each of the original Avengers. They looked each other in the eye, as it were, and took each other's measure. As a result of these efforts, these leaders built the teams, or set the foundations for them, long before they were needed.

At the end of *Captain Marvel*, we see Fury fresh off his "there are more things in heaven and earth, Horatio, than are dreamt of in your philosophy" moment.[4] His experiences inspired him to create "The Avenger Initiative," crafted as "a response team comprised of the most able individuals humankind has to offer. The initiative will defend Earth from imminent global threats."[5] This becomes the ethos of the Avengers: recruiting, empowering, and collaborating with people under the banner of a shared mission.

Every individual in all the associated Marvel storylines constantly reassessed their own perception of individual value and ableness. Some people's value or ability were more obvious (e.g., thunder deity, scientifically engineered warrior, billionaire/genius/playboy/philanthropist) whereas others were more subtle (e.g., empath, sentient tree, weapons-obsessed raccoon). They did not underestimate or dismiss anyone based on their own biases or preconceived notions, partly because they understood that everyone contains multitudes.[6] As these stories evolved, characters with less-obvious value propositions turned out to be important catalysts, ready with a burst of twinkling lights, pent-up rage from a Tragic Backstory™, or a cybernetic eye stolen during a stint in prison.

None of these characters completely abandoned their sense of self. In fact, it is each one's individuality that strengthens the whole. Each individual was unique, and they were there for a reason: they were leaders; they had special abilities; or, they represented the last remnants of a dwindling race. Over time, they gained operational proficiency and built a commitment to the other members of their team that rendered their loyalty a weapon in its own right.

Each of these characters has something more important in common—they know they are different. They are not the kind of normal that allows them to sit back and watch things happen. They are not the everyday hero who works, in ways both large and small, to make the world a better place. They may be misfits, but, by virtue of their inherent capabilities, their associations, and their senses of self, they are "most able."

Misfits know they can do it alone, and that doing it alone might even be easier for them; they also know how powerful that craving for connection can be, recognizing it both as a strength and a liability. This is why misfits are so selective and place so much value on meaningful connections. Misfits have experienced the travails associated with trying to fit in—and they have likely failed at it.

When a misfit has decided not to hide their light under a bushel, they have bravely accepted all that entails. Misfits have the courage to risk disconnection. They even expect disconnection, testing the boundaries of themselves and others to see who "gets it," who sticks around, and who walks away.

So, when misfits find one another and choose to travel in packs, it is because of a profound connection. It is because they as individuals—thrown together by circumstance, a common problem, or simply because they enjoy challenging one another—have found a group that both accepts their individuality and meets their need for community. They become united by overarching goals while still retaining the integrity, authenticity, and boundaries of their individual selves. They don't get absorbed into a collective; they lend themselves to a cooperative effort.

The power of being oneself should never be underestimated, nor should the power of being oneself in a group of one-selves. When a team accepts, even embraces, the differences in their personalities, it inspires the truest sense of belonging. According to the influential podcaster and social worker Brené Brown, belonging is less about fitting in and more about being who we are.[7] When an individual feels a sense of belonging, they are better equipped to extend trust and share their creative solutioning.

Dance off, Bro: New Approaches to Old Problems

When the Guardians of the Galaxy met each other, and when the Avengers met the Guardians, they did not underestimate anyone's capabilities. They represented a variety of backgrounds, ethnicities, and capabilities and had their own experiences, skills, and perspectives from which to draw upon. They set aside their preconceived notions and risked giving each the opportunity to try, to fail, and to prove themselves. They assumed that each one was "able," even if only because they passed the initial test: demonstrating their willingness to risk their lives for the greater good.

The leaders in these groups saw these misfits as "missed-fits." They saw that the perceived opposition to the status quo did not negate their ability to be effective contributors, nor did it undermine their commitment to the shared goal. As a result, they recognized, supported, and empowered one another, becoming a team built on meaningful connections. That gave everyone the space to be themselves and still do good work, even if that goodness was accomplished in unpredictable ways.

In the 2014 film, *Guardians of the Galaxy*, the team becomes the Guardians because they put aside their own individual goals to focus on a collective mission with larger impact. Drax still seeks to avenge his family, Quill still wants to steal things, Rocket still wants to make money and blow things up, but they all know that the priority must be keeping Ronan from getting the power stone. However, all the traditional systems and approaches failed.

In an effort to regain the advantage before it was too late, Rocket crashed a spaceship into the bad guy (and members of his own team), which was an act that was most certainly not part of the conventional order of battle. It achieved its purpose and, amidst the confusion, Quill distracted Ronan by challenging him to a dance battle, another act not typically present in combat operations. Yet it worked and provided the Guardians with just enough time to collect themselves and, ultimately, come together to defeat the threat.

We Leave No One Behind: Building Trust Across Diverse Teams

There are some compatriots who, once you get to know them, become your tribe, your people, your fellowship. They are the ones who say "I'm in" before they get any details of what you're asking—they do it just because if you're in, they're in. And, that trust goes both ways.

In film, team-bonding moments are often condensed into a montage. In real life, that time spent on team building is critical, even if it is time consuming. It takes exposure and communication to build trust and confidence with one another. But that trust can be earned and nurtured when teams are comprised of strangers. The best teams work together "not by asserting their identities in conflict with one another, but by acknowledging themselves as a space in which differences could flourish."[8]

In Charles Feltman's *The Thin Book of Trust*, trust in the workplace is defined as "choosing to risk making something you value vulnerable to another person's actions."[9] From Feltman's perspective, the decision to extend trust is a risk assessment, and one that can be made by exploring four key distinctions: sincerity, reliability, competence, and care. These distinctions make it possible to assess the level of trust in smaller ways, and to do so not by making trust a zero-sum game, but by exploring opportunities to address areas where gathering more information or repairing a relationship might change the overall perception.

The distinction of sincerity speaks to the assessment that a person can be taken at their word and that their actions will align with those words. Reliability means that someone will honor their commitments, no matter what. Competence is exactly as it seems: that someone has the ability to do what needs to be done. At least one of these distinctions must be demonstrated in some way in order for individuals to have basic trust in one another, as evidenced by anyone who has ever done a group project for school.

The Guardians of the Galaxy and the Avengers have already expanded to include one another. In *Avengers: Infinity War*, Thor had encountered the Guardians and evaluated whether he could trust them. He sensed their sincere desire to protect the galaxy and judged their reliability and competence as he learned what they had done before. He recognized them. This led him to take some members on an important side quest while urging the others on to their next objective, advising them to look for the Avengers.

The Guardians who did not travel with Thor came across some of the Avengers by accident. They were all drawn to the same place in search of Thanos and, during this encounter, they made two discoveries. First, they realized they were bound by the proverb, "the enemy of my enemy is my friend." However, the relationship deepened when Thor's name served as a shibboleth indicating that they not only had a common enemy, but a common friend. That allowed them to extend a measure of trust to one other and work together. However, they worked without a strong sense of cohesion, something that led to calamity as the finer points in their distinctions of trust failed to be fully realized.

That brings us back to the fourth of Feltman's distinctions—care—which must happen naturally. A person can get a sense of the other three distinctions by meeting people and checking their bona fides. For care, people must believe that others are acting out of a genuine consideration for the interests of others. Individuals must believe that everyone is in it for more than just their own glory. That sense of caring cannot be forced. It must be genuine.

We see this when Quill is rallying the team to fight in *Guardians of the Galaxy*.[10] They have already proven their competence as warriors, but this moment amplifies and confirms the other distinctions. Quill says, "I, for one, am not going to stand by and watch as Ronan wipes out billions of innocent lives." This speaks to his sincerity and reliability, even in the face of almost certain death.

Then Gamora says, "I have lived most of my life surrounded by enemies. I will be grateful to die among my friends." Those words, especially when spoken by a character who has evolved to display more emotional capacity, demonstrates deep caring for those with her—and the pathos of her emotional vulnerability inspires the others to agree. Even Rocket, hardly known for his own effusive outpourings of sensitivity, reciprocates that caring in his own way: "Oh, what the hell. I don't got that long a lifespan anyway. Now I'm standing. Y'all happy? We're all standing up now."

It takes time for relationships to embody all the distinctions of trust. Even if teams know that they are sincere in their commitment to the cause, that they will honor that commitment, and that they will use all their capabilities in service to it, that may not be enough to foster a lasting trust that extends to all situations. When teams come to care for one another, to feel a sense of belonging, they are no longer working alongside one another; they are working *together*.

We Are Groot: Containing and Leading Multitudes

Systems cannot recognize the beauty in individual multiplicities. Individuals can—and should—because getting to know people is never a waste of time. It is our complexity that makes us interesting and, when we recognize the value inherent in every individual, makes us stronger when we work together.

As for what this means for leaders at any level and how this might inform a leadership approach, that becomes a question for the individual. Ideally, leaders will focus on building and protecting their teams, valuing them as individuals and keeping them from becoming a process or a system.

However, all leaders (in this realm) are human. They make their choices. They are fallible; they withhold information, manipulate those around them, and let their emotions take over in crucial moments. All leaders, regardless of their positional authority or influence, have to decide what kind of leader they want to be—and work at every moment to bring their best to the mission.

Notes

1 "Ragtag Bunch of Misfits," TV Tropes. https://tvtropes.org/pmwiki/pmwiki.php/Main/RagtagBunchOfMisfits.

2 Lois Kelly, Carmen Medina, and Debra Cameron, *Rebels at Work* (New York: O'Reilly Media, Inc., 2014).

3 "About," Rebels at Work. https://www.rebelsatwork.com/how-we-can-help/about.

4 William Shakespeare, *The Tragedy of Hamlet* (London: The Folio Society, 1954), Act One, Scene Five.

5 *Captain Marvel*, directed by Anna Boden and Ryan Fleck (Los Angeles: Marvel Studios, 2019).

6 Walt Whitman, "Song of Myself (1892 Version)," *Poetry Foundation*. https://www.poetryfoundation.org/poems/45477/song-of-myself-1892-version.

7 Brené Brown, *Daring Greatly: How the Courage to Be Vulnerable Transforms the Way We Live, Love, Parent, and Lead* (London: Penguin Books Ltd, 2012).

8 Edward Thornton, "Two's a Crowd," *Aeon*, March 2018. https://aeon.co/essays/a-creative-multiplicity-the-philosophy-of-deleuze-and-guattari.

9 Charles Feltman, *The Thin Book of Trust: An Essential Primer for Building Trust at Work* (Bend, Oregon: Thin Book Publishing, n.d).

10 *Guardians of the Galaxy, Volume One*, directed by James Gunn (Los Angeles: Marvel Studios, 2014).

CHAPTER 12

The Ordinary, Everyday Superhero

Mike Burke

The Dark Knight. The Caped Crusader. The Defender of Gotham. I was eight years old when my family got cable television for the first time, and in short order, Batman became a staple in my life. He was my first superhero, eventually coming to be a central figure in the formative years of my youth. My afterschool ritual was an episode of *Batman: The Animated Series*. I lived and breathed Batman. He was many things to many people, but to me he was the leader that I wanted to be.

Batman is a highly trained martial artist, incredibly wealthy, and—with family butler Alfred Pennyworth at his side—a master detective and strategist. For 75 years we watched Batman escape every seemingly inescapable situation. No matter how malevolent the foe or incredible their powers, Batman took the fight to them and emerged victorious. He was so well prepared that he had plans for his plans; he never took a situation at face value, always looking for the ever-elusive—and unlikely—outcome that lurked in the shadows. And when he rose once again in triumph, everyone was shocked, amazed, and thoroughly entertained. Except for the always stoic Batman.

The Relatable Superhero

> "You're not brave ... men are brave. You say that you want to help people, but you can't feel their pain ... their mortality ... It's time you learn what it means to be a man."
> —*BATMAN V SUPERMAN: DAWN OF JUSTICE* (2016)

At some point in our lives, we've all imagined a world where we were endowed with superpowers. What would we do if we could fly, read minds, or traverse the globe in seconds? What if we had adamantium claws, impenetrable skin, or could wield sorcery? There are an infinite number of possibilities, all fantastic and wonderous. Which, unfortunately, can make superheroes sometimes seem distant and unrelatable. Not so with Batman.

Batman is an unlikely superhero, an ordinary human with extraordinary abilities, a reluctant leader who epitomizes personal sacrifice, courage, and integrity. He's just a regular guy fighting the good fight: not a demi-god, not an AI-empowered superbeing, not the product of scientific experimentation. His mortality provides him with depth and makes him relatable. His very human limitations make him seem *normal*. When you strip away the cape, cowl, and tool belt, Batman is just an (extra)ordinary human. He's not invincible. He has no otherworldly powers. He doesn't have access to alien technology. But he does have a honed set of skills; he possesses a keen ability to outthink and outmaneuver his enemies.

Batman is very much human and vulnerable in any number of ways. A timeless element of the Batman lore has always been Alfred, whose stalwart presence provides Bruce Wayne with honest and sometimes brutal feedback, another perspective to help him overcome his own human limitations. Alfred is a subtle reminder that as leaders, we can always learn from others, that we need to be humble enough to accept those lessons and remain open sometimes to ideas that challenge our beliefs. We must strive to create environments that facilitate input and feedback, that foster open dialog and the exchange of ideas. None of us is as smart as all of us. Creating teams that understand this and incorporate feedback isn't always easy, but we must do it to leverage the collective wisdom of the group.

At his core, Batman is one of us. We relate to him. He is flawed, imperfect, and entirely human. We can't help but admire this; as humans, we want to know that someone has taken the uncontrollable and placed parameters around it, finding a way to make the impossible possible so that we can have a shred of hope. He is a mirror into our souls. A very relatable mirror.

Past as a Prologue

"Our scars can destroy us, even after the physical wounds have healed. But if we survive them, they can transform us. They can give us the power to endure, and the strength to fight."

—*THE BATMAN* (2022)

Batman's origin story has been told countless times since his first appearance in *Detective Comics*, but none is more revealing than the early scenes of the 2005 film, *Batman Begins*. After young Bruce—just eight years old—is upset during a performance of Boito's *Mefistofele*, Thomas Wayne leads the family outside the opera house and into Gotham's "Crime Alley," where he and Bruce's mother are summarily robbed and murdered. This tragedy sparks something deep within Bruce. It fuels his inner strength and feverish desire for justice. It drives him to become more.

Like so many great leaders of our time, his origin story is rooted in hardship and adversity. Though most of us aren't witnesses to the murder of our parents, we can all relate to feeling powerless at some point in our lives. Maybe it was the bully who made our lives a living hell as a child, a sibling who lorded over us during our youth, or a toxic and abusive superior in the workplace. Afterward, we told ourselves that we'd handle things differently *the next time*. We'd fight back for once, tell our parents, or quit our jobs in protest. We'd finally summon the courage to stand up for ourselves and serve justice.

Bruce felt similarly, and it haunted him his entire life. The effect of his trauma drove him to be different. He relentlessly and tirelessly trained his body, mind, and spirit, always pushing to be a better version of himself, so when the Bat Signal was raised above the Gotham skyline, he brought more to the fight than the time before. Unlike his counterparts, he couldn't just show up and be a superhero—he was an otherwise ordinary human being driven by pain and an unwavering quest for justice. He understood that we don't rise to the level of our expectations, we fall to the level of our preparation.

He couldn't stop if he wanted to. He fights a constant—and losing—battle to suppress the trauma of his past. As leaders, the experiences of our past shape who we become. They color our perceptions and interactions, sometimes even to the detriment of those around us. Batman's past often makes him inapproachable as a leader figure; his dark mystique and brooding manner is frustrating—to say the least—to others at times. As leaders we need to be vigilantly self-aware, to understand why we do what we do and how our biases can cause blind spots in our logic and actions and create barriers for those we lead. We can't control our pasts, but we need to acknowledge them.

The Reluctant Leader

> "Because he's the hero Gotham deserves, but not the one it needs right now. So, we'll hunt him. Because he can take it. Because he's not our hero."
>
> —*THE DARK KNIGHT* (2008)

Great leaders through history have shown a rare ability to turn the tide of battle, exhibiting undaunted courage in the face of overwhelming odds. These leaders weren't born of title or position, but spurred others into action through individual acts of bravery. They rose above the fray when a situation reached *critical mass*, proving their mettle and, in turn, inspiring others to follow.

Batman tends to be a solitary figure. He doesn't seek out the mantle of leadership or yearn for the company of others. He does so reluctantly, with the pragmatism of a man who recognizes when he can no longer go it alone. Nevertheless, *with great power comes great responsibility*. When the Justice League—an alien demi-god, a cybernetic superhuman powered by alien technology, a warrior princess from another time, and a faster-than-light being—coalesces as a team, they turn to Batman for leadership. Batman may be an ordinary human, but his indomitable courage inspires confidence in others. They believe in him in a way that transcends his own doubts and human limitations. They rally to him in times of crisis. They also see something in him that he might not see himself.

Each member of the Justice League shares some form of past trauma. A home planet destroyed. A life shattered. A love lost to time. A family torn apart. Batman understands trauma. It drives a compassion so deep that even he fails to recognize it at times. But the other members see it, embrace it, and honor it. He is not the strongest or fastest. He cannot "leap tall buildings in a single bound." He is just a man. A man whose courage and determination, whose ability to lead them through the most difficult of situations earns him the mantle of leadership.

His very humanity—and the innate frailties that come with it—makes him an ideal leader. He recognizes and acknowledges his own physical limitations. He knows that he's the weakest link in the chain that binds the team. He understands that if he fails, he'll likely be the first to die. As a result, he's an *all-in* leader. He throws himself into the fray like no other member of the Justice League, consistently demonstrating "courage in the face of overwhelming odds." To do anything less will likely bring defeat because the team is only as strong as its weakest link. They may be Earth's mightiest heroes—at least in this superhero universe—but the strength of the team lies in the cohesion among the individual members. Break that cohesion and the team fails. This is the essence of crisis leadership. You set aside your fears and doubts. You put your reluctance behind you. You lead the way knowing that others will follow. You lead the way with the knowledge that your courage will bring out the best in others. You lead the way confident that your combined efforts will overcome adversity.

This trait is what serves teams best. It's not about glory or recognition, it's rising to the moment and being the leader people need when it matters most. It's becoming the leader that everyone else sees, even when you do not. It's putting the needs of the many ahead of the needs of the few, or the one.

The World's Greatest Detective

> "A hero can be anyone."
>
> —*THE DARK KNIGHT RISES* (2012)

In the first act of the 2017 film, *Justice League*, Bruce is traveling the world to recruit potential members for the superhero team needed to take on the looming threat of Steppenwolf. Barry Allen (aka The Flash) is peppering Bruce with questions as they get into the latter's gull-wing Mercedes-Benz AMG Vision Grand Turismo (which has a sticker price north of $1.5 million), when Allen offhandedly asks about his particular superpowers. "I'm rich," Bruce answers flatly.

But Bruce is much more than rich. He's tenacious. He's driven. He's a natural leader. Yet none of these are superpowers. Batman's true superpower is what former Secretary of Defense and retired Marine general James Mattis referred to as "the most important six inches on the battlefield." Bruce is a genius. His cognitive skills allow him to match up effectively against any superpowered opponent.

Since his first appearance in *Detective Comics* #27 in May 1939, Batman's mind has always been subtly revealed as his true superpower.[1] His mortality made him relatable, but his intellect gave him credibility, earned him respect, and made him a leader. Even as his character evolved over the decades—changing suits, adding gadgets to his ubiquitous tool belt, and revealing more and more of his backstory—that single trait has remained consistent. He could, literally, out-think any foe.

But it doesn't come easy. Batman is a meticulous planner. He understands people and human nature, something that often evades the otherworldly members of the Justice League. He relates to their motivations, their problems. He studies his enemies in minute detail. His mind never rests—he knows that any weakness in his planning and preparation will be exploited. He explicitly understands that to emerge victorious in battle against a superior foe demands flawless plans and equally flawless execution. His obsession drives him to explore—and re-explore—every possible contingency. He leaves nothing up to luck.

In the most volatile days of the Global War on Terror, if you stepped into any military command center, amid all the brightly lit screens and briefing boards, you would have seen planners agonizing over contingencies. You might have seen briefing slides that addressed all the possible contingencies for an ongoing operation, with leaders gathered around and debating the likelihood of the events that would spur those contingencies. This is the great detective in the Batcave, his own version of a military command center. Exploring every contingency, mentally walking through every imaginable possibility.

Batman is the ultimate contingency planner. He must be because he is also surrounded by individuals whose own powers surpass the human limitations of his own physical abilities. With great power also comes great risk. If any member of the Justice League should turn against the others, that risk explodes exponentially. Any one of them could wreak havoc on the world, endangering far more than the citizens of Gotham. A fact not lost on the world's greatest detective.

In the 2000 *Justice League of America* multi-issue story arc, *Tower of Babel*, Batman contends with the risk of what the military defines as an "insider threat," the possibility that one or more of the team might break ranks and threaten the world.[2] Perceiving that a potential betrayal is at hand, he secretly studies each of the other members, identifying their potential weaknesses and developing *cautionary* contingency plans—and weapons—to neutralize them, if necessary. The true threat, it is later learned, comes from Ra's al Ghul, who steals Batman's plans and is able to defeat several members of the Justice League before the plot is exposed and order restored.

For the Justice League, this is a tipping point. Due to Batman's secretive planning and the subsequent consequences, many of the team feel that *his* betrayal warrants expulsion from the League. Others see the logic in his actions—the world's greatest detective had sound cause for concern. Superman is left to cast the deciding vote. Batman, ever the solitary figure, walks away from the Justice League before the last Son of Krypton can reveal his decision.

The People Person

> "I'm not really a people person. But when you need help—and you will—call me."
> —*JUSTICE LEAGUE (2001)*[3]

In the film version of the Justice League, each member of the team represents an actual personality you may encounter in life. Superman is the superior being, someone who transcends the group. He possesses more strength and power than the others and is typically the key to overall success. But he is conflicted about humanity and sometimes struggles to understand humankind. Wonder Woman is the hero out of time, brought up in an ancient warrior society isolated from the rest of the world. She is raised to be their champion but yearns for a life of peace and tranquility. Aquaman is the rebel, first to fight and last to apologize. He charges headlong into any conflict without so much as a passing thought. Cyborg is the brooding hero, haunted by the trauma that left him a shell of his former self and angry at the world that allowed it to happen. The Flash is the comedic sidekick—happy to be included but unsure of himself and the powers he possesses.

Each one has their own particular issues, often specifically driven by parental roles in their lives. And, in turn, those issues lie at the heart of their individual strengths and weaknesses, the genesis of their powers. While those powers often make them somewhat unrelatable, their issues have the opposite effect—they allow us to relate to them on a level we might not otherwise. And the better we relate to those characters, the stronger our connection to them.

Then there's the Batman. The loner. The dark personality. No one is ever quite sure what's happening behind the mask. He's, well … complicated.

Sometimes the best leaders are not the strongest or the fastest, the bravest or the smartest. Sometimes, the best leaders are those who simply understand others. Batman doesn't have heat vision. He can't fly. He doesn't own a truth rope. He can't talk (or do much else) to fish. He's just an ordinary human being with a problematic past and a lot of complicated family issues. In other words, the ideal person to lead a team of similarly challenged superheroes.

Through personal example and sacrifice, the team forms around him. They trust his instincts, his seemingly tireless drive. They respect his mind, his ability to see the infinite possibilities in the threat matrix. But what makes him an ideal leader for the Justice League is his innate sense of empathy. He understands how Clark Kent's grief for the loss of family—both of them—fuels his passion to do the right thing. He sees parts of himself in Wonder Woman—alone, separated in time from those who matter most. Like Aquaman, he also has a deeply rebellious side, one that drove him to seek the answers in the League of Shadows. He respects Cyborg's brooding personality and the anger and frustration that feeds it. And like the Flash, he too spent his youth isolated from family, searching for meaning in life.

Batman's empathy may indeed be his greatest strength.

That empathy is what ultimately draws the Justice League together, binds them as a team. It isn't just shared trauma, it's his ability as a leader to use empathy to connect with each of the team members on an individual level and unite them as a superhero team. In a 2021 *Forbes* article, author and researcher Tracey Brower notes, "Empathy has always been a critical skill for leaders, but it is taking on a new level of meaning and priority." Empathy is the glue that holds the team together, but it also allows them to optimize performance, increase their ability to engage as a group, and spurs innovation. When you're dealing with the stress of facing down the world's challenges every day, "empathy can be a powerful antidote."[4]

Leadership is a crucible. Even with some of the greatest superheroes around him, success was never guaranteed. The possibility of failure cast a dark shadow over the Justice League time and again. Through it all, Batman never allowed it to paralyze him. Instead, he reached deep within himself and drew on his own experiences to bring together an amazing team of superpowered individuals and form them as a cohesive team. To do that, you must be a people person. And as hard as it may be to imagine, Batman is a people person.

Years later, I still hear the words of the late Kevin Conroy—the voice of Bruce in *Batman: The Animated Series*—echoing in my thoughts. I continue to view Batman with admiration, comparing my two decades of leading across the world to his. Why? Because Batman is human. Like the rest of us, a mere mortal. Like Batman, we've all struggled at some point in our lives. Our own origin stories are often just as dark and complicated. Maybe we didn't witness our parents dying in a dark Gotham alley, but trauma is relative to our perspective. As leaders, we don't let the circumstances of our past become an excuse, instead we use them to better ourselves, build stronger teams, and strive to make the world a better place, one battle at a time.

In our own way, we're all Batman.

Notes

1   Launched in 1937, *Detective Comics* was the final publication created by Major Malcolm Wheeler-Nicholson, a World War I veteran and comic entrepreneur, who pioneered the American comic book. The publishing company he founded, National Allied Publications, would eventually evolve into DC Comics, one of the two largest publishers of comic books in the world today.

2   Mark Waid, *Justice League of America*, "Tower of Babel," #43–46 (Burbank: DC Comics, 2000).

3   Not to be confused with the 2017 film, *Justice League*, this quote is from Season 1 of the 2001 animated series, *Justice League*.

4   Tracy Bower, "Empathy Is the Most Important Leadership Skill According to Research," *Forbes*, September 19, 2021.

PART III

GREEN LANTERN'S LIGHT!

"In brightest day, in blackest night, no evil shall escape my sight. Let those who worship evil's might, beware my power, Green Lantern's light."

—OATH OF THE GREEN LANTERN CORPS

CHAPTER 13

The River of Truth

Matt Lancaster

> Doesn't matter what the press says. Doesn't matter what the politicians or the mobs say. Doesn't matter if the whole country decides that something wrong is something right.
>
> This nation was founded on one principle above all else: the requirement that we stand up for what we believe, no matter the odds or the consequences.
>
> When the mob and the press and the whole world tell you to move, your job is to plant yourself like a tree beside the river of truth, and tell the whole world …
>
> … "No, YOU move."
>
> —CAPTAIN AMERICA, *AMAZING SPIDER-MAN* #537

I remember reading these words in my friend's basement at the height of my superhero obsession, somewhere in the late 2000s. The local bookstore had started stocking trades and we had just discovered Marvel's *Civil War* run. Hype for the movies was building—this was in the days after Sam Raimi's take on Spider-Man and the first *Iron Man* film—and these words hit at the exact right time and place in my life.

I was an upperclassman in high school, trying to figure out how to get away from home and what I was going to do with the rest of my life, and we were caught in that bittersweet adolescent fugue of realizing the world is not what your parents and teachers made it out to be but also that you have no idea what it *should* be. We were not yet brave enough to follow Cap's sage wisdom, but we aspired to that level of self-confidence and righteousness in the face of our rapidly changing worldview.

Spider-Man's reply to this riff on a Mark Twain quote is to pause before asking, "Can I, like, carry your books to school? For the rest of my life?"[1]

We felt that.

Perhaps one of Cap's most famous lines, this dialogue has inspired countless online discussions and moments of self-revelation. It even featured (albeit, delivered by an entirely different character) in the *Captain America: Civil War* film, the one that introduces the prospect of fratricide to the series.[2] There is something for everyone:

A healthy dose of rose-colored patriotism.

The promise of vindication in the face of criticism, doubt, and competing belief systems.

Courage to stand up for what's right.

The fantasy of a heroic stand against opposing forces.

These words, penned in December of 2006 by J. Michael Straczynski, would inspire people like me for years to come. These words catapulted Captain America to the top of my list of favorite superheroes, and these words inspired me as I set out to begin my life. Over the years, I would revisit these words—through pinned Facebook and Goodreads quotes, as an ever-present sticky note on my laptop in college, and when trying to impress girls as being a "nerd" became popular in the early 2010s. Cap's self-assurance was exactly the shield (a little pun intended) that my emerging and conflicted identity needed to defend itself from those who would threaten or question it. As I left home and railed against the small-town values and beliefs I had been surrounded by, I was confident in the belief that my approach to the world was good and right.

One can see the problem here.

Captain America is not the strongest superhero, nor is he the most skilled fighter. From the power grid standpoint, his claim to fame is that he is substantially stronger, faster, and more resilient than a baseline human.[3] What he lacks in extradimensional power, divine wrath, and alchemical fury, he more than makes up for with an iron will and the charisma required to lead people into uncertain odds based solely on purity of belief.

Charisma and willpower can only take a leader so far, however. They can rally people of similar beliefs to one's banner initially, but what happens when a threat to that belief system arises that cannot be neatly categorized as "evil?" After the initial fervor and excitement dies down, what keeps people committed to the cause—especially in the face of adversity? In fact, when a leader starts thinking of opposing viewpoints as "the mob and the press," what happens to their credibility?

Cap's comments to Spider-Man came at a crucial time in my life. They shaped my view of leadership and my values, and I didn't realize until it was almost too late the danger of always standing up for "what we believe."

The *Civil War* event in Marvel Comics spanned seven core issues between 2006–2007, with multiple tie-in issues across its flagship characters/series throwing everyone into the proverbial pool.[4] Interested readers may wish to start with the 192-page trade paperback simply titled *Civil War*.

While the event is featured in—and even directs the course of—the MCU films, the origins of this superhuman conflict are somewhat more sinister in the comics.[5]

A small-time team of superheroes known as the New Warriors is filming a battle in Stamford, Connecticut, against a group of villains recently escaped from the Raft. One of the baddies is known as Nitro, who features the predictable ability to explode and reform himself at will, causes a blast that destroys the New Warriors, a staggering amount of civilians, and 60 schoolchildren at a nearby elementary school.

This "preventable" tragedy (the New Warriors were outclassed by those they took on but did so anyway to drive ratings for their reality show, and one of them was found to have taunted Nitro into the bombing) triggers the United States government to introduce the Superhuman Registration Act in an effort to track, curb, and direct the activities of those who place themselves above the confines of humanity and the law.

Marvel has long tied the issues that their characters face to those of their readership, and our history is darkly colored by similar efforts to categorize and ostracize the fearsome "other"—the Holocaust, Rwandan genocide, redlining and white flight, and Japanese internment camps to name only a few.[6] Naturally, the Act served as a catalyst for the superhuman Civil War.

Like in the 2016 film *Captain America: Civil War*, Steve and Tony head up opposing sides of the issue. While Iron Man had originally been an anti-registration advocate, even going so far to stage an attack against himself to demonstrate why persecution against "mutants" was a singularly bad idea, he finds the Stamford incident to be utterly indefensible and begins advocating for the oversight, training, and policing that the Act would provide, as well as for those superhumans who have yet to reveal their true identities to do so.[7] Captain America—always a champion of the people before the government in a sort of libertarian's utopic ideal—argues that if the government (read: S.H.I.E.L.D.) can control the heroes, they can control who is labeled the villains.

Tensions come to a head as Cap evades arrest and forms the Secret Avengers, and Iron Man is tasked with taking him down. Both sides give up their moral high ground as pro-registration forces hire killers such as Bullseye and Venom to seek out those who will not accede, while anti-registration revolutionaries respond in kind by bringing Punisher into the fold, who takes it upon himself to murder potential allies based on his own judgment of their past actions.[8] Lynchings, beatings, and isolated murders of resistance members give way to open conflict the world over.

The final battle devastates New York City for the umpteenth time, and just as Steve is about to deal his former friend Tony a finishing blow, a group of civilian first responders (the real heroes, as Marvel so often implies) force him to survey the damage his rebellion has caused to those he swore to protect, and he surrenders.

Like many Marvel events and story arcs, *Civil War* is aptly placed both in context and history. Having been published just five years after the events of the September 11 attacks and the establishment of the PATRIOT Act, it explores the consequences of government surveillance and intervention giving way to overreach and witch-hunting. It finished six years prior to the Boston Marathon bombing, which tragically showcased how dangerous the court of public opinion can be when several young people were erroneously identified as the culprit on social media giant Reddit.[9] It highlights the incompatibility of individualism and isolationism in a crowded world and complicated political environment with as many players as there are stakes.

Most importantly to this author, it explores the concept of truth. What is your truth, what is mine, and how do we navigate the space between? Captain America nobly planted himself beside the river of his own truth, and it led to even more death and conflict—but would it have mattered if he capitulated?

Establishing values and communicating them is an important early step for leaders, but being married to one's own viewpoint (or worse—demonizing that of others) is a surefire way to undermine that leadership.

We would like to believe that those who seek leadership positions do so out of noble intent—to share skills or experience for the benefit of all, to use their status and resources to serve those without, or to advance an organization's prospects through shared commitment to a common cause. Indeed, most do—the ranks of corporate executives, non-profit directors, government officials, and educational administrators are made up of far more folks who would do good than tyrants and despots, and these latter do not maintain their prestige in the public eye for long.

But, as the centuries-old proverb goes, "The road to hell is paved with good intentions."

Captain America's intent *was* good—to protect both the common people and their superhuman champions and to fight against political and institutional corruption. He may have even been right. It was his approach—his staunch adherence to his own definition of "right" above all else—that was his downfall and that led in part to such destabilization and chaos. Our own society is full of examples of this kind of misguided virtue signaling.

As a native Kansan, I remember well the tenure of former governor Sam Brownback. Elected in 2011, Brownback championed conservative ideals in the state of Kansas until leaving office in 2018 as one of the least popular governors in the nation, boasting a 66 percent disapproval rating and facing legislative repeals of his own gubernatorial acts.[10] He went on to serve as former president Donald Trump's Ambassador at Large for International Religious Freedom, but is remembered across the state on both sides of the political aisle for his "red-state experiment."

Brownback slashed the income tax in Kansas with the intent of establishing economic growth by increasing his citizenry's capacity to invest and spend and businesses' capacity to hire and grow—a tactic of supply-side economics and common value of his Republican party. As he signed these historic tax cuts into law in May 2012, he referred to them as a "real live experiment."[11]

As the years went by, members of his own party cautioned him against the catastrophic effects these cuts were having on the state's economy and urged him to roll back the cuts. The state faced a budget deficit of hundreds of millions of dollars. Rather than heeding those around him, Brownback stuck to his guns, and many state agencies—most notably the areas of education and transportation—took hits that would take years to recover from. As the experiment continued to fail, he was forced to borrow from the state pension fund and other self-sustaining areas to prop up his general budget, leading to a bi-partisan coalition rolling back most of his dramatic tax reforms despite his veto of the measures shortly before he left office.[12] Among the many controversies plaguing his tenure as governor, his legacy has been defined by the way he continued to tank the Kansas economy and its infrastructure despite a wealth of criticism from around the nation.

Brownback planted himself like a tree beside the river of the "Reagan Formula," and his people suffered for it.

Regardless of politics, most readers will remember the days of walking into a Blockbuster store on a Friday afternoon and picking out a movie or two—and perhaps a bucket of popcorn—for the weekend. It was a summer ritual for my family, and one that has been lost like so many others to the rose-colored haze of nostalgia. In the span of roughly a decade, Blockbuster went from a titan of home entertainment boasting 9,000 stores to one of the most well-documented failures of the "old days."

The video rental chain had multiple opportunities to see the writing on the wall. It walked away from a buyout of the fledgling startup known as Netflix. It stuck to an outdated revenue model centered on pricing that big box retailers were undercutting and late fees that competitors stopped charging. It brought on investors and executives that scoffed at the move to online business in favor of brick-and-mortar stores. Blockbuster adhered to an outdated business strategy and financial model in the face of a changing landscape, perhaps favoring the stability of what it had known and done best for years.[13]

No matter the odds or consequences, Blockbuster refused to pivot, and so it failed.

The rise and fall of former president Donald Trump is perhaps an unprecedented tale of the modern era—and, based on the violence and fallout of his succession in the Oval Office—hopefully unlike anything the United States will see again. The president's antics, personality, and politics aside, the events of January 6, 2021, speak to the potential dangers of leadership built on infectious charisma and ironclad resolve.

At the time of this writing, Trump's involvement with the attack on the United States Capitol has yet to be officially determined, though the former president has been subpoenaed to speak before the investigative committee. But, in a dark mirror to the First Avenger's adherence to his own principles no matter the odds, Trump's leadership undoubtedly added fuel to the insurrectionist fire.

In the days, weeks, and months following the election, Trump repeatedly took to social media decrying the results and making (ultimately baseless) claims of fraud and abuse of power. He spoke of president-elect Joe Biden and his party as a king does of a usurper, and refused to concede even as many of his allies quietly accepted the outcome. After the debate leading up to the election, he cryptically advised his more militant supporters—those of the white nationalist group the "Proud Boys," for example—to "stand back and stand by," rather than condemning the looming threat of violence outright. On the day of the Capitol riot, Trump knew that many attendees of his "Save America" rally were armed, and stoked them to a near-religious fervor using language revolving around fighting, then resisted deploying the National Guard to quell the insurrection once his followers had breached the Capitol building, erected a gallows, and begun calling for the death of then vice-president Mike Pence among others.[14]

Donald Trump's presidency and legacy may be defined by his ability to motivate the masses that others had forgotten. In a vacuum, his persona could be called "charismatic" to say the least, as evidenced by the fact that years after his election loss and impeachment and in the midst of a criminal investigation one can still see his flag flying high in communities across the nation.

In the face of defeat and after the world told him to move, Trump told the mob and the press, "No, *you* move," and it very nearly led to a violent overthrow of the United States Capitol.

Fortunately, the consequences of this kind of individualistic and idealistic leadership are recorded plainly for us to reflect on.

Captain America, upon seeing the destruction his faction's desperate need for vindication had wrought upon those he served, ultimately surrendered. Does this mean that Tony was right all along? Unlikely—the Human Torch was beaten into a coma outside of a nightclub, and one of the survivors of the New Warriors, Speedball, was shot en route to the courthouse where he would agree to register. The unfortunate truth of *Civil War* is that neither was completely right, and that there may not *be* a "right."

Brownback left office and his state in ignominy, after causing devastating damage to the Kansas economy and financial infrastructure. Had he been open to the counsel of policymakers in and outside of his party, could his vision of the "red-state experiment" had a more positive outcome? Perhaps not, but the manner in which his office handled the criticism and obvious financial blowback leaves Kansas unlikely to try it again.

Blockbuster has been reduced to one physical holdout and a fading collective memory. Had it considered the changing times and the dawn of online commerce, would it still be a major player? It is likely that the entertainment streaming ecosystem would look substantially different than it does today had it been founded on Blockbuster's brick-and-mortar success with the innovation that Netflix brought to the table.

Trump stands accused of inciting insurrection and the legal, cultural, and socioeconomic damage done to our nation from the five-hour riot will not be fully understood for some time. Had he accepted his defeat and helped facilitate a peaceful transition of power from the announcement of the election results, would the nation still stand so close to the precipice of civil strife? Perhaps this is the way politics will be from now on, though one can hope for a return to some sort of civility.

Though one can imagine that Captain America would have something to say about being compared to Reaganomics, corporate strife, or Donald Trump, each of them illustrates how adhering too closely to one's personal values and blinding oneself to legitimate counterpoints from the opposition leads to a breakdown of order and a failure of leadership. While Cap's call to stand for "what you believe in" is a noble one, it can be misguided, and there are lessons to be learned from his downfall.

Steve's eventual acceptance of the pro-registration movement is a result of being confronted with the pain and suffering inflicted on the "little guys"—the first responders who have to clean up the damage, the world population that is suffering at the hands of the real villains now that the world's superheroes are embattled with each other, and the ordinary civilians who have died in droves. The power comes from the people, and the ultimate responsibility is to them. This is the first humbling lesson that aspiring leaders must come to terms with and the one that is easiest to express and most difficult to swallow.

Leadership is service.

Whether one is voted in, promoted, or simply takes charge in a leaderless environment, it is easy to assume that the talents, skills, values, and charisma that put them there is enough to sustain effective leadership. This is not the case. Being a true leader of people—one they come to rely upon, one that brings about effective change and success in an organization, and one that can hang their hat on a good day of work or conversation or initiative, means knowing when to set aside what you know to be right. It is knowing which hills to die on, which rivers to plant yourself besides, and when you may have hitched your horse to the wrong buggy.

I have experienced this all too often in my own roles as an educational leader—assuming that because we all belong to the same organization and want the same outcomes for our students, that we all agree on the best way to get there (and that the best way is my way). I am often wrong.

Leaders must listen to the people they serve and to external input. As in all things, there is a balance; spending one's time listening to constant griping is unproductive, as is taking everything that detractors would say personally and so suffering from analysis paralysis. We start with our values, we communicate those values, and then we work to align them with those under our leadership so that the end result is something greater than any of us could have imagined on our own.

Being a leader means being willing to be wrong, and to accept that others may know something more than you, as simple as that sounds. Being a leader means to stand up not only for what you believe in, but for what your people believe in as well. Being a leader means that when the mob and the press and the whole world tell you to move, it might be because you aren't seeing the whole picture. And if Captain America can learn that I think our leaders can, too.

Notes

1   Mark Twain, *The Bible According to Mark Twain: Irreverent Writings on Eden, Heaven, and the Flood by America's Master Satirist*. Ed. Howard G. Baetzhold and Joseph B. McCullough (New York: Simon & Schuster, 1996).

2   In this film, the Superhuman Registration Act is replaced by the Sokovia Accords, proposed by the U.N. after the catastrophic events of *Avengers: Age of Ultron*. The line is delivered by S.H.I.E.L.D. agent Sharon Carter at the funeral of her great-aunt and former director Peggy.

3   A matrix by which Marvel characters may be informally categorized according to their relative powers and abilities, available at https://marvel.fandom.com/wiki/Power_Grid.

4   Marvel often uses "events" to focus and advance their overall narrative—some popular events include *Civil War, Secret Wars*, and *Infinity Gauntlet*.

5   The conflict stemming from the movie *Captain America: Civil War* has major implications on the rest of the films in the third phase of the MCU, including both *Avengers: Infinity War* and *Avengers: Endgame*.

6   Brian Hiatt, "Stan Lee on the X-Men and more: The lost interview," *Rolling Stone*, November 12, 2018. https://www.rollingstone.com/culture/culture-features/stan-lee-dead-x-men-lost-interview-754889/.

7   *Amazing Spider-Man* #529–531.

8   Super-villains Goldbug and Plunderer show up to join Captain America's cause, but the Punisher kills them, leading to Cap attacking him and kicking him out of the group.

9   "Reddit apologises for online Boston 'witch hunt'," *BBC*, April 23, 2013. https://www.bbc.com/news/technology-22263020.

10 Cameron Easley, "America's most and least popular governors—July 2017," *Morning Consult*, July 18, 2017. https://morningconsult.com/2017/07/18/americas-least-popular-governors-3/.

11 Peter Coy, "Kansas tries to shrink its way to prosperity," *Bloomberg Businessweek*, April 17, 2014. https://www.bloomberg.com/news/articles/2014-04-17/kansas-governor-brownbacks-lab-for-steep-tax-and-budget-cuts.

12 Russell Berman, "Kansas Republicans sour on their tax-cut experiment," *The Atlantic*, February 24, 2017. https://www.theatlantic.com/politics/archive/2017/02/the-republican-blowback-against-sam-brownback-kansas/517641/.

13 Tricia McKinnon, "8 reasons why Blockbuster failed & filed for bankruptcy," *Indigo9 Digital*, March 28, 2022. https://www.indigo9digital.com/blog/blockbusterfailure

14 Dana Bash, Jake Tapper, and Jeremy Herb, "The committee is arguing Trump had a 'seven-part plan' to overturn the election. Here's what that means," *CNN*, June 28, 2022. https://edition.cnn.com/politics/live-news/january-6-hearings-june-28

CHAPTER 14

They Only Lack the Light to Show the Way

Superman and Transformational Leadership

Eric V. Muirhead

"They can be a great people, Kal-El, if they wish to be. They only lack the light to show the way. For this reason above all, their capacity for good, I have sent them you: my only son."

—JOR-EL TO SUPERMAN (KAL-EL) IN THE FORTRESS OF SOLITUDE[1]

Christopher Reeve's Superman is my favorite superhero. He was also my first. Almost four decades later, my mother still recounts with glee when I was two years old, and she took me for a haircut. I (allegedly) told the stylist that "I wanna look like Superman!" I still have vivid memories of running around the hardwood floors in my childhood home wearing a pair of Superman footed pajamas and trying to get the Velcroed red cape to flap behind me. As a toddler, I demanded that we rent the 1978 movie so many times, my mother finally gave up and purchased it on VHS (the first film I ever owned). I played for hours with my favorite Superman action figure: lifting wooden blocks off other characters and carrying the villains who caused the destruction "off to jail." I still have that action figure, and he is standing on my desk next to me as I write this chapter to keep me honest.

Something in Reeve's portrayal of a man who was so powerful, yet still so altruistic, resonated deeply in my young mind. I like to think Superman's lessons helped make me the person I am today. As I have grown over the past 36 years and (somewhat) matured, I have come to understand that the true power of Reeve's breakthrough performance is not its special effects, acting, or the sort of moral ambiguity that has become commonplace in the contemporary superhero genre. Rather, this story is special because of the protagonist's devotion to doing the right thing *for right's sake*. Richard Donner's *Superman* is a brilliant allegory for the power and importance of transformational leadership in our contemporary society.

"Transactional" Versus "Leadership Theory"

For the purposes of this chapter, we will examine two styles from the "Full Range Leadership Model" developed by scholars Bernard Bass and Bruce Avolio: "transactional" versus "transformational" leadership. Bass does not ascribe a value judgment to which style is superior. In fact, he suggests that both styles can co-exist and augment each other in a single leader as different human beings respond to different motivations at different times.[2] However, Bass also states that more transformational leaders tend to be viewed by subordinates as making "more of a contribution to the organization," and their subordinates "exerted a lot of extra effort" for them.[3] Meanwhile, more transactional leaders tend to be viewed as statistically less effective while subordinates "exerted much less effort" under their charge.[4] This data suggests that while transactional leaders lean on extrinsic penalties and incentives to motivate others, transformational leaders find ways to intrinsically motivate others to improve both themselves and their organization.

Transactional leaders center their efforts on the accomplishment of specific tasks for specified rewards. For example, if a subordinate completes "X" assignment, they will receive "Y" compensation (wages, time-off, possibility of promotion, etc.) Conversely, if a subordinate fails to complete "X" assignment, they will receive "Z" punishment (loss of pay, loss of time off, fines, etc.).[5] Transactional leadership focuses on basic "cost versus benefit" thinking. As a result, it is often the simplest and least uncomfortable style for young or inexperienced leaders to adopt.[6] However, this also means that subordinates focus their decision-making around a "cost versus benefit" framework and, as a result, are extremely unlikely to place the needs of others or the organization above their own. In addition, transactional leaders focus on maintaining a "status quo" in operations and discourage innovative ideas in favor of tried and tested methods.[7] Though relatively simple to maintain, transactional leadership often centers on the needs and desires of the leader and can easily result in loss of enthusiasm, general cynicism, and lack of personal satisfaction in a subordinate's work.

On the other hand, transformational leadership focuses on the needs and desires of a group's members. Rather than simply maintaining a status quo, transformational leaders produce positive changes and reforms at all levels of an organization.[8] They do this through three characteristics identified by Bass: charisma, inspiration, and intellectual stimulation.[9] Each of these attributes must be present for a leader to be considered transformational.

Transformational leaders display charisma through key personal traits that instill in followers an intense desire to follow their example. They are emotionally expressive: unafraid to portray their true feelings, thoughts, and desires to others and openly share their excitement at the possibility for positive change.[10] They possess intelligence, personal insight, and the eloquence to convey their ideas simply and powerfully to those around them.[11] Charismatic leaders are also energetic and active, and they display insight into the needs, hopes, and values of their followers.[12] Finally, they are confident in their own abilities and the desire to do what they believe is right regardless of the expectations and limitations externally imposed on them.[13]

Transformational leaders are also inspirational. They understand the challenges facing those around them and boldly set goals to help everyone collectively overcome obstacles.[14] Inspirational leaders actively work to tear down petty distinctions between individuals. They unite followers together as a single group and are dedicated to achieving collective goals through empowering everyone to give their best effort.[15] Inspirational leaders achieve this by demonstrating repeated competence in their own abilities.[16] In this way, they actively expand what others think is possible. Finally, inspirational leaders are adept at adopting symbols which resonate with followers and immediately convey their ideals and vision.[17] They allow others to freely adopt their symbol to broaden and strengthen their coalition, creating a welcoming and inclusive atmosphere.[18] Once they have inspired others, transformational leaders do not sit idle. Rather, they work to continue improvements through the process of intellectual stimulation.

Intellectual stimulation is the continuous search for new possibilities and outcomes. Transformational leaders do not isolate themselves from those they lead. Instead, they believe that leadership consists of a never-ending dialogue to discover what changes are necessary for continued organizational improvement.[19] This dialogue also encourages followers to grow, develop, and take more ownership of their future rather than simply becoming dependent on the leader's constant direction.[20] As a result, followers become empowered to become new leaders themselves.

While groups led by transactional leaders are stable, they also tend to stagnate rather than change to meet the evolving needs of their members. In contrast, organizations led by transformational leaders are dynamic: constantly advancing, expanding, and creating new leaders dedicated to propagating the organizational vision.

The World of *Superman* (1978)

Based on a story written by Mario Puzo, author of *The Godfather*, Richard Donner's *Superman* builds on the established mythology of the character. The planet Krypton orbits a distant, dying star in another galaxy. The dim light of their fading red sun has left the world cold and barren, but the ancient and advanced Kryptonian species evolved a "dense molecular structure" allowing their culture to survive for untold millennia.[21] During that time, Kryptonians have explored many other worlds and regard themselves as the pinnacle of civilization and culture.

In 1948, 30 years before the main events of the film, leading Kryptonian citizen and scientist, Jor-El, informs the ruling council of his discovery that the planet is less than a month from destruction. The politicians glibly dismiss his findings and order both Jor-El and his wife, Lara, to remain on the planet to prevent a panic. Unwilling to challenge the council's authority, Jor-El and Lara acquiesce to their deaths, but not before launching their newborn son, Kal-El, in a spacecraft towards an undeveloped and barbarous planet in the Milky Way known as Earth.[22] Lara initially protests, stating that humans are "primitives, thousands of years behind us!"[23] However, Jor-El convinces her by stating that their son will appear human and when his physiology interacts with the young, yellow sun of Earth, Kal-El will be "fast, [and] virtually invulnerable."[24] Jor-El also reminds her that Kal-El will "never be alone" because he has included the sum total of all Kryptonian knowledge embedded in a collection of data crystals stowed aboard the lifeboat.[25] As the last son of Krypton lifts off to his parents' tearful farewell, the red sun's gravity rips apart Kal-El's home planet before igniting into a supernova that destroys the entire system.

After three years in suspended animation, little Kal-El crash lands into the Kansas prairie. Jonathan and Martha Kent, a kind, yet childless couple, are making their way home from church. The impact of Kal-El's ship runs them off the road and blows out their tire. Martha immediately believes a baby falling from the sky is an answer to their prayers, but Jonathan is concerned that the child could bring unwanted attention and government troubles into their lives.[26] However, the decision to keep little Kal-El is finalized when the truck Jonathan is repairing falls of the jack and nearly crushes him until the toddler easily catches it and lifts it off the ground with a smile.[27]

Over the next 18 years, Kal-El (now known by his human name "Clark") grows up in rural America. However, the teen is torn between respecting his concerned parents' desire for secrecy and his own desire to use his amazing abilities for personal gain. In what will become Clark's last conversation with his human father, Jonathan Kent reassures his son saying, "*You are here for a reason* ... but I do know one thing, it's not to score touchdowns."[28] Sadly, just a few moments later, Jonathan collapses and dies from a pre-existing heart condition. Clark is emotionally destroyed, having now lost his most powerful role model, and bemoans the fact that despite "all those things I can do, all those powers, and I couldn't even save him."[29] The next day, with Jonathan's final words ringing in his mind, Clark takes the last remaining crystal from his childhood spacecraft, bids goodbye to Martha, and travels north to the Arctic.

Near the North Pole, in terrain that closely mimics Krypton, Clark throws the crystal into the Arctic Ocean, which immediately transforms the ice and snow around it into the "Fortress of Solitude" a re-creation of his home world's architecture. Once inside, a holographic representation of Jor-El's preserved consciousness informs Clark of his real identity, potential, and his mission: not to "interfere with human history" but to be the "light to show the way" and help humanity discover its true potential through his leadership.[30] Over the next 12 years, Clark stays with Jor-El studying Kryptonian knowledge and moral philosophy before ultimately emerging from his seclusion as Superman.

The city of "Metropolis" was a fictional reflection of contemporary New York City. While Clark was in seclusion from 1966 to 1978, the United States suffered the simultaneous traumas of Vietnam, Watergate, an escalating nuclear arms race with the Soviet Union, and the Energy Crisis all while struggling with its moral compass during the Civil Rights Movement, Gay Rights Movement, and Second Wave Feminism. New York City of the late '70s (and presumably its comic book counterpart) was drowning in violent crime, dealing with the aftermath of psychotic serial killers such as the Son of Sam, and awash in poverty, drugs, and exploitative prostitution.

Re-watching *Superman* as an adult historian reveals the deep cynicism about the future of America that pervaded 1970s America. Pimps, thieves, and sex workers fill the background on streets and in police stations. On Clark's first day of work at *The Daily Planet*, Lois Lane has just completed a "dynamite expose on the sex and drug orgies in [a] senior citizen's home," and is wrapping up an "East Side Murder" piece entitled "An Ode to Spring." She also pitches an ongoing series to the chief editor, Perry White, called "Making Sense of Senseless Killings."[31] Everything culminates when Clark and Lois are mugged at gunpoint just a few blocks from Grand Central Station. Lois would have been brutally shot in the back if Clark did not literally catch a .38 slug with his bare hands before faking a fainting spell.[32]

Of course, all these horrors pale in comparison to the film's antagonist, Lex Luthor, who takes the form of the *ultimate* villain: a narcissistic, big-city millionaire real estate swindler who surrounds himself with busts of Octavian, portraits of Mussolini, a sycophantic dullard henchman named Otis, and his indifferent, materialistic girlfriend, Miss Teschmacher. In his subterranean headquarters beneath Midtown, Luthor dreams of hijacking a pair of nuclear missiles and using them to destroy the State of California, ultimately gaining control of the entire U.S. West Coast through defrauding indigenous land holdings.[33]

This bleak world view would have not been strange to the audiences watching *Superman* when it premiered in 1978. How could one person, even one with Superman's powers, hope to change it? The true genius of this film, however, is that its creative team understood that Jerry Siegel and Joe Shuster originally created the character 40 years before during another terrible period of American history: the Great Depression. Perhaps Superman's eternal optimism, perpetual virtue, and selflessness could transform another period's enduring malaise into new hope for change?

Superman as Transformational Leader

Not surprisingly, Superman's big reveal comes in a critical moment where Lois Lane's life is in jeopardy. After an evening soliloquy lamenting the banality of most people's lives, Lois rebuffs a dinner invitation from Clark because she wants to helicopter to Metropolis Airport. Her mission is to meet Air Force One and ask the

President questions "that he would rather duck," presumably about poor government performance or possible scandals.[34] Clark then heads home alone while being ignored and belittled by many of his co-workers for his polite yet humble demeanor.

Meanwhile, Lois' helicopter clips a cable while taking off from *The Daily Planet*'s rooftop, careens to the edge of the skyscraper, and leaves her hanging helplessly 50 stories over the street. A crowd of reporters, emergency workers, and onlookers gather below, but do nothing to help. They merely gawk at her misfortune and (presumably) her impending grisly death. Meanwhile, Clark steps out on the sidewalk below, quickly realizes what is happening, and springs into action. He transforms into Superman, flies skyward just in time to catch a falling Lois in his arms, and smiles as actress Margot Kidder flawlessly delivers the famous line, "You've got me? WHO'S GOT YOU?"[35] Then, after the helicopter comes crashing down toward them, Superman easily grabs the aircraft with one hand and delivers both Lois and the disabled chopper back onto the building's helipad. Superman politely departs after calmly delivering an impeccable speech on airline safety that the Federal Aviation Administration would admire.[36] In my opinion, it is the perfect superhero scene than has never been topped (except possibly by Superman crushing General Zod's hand in the sequel, but that is another essay). From John William's triumphant score to Superman's humility contrasted with his unbelievable physical powers, the helicopter rescue scene set the stage for the modern cinematic superhero and showcases everything that makes Superman a true transformational leader.

From the moment Superman first reveals himself, both to the characters onscreen and the audience members off screen, he displays all the characteristics of transformational leadership: charisma, inspiration, and intellectual stimulation. This agrees with the organizational change model of Harvard Professor John Kotter, who argues that "behavior change happens mostly by speaking to people's feelings" and it is crucial for leaders to rapidly create "victories that nourish faith in the change effort."[37] Beyond simply doing what is right, Superman understands that others must see him doing right to create positive change.

Superman's charisma is undeniable. He is eloquent, bold, and always tells the truth. In a follow-up interview with Lois, he clearly states that his vision is to fight for "truth, justice, and the American Way."[38] Even after Lois belittles him, stating "you're going to end up fighting every elected official in this country," he gently corrects her, stating that he "never lies."[39] Through his honesty and linking his espoused values to concrete actions, Superman begins to win over even the most skeptical observers with his genuine desire to help others and improve the world around him.

Next, Superman is one of the most inspirational heroes ever created. He is an expert at linking positive acts that people once believed impossible to his stated vision for the world. At the film's climax, Luthor boasts that even Superman won't be able to stop his plan to obliterate the West Coast. Superman then proceeds to save the Eastern seaboard and race to the Pacific just in time to plunge into the Earth's mantle and lift the entire state of California before it falls into the ocean. The words of a reporter earlier in the film reinforce this point, "I just cannot believe it."[40] That is the whole point. Transformational leaders bring others to their cause by showing others that the perceived impossible is possible with the right effort.

However, what separates Superman's humility from toxic narcissists like Lex Luthor is the fact that Superman quickly divorces himself from his deeds. He understands that true heroes do not get to decide what is a "big" or "small" problem but must try to help everyone's perceived issues equally: including taking a break from busting armed robbers and saving the President to help a distraught little girl whose cat is stuck in a tree.[41] The famous "S" on his chest does not only belong to him: he offers it freely to the world as a symbol for all humanity to unite behind.

Finally, Superman believes in the concept of intellectual stimulation by constantly empowering those around him to help answer his call to service. Despite his immense power, Superman never fails to defer to lawful authority. He understands that enduring positive change comes about not through the efforts of the individual, but through collaboration and cooperation. From always dropping off bad guys with helpful police officers to working with the employees of a hydroelectric dam when a man-made earthquake threatens their facility, Superman knows that everyone has their part in the solution. Perhaps the final scene of the film sums up this concept best. After dropping off Lex Luthor into pre-trial confinement, the prison warden states, "This country is safe again, Superman, thanks to you!"[42] Superman smiles and immediately responds: "No, Sir. Don't thank me, Warden. We're all part of the same team!"[43]

I can already hear the critics of this article stating that Superman's lessons for real world leadership are limited because he is a "god" with unlimited powers. That there is no way any human being could be that strong, that brave, or have those gifts without descending into despotism. However, the genius of *Superman* (1978) is that its hero's moral code isn't just born on Krypton. Indeed, Kryptonians exhibit the same flaws and weaknesses of our own species. The film begins during a trial for sedition in the aftermath of a planet-wide coup attempt. Also, for all their knowledge, Kryptonian political leaders walked blindly into their own planet's destruction, ignoring any warnings to the contrary.

Superman was not born a hero. He was created in the farm fields of Kansas and the classroom of the Fortress of Solitude. Even today, when our world seems to have much in common with the violence, corruption, and uncertainty of 1978 Metropolis, Superman teaches that any of us can become a transformational leader if we take pride in our ourselves and our heritage, work hard, and put aside our own egos to be "the light to show the way."

Notes

1   *Superman*, directed by Richard Donner (Los Angeles: Warner Brothers Pictures, 1978), DVD.
2   Bernard M. Bass, *Bass and Stogdill's Handbook of Leadership: Theory, Research, and Managerial Applications*, 3rd ed. (New York: The Free Press, 1990), 220.
3   Ibid., 218.
4   Ibid., 218–219.
5   Bernard M. Bass, *Bass and Stogdill's Handbook of Leadership: Theory, Research, and Managerial Applications*, 4th ed. (New York: The Free Press, 2008), 50, 263.
6   Ibid.
7   Johnson Hackman and Craig Michael, *Leadership: A Communication Perspective* (Long Grove, Illinois: Waveland Press, 2009), 102–104.
8   Bass (1990), 215.
9   Ibid., 218.
10 Ibid., 190.
11 Ibid., 191.
12 Ibid.
13 Ibid.
14 Ibid., 207.
15 Ibid., 207, 213.
16 Ibid., 210.
17 Ibid., 209.
18 Ibid., 209–210.
19 Ibid., 216.
20 Ibid.
21 *Superman*, Donner.
22 Ibid.
23 Ibid.
24 Ibid.
25 Ibid.
26 Ibid.
27 Ibid.
28 Ibid.
29 Ibid.
30 Ibid.
31 Ibid.
32 Ibid.
33 Ibid.
34 Ibid.
35 Ibid.
36 Ibid.
37 John Kotter as quoted in Alan Deutschman, "Change or Die," *Fast Company.com*, May 1, 2005, at https://www.fastcompany.com/52717/change-or-die.
38 *Superman*, Donner.
39 Ibid.
40 Ibid.
41 Ibid.
42 Ibid.
43 Ibid.

CHAPTER 15

Could the Sokovia Accords
Save the (Real) World?

Theresa Hitchens

"If we can't accept limitations, we're no better than the bad guys," Tony Stark says. "The safest hands are still our own," Steve Rogers replies.

And so begins the 2016 Marvel Cinematic Universe movie *Captain America: Civil War*. The film centers on the deep ethical rift between the two leaders of the Avengers—Tony Stark, aka Iron Man, and Steve "Cap" Rogers, aka Captain America—piqued by a UN effort to establish a treaty of sorts between the governments of the world and "enhanced" humans, or in other words superheroes.

The UN's rationale, endorsed strongly by the government of the United States where the Avengers are based, is that superhero actions require oversight and control because their powers, even when used against threats to humanity, can destroy cities, countries, and perhaps the entire world. "For the past four years, you operated with unlimited power and no supervision. That's an arrangement the governments of the world can no longer tolerate," says US Secretary of State Thaddeus Ross in confronting the Avengers with the UN demands.

An incident in Lagos where a delegation from Wakanda[1] is caught in the crossfire of an Avenger's intervention in a humanity-threatening criminal scheme serves as the trigger for the UN move, the linchpin incident for the plot of *Civil War* occurred in the previous movie in the series, *Avengers: Age of Ultron*. In that 2015 film, the Avengers must defeat the eponymous Ultron, an artificial intelligence (AI) created by Stark to provide global protection. But soon after being awakened, the AI turns on the Avengers and spirals out of control threatening all humanity. The resulting battle essentially destroys the fictional Eastern European country of Sokovia, resulting in a worldwide uproar.

Thus, the legal instrument that will place the Avengers under the direct supervision of the United Nations is dubbed the "Sokovia Accords." The heroes are asked (in reality, ordered) to sign the accords or retire and hang up their metaphorical spurs.

Further, those who do not sign and later decide to take action without a UN mandate will be considered lawbreakers and subject to arrest.

As the movie's title implies, the members of the Avengers are split into two groups based on their view of the accords.

Tony convinces half of the team that there is value in accepting the restrictions, partly out of concern about the potential for abuse of power, but also to stave off efforts to impose worse constraints on superpowered humans. "We need to be put in check," he says bluntly.

Cap and his followers take the opposing view, both out of a distrust of authority and a belief that the individual members of the Avengers will make the right choices if given the freedom to do so.

Civil War, at its heart, is an allegory for the constant ethical struggle in societies, particularly democracies, between security and liberty, as argued by philosopher Mark D. White in his book *A Philosopher Reads ... Marvel Comics' Civil War*. White argued, "if we peel away the superhero façade, under the capes and masks we see the same debates in the Marvel Universe as we do in the real world. These include conflict between liberty and security in the political realm as well as defending the right and advancing the good in the personal realm."[2]

But at the crux of *Civil War* is the precise question of whether individuals with world-destroying powers should somehow be collectively regulated by representatives of the rest of the world they might imperil. That question applies to a particularly thorny conundrum of international security today: the existence of nuclear weapons in the hands of a select few.

Interestingly, the film makes a comparison between the superheroes themselves and nuclear weapons. For example, when lecturing the Avengers on the need for the Sokovia Accords, Ross decries that the team has no idea where Thor (the god-prince of the planet Asgard, based on Norse mythology) and Bruce Banner, aka the Hulk, currently are or what they are doing.

"If I misplaced a couple of 30-megaton nukes, you can bet there'd be consequences," he says.

While the analogy to the leaders of nuclear-armed countries is not perfect, in that *Civil War*'s ethical debate is primarily focused on individual human rights, there is enough of a parallel to tease out some implications for real-world global security. What responsibilities do nuclear-armed states, and their leaders, have to the rest of the 8 billion humans on Earth concerning the use of potentially planet-busting nukes? What actual collective controls should, or even could, be put on those leaders' decisions regarding nuclear weapons use or directly on their arsenals?

As of November 2022, there are nine (known) men in the world who have their fingers on nuclear buttons—none of whom face any real constraints, legal or otherwise, upon their ability to trigger Armageddon. Of those nine countries possessing nuclear weapons, five of them are sanctioned to do so under international law via the 1968 Treaty on the Non-Proliferation of Nuclear Weapons (NPT).[3] Those countries are China, France, Russia, the United Kingdom, and the United States. The four others possess nuclear weapons but have not been officially blessed to do so under international law: India, Israel, North Korea, and Pakistan.

India, Israel, and Pakistan are not signatories to the NPT, so arguably they are not bound by its strictures (although there have been legal arguments surrounding their status citing customary international law).[4] Both India and Pakistan openly tested nukes in the late 1990s, and the international community has essentially accepted their status as nuclear weapon states. Israel is known to have possessed nuclear weapons since the 1960s[5] but has never admitted to doing so.

North Korea, by contrast, signed the NPT in 1985 but withdrew in 2003 after the discovery of its clandestine effort to develop nuclear weapons. Thus, Pyongyang is considered by many, if not all, nations as operating outside international law and therefore subject to economic sanctions. Hence the on-again, off-again effort by the United States to negotiate a deal with North Korea that would trade economic relief and assistance for disarmament.[6]

In all those countries, the decision to use a nuclear weapon is solely up to the head of state. Read that again: solely up to the head of state, however intelligent, rational, or completely crazy that person may or may not be. In most nuclear weapons states, a decision by a president or prime minister would be conveyed to senior military leaders, who in turn would authorize weapons operators to perform the actual launch. So, in theory, those national military officials could serve as an obstacle to actions they deemed irrational or illegal under either national law or the international law of armed conflict.[7]

But in practice, military officers who refuse to take orders from those at the top of their chain of command face dismissal or worse, depending on the country in question (one only needs to look to North Korea to see examples of worst-case consequences[8]). Indeed, in the United States during the Trump administration, several top military leaders were ousted, resigned in protest, or considered doing so because of presidential decisions they deemed grossly misguided, dangerous, or outright illegal.[9] Additionally, there is little de facto international control over how those nine nuclear states deploy or use their arsenals. Outside of the general prescriptions against the threat or use of force absent an armed attack in the UN Charter[10] and those included in the law of armed conflict, there are no legally binding constraints on the use of nuclear weapons on those countries or their leaders.

The International Court of Justice in a landmark 1996 case essentially found that while international law nowhere authorizes the use of nuclear weapons, it also nowhere prohibits it.[11]

In 2017, 122 nations signed the UN Treaty on the Prohibition of Nuclear Weapons[12] that pledges signatories not to develop, test, produce, acquire, possess, stockpile, use or threaten to use nuclear weapons. That treaty went into force in

January 2021. However, the negotiations were boycotted by all nine nuclear weapons states and many of their allies, including most NATO countries[13]—making its relevance to nuclear decision-making moot.

The NPT commits the five signatory nuclear weapon states to take collective steps toward complete nuclear disarmament, as well as efforts to prevent their arsenals and know-how from leading to proliferation by other states. Yet, while the United States and Russia have concluded a series of bilateral nuclear arms treaties designed to limit or reduce their arsenals, neither China, France, nor the United Kingdom have signed similar treaties.

In addition, despite those treaty obligations, the five NPT weapons states[14]—as well the other four de facto nuclear weapons states outside the treaty—all continue to pronounce nuclear weapons as central to their national security and are undertaking expensive weapons modernization programs, according to a comprehensive report by the Stockholm International Peace Research Institute.[15] This means that the total number of nuclear weapons at the start of 2022, an estimated 12,705, is expected to rise in the coming years, SIPRI reported in a June 13, 2022, press release.

> "All of the nuclear-armed states are increasing or upgrading their arsenals, and most are sharpening nuclear rhetoric and the role nuclear weapons play in their military strategies," said Wilfred Wan, director of SIPRI's Weapons of Mass Destruction Program. "This is a very worrying trend."

Indeed, Russia has used nuclear saber-rattling, at least indirectly, to deter other nations from intervening in its ongoing war with Ukraine.[16]

In fact, none of the nuclear weapon states have proven to be willing to negotiate sovereign control over their nuclear arsenals over the years. However, some (including the United States[17]) have agreed to limited inspections by the International Atomic Energy Agency. And the three countries with the largest nuclear arsenals—Russia, the United States, and China—all have formidable conventional might, and all three still can harness considerable economic power to achieve their geopolitical goals, including their hold on their nuclear arsenals. Further, they each have unilateral veto power on the UN Security Council, although the United Nations has been working since its establishment in 1946 to eliminate nuclear weapons, with obviously little success.

Proponents of nuclear weapons in the US and Western countries often argue that while total nuclear disarmament would be ideal, it will never occur. In our imperfect world of geopolitical conflict, they assert, nuclear weapons instead have contributed to upholding international peace and security, and will continue to do so, by preventing war among the major world powers. Under this logic, the existence of nuclear weapons inherently deters their use due to fears among their possessors of mutual annihilation.

This argument is a riff on Cap's conviction that each of the Avengers can be counted on to make the right decisions—rational leaders will refrain from nuclear use because that would be self-destructive, if nothing else. But just as Tony argued in *Civil War* with regard to superpowered humans, no one can guarantee that all national leaders with nuclear buttons will always act rationally—and there is a good deal of evidence to show there have been, and still are, some who are dangerously far from rational.

Nonetheless, in Marvel's *Civil War* it proves infeasible for the United Nations and the world's governments to constrain the actions of the superpowered Avengers. So, Cap goes into hiding with his allies after freeing them from a UN high-security prison, leaving Tony in the near-empty Avengers' compound with only two members of the team who continue to support the Sokovia Accords. The film ends in a poignant scene, as Tony reads a letter from Cap that is both an explanation of his actions and an olive branch—but not an apology for his opposition to the accords.

In the real world, it likewise is questionable whether something akin to a nuclear version of the Sokovia Accords could be made to work, simply because it remains highly unclear what persuasion or power the rest of the world could bring to bear upon the leaders of nuclear weapon states to even bring them to the table. So, for the moment anyway, it is simply a fact that all human beings live in the shadow of extinction at the hands of nine men, over whom they have little or no meaningful political, legal, or even moral sway.

Perhaps, however, there is value in putting time and effort into considering how to do so—just as *Civil War* makes clear that Tony's thwarted desire to find a way to legitimize and constrain superhuman violence, as well as prevent superhero abuse of power, is a worthwhile and logical aim. For example, it isn't inconceivable that some of today's nuclear powers might be convinced that it is in their security interest to create higher national barriers to nuclear weapons use—and to urge their counterparts to do the same. This, in turn, could serve as a step toward consideration among the nuclear powers about how to improve collective speed bumps to nuclear escalation. Meanwhile, those majority of countries (and people) without nuclear weapons at their command could begin to develop ideas for how to reduce the benefits and increase the political and economic costs of those who do. In this vein, the 2017 Nuclear Ban treaty could serve as a forum.

As the crippled James Rhodes, aka War Machine, tells Tony at the end of *Civil War*, sometimes the hard fight needs to be fought because it is "the right thing to do."

Notes

1   The fictional African country featured in Marvel's 2018 and 2022 "Black Panther" movies.
2   Mark D. White, *A Philosopher Reads Marvel Comics Civil War* (Aberdeen, UK: Ockham Publishing, 2016), 11.
3   See: https://www.un.org/disarmament/wmd/nuclear/npt/text.

4   Customary international law stems from state practice, independent of treaty law. For a detailed explanation, see the International Committee of the Red Cross website, https://www.icrc.org/en/war-and-law/treaties-customary-law/customary-law.

5   See: Nuclear Threat Initiative website, https://www.nti.org/countries/israel/.

6   "North Korean Nuclear Negotiations, 1985–2022," *Council on Foreign Relations*, Washington, D.C., https://www.cfr.org/timeline/north-korean-nuclear-negotiations.

7   For a comprehensive review of international law applicable to conflict and warfare, see the website of the International Committee of the Red Cross, https://www.icrc.org/en/war-and-law.

8   "North Korea Defence Chief Hyon Yong-chol 'executed'," *BBC News*, May 13, 2015, https://www.bbc.com/news/world-asia-32716749.

9   Susan B. Glaser and Peter Baker, "Inside the War Between Trump and His Generals," *The New Yorker*, Aug. 15, 2022, https://www.newyorker.com/magazine/2022/08/15/inside-the-war-between-trump-and-his-generals.

10 See: https://www.un.org/en/about-us/un-charter/full-text.

11 "Legality of the Threat or Use of Nuclear Weapons," International Court of Justice, July 8, 1996, https://www.icj-cij.org/en/case/95.

12 "Treaty on the prohibition of nuclear weapons," United Nations Office of Outer Space Affairs website, https://www.un.org/disarmament/wmd/nuclear/tpnw/.

13 "Treaty on the Prohibition of Nuclear Weapons (TPNW)," Nuclear Threat Initiative website, https://www.nti.org/education-center/treaties-and-regimes/treaty-on-the-prohibition-of-nuclear-weapons/.

14 For the US position, see the 2022 National Defense Strategy/Nuclear Posture Review released by the Biden administration Oct. 25, 2022, https://www.defense.gov/National-Defense-Strategy/.

15 "Global nuclear arsenals are expected to grow as states continue to modernize–New SIPRI Yearbook out now," Stockholm International Peace Research Institute (SIPRI) press release, June 13, 2022, https://www.sipri.org/media/press-release/2022/global-nuclear-arsenals-are-expected-grow-states-continue-modernize-new-sipri-yearbook-out-now.

16 "Biden Warns Russia Against Using Nuclear Weapons as 'Dirty Bomb' Accusations Fly," *The New York Times*, Oct. 25, 2022, https://www.nytimes.com/live/2022/10/25/world/russia-ukraine-war-news.

17 "Agreement Between the United States of America and The International Atomic Energy Agency for the Application of Safeguards in the United States (and Protocol Thereto)," US Department of State website, https://2009-2017.state.gov/t/isn/5209.htm.

CHAPTER 16

A Fitting End for His Kind

On Justice, Retribution, and Vigilantism in Gotham City

Jo Brick

> "It is better for the law to rule than one of the citizens ... so even the guardians of the laws are obeying the laws."
>
> —ARISTOTLE[1]

Batman is the embodiment of justice and vengeance, dispensing with criminal elements and providing hope to the long-suffering citizens of Gotham City. This is why Gotham City is big on justice but has very little rule of law. The corroding effects of deep-set corruption in Gotham's law enforcement and judicial systems set the ideal conditions for a masked vigilante—Batman—to take the law into his own hands to make up for the failures of Gotham's justice system. Like other denizens of Gotham, he has suffered the pain of crime—losing his parents to a petty thief in an alley as a child. His outrage fuels his justification to bring down criminals wherever he finds them. The problem is that there is a price for his actions. He is a hero to many, and he legitimizes acting outside the rule of law, which has many consequences that manifest in the form of his nemesis: the Joker.

Christopher Nolan's Batman trilogy—*Batman Begins*, *The Dark Knight*, and *The Dark Knight Rises*—is a series of parables about the dangers of the loss of trust in policing and judicial institutions caused by the absence of the rule of law. Two key themes arise from the Batman "Nolanverse"—the symbiotic relationship between justice and retribution and the tension between vigilantism and the rule of law. These themes highlight lessons for our world about the centrality of law and the legitimacy of institutions to the stability of nations.

The rule of law is a central tenet of jurisprudence, or the philosophy of law. Former British Lord Chief Justice Tom Bingham defined the rule of law as: "The core of the existing principle is, I suggest, that all persons and authorities within the state, whether public or private, should be bound by and entitled to the benefit of laws publicly made, taking effect (generally) in the future and publicly administered in the courts."[2] Most importantly, the rule of law is a fundamental pillar for the stability and order on which society depends and is necessary to achieve justice. Indeed, if justice is the goal, the rule of law is the means. Acting based on the rule of law provides legitimacy to dispute resolution mechanisms in society. Its absence leads to fear and chaos and the erosion of trust in vital social institutions.

Batman—Justice and Retribution

DC Comics celebrated the 80th anniversary of Batman in 2019.[3] The first Batman story, "The Case of the Chemical Syndicate," was published in *Detective Comics* #27 on March 30, 1939, and conceived by comic book artist Bob Kane and writer Bill Finger. In the Caped Crusader's first story, Batman fights an armed criminal, eventually knocking him into a vat of acid. As the man splashes into the green liquid below, Batman says to Detective Rogers, "A fitting end for his kind."[4] It is clear from the beginning that the ideas of justice and retribution lie at the heart of Batman's story.

However, it was not until *Detective Comics* #33 that Batman's origin story involving the murder of his parents began to take shape.[5] This origin story lies at the heart of everything Batman does, and it is either ignored, hinted at, or explored in depth across the spectrum of Batman stories available today.[6] Amongst a crowded field of Batman media, the *Nolanverse* stands out for its layered exploration of Batman and the man behind the mask, Bruce Wayne. Nolan's work explores the psyche of Wayne/Batman by exhuming the shattered soul of this central character and how the weight of his parents' death continues to underscore almost every decision in his life.

The first act of *Batman Begins* explores Wayne's inner struggle with outrage and the need for retribution. Professor Michael Sandel defines outrage as "the special kind of anger you feel when you believe that people are getting things they don't deserve. Outrage of this kind is anger at injustice."[7] Henri Ducard (aka Ra's al Ghul of the League of Shadows) takes advantage of Wayne's sense of outrage and begins to groom him for membership in the League:

> WAYNE: My anger outweighs my guilt.
> DUCARD: You have learned to bury your guilt with anger. I will teach you to confront it and to face the truth.[8]

Instead of joining forces with Ducard, Wayne returns to Gotham City for the trial of Joe Chill—the petty thief who killed his parents—hoping to assuage his outrage for the killer. But Chill has made a deal with the District Attorney and is due to be set free in exchange for information about Carmine Falcone, a powerful Gotham mob boss. Wayne intends to impose his own sense of justice, bringing a pistol to court and intending to shoot Chill. Outside the courtroom, he waits for Chill, gun in hand, only to witness Chill being gunned down by one of Falcone's thugs. Justice denied.

In a subsequent scene, Wayne rides in a car with Rachel Dawes, his childhood friend and a Gotham Assistant District Attorney. Their discussion discloses Wayne's inner struggle:

> BRUCE: My parents deserve justice.
> RACHEL: Well, you're not talking about justice; you're talking about revenge.
> BRUCE: Sometimes they're the same.
> RACHEL: No, they're never the same, Bruce. Justice is about harmony; revenge is about you making yourself feel better. This is why we have an impartial system.
> BRUCE: Your system is broken.
> RACHEL: You care about Justice? Look beyond your own pain, Bruce. This city is rotting ... As long as he keeps the bad people rich and the good people scared, no one will touch him. Good people like your parents who stood against injustice. They're gone. What chance does Gotham have when the good people do nothing?
> BRUCE: I'm not one of your good people, Rachel.
> RACHEL: What do you mean?
> BRUCE: All these years, I wanted to kill him. Now I can't (takes out gun).
> RACHEL [slaps Bruce]: Your father would be ashamed of you.[9]

Interestingly, retribution is a principle that underscores the justice system. In the Australian criminal law jurisdiction, many legal cases recognize the importance of retribution as a principle of sentencing. For example, in the New South Wales Court of Criminal Appeals, Chief Justice Hunt says, "Retribution, or the taking of vengeance for the injury which has been done by the offender, is also an important aspect of sentencing."[10] However, in the Supreme Court of Canada, Chief Justice Lamer made a distinction between *vengeance* and *retribution*:

> [Vengeance is] an uncalibrated act of harm upon another, frequently motivated by emotion and anger, as reprisal for harm inflicted upon oneself by that other person ... [retribution is] an objective, reasoned, and measured determination of an appropriate punishment which properly reflects the moral culpability of the offender and the normative character of the offender's conduct.[11]

This distinction is at the heart of the tension between Batman and Ra's al Ghul. The Leagues of Justice and Shadows are focused on restoring what they call *true justice*—vengeance by another name. As Ra's al Ghul says, "If someone gets in the way of true justice, you simply walk up behind them and stab them in the heart."[12] Philosopher A. C. Grayling considers that such an impulse for revenge is primitive and, based on personal emotion, is unlikely to restore balance and invite further retaliation.[13] This is the core issue of why justice cannot be a private matter, to be resolved by a single citizen at their whim. Instead, social institutions—the legal and judicial systems—have been established to provide an impartial and objective method for conflict resolution. In these mature systems, the rule of law governs the behavior of the collective, where it is better for "a fitting end" for an offender to be determined by law than by the actions of a single vigilante.

The Caped Crusader Versus the Rule of Law

> "Wherever law ends, tyranny begins."
>
> —JOHN LOCKE[14]

With systemic corruption and rampant crime plaguing the city, the Gotham of *Batman Begins* lends a prophetic tone to Locke. In a second act scene where Wayne confronts Falcone in a dark nightclub, the mob boss brags that he has judges and policemen on his payroll, and he tells his men to escort Wayne out of the club. The existence of Batman is itself a manifestation of the failure of the effectiveness and legitimacy of Gotham's legal system. Batman himself operates outside the law and is often pursued by the Gotham City Police Department, despite a close working relationship with Commissioner Jim Gordon.

The Bat Signal, an iconic symbol above Gotham's skyline, is Gordon's principal means of alerting Batman that the city needs him. Conveniently located atop the Gotham City Police Headquarters, the Bat Signal symbolizes hope for justice among the city's citizens while striking fear in those who might spur Batman's thirst for justice.[15] This is at the core of the problem of relying on one man for a dependable and impartial form of justice and highlights the importance of stable and legitimate social institutions to sanction criminal behavior on behalf of the broader society. These social institutions embody the rule of law.

A form of justice can survive without the rule of law, but it is likely arbitrary, inconsistent, and subjective. Justice without the rule of law favors the powerful forces who can corrupt the system and bend it to their will. The destabilization of regulatory social institutions—such as the legal system—is generally the first step in undermining the rule of law. Grayling states, "History is dogged by the tragic fact that, whenever individuals or countries become powerful, they apply the crude and ancient principle that might is right, and concomitantly refuse to subordinate their power to wider and higher law."[16] In Gotham City, criminal organizations and an endless array of supervillains operate outside the law or undermine it from within. In *Batman Begins*, the Chief Administrator of Arkham Asylum, Dr. Jonathan Crane, exemplifies this phenomenon. In his role at Arkham, Crane is working with Falcone to provide access to a fear toxin that allows him to commit potential witnesses to the asylum, subverting their ability to participate in criminal trials.[17] As the villain Scarecrow, he plots with Ra's al Ghul to introduce the fear toxin into the city's water supply to create mass hysteria and, ultimately, destruction.

But Batman also operates outside the law. While this may be rationalized by Commissioner Gordon and the Gotham citizens who support his quest for justice, there is a price to be paid for acting outside the system. That price is the legitimacy that Batman's actions give to other Gotham citizens who also decide to act outside of the law. For example, in the first act of *The Dark Knight*, Batman interrupts a group of amateur vigilantes called The Batmen, who are in the midst of attempting to capture Scarecrow. One of the group, Brian Douglas, is later captured by the Joker on the mistaken belief that he is the real Batman. When The Joker asks Douglas why he dressed up like Batman, Douglas says it is because Batman is a symbol of the fight against criminals like the Joker.[18] There are sounds of a struggle, with Douglas screaming out. Douglas is then found hanging from a rope outside the Mayor of Gotham's office, intimating that the Joker killed him. A playing card is attached to Douglas' body with the message, "Will the real Batman please stand up."

Gotham City's District Attorney, Harvey Dent, symbolizes the rule of law. In *The Dark Knight*, Dent is celebrated as the successful DA who has brought mob bosses and corrupt government officials to justice. Unfortunately, he becomes the Joker's target, who kidnaps Dent and girlfriend Rachel Dawes. The Joker places them in separate warehouses in the city with timers set to explode simultaneously, cunningly designed to force Batman and the Gotham City Police into a terrible choice: save Harvey or Rachel? Batman chooses to rescue Rachel, but Joker has tricked him into instead rescuing Harvey, whose face is burned and disfigured in the ensuing explosion. Rachel dies.

On recovering from his injury, Dent learns of both the choice and its cost. Dent blames Batman and Commissioner Gordon, and as Two-Face, seeks revenge for Rachel's death by kidnapping Gordon's family and holding them hostage in the warehouse where Rachel died. Dent blames Gordon for not standing up to corruption and threatens Gordon's young son. Batman intervenes.

> BATMAN: You don't want to hurt the boy, Harvey.
> DENT: It's not about what I want. It's about what's fair! You thought we could be decent men in an indecent time. But you were wrong. The world is cruel and the only morality in a cruel world is chance. Unbiased, unprejudiced, fair![19]

In his decision to act outside the law, Batman has triggered a chain of events by actively destroying criminal organizations as a way to avenge his parents' death. He has created a norm in Gotham society to act outside the law and has spawned other events that can be traced to Two-Face's actions against Gordon's family. Dent is no longer the embodiment of the law and becomes the personification of vengeance. Once the genie of vengeance is out of its bottle, it is difficult to contain within the boundaries of the law.

Law, Legitimacy, and Lessons for our World

The demise of Harvey Dent in *The Dark Knight* was the goal of the Joker. However, in a scene where Batman has tied up the Joker at a building construction site and hangs him upside down, he states his true intention to Batman.

> BATMAN: This city just showed you that it's full of people ready to believe in good.
> JOKER: Until their spirit breaks completely. Until they get a good look at the real Harvey Dent and all the heroic things he's done. You didn't think I'd risk the battle for Gotham's soul in a fistfight with you! No! You need an ace in the hole—mine's Harvey Dent.
> BATMAN: What did you do?
> JOKER: I took Gotham's White Knight, and I brought him down to our level. It wasn't hard. You see, madness, as you know, is like gravity—all it takes is a little push! (Laughter).[20]

The Joker had created a situation where Dent lost someone he loved (Rachel) to incite outrage and a desire for revenge in the heart of Gotham's successful District Attorney. In his personal loss and anguish, Dent did not turn to the law to address the wrong he suffered but sought to satiate his desire for vengeance. Dent's descent from being the White Knight of Gotham to the villain Two-Face is a metaphor for the fragility of the rule of law and its social institutions. The allegory of Harvey Dent also demonstrates how easy it is to undermine the legitimacy of the rule of law and its supporting social institutions where fear and anger—whether in an individual or in society writ large—combine with the desire for vengeance. A. C. Grayling stated: "Desire for revenge is most dangerous when felt by individuals additionally oppressed by fear, anger, and a sense of impotence in the face of perceived injustice. Most of the world's flashpoints are thickly wreathed in such combustible vapors."[21]

There are many examples in our world where society's fear and anger, coupled with its desire for vengeance, have undermined the rule of law. One example is the use of torture to extract information from detainees during the War on Terror. The release of the U.S. Senate Select Committee on Intelligence's report on torture in December 2014 revealed the use of torture by CIA interrogators, who were authorized to do so by senior elected leaders.[22] The rationale for these practices was to obtain actionable intelligence to prevent terrorist attacks. The authority for these practices was given in the climate of fear that followed the September 11, 2001, attacks. In retrospect, it is easy to see how the climate of fear after an attack that was so shocking in its magnitude and consequence could result in such authorization. Similarly, a 2014 study co-authored by Avani Mehta Sood, a social psychologist and former Professor of Law at the University of California, Berkeley, found that the American public supported extreme interrogation, not just to obtain information to prevent attacks but also as a proxy for punishment.[23] This example demonstrates that the gravity of the circumstances, exacerbated by fear and vengefulness, makes it easy to give society "a little push" away from the rule of law and toward arbitrary retribution. The ease with which this can occur emphasizes the need to be vigilant in protecting and enforcing the social and legal institutions that embody the rule of law.

Conclusion

"There is nothing so urgent as the desire for revenge, when the real or perceived injury has been done to oneself or one's community, and there is nothing so sweet as the angry pleasure it gives once enacted."

—A.C. GRAYLING, *THE MEANING OF THINGS*[24]

Christopher Nolan's approach to the Batman story brings both Bruce Wayne and his alter ego to life in a vivid manner that makes it seem that they exist in our world, making them—and all of the other Gotham characters—much more than superheroes and supervillains. They each must navigate the chaotic moral and ethical challenges the world presents, in all its messiness and consequence, without any possibility of being saved by a surprise contraption in a utility belt or other deus ex machina. As a result, the *Nolanverse* provides a rich backdrop against which to examine the fundamental philosophical and institutional prerequisites for a stable and prosperous society. Nolan's conception of Gotham City—its economic and social decay caused extensively by the corruption of law enforcement and judicial institutions—is a perfect setting for Batman to wrestle with the concepts of justice and retribution and the rule of law and legitimacy. In Batman's struggle to seek justice rather than revenge, we can see our own struggle. While revenge is sweet and immediate, its consequences are corrosive. Perhaps it is Wayne's butler, Alfred Pennyworth, who we should aspire to emulate: He is the magnanimous and wise mentor to the Caped Crusader and is perhaps the true superhero of Gotham City.

Notes

1   Quoted in Tom Bingham, *The Rule of Law* (London: Allen Lane 2010), 3.

2   Ibid., 8.

3   DC Comics, "Batman, a History of Heroics: The Beginning," last modified March 19, 2019, https://www.dc.com/blog/2019/03/19/batman-a-history-of-heroics-the-beginning.

4   Ibid.

5   Ibid. It was only in 2015 that DC Comics and Warner Bros granted Bill Finger co-creator credit for Batman after a dispute that lasted 75 years: Charlie Jane Anders, "Who really created Batman? It depends what Batman means to you," last modified May 8, 2017, Wired online: https://www.wired.com/2017/05/batman-and-bill-who-is-batman/.

6   For an overview of the breadth of Batman movies, see: Charlie Jane Anders, "Fun Batman or Dark Batman? Hell, why not both," last modified February 10, 2017, *Wired* online https://www.wired.com/2017/02/fun-batman-vs-dark-batman/.

7   Michael J. Sandel. *Justice—What is the Right thing to Do?* (London: Penguin, 2010), 7.

8   *Batman Begins*, directed by Christopher Nolan (Los Angeles: Warner Bros., 2005).

9   Ibid.

10   *R v Gordon* (unreported, NSW Court of Criminal Appeal, February 7, 1994), per Hunt CJ at 468.

11   *The Queen v CAM* [1996] 1 Supreme Court Reports 500, per Lamer CJ at 80.

12   Nolan, *Batman Begins*.

13 A. C. Grayling. *The Meaning of Things. Applying Philosophy to Life* (London: Weidenfeld & Nicholson, 2007), 89.

14 Quoted in Bingham, *The Rule of Law*, 8.

15 The Bat Signal first appeared in *Detective Comics* #60 in 1942. Nick Mindicino, "Forever Shining, the One and Only Bat Signal," last updated September 16, 2020, DC Comics Blog, https://www.dc.com/blog/2020/09/16/forever-shining-the-one-and-only-bat-signal.

16 A. C. Grayling. *The Heart of Things. Applying Philosophy to the 21st Century* (London: Phoenix, 2006), 146.

17 Nolan, dir. *Batman Begins*. See also "Scarecrow" entry, https://villains.fandom.com/wiki/Scarecrow_(Nolanverse).

18 *The Dark Knight*, directed by Christopher Nolan (Los Angeles: Warner Bros, 2008). See also Brian Douglas' entry in *Batman Fandom* wiki, https://batman.fandom.com/wiki/Brian_Douglas.

19 Ibid.

20 Ibid.

21 Grayling, *The Meaning of Things*, 90.

22 Adam Gopnik. "Fear and Torture," *The New Yorker* online, last updated December 10, 2014, https://www.newyorker.com/news/daily-comment/fear-torture.

23 Avani Mehta Sood, "Was revenge a hidden rationale for torture?" *Los Angeles Times* online, last updated December 23, 2014, https://www.latimes.com/opinion/op-ed/la-oe-sood-torture-punishment-20141224-story.html. See also Kevin M. Carlsmith, Avani Mehta Sood, The fine line between interrogation and retribution, *Journal of Experimental Social Psychology*, Volume 45, Issue 1, 2009, 191–196, https://doi.org/10.1016/j.jesp.2008.08.025.

24 Grayling, *The Meaning of Things*, 89.

CHAPTER 17

Injustice for All

The Parallel Downfalls of the Justice League and the Delian League

James Groves

Fear. Honor. Interest. These three ingredients are the recipe for Superman's brutal fall from noble superhero to murderous tyrant in DC Comics' *Injustice: Gods Amongst Us* series and lead to the irreparable downfall of the Justice League. They are also the ingredients for the similarly ignoble fall from grace undertaken by Athens in Thucydides' *The Peloponnesian War* and subsequent downfall of the Delian League and their once-noble Athenian leaders.

At first glance, the dark and brooding superhero world portrayed in the *Injustice* series—complete with beautifully rendered panels of comic book artwork, an accompanying animated film, and an award-winning companion computer game—is as far away from *The Peloponnesian War* as any two written works could possibly be.

Not only is Thucydides' magnum opus generally considered the exclusive property of academics and students of history and strategy, but it has been described by many as "difficult, complex and, occasionally, obscure."[1] As if forecasting such review from future audiences, Thucydides himself wrote in the 5th century BC that he had written his work "not as an essay which is to win the applause of the moment, but as a possession for all time."[2] Although the authors of these two source materials are separated by two and a half millennia and the audiences are perhaps—at face value—equally distant, there are significant parallels between the two.

In brutally simple terms, both *Injustice: Gods Among Us* and *The Peloponnesian War* describe war. Not a glorious, romanticized story of war complete with Alexandrian leadership and *deus ex machina* escape mechanisms for the heroes, but an inglorious and painful war story that leaves audiences despairing for the heart-rending bloodiness of it all. They both describe what is, in many ways, a civil war. A series of battles fought by neighbors, by belligerents who have so much more to gain through cooperation than through conflict, and whose meeting in combat feels desperately unfulfilling rather than gloriously valiant.

In *The Peloponnesian War* we see a historical maritime power, Athens, waging war against a land power, Sparta. In *Injustice: Gods Among Us,* we see a fictional alien being, Superman, waging war against a mighty human, Batman. Each is seemingly invincible in their preferred domain, leading to a very drawn-out and costly series of encounters that result in the deaths of leading characters, their loved ones, and countless non-combatants.[3] In this way, both stories describe war on an epic scale but through a very personal lens. They show us that war takes a personal toll on each of its combatants and that ethical questions are faced by all who live by the sword.

In this sense, we can already begin to see the concepts which bridge DC Comics' and Thucydides' great works and identify some unexpected but fascinating common ground. Indeed, *Injustice: Gods Among Us* and *The Peloponnesian War* both discuss three specific themes that carry timeless value. First, parties go to war based on fear of a change or an imbalance in the status quo. Second, parties will fight over national or personal honor to defend what they treasure or avenge what they have lost. Third, parties will go to war simply to advance their interests.

Fear: "The Growth of Power … Made War Inevitable"

The opening panels of *Injustice: Gods Among Us* show Superman at his most human. The Man of Steel, faster than a speeding bullet, more powerful than a locomotive, able to leap tall buildings in a single bound, wakes to what he describes as the "single greatest sound [he has] ever heard … the sound of two heartbeats coming from one person."[4] The giddy nervousness of newly realized parenthood is endearing, and we, the audience, share Superman's excitement when he rushes to tell Batman, his closest friend, the news that he and his wife Lois Lane have only just learned themselves. This is Superman at his compassionate and collaborative best; despite his Kryptonian heritage, he feels the same elation, the same joyous impatience of parents-to-be across the human race, and we love him all the more for it.

His joy turns to panic within a couple of comic panels as Joker kidnaps Lois and Superman pleas for his friends' help. We see just how implicitly motivated and unified the Justice League is when all of them—men, women, demigods, and cyborgs—stop what they are doing and join the search for Lois. With the simultaneous tragedies of his wife and unborn child's death and a nuclear bomb detonating in his adopted city of Metropolis, Superman's emotional, ethical, and moral regulation is similarly extinguished.

An overwhelming desire for revenge sparks an explosion within Superman. He not only murders the Joker on sight but sets out on a crusade to create peace—by force—across the globe. He fears more innocent cities, like Metropolis, and more innocent individuals, like his wife and baby, will perish if he does not act swiftly and surely. So, he calls for "an immediate world-wide ceasefire" and orders "all hostilities will stop, or I will stop them."[5] Although his Justice League comrades met his savage and illegal murder of the Joker with reluctant sympathy, Superman's subsequent unilateralism in violently resolving all the world's wars sets him on a path they cannot follow. "The Justice League cannot be the world's police force," Batman states in the *Injustice* film, "if we continue on this path, we become tyrants."[6]

This differing perspective is the beginning of the end for the Justice League and illustrates the first parallel with *The Peloponnesian War*. The rise of Superman's use of power to levels beyond what is acceptable to his superhero colleagues removes all trust they have in one another and leads them to fear the worst in him if they leave his powers uncontested and his ambitions unchecked. In addition, Superman fears more innocents will needlessly die if he does not forcefully intervene. This echoes Gwynne Dyer's summary of *The Peloponnesian War* in that "the potential for war became the reason for war" and that conflict "escalated rapidly to a war of annihilation because neither side was willing to back down."[7]

The Justice League traditionally sought to exert a rules-based order by deterrence and defensive might. Any external threats would be defeated through a collective response. Similarly, the early days of the Delian League saw all members contribute to a fleet-in-being that was maintained and kept ready to defend against Persian incursions. Over time, the character of the Delian League changed, and Athenian leadership evolved to coercive power over its neighbors and liberal use of aggressive interventionism.[8] Their increasingly unrestricted use of power and unilateral actions echoes Superman's ultimatums delivered to the United Nations without consulting the Justice League and his desire to decide the outcomes of world affairs single-handedly.

The sudden and seemingly unstoppable rise of Superman's power created fear in the Justice League. "You have to stop what you're doing," Batman argues to Superman, "you can't put yourself above us." Superman's continued unilateralism spells doom for the unity of the Justice League and, ultimately, compels a reluctant and Spartan-like Batman to enter into war against the now-unbridled and increasingly Athenian Superman.

Honor: "No Concessions to the Peloponnesians!"

Honor and its resultant acts of justice, protection, and even retribution are salient themes in *The Peloponnesian War* that can also be found in *Injustice: Gods Among Us*. For superheroes and ancient Greek warriors alike, to be a bystander to injustice or to fail to act honorably in the face of evil is anathema. Both works feature eminent speeches by demigods and demagogues which urge their audiences to action—specifically to take arms against the foe—on the pretext of honor.

Thucydides describes Pericles as "the best man" in Athens, a man who under-stands "the needs of the state" and who "gauged the power of his country."[9] With such moral authority clearly evident, Pericles appeals to his fellow Athenians' sense of honor in their obligation to live up to the ideals of their polis. "Our city is worthy of admiration," he says in his famous Funeral Oration, "we are a pattern to others ... as a city we are the school of Hellas."[10] Athenian honor thus established, this same orator rouses his peers to war in another speech which commences with the battle cry "there is one principle ... the principle of no concession to the Peloponnesians" and concludes with the simple proclamation that "war is a necessity."[11]

Wonder Woman's credentials and appeals to her colleagues' sense of honor are similarly developed in her landmark Justice League Watch Tower speech. First, she creates a shared sense of unity by appealing to the assembled superheroes' collective mourning. "Every one of us lost friends and loved ones in Metropolis," she says. "Superman has not been mourning," she continues, "He has been fighting ... he took a tragedy and began to act to make sure it could never happen again."[12] Wonder Woman then uses this symbolic act from Superman to appeal to her peers' sense of honor. In a very Periclean climax to her oration, she declares, "I believe in what has been started. I believe we cannot just save the world but change it for the better ... and I will not stand by."[13]

Pericles and Wonder Woman deliver a number of monologues throughout *The Peloponnesian War* and *Injustice: Gods Among Us*. However, the most stirring and memorable of these orations explore the significance of honor and its ability to inspire combatants into action and rouse entire nations to war. For the Athenians, their sense of honor drove them to pursue increasingly unsustainable goals in military campaigns and unequal distributions of power, resulting in the downfall of the Delian League. For the DC superheroes, their sense of honor allowed them, in one meeting in the Watch Tower, to determine whether they stood in support of Superman and his sudden rise in power, or against him due to his unjust global domination, resulting in the downfall of the Justice League.

Interest: "The Strong Do What They Can and the Weak Suffer What They Must"

Political realism, the view that states relentlessly act in pursuit of their interests, is perhaps the most striking of all the themes that bridge both *Injustice: Gods Among Us* and *The Peloponnesian War*. Tragedy has unhinged Superman and driven him to use his full panoply of superpowers to achieve his newly desired endstate of zero tolerance to violence. When we see him address the United Nations and declare, "I am calling for an immediate world-wide ceasefire ... All hostilities will stop immediately, or I will stop them," we are confronted with an agent who has unilaterally decided that the status quo of the global balance of power is over. He has subordinated international free will to his wishes. By setting an immediate example, he issues a three-hour ultimatum to the leaders of Israel and Palestine to agree to peace terms or, he threatens with red eyes glowing, "they will be agreed for you."[14] He sends similar messages to warring factions in Burma, Syria, and Sudan, terrifying all parties into submission to conform the planet to his idealist view of Earth's future.

Such aggressive and liberal use of 'hard power' to achieve his goals, regardless of how unsustainable they may be, links Superman's actions to the Athenians. Thucydides describes this in the vignette commonly known as the Melian Dialogue. In 416BC, Athens deployed an armed expedition to Melos to force their subjugation to Athenian rule. The Melians refused, citing that justice and the pursuit of what is "right and fair" should guide a nation in its behavior. The invading Athenians fundamentally disagree with this worldview. Thucydides gives us the timeless quote from their delegation: "the strong do what they can and the weak suffer what they must."[15] This blunt declaration of hubris is compounded by the same Athenian delegation, which openly states, "we have come here in the interest of our empire."[16] Before they withdraw from the dialogue and commence their siege of Melos, the Athenians' parting comments that gods and men "rule wherever they can" leave us in no doubt that they not only feel they are vindicated in their actions, but that they are in fact acting in the only way they can.[17]

Superman's actions in the Injustice series can be interpreted as driven by a perverse honor derived from his desire to avenge Lois' murder. He is undoubtedly acting through self-interest in doing so. He has neither the patience nor the faith to permit the world's leaders to resolve their differences, nor does he feel the world's criminals deserve anything other than the punishments he decides. Batman's warnings to him are rebuffed with explosive anger. "You'd do exactly what I'm doing if you were me," Superman argues, "if you could do what I can."[18] His few remaining followers enable this self-interested behavior, Wonder Woman in particular, encourages Superman to dismiss the reservations of those who are not entirely behind him. "Don't worry about what they think," she tells him in affirmation, "you did what needed to be done."[19] The strong, according to Superman and his supporters at least, indeed do what they can.

The exploration of self-interest in both *Injustice: Gods Among Us* and *The Peloponnesian War* is fascinating and salient. There is no need for subtlety from the authors of either work in describing the protagonists' and antagonists' views on power and its ethical use by those who wield it. For example, the brazen attitude of the Athenians in the Melian Dialogue and their sense of pre-ordained righteousness based on their control of power in the relationship has become a case study in realism. Similarly, Superman's uncompromising ultimatums and threats of demonstrably assured destruction to achieve his desired outcomes from all political interactions are the DC Comics version of this ancient concept. Both works establish fear, honor, and interest as the themes explored in brutal, far-reaching, and heart-breaking examples as enduring reasons why parties go to war.

Conclusion: The Heart Break of Parallel Downfalls

The differences between DC Comics' *Injustice: Gods Among Us* and Thucydides' *The Peloponnesian War* are multi-faceted and immediately apparent. Thucydides' work is weighty, occasionally difficult to absorb, and often easy to dismiss as a fascinator of academia only. On the other hand, DC Comics has a reputation for over half a century of telling the stories of exciting, inspiring, and highly appealing superheroes in action. However, their common ground is significant and is home to several profound lessons.

Thucydides tells us in Book 1 of his great work that the Athenians, like all great powers, were subject to the three timeless motives of fear, honor, and interest when acting to preserve their strength. Although the Athenians say this about themselves, Thucydides illustrates the validity of this statement across three critical tracts in *The Peloponnesian War*, and they are echoed with astounding reverberation throughout *Injustice: Gods Among Us*.

Thucydides' work develops the concept of fear almost immediately. Within the first few pages, we read that "the growth of the power of Athens, and the alarm which this inspired in Sparta, made war inevitable." Similarly, we see Superman's willingness to use his powers to their fullest extent within the first few pages of DC Comics' story. However, the alarm that this inspires in the remainder of the Justice League makes them determined to stop him by any means possible.

The ancient Greek general Pericles uses honor to inspire his fellow Athenians during low points in the Peloponnesian War and rouse them to clear-eyed determination to see the war through to its completion, regardless of personal cost. Similarly, the Amazonian demi-goddess Diana, known as Wonder Woman, uses honor as a tool to connect with the Justice League after the tragedy of Metropolis, to urge them to sympathize with Superman and to appeal to their shared sense of justice and virtue. Of course, neither Pericles nor Wonder Woman are entirely blameless in their roles within their respective wars; however, they both successfully use honor and language built around honorable themes as demagogic levers to spur their peers to military action.

The Athenian's relentless pursuit of self-interest is displayed throughout the Melian Dialogue and illustrates their instinctive use of power to achieve their ends. Superman shares their view that 'the strong do what they can' as evident in his unilateral application of justice and the series of ultimatums he issues to the world's governments.

The downfall of the Delian League, as described by Thucydides in *The Peloponnesian War*, can be broadly understood and, for some themes, clearly recognized in the downfall of the Justice League, as described by DC Comics in *Injustice: Gods Among Us*. The parallels are striking once we see them, and the lessons are eternally pertinent as they span millennia and genres. Fear, honor and interest not only lead to the fall of great heroes and admirable alliances, they ultimately and inevitably lead to injustice for all.

Notes

1 Robert B. Strassler (ed), *The Landmark Thucydides: A Comprehensive Guide to The Peloponnesian War* (New York: Free Press, 2008), xxv.
2 Ibid., 1.22.4.
3 Professor Hunter Rawlings in *Classics* podcast, ep 12—Thucydides' History of the Peloponnesian War, Part 1.
4 DC Comics, *Injustice: Gods Among Us* (New York: DC Comics, 2013), Vol 1, Pt 1.
5 Ibid., Vol 1, Pt 2
6 *Injustice*, directed by Matt Peters (Los Angeles: Warner Bros. Animation, 2021).
7 Gwynne Dyer, *War* (New York: Crown Publishers, 1987), 42.
8 Williamson Murray, *Successful Strategies: Triumphing in War and Peace from Antiquity to the Present* (Cambridge: Cambridge University Press, 2014), 15.
9 Strassler, 2.65.4–5.
10 Ibid., 2.37–41.
11 Ibid., 1.140–144.
12 DC Comics, *Injustice: Gods Among Us* (New York: DC Comics, 2013), Vol 1, Pt 3.
13 Ibid.
14 DC Comics, *Injustice: Gods Among Us* (New York: DC Comics, 2013), Vol 1, Pt 6.
15 Strassler, 5.89.
16 Ibid., 5.91.
17 Ibid., 5.105
18 DC Comics, *Injustice: Gods Among Us* (New York: DC Comics, 2013), Vol 1, Pt 4.
19 *Injustice*, Peters.

CHAPTER 18

It's Not Just Black and White

Widow's Redemption Story

Alyssa Jones

"In these troubled times, we need leaders who understand the importance of redemption. We need leaders who have faced adversity and risen from its ashes."

—JOHN FERRITER

Technology in the 21st century, including social media, has the paradoxical effect of keeping us locked in an unending present while simultaneously building an archive that will never vanish. As a result, we experience high degrees of anxiety, depression, and loneliness, in addition to difficulties in growing and evolving, which are our primary goals and the foundation of our spiritual and philosophical traditions. Yet, beyond the more well-known instincts of survival—sex and power—there is an instinct that drives us to adapt and grow through our mistakes, through pain, and through self-discovery. Author and entrepreneur Arianna Huffington referred to this penchant for adaptation as our fourth instinct, the "highest common denominator" that enables one to have an impulse to fulfillment.[1]

This impulse is the driving force behind the story arc of Natasha Romanoff, better known as the Black Widow in the Marvel Cinematic Universe (MCU). Across multiple films and countless television programs, Natasha's journey to—and struggles with—redemption is documented for viewers, all while she works to come to terms with who she is and how others perceive her. Natasha's path to redemption serves as apt metaphor for the crucible experiences that forge our greatest leaders, in this case a superhero with a dark and somewhat checkered past.[2]

The path to redemption—or the fight for redemption—can present both obstacles and opportunities on our journey to become the best version of ourselves possible. We do not simply find redemption. We navigate the obstacles life presents, overcoming those challenges while forging onward in pursuit of the opportunity to achieve our goals. We pick ourselves up when we fall and transform the greatest of those challenges into positives that become central to how we live, lead, and learn. Natasha's redemption arc is a stirring example of how we can leverage a traumatic past to become more, and maybe along the way find peace with our past.

The Roots of Redemption

The term "redemption" derives from the Latin *redimere*, which conveys a general sense of repurchase or deliverance. Key among its various meanings, however, is the religious concept of *release* from past sins. Redemption frees us from our darkest moments, allowing us to flourish in our quest for fulfillment. In his book, *The History of Redemption*, Ronnie Smith wrote that redemption often seems like an abstract concept.[3] For most of us, redemption appears as a flourishing life, a day-to-day existence overflowing with joy and fulfillment. However, a deep appreciation for redemption's release does not come without an equally deep sense of the effect of the sins of the past. Only if you appreciate the consequences of your own fall can you begin to truly appreciate the grace of what appears to others as the everyday realities of life.

Redemption is a release. It delivers us. And that is precisely what our contemporary society makes increasingly difficult. We cannot move on from our worst experiences, improve ourselves, or make the world a better place, since doing so would allow our wounds to close and the healing process to begin. Although we profess to value a "growth mindset," we embrace the stagnant mentality of our own irredeemability.[4] Our society has reached a point where we believe in a frozen ideal, a state of arrested development from which improvement or growth is thought to be inconceivable; we celebrate our own unworthiness. Because forgiveness, reconciliation, and redemption are essential components for growth, we cannot advance either personally or as a society if we are not permitted to atone for our errors, make amends, and change for the better.

The Founding Fathers of the United States understood this clearly. They included amendments in the Constitution because—as history has proven—the great documents we live by presume progress, whether through the never-ending quest for "a more perfect union" or Dr. Martin Luther King's "arc of the moral universe" bending toward justice.[5] Human growth is required for actual systemic change to occur. The "line dividing good and evil flows right through every human heart," as Aleksandr Solzhenitsyn put it, "not through states, not between classes, nor even across political parties."[6] King was very aware of this concept and made it plain that to change society, "you've got to change the heart."[7] And that growth towards redemption can be challenging.

The Road From Perdition

Across the entire *Avengers* story arc, Natasha struggles to atone for her past, going to any lengths necessary to disassociate herself from her veiled, often shadowed history. There is a cold streak in the Black Widow that belies Natasha's true self. She is singularly focused in pursuit of her mission, withholds key information from those closest to her, and exposes herself—and others—to danger seemingly without concern. The Black Widow holds herself to an exacting and unforgiving standard and can be harsh—and deadly—to those unable to meet that same standard.

Other Marvel superheroes considered themselves flawed before choosing the path of the hero. But Natasha was not just flawed; she was a cold-blooded killer, an unapologetic villain. Her past haunts her, as do the moral compromises she made along the way. As the event of *Captain America: The Winter Soldier* unfold, Natasha learns that HYDRA has compromised S.H.I.E.L.D. and begins to understand just how compromised she has always been. She feels the friction between who she was and who she is. Or, as she secretly worries, whom she pretends now to be.

At her core, Natasha is driven by her own inescapable feelings of unworthiness, and her inner shame is revealed gradually across her entire redemption arc. Her "dripping red ledger" is ever-present in her thoughts, and she is continually reminded of her past mistakes by those with whom she interacts. During one particularly lighthearted scene in *Avengers: Age of Ultron*, Natasha refuses to attempt to lift Thor's hammer, Mjölnir, a revealing moment that reflects her own fears of unworthiness.[8] In *Captain America: The Winter Soldier*, the World Security Council Secretary, Alexander Pierce, points out that the truth about her past would be revealed to the public if she exposed S.H.I.E.L.D.'s secrets. And in *The Avengers*, Loki laid bare her state of mind in a brutal conversation when he said, "You lie and kill in the service of liars and killers. You pretend to be separate, to have your code. Something that makes up for the horrors. But they are a part of you, and they will never go away!"[9] This inescapable sense of unworthiness follows Natasha to Vormir during *Avengers: Endgame*, where she sacrifices herself to obtain the Soul Stone, the last of the Infinity Stones necessary to restore the known universe from the genocidal effects of *The Snap*. In the truest sense of Christian redemption, her death—an incredible act of unselfish nobility—is necessary to save everyone else.

But *Avengers: Endgame* lacked a proper memorial for such an important character. The closing scenes of the film acknowledged her sacrifice and absence but focused more on closing the story arc of Tony Stark, who had also sacrificed himself to stop Thanos and restore the lives he had snapped away at the end of *Avengers: Infinity War*. Natasha needed—no, deserved—a funeral. For that, we have the 2021 film, *Black Widow*.

The Path to Redemption

The movie opens in 1995, introducing the seemingly idyllic family of Alexei Shostakov and Melina Vostokoff and their daughters Natasha and Yelena, living an all-too-typical life in an otherwise unremarkable Ohio neighborhood. But perceptions can be deceiving, and the family is anything but idyllic. In reality, Alexei and Melina are Russian agents sent into deep cover to infiltrate and destroy the HYDRA-occupied North Institute within S.H.I.E.L.D., and their "daughters" are surrogates provided by General Dreykov to complete the ruse. After destroying the Institute, the "family" escapes to Cuba, where Dreykov takes possession of the girls and betrays Alexie, incarcerating him in the infamous Seventh Circle Prison for criticizing the Russian government.

The girls, as we soon learn, aren't even sisters. They are part of Dreykov's Red Room, a classified Russian training program in which he uses psychological conditioning and mind control to transform young women into obedient, elite assassins known as Black Widows. Purchased or stolen from their true families by Dreykov, the girls are merely tools. Yelena reveals the depth of Dreykov's sinister program early in *Black Widow*:

> Dreykov and his network of Widows. He takes more every day. Children who don't have anyone to protect them. Just like us when we were small. Maybe one in twenty survives the training, becomes a Widow. The rest, he kills. To him, we are just things. Weapons with no face that he can just throw away.[10]

Yelena and Natasha are eventually separated, and Natasha becomes Dreykov's principal operative. Eventually targeted by S.H.I.E.L.D., Natasha is recruited by Clint Barton, who helps her to defect. Once clear of Dreykov's influence, Natasha returns in hopes of sparing Yelena the worst of the Red Room, destroying the training academy and assassinating the general, but also killing his daughter Antonia in the process. Or so she believes.

Several years later, following the battle between the Avengers at Leipzig/Halle Airport depicted in *Captain America: Civil War*, Natasha is a fugitive, fleeing to a safe house in Norway after violating the Sokovia Accords. After receiving a package from Yelena, she reunites with her pseudo-sister in Budapest, who reveals that Dreykov is indeed alive and the Red Room is still very much in operation.[11] For Natasha, this revelation only further reinforces her immense feelings of unworthiness. Even as she and Yelena work to bring an end to Dreykov and the Black Widow Program, she knows in her heart that she failed to protect the one person closest to her, the "sister" fighting by her side.[12]

We see that same sense of irredeemability resurface throughout Black Widow. As the film narrative progresses, we are offered more insights into the complexities of Natasha's character and her ongoing struggle to prove her worthiness. The family portrayed by Alexei and Melina is anything but functional and—comedic elements aside—their eventual reunion only serves to underscore the wounds inflicted upon her psyche as a result of their betrayal. Her disgust upon seeing Alexei—Dreykov's vaunted Red Guardian—again after orchestrating his escape from Seventh Circle Prison reflects the depth of those wounds. His only concern is for his own welfare, not the "daughters" he sacrificed to Dreykov's Red Room. His pride for Natasha is disturbingly misplaced, and his praise for her murderous past slices to her soul: "You have killed so many people! Your ledger must be dripping [with blood]—just gushing! I couldn't be more proud of you!"[13] But their "mother," Melina offers probably the most telling reason those wounds cut so deep: "Why does a mouse born in a cage run on that little wheel? Do you know I was cycled through the Red Room four times before you were even born? Those walls are all I know. I was never given a choice."

The same deep-seated aspirations to be worthy manifest in Natasha's interactions with Yelena, pushing her away and not acknowledging her love for her sister. Natasha sincerely believes that Yelena is better off without her. Learning that she not only failed to kill Dreykov but doomed her sister to the worst the Red Room offered was a final slap in the face. Even discovering Antonia's survival—horribly scarred and transformed into the soulless assassin Taskmaster—could not appease her guilt. If nothing else, it was another painful reminder that she cannot just wipe away the mistakes of her past, regardless of how much good she does. In her mind, she can never be fully redeemed from the actions of her own past.[14]

It is not until Natasha finally accepts the unconditional love of her adopted sister that she finds her path to redemption. Then, in the closing act of Black Widow, Natasha—with the timely assistance of Yelena—risks her own life to free the other girls from Dreykov's hold. She brings a final end to the general's reign of terror, setting in motion the destruction of his secret airborne training facility. Then, with the Red Room collapsing around her, Natasha chooses to spare the life of her enemy, to free Antonia from her prison. Natasha finally becomes the hero her Black Widow persona represents. She is redeemed.

The Price of Redemption

The cinematic events that follow Black Widow on the MCU timeline capture a significant and distinct change in Natasha. The evolution of her character reflects an Avenger at peace with her present, released from the sins of her past. Through the narrative arc of the final two Avengers films, the Black Widow we see is not the same Black Widow we met early on in Iron Man 2. Hers is a classic tale of redemption, someone trying to correct a past wrong through actions in the present. Redemption stories are part of the human experience, retold over time in films ranging from It's *a Wonderful Life* to *Star Wars: Return of the Jedi*. We love a good redemption story, and Natasha's story arc doesn't disappoint.

Natasha Romanoff was long known as a great operative, first as an agent of S.H.I.E.L.D. and later as a member of the Avengers. But she also had a life before being considered a hero. "Persuaded by a force that will stop at nothing to bring her down. Dealing with dark parts of her ledger when a dangerous conspiracy with ties to her past arises and dealing with her history as a spy."[15] In her heart, Natasha knew that she did not deserve redemption. The Christian faith teaches us as much. And yet, through unearned grace, we are all offered redemption—or, at least, a chance for it. We understand that redemption exists, and by changing our actions, we can seek release from past sins. Natasha aims to make the most of that second chance and tries, each and every day, to be better. That is what makes her a superhero.

Though her self-sacrifice in *Avengers: Endgame* served as a tragic—and necessary—close to Natasha's arc of redemption, it wasn't until Marvel Studios released *Black Widow* in the summer of 2021 that we felt a final sense of closure. Her redemption was not from society but from the sins of human culture. When she joined S.H.I.E.L.D., she was forsaking atonement for her past mistakes. When she downloaded S.H.I.E.L.D.'s secrets in *Captain America: The Winter Soldier*, she also downloaded her own, representing—in a sense—a symbolic public confessional. Her entire career—spanning from *Iron Man 2* through *Black Widow*—marks a determined effort to reconcile with her past as best she can.[16]

The closing scenes of *Black Widow* undeniably demonstrate that Natasha was truly one of *Earth's mightiest heroes*. Despite a decidedly dark past and a noticeably violent, bloody "red ledger," Natasha was an exemplar for us all. We can atone for our past mistakes by being the best versions of ourselves possible, showing grace to those in need, and living lives of charity and compassion. Like Natasha, our ledgers can be wiped clean by accepting redemption, becoming the heroes others need us to be.

Notes

1   Arianna Huffington, "A Culture Without the Possibility of Redemption is a Toxic Culture," *Thrive*, August 23, 2021. https://thriveglobal.com/stories/arianna-huffington-cancel-culture-redemption-forgiveness-growth/.

2   Warren Bennis and Robert Thomas, "Crucibles of Leadership," *Harvard Business Review*, September 2002.

3   Ronnie Smith and Chris Koelle, *The History of Redemption* (Austin: The Austin Stone Community Church, 2010).

4   Huffington.

5   Ibid.

6   Aleksandr Isevich Solzhenietisyn and H. T. Willetts. *One Day in the Life of Ivan Denisovich* (New York: Farrar, Straus and Giroux, 2005).

7   Huffington.

8   According to Marvel canon, Mjölnir is inscribed with the words, "Whosover hold this hammer, if he be worthy, shall possess the power of Thor." Thor's own unworthiness to weild Mjölnir is a central element of the thunder god's story arc in the MCU.

9   Amy Coknour, "Black Widow: Redeeming the Past," *Love Thy Nerd*, July 23, 2021. https://lovethynerd.com/black-widow/.

10 *Black Widow*, directed by Cate Shortland (Los Angeles: Marvel Studios, 2021). https://www.disneyplus.com/movies/black-widow/3VfTap90rwZC.

11 Budapest figures prominently in Marvel canon as the nexus of several story arcs across the MCU.

12 Coknour.

13 Ibid.

14 Ibid.

15 "Black Widow (Natasha Romanova)," in Comics Powers, Villains, History | Marvel. *Marvel Entertainment*. Retrieved September 20, 2022, from https://www.marvel.com/characters/black-widow-natasha-romanova/in-comics.

16 Paul Asay, "Black Widow's Quest for Redemption Might Make Her Marvel's Best Hero," *Watching God*, July 9, 2021. https://www.patheos.com/blogs/watchinggod/2021/07/black-widows-quest-for-redemption-might-make-her-marvels-best-hero/.

CHAPTER 19

Black Vibranium in the Hour of Chaos

Aaron Rahsaan Thomas

There were two men. The first, born in 1909 to a tribal family in the Nkroful region of the Gold Coast; a territory since demarcated and labeled as a country, Ghana, by Western entities. This man grew up in a rural area near the French colonized Ivory Coast, raised by his mother and extended family in a traditional matrilineal system where rituals are passed down through the mother's side of the family. Due to the naming customs of the Akan people, this man was given the first name, Kwame, a name granted to males born on a Saturday. He inherited a surname from his father's side of the family, Nkrumah, which means ninth-born child, as his father took multiple wives and had other children.

Initially poor and illiterate, Nkrumah enjoyed a mostly carefree life in a colonialized system. As a child, he played in the bush and along the coast, learning to fish in the Atlantic Ocean. Supported by his family, he would pursue higher education abroad in the United Kingdom and United States, where he was heavily influenced by texts from African American intellectuals such as W. E. B. Dubois and Marcus Garvey. It is partially through this education that Nkrumah was introduced to theories on leadership and Pan Africanism, the political union of indigenous inhabitants of the African continent. This inspiration is the foundation that launched Kwame Nkrumah's rise to become the first president of Ghana and the historical and international face of Pan Africanism. His political work served as motivation for others, even stretching into the world of pop culture, comic books, and graphic novels. Discussing his influence on the world stage in a 1957 autobiography, Nkrumah stated:

> Just as in the days of the Egyptians, so today God had ordained that certain among the African race should journey westwards to equip themselves with knowledge and experience for the day when they would be called upon to return to their motherland and to use the learning they had acquired to help improve a lot of their brethren.... I had not realized at the time that I would contribute so much towards the fulfillment of this prophecy.[1]

Just as Nkrumah's political career would come to a sudden end in 1966, a second man was born the same year. A fictional character created by two Jewish cartoonists,

Stanley Lieber, now known as Stan Lee, and Jacob Kurtzberg, now known as Jack Kirby. This character was designed as a reflection of a 1960s interest in exploring African roots and black consciousness, influenced in large part by movements inspired by Nkrumah. Having personal friends who were African American, Stan Lee and Jack Kirby chose to become aware of the dearth of black comic book heroes in existence. The character they created was given a first name, T'Challa, a popular name in West Africa. But the world knows him better as Marvel's Black Panther.

Early in T'Challa's comic book existence, he served as a mysterious sidekick to the Fantastic Four, a white American family introduced to portray relationship and soap opera dynamics in a comic book hero world. The mystery surrounding T'Challa was often used for suspense; he wore all black with a full mask over his face long before other characters did. But, some of these decisions were also made in the interest of business. The full mask hid controversial black skin from some of Marvel's more aggrieved readers. And, although the Black Panther was created a few years before the revolutionary group of the same name gained public prominence, it was decided that his name would change to the Black Leopard for a short period to avoid perceived affiliation. By the start of the 1970s, Marvel's gamble on this character paid off as T'Challa grew popular enough to launch his own comic in 1973.

Rather than assigning a specific tribal origin to T'Challa, he was given a combination of African details. In effect, his story became the first Pan African comic book origin. Possessing a West African name, T'Challa exhibited heightened abilities, a genius-level intellect, and was presented as the king of a fictional home nation of Wakanda; a territory demarcated and labeled as a country, given a name born from a 1960s-era fascination with the Swahili language. Landlocked and hidden from most of the world, Wakanda would come to symbolize a mix of Afrofuturistic technology, traditional custom and fashion from various nations within the African continent. Wakanda would eventually become more than a fictional destination for comic book readers, rather a symbol of what might be possible in light, or despite of, the era of colonialism. A fictional black utopia in the vein of Zamunda, a country created for the 1988 Eddie Murphy film, *Coming to America*. In many ways, T'Challa and Wakanda signify the potential of the Pan African dream. T'Challa's existence and even more so, his modern evolution through comics, animation, and film is inspired by the same African American intellectuals Kwame Nkrumah studied. The texts of W. E. B. Dubois and Marcus Garvey would inform modern intellectual Black Panther storytellers such as Ta-Nehisi Coates,[2] Reginald Hudlin,[3] and Ryan Coogler[4] as they expanded an aspiration elevated by Nkrumah.

At the heart of Nkrumah and T'Challa's life journeys resides a personal mandate to protect a people, its citizens, and resources, preferring to use diplomacy and intellect above all other methods. In a way, the nations of Ghana and Wakanda are both imaginary constructs, in that the names, locations, and physical perimeters of each country were created and determined by elements that are non-indigenous to the African continent. The arbitrary nature of created national boundaries is a key element in the idea of Pan Africanism. In the case of Nkrumah, the Akan people of which he was born and raised reside over the land mass of several nations. Their culture and traditions cross government boundaries, which is to say that if a person is of the Akan people, their legacy is not restricted to Ghana, Nigeria, the Ivory Coast, or a host of other established West African countries. Family and tribal lineage becomes varied and muddled, which is a concept that some African Americans, the descendants of slaves whose history was often destroyed or lost to time, relate to.

Nkrumah's plan was to pursue an African culture that united people as a country, in addition to tribal heritage. One of his goals was to diminish tribalism, a foundation of loyalties that was once held more sacred than loyalty to the country, itself. In his book, *Africa Must Unite*, Nkrumah wrote: "We were engaged in a kind of war, a war against poverty and disease, against ignorance, against tribalism and disunity. We needed to secure the conditions which could allow us to pursue our policy of reconstruction and development."[5]

Accordingly, as the Black Panther storytelling mantle was passed from Stan Lee and Jack Kirby to modern black artists, the idea of T'Challa and Wakanda evolved, starting to reconcile notions of a larger African diaspora. In short, Wakanda is whatever the reader or viewer wants it to be. Certainly, there are constructive elements that result from this approach, an aspirational idea of what successful Pan Africanism could result in. But there are also criticisms. In contrast to the approach of other comic book publishers and movie studios, Marvel Comics has mostly defied a stark theme of good guy vs. bad guy narratives to eschew stories that sometimes exist in ethically and morally challenging gray areas. Marvel looks to place imperfect everyday people at the center of flawed real locations, facing everyday, grounded challenges, even as these characters use fantastic powers to achieve the impossible. These stories are the definition of escapism and often serve as comfort food for the reader or viewer. However, when tied to the dreams of an actual continent, this portrayal also risks oversimplifying actual challenges that Nkrumah sought to rectify.

Nkrumah's strategy was to supplant colonialism with African socialism. It was an idea of pursuing a federal United States of Africa, with interlocking regional governments, ruling separate states using restricted sovereignty. Limited with a low amount of capital funding, his theory was to build a new nation by constructing a democratic regime within a socialist or communist system, synthesizing traditional aspects with modern thinking.

Nkrumah looked to industrialize Ghana's economy. The idea was that if Ghana escaped colonialism by reducing dependence on foreign money, imports, and supplies, it could become truly independent. Initially, Nkrumah's ideas were effective in gathering support. In 1957, Ghana became the first of Britain's African colonies to gain majority-rule independence. In the process, it became a beacon of Pan Africanism, and Nkrumah's stature as a leader grew beyond measure. When he spoke at the first session of the Ghana Parliament on Independence Day, he stated: "The new African is ready to fight his own battles and show that after all the black man is capable of managing his own affairs."[6]

The end of the first *Black Panther* film, written by Joe Robert Cole and Ryan Coogler and directed by Coogler, saw T'Challa, portrayed by the late, great actor Chadwick Boseman, face a similar coming-out party for Wakanda on the world stag.[7] However, challenges lay ahead for governing in the public sphere. In the sequel to *Black Panther*, subtitled *Wakanda Forever*, the main threat resulted from the sudden spotlight on the country's invaluable natural resources. For Ghana, the real-life challenges came from within. As president, Nkrumah adopted social democratic policies. He created a welfare system, started community programs, and established schools funded by the state. But, to make these achievements possible, he also charged high taxes on the working class and acted on a desire to bypass a British-trained judiciary, which he distrusted, viewing them as opposing his vision for an independent African nation. This distrust would manifest itself in the form of arresting select citizens without a proper trial. According to David Birmingham, a Nkrumah biographer: "No single measure did more to bring down Nkrumah's reputation than his adoption of internment without trial for the preservation of security."[8]

A manipulated national legal system is not something that Black Panther has tackled in depth yet, but controversial decisions made by well-meaning leaders is a consistent theme for T'Challa and the Wakandan kings who came before him. For instance, the decision to remain secluded from the world, even at the expense of not aiding others in need, resulted from a concern that their natural resources would be coveted by other nations. In part, this is based on actual fears from the colonial era.

In the turbulent 1960s, President Nkrumah reasoned that there would be no peace at large until African nations made peace amongst themselves. However, in a world dominated by a Cold War fueled by American and Russian Soviet allies and proxies, sharp lines were drawn literally and financially. Where African nations supplied a great percentage of the world's petroleum, gold, diamonds, and cocoa, most of the profit rarely benefitted source nations, an arrangement partly inherited from the colonial era and in large part protected by Western elements with an interest in keeping purchase prices as low as possible. Consequently, the idea of Pan Africanism was seen as a direct financial threat to world order, making Nkrumah's dream a dangerous political prop used to help justify strategic and purposeful regional destabilization. In a sense, African nations were looking to unionize, while corporate business entities had zero interest in allowing it to happen. The result of this was to use Nkrumah's socialist leanings to undermine and target him as an enemy of the state. In the U.S., he was defined as a communist for wanting to build a new country that provided free education and healthcare. And, in Soviet Russia, he was viewed as an American-educated democratic sympathizer, keen to side with the United States if forced to make a choice. These forces, strengthened by poor results from short-sighted internal decisions from Nkrumah himself, made him vulnerable and the priority of a military coup that unseated him from power in 1966 while he was out of the country on a diplomatic visit.

T'Challa's Wakanda found its own challenges in governing after coming out to the world. As a prosperous African nation that mostly kept to itself, this notion for Wakanda was used in comics to logically explain how such an advanced and well-adjusted country could exist on a continent that has been ravaged by colonizers for centuries. However, as the story of T'Challa and Wakanda changed hands with new authors throughout time, some storytellers employed actual African history in a way that few comics had before. Layers were added referencing grounded problems facing the continent. For instance, the source of Wakanda's prosperity is its own natural resource, the rarest metal on earth, known as Vibranium. Deposited by a meteorite 10,000 years ago, Vibranium is nearly indestructible and channels and redirects sound and energy in useful and sometimes destructive ways. Consequently, Vibranium is one of the most desired elements on the planet. A sample of this metal is what makes Captain America's shield invulnerable. A mixture of Vibranium is what creates the Adamantium steel that fortifies Wolverine's unbreakable claws and skeleton.

It is the pursuit of Vibranium that now drives the Black Panther narrative in the Marvel Cinematic universe, as well as many of his current comic book stories. Where storytellers take this narrative in the future should be fascinating.

The stories of Nkrumah and Ghana, and T'Challa and Wakanda, are still growing into maturity. Though Nkrumah passed away in 1972 from pancreatic cancer, the foundation he built continues to determine the path of a country that is still less than 70 years old. To put this in perspective, consider where the United States was in the year, 1841. In the timeline of nations, Ghana is a country in its infancy. The fictional Wakanda has been established much longer, yet the stories exploring this land and its rulers feels full of potential, as though the most layered and interesting aspects lay ahead of us as readers and viewers. Considering this, a lyric from the rap group Public Enemy's iconic song *Black Steel in the Hour of Chaos* comes to mind:

> And to my rescue, it was the S1Ws
> Secured my getaway, so I just got away
> The joint broke from the black smoke
> Then they saw it was rougher than the average bluffer
> 'Cause the steel was black, the attitude exact
> Now the chase is on, telling you to c'mon
> 53 brothers on the run, and we are gone.[9]

Notes

1   Kwame Nkrumah, *Ghana: The Autobiography of Kwame Nkrumah* (Nashville, Tennessee: Thomas Nelson & Sons, 1965).
2   This is a reference to "A Nation Under Our Feet," a Black Panther graphic novel written by Ta-Nehisi Coates (2016).
3   This is a reference to the 12-part animated series, "Black Panther: Who Is the Black Panther?" (2010) and the graphic novel "Black Panther by Reginald Hudlin: The Complete Collection Vol. 1" (2017).
4   This is a reference to two Marvel Cinematic Universe films directed by Ryan Coogler, *Black Panther* (2018) and *Black Panther: Wakanda Forever* (2022).
5   Kwame Nkrumah, *Africa Must Unite* (Bedford, UK: Panaf Books, August 2007).
6   The full speech in text and captured in video can be found at ghanaweb.com.
7   This is a reference is to T'Challa's address to the United Nations at the end of the Black Panther film.
8   David Birmingham, *Kwame Nkrumah: The Father of African Nationalism* (Athens, Ohio: Ohio University Press, December 1998).
9   Public Enemy, "Black Steel in the Hour of Chaos," from the album of the same name (1988).

PART IV

IT'S CLOBBERIN' TIME!

"Oh well, it ain't time yet for my beauty sleep, so I guess—It's clobberin' time!"
—BEN GRIMM (THE THING) IN *THE INCREDIBLE HULK* #122 (1969)

CHAPTER 20

Who Runs the World? Squirrels!

The Unbeatable Squirrel Girl and Peaceful Conflict Resolution

Kelsey Cipolla

In the vast Marvel universe, one hero has bested everyone from world destroyers like Galactus and Thanos to world-class heroes like the Avengers: the Unbeatable Squirrel Girl, known to her friends and family as Doreen Green, Empire State University computer science student.

Green possesses the powers of a squirrel and a girl—the former includes the proportional strength of a squirrel, which makes her tremendously strong; the ability to jump great distances; a knack for conversing with squirrels often used to rally them to her aid; and squirrel-like physical attributes such as retractable claws and knuckle spikes, enhanced teeth and, perhaps most notably, a long, bushy tail. But although those traits make her a formidable opponent, it's the "girl" side of her identity, which is to say the human, emotionally intelligent side, that sets her apart in the crowd of heroes.

No matter how high the stakes get, Doreen relies on her unfailing sense of empathy and compassion, ability to resolve sticky situations through communication, and strong connections with her community. In a comic landscape (and world) where violence is so often depicted as the answer, she shows another way forward through peaceful conflict resolution tactics and relationship building.

As Doreen tells one assumed enemy turned ally as she prepares to train him in her ways: "We are going to empathize *so hard* with conflicting points of view and reach mutually acceptable compromises, *you just wait*."[1]

Squirrel Power

Squirrel Girl's first act of conflict resolution in the modern era was presumably forgiving her character's snarky origins. Introduced in 1991 by writer Will Murray and artist Steve Ditko, she occasionally popped up in comics, defeating formidable foes off-panel as a running joke.[2] After all, what could be more ridiculous than a teenage girl with squirrel powers doing what the big-name heroes couldn't, even in a fictional universe where seemingly anything is possible?

Thankfully, writer Ryan North and artist Erica Henderson brought Doreen to life anew in *The Unbeatable Squirrel Girl* comic series, which debuted in January 2015. Their take overflows with ridiculousness, but this time around the protagonist is in on the jokes, and cracking lots of her own—fittingly, she's got a thing for nut-based humor.

The series gave longtime comic fans and newbies alike a lot to celebrate, from the realistic way Henderson drew Doreen Green's physique to the diverse cast of supporting characters. But perhaps most importantly, readers got a front-row seat to see how Squirrel Girl has been beating villains all this time: by trying to understand their motivations and help them arrive at a mutually beneficial solution.

It's a tactic we see right from Issue 1 when Kraven the Hunter picks the wrong squirrel to mess with. (Not Squirrel Girl, to clarify—her friend Tippy-Toe, who is a literal squirrel.) After trying to peacefully intervene on behalf of Tippy-Toe, Squirrel Girl and Kraven are trading blows when she has an epiphany: "Wait … Maybe the question isn't, 'How do I beat him?' Maybe the question is, 'Dude, why are we even fighting in the first place? What does Kraven want?'"[3]

It turns out, Kraven is frustrated he can't kill Spider-Man, who he considers the world's most dangerous prey. But Doreen is quick to point out there are other creatures for Kraven to turn his attention to, like Gigantos, superpowered and super evil aquatic creatures. The world's greatest hunter heads under the sea, and he and Squirrel Girl part civilly, later even becoming something approaching friends.

It's a pattern we see play out time and again with Squirrel Girl: An enemy's dastardly behavior is simply their way of trying to meet a need, and they can be put on a different path when she takes the time to listen.

One of Marvel Comics' most enduring and difficult to defeat villains, Galactus, is prevented from eating Earth when Squirrel Girl finds him an uninhabited planet filled with high protein nuts to snack on instead.[4] Hippo the Hippo gives up bank robbing when our favorite crime-fighting rodent-human suggests he look into a career that makes use of his natural strength to help pay his living expenses: demolition.[5] And Brain Drain, a Hydra-aligned cyborg, turns out to have just been badly programmed by aliens that had a minimal understanding of the human race; using their computer science know-how, Doreen and her roommate, Nancy, fix him up and give him the capacity for self-improvement, which he uses to join them in fighting crime and as a student at ESU.[6]

Like I'm the Only Squirrel in the World

Squirrel Girl has some tactical advantages that allow her to begin interactions with adversaries by trying to find common ground—namely, all her powers that ensure if an opponent feels more like punching than talking, our heroine can hold her own. (Unbeatable isn't in the title for nothing.)

But diplomacy—sans squirrel abilities, that we know of—has existed since ancient times. Records of diplomatic correspondence between Egyptian pharaohs and other rulers date back to 14th century BCE, and treaties concerning empires surviving from 1259 BCE. Even one of literature's first great heroes, Odysseus, was renowned for his diplomatic skill and ability to talk his way out of situations.[7] The term diplomacy is generally applied to appointed representatives of state aiming to influence international affairs, which requires navigating myriad challenges, from maintaining the appearance of strength during negotiations to avoid future threats to fostering positive relationships over long periods of time in the face of changing regimes.

Though it's safe to say heads of state are generally opposed to having the planet they rule on eaten, Squirrel Girl doesn't officially act on behalf of any nation. Rather than viewing her actions as those of a diplomat, it's more appropriate to look at her as a master at conflict resolution, a process with boundless applications, from disputes among friends to navigating international incidents.

Researcher J. L. Steele defined conflict resolution by breaking it down into its component parts: First, there must be two or more parties who have a mutual problem "in which there is a behavior (or threat) designed through the exercise of power to control or gain at the other's expense." Meanwhile, "resolution involves the breaking into constituent parts and developing a consonant solution to the problem at hand."[8] As a discipline, its goals are deceptively straightforward: "the development of means which will prevent broad aggressive action."[9] But as anyone can glean from their own personal experiences with conflict, developing those means is the challenge—and this is where we can all learn from Squirrel Girl.

Instead of approaching negotiations from a place of distributive bargaining, where one person's gains are another person's losses, Doreen seems to operate along the lines of the Conflict Resolution Model (CRM-A). Formulated by a group of Australian psychologists, the model favors the development of a more integrative solution—what we would call a win-win.[10]

Here's a squirrely example: In her initial conflict with Kraven, a distributive bargain might have looked like Squirrel Girl sacrificing Tippy-Toe to avoid a fight, or her simply killing Kraven to ensure he could never harm any of her rodent friends—not much of a bargain in either scenario.

We can see how their actual interaction instead mirrors the four stages of CRM-A, which include developing expectations for a win-win solution; defining the issue in terms of underlying concerns, needs, or interests; brainstorming creative options; and, finally, combining options into win-win solutions.[11]

Squirrel Girl begins the interaction by setting expectations, first politely asking Kraven to release Tippy-Toe and then later very clearly stating that she wants to talk, not to fight him. This gives Kraven a chance to reframe what's happening—unlike in his past encounters with superheroes, Squirrel Girl *wants* to hear him out. Squirrel Girl then lays out the issue behind their conflict: Kraven's unmet hunting aspirations, delivered with only moderate sass (researchers advise avoiding criticism in this process, but hey, Doreen has an audience to amuse here). Still, she gives Kraven a chance to share his thoughts, which is important since "the likelihood of a satisfactory outcome is improved when each person feels listened to and valued."[12]

Brainstorming creative options is something of a specialty of Doreen's, and in this instance, it comes in the form of suggesting another form of prey, one that has already been identified as a threat to society. Ideally, brainstorming would involve developing a variety of options, but a comic book only has so many pages, and given all we know of Doreen, there's no doubting she could have come up with some backups had Gigantos not piqued Kraven's interest.

And just like that, a violent clash de-escalates into a mutually beneficial scenario, with Tippy-Toe safe and Kraven heading off to better the world with a renewed sense of purpose.

While Doreen proves naturally adept at CRM-A, in the real world it can take some practice. In studies examining the efficacy of the model, some participants first received training around the process and how to communicate before they were paired up and tested in a conflict scenario and assessed based on cooperation, appropriate assertiveness, active listening, and brainstorming options. Participants who received the training showed significantly higher skill levels, but the overall performance of pairs was still markedly better when one person had received the training compared to pairs comprised of two untrained participants.

In short, it may take two to tango, but having one person who knows how to lead can make the dance much smoother. This also explains why Squirrel Girl sees positive results even when she's the only one used to engaging in thoughtful conflict resolution—her (CRM-)A game helps all involved parties communicate and cooperate better.

Squirrel, You Really Got Me Now

Of course, not everyone can be reasoned with, and there aren't a ton of harmless alternatives to commonly held villain goals like establishing oneself as a global dictator. In those scenarios, Squirrel Girl relies on her community. That includes squirrels (more helpful in a fight than you might think), other super-powered allies, and kind and intelligent regular folks, like her mom, roommate Nancy, and her ESU classmates.

Relying on others might seem like a simple strategy, but it can have monumental impacts. In geopolitics, countries or kingdoms forming alliances often alter the course of their histories,[13] and the same is true in comics, where team ups and superheroes working collaboratively often prove key to winning an otherwise impossible conflict. Doreen has particularly strong relationships because of how she not only empathizes with everyone she meets but also empowers them.

In professional settings, empowering employees—which might include delegating authority and decision making, sharing information and asking for input—"is associated with stronger job performance, job satisfaction, and commitment to the organization," with research indicating empowering leaders positively influence employee creativity and culture while also receiving more trust from those they oversee.[14] We see it having a similarly positive effect across Doreen's personal and professional relationships, starting with her smallest allies: squirrels.

Squirrels rush to Doreen's defense frequently, starting in her Marvel debut when she helps free herself and Iron Man from Dr. Doom's ship by overrunning it with squirrels who chew through the wiring, keeping them captive before swarming Doom himself.[15] It's important to note in scenarios like these, she's using her ability to verbally communicate with them to ask for their help, not forcing them to her aid using telepathic contro.[16] Rather than coercing them, she's taken the time to empower them and build trust. The squirrels are helping Doreen fight crime, but she's helping them too, defending them from threats, serving as their link to the human world, and giving them the opportunity to solve problems and make a difference alongside her.

Squirrel Girl also has her fair share of superpowered allies, including teammates from her stints as a member of the Great Lakes Avengers and New Avengers; familiar superhero faces such as Ant-Man, Thor, and Iron Man; and her fellow computer science-studying, crime-fighting classmates Brain Drain, Chipmunk Hunk, and Koi Boi (the latter two have animal-themed powers that mimic Squirrel Girl's own, in case you were wondering). And, as established, Doreen even shows a knack for turning her foes into friends. But her relationships with them go beyond fighting together; we see her checking up on them outside of conflicts, inviting them to her birthday celebration, and taking a genuine interest in their lives, not just their heroics.

All the relationship building she does throughout the series comes to a poetic conclusion in the final issues of *The Unbeatable Squirrel Girl*, when her enemies reveal to the world that Squirrel Girl is actually Doreen Green and her home is destroyed. Fighting against seemingly insurmountable odds, the community she's created along her hero's journey appear to fight at her side—and when that doesn't get the job done, Galactus himself shows up, quipping, "This deus is here to ex machina, so let's get to it."[17]

Yes, it's convenient to have one of the cosmos's most powerful entities on your side, but Squirrel Girl shows you certainly don't have to be a god to make a difference, and even a regular person can play a big role.

When Doreen and a number of her classmates mysteriously disappear from their present day and find themselves in the 1960s, creating a timeline where superheroes haven't yet gone mainstream and a time-traveling Dr. Doom can seize control of the world with minimal resistance, they band together. Pooling their knowledge of technology, they build electromagnetic pulse devices to disrupt Doom and his army's suits. After that fails, it's the students' shared understanding of C++, a coding language, that allows them to communicate covertly and ultimately defeat Doom.[18]

While her collection of allies might seem nonsensical at first glance, the strength of Doreen's community is its diversity—whether she needs a squirrel to crawl down a bad guy's pants[19] or some local pals to keep the city safe while she's on an interdimensional vacation,[20] there's somebody she knows she can count on because she's empowered them to step up.

In a Nutshell

A character who started as a punchline now has a permanent place in the hearts and minds of readers thanks to *The Unbeatable Squirrel Girl*, which offers so much more than crime fighting, laughs, and fun facts about squirrels—although those things are present, too.

As Doreen tells Tippy-Toe early on, "I want to be the best me I can be, and there's more to being a superhero than just punching the strongest, you know? I want to be able to help people."[21] Throughout the series' 50 issues (plus some appearances outside her own title), Squirrel Girl does that, showing us along the way how to build community, even with our enemies, and resolve conflicts with empathy and creativity.

Is Doreen, at times, a little naive? Absolutely, and certain nemeses are quick to call her on it, seeing it as both pretty annoying to them personally and a weakness that can be exploited. But Squirrel Girl shows you don't have to be dark and gritty to create change; in fact, leaning into positivity can often be a more effective solution—and a lot more fun.

Notes

1   Ryan North, Will Murray, Erica Henderson and Rico Renzi, "Issue 14," in *The Unbeatable Squirrel Girl: Vol. 5: Like I'm the Only Squirrel in the World* (New York: Marvel Comics, 2017).

2   John Kelly, "A Modern Marvel: The Latest Hit Comics Character Is the Unbeatable Squirrel Girl," *The Washington Post*, April 13, 2016, https://www.washingtonpost.com/local/a-modern-marvel-the-latest-hit-comics-character-is-the-unbeatable-squirrel-girl/2016/04/13/8c0198ac-00c2-11e6-9d36-33d198ea26c5_story.html.

3   Ryan North and Erica Henderson, "Issue 1," in *The Unbeatable Squirrel Girl: Vol. 1, Squirrel Power* (New York: Marvel Worldwide, Inc., 2016).

4   Ryan North and Erica Henderson, "Issue 4," in *The Unbeatable Squirrel Girl: Vol. 1, Squirrel Power* (New York: Marvel Worldwide, Inc., 2016).

5   Ryan North, Erica Henderson and Rico Renzi, "Issue 6," in *The Unbeatable Squirrel Girl, Vol. 2: Squirrel You Know It's True* (New York, NY: Marvel Worldwide, Inc., 2015).

6   Ryan North and Erica Henderson, "2015B Issue 1," in *The Unbeatable Squirrel Girl: Vol. 3, Squirrel, You Really Got Me Now* (New York: Marvel Worldwide, Inc., 2016).

7   Robert F. Trager, "The Diplomacy of War and Peace," *Annual Review of Political Science* 19, no. 1 (November 2016), 205–228, https://doi.org/10.1146/annurev-polisci-051214-100534.

8   J. L. Steele, "Conflict Resolution," Operational Research Quarterly (1970–1977) 27, no. 1 (1976), 221, https://doi.org/10.2307/3009141.

9   Ibid.

10 John Davidson and Christine Wood, "A Conflict Resolution Model," *Theory Into Practice*, Winter, 2004, Vol. 43, No. 1, *Conflict Resolution and Peer Mediation* (Winter, 2004), pp. 6-13.

11 Ibid.

12 Ibid.

13 Robert F. Trager, "The Diplomacy of War and Peace," *Annual Review of Political Science* 19, no. 1 (November 2016), 205–228, https://doi.org/10.1146/annurev-polisci-051214-100534.

14 Lee, Allan, Amy Wei Tian, and Sara Willis. "When Empowering Employees Works, and When It Doesn't." *Harvard Business Review*, August 31, 2020. https://hbr.org/2018/03/when-empowering-employees-works-and-when-it-doesnt.

15 Michael Higgins and M. C. Wyman, "Marvel Super-Heroes Winter Special #8 Vol. 2" (New York: Marvel Comics, 1991).

16 Ryan North, Will Murray, Erica Henderson and Rico Renzi, "Issue 13," in *The Unbeatable Squirrel Girl Vol. 5: Like I'm the Only Squirrel in the World* (New York: Marvel Worldwide, Inc., 2017).

17 Ryan North, Derek Char, Erica Henderson and Rico Renzi, The Unbeatable Squirrel Girl Issue No. 50 (New York, Marvel Worldwide, Inc., January 2020).

18 Ryan North and Erica Henderson, "2015B Issues 4–5," in *The Unbeatable Squirrel Girl: Vol. 3, Squirrel, You Really Got Me Now* (New York: Marvel Worldwide, Inc., 2016).

19 Ryan North and Erica Henderson, "2015B Issue 7," in *The Unbeatable Squirrel Girl: Vol. 4, I Kissed a Squirrel and I Liked It* (New York: Marvel Worldwide, Inc., 2016).

20 Ryan North, Erica Henderson Chris Schwiezer and Rico Renzi, "2015B Issue 21," in *The Unbeatable Squirrel Girl: Vol. 6, Who Run the World? Squirrels!* (New York: Marvel Worldwide, Inc., 2017).

21 Ryan North and Erica Henderson, "Issue 1," in *The Unbeatable Squirrel Girl: Vol. 1, Squirrel Power* (New York: Marvel Worldwide, Inc., 2016).

CHAPTER 21

Your Cape and Cowl, Mr. Bond?

Mitch Brian

"Ladies and Gentlemen of the 21st century, let's get ready to rumble!" The contestants spring from their corners: the Gotham Grappler clad in cape, cowl, and body armor versus the Smasher from Scotland in a tightly tailored Tom Ford suit. A pair of cinematic reboots circling, clashing, and intertwining. Neither possesses superpowers, although bouts in the previous century included maneuvers and stunts that were nothing short of ridiculous. But in this match, the action is hard, the technology grounded, and the anxieties stem from psychological trauma and social chaos of post-9/11 global terrorism. Over the course of eight films from 2005 to 2021, they will capitalize on each other's strengths and weaknesses while earning their corporate sponsors more than $5.3 billion. This is a match between The Batman and James Bond. And in the end, one combatant will die.

Obligatory Origin Stories

The cinematic success of both James Bond and Batman came after some false starts. Ian Fleming's novels were adapted into popular comic strips (1958–1966), a now-lost 1955 radio drama, and an underwhelming 1954 black-and-white live TV production (as American secret agent Jimmy Bond). Four years after Batman's comic book origin in 1939, he would fight crime in a pair of low-budget movie serials (1943 and 1949) and then in 1966 strike TV gold in a colorful, campy bi-weekly series that spawned its own big screen iteration using the same cast, sets, and locales.

But Batman's path to TV, with its pop sensibilities, gadgets, and deadpan humor, was a trail that had been blazed by none other than 007. In 1962, *Dr. No* exploded onto screens with its vivid Eastman Color combo of sex, violence, and exotic locations, becoming nothing short of a cultural phenomenon. Six films would span the 1960s, their budgets and box office swelling, spawning merchandising and countless imitators, and laying the groundwork for blockbuster franchises to follow. Ten more 007 adventures would encompass the 1970s and 1980s.

Bond films set the trends in their first decade, but the subsequent years saw the series following trends, embracing self-parody and bouncing Bond off of the hottest genres of the day. Blaxploitation (*Live and Let Die*, 1973), kung-fu (*Man with the Golden Gun*, 1974), science fiction (*Moonraker*, 1979), techno-thriller (*For Your Eyes Only*, 1981), retro-serial adventure (*Octopussy*, 1983) and even TV's *Miami Vice* (*Licence to Kill*, 1989) all allowed Bond to do what nobody does better: make it out alive and onto the next adventure. James Bond was a survivor.

Meanwhile Batman failed to throw off its camp TV chains, only to wind up on Saturday morning cartoons for the rest of the 1960s and '70s (*Super Friends*, 1973–1986). But in the comics of the '70s, thanks to writers such as Dennis O'Neil and Len Wein, a more serious Batman thrived on the mean streets of Gotham. Frank Miller's 1986 graphic novel *The Dark Knight Returns* and 1987 series *Batman: Year One* redefined the character with decidedly adult, violent tones that would influence cinematic versions to come.

The Gauntlet Thrown Down

In 1989, buoyed by the success of the *Superman* films, everything changed. The blockbuster formula Hollywood had been striving for through the 1980s found its apotheosis in Warner Bros. big screen *Batman*. Like the Bond films of the '60s, it had it all: a well-known intellectual property, merchandising tie-ins, a massive ad campaign, star power (Michael Keaton and Jack Nicholson), and even radio-ready songs (by Prince). Director Tim Burton brought a quirky, art school German expressionist sensibility to the first pair of films, resulting in a mashup of film noir and Edward Gorey. Those dark shadings exploded into garish neon colors when director Joel Schumacher took over, subbing in Val Kilmer and then George Clooney into the nipple-enhanced Batsuit, returning to the star-studded camp fest of the '60s TV show.

Bond fared better in the '90s, retooled with Pierce Brosnan as Bond, Judi Dench as a female M, and Desmond Llewelyn hanging on as Q to provide some continuity. There were hints of political relevance in 1995's *Goldeneye* in the wake of the Soviet Union's fall and 1997's *Tomorrow Never Dies* hinted at anxieties over the Hong Kong handover. But as Bond hurtled through the air to catch up with a plane, drove an invisible car and para-surfed on a tsunami, this new "SuperBond" became *almost* as ridiculous as Schumacher's Batman. Nevertheless, Brosnan's Bond bested the Bat, with the four 007 films scoring $2.6 billion over the competing caped crusader's quartet totaling $1.8 billion.

The Vigilante Versus the Assassin

The attacks on the World Trade Center and The Pentagon and the crash of United 93 brought a sobering start of the 21st century. The collapsing buildings and billowing smoke engulfing fleeing citizens provoked the oft-repeated phrase, "It was like something out of a movie." The trauma and confusion in the days, weeks, and months after reverberated through popular culture. Director Cameron Crowe resisted studio pressure to remove the Twin Towers from his film *Vanilla Sky* (2002). One studio executive boldly pronounced we would never see falling buildings in movies again. Firemen raising the American flag atop the WTC rubble evoked the Marines at Iwo Jima. American Special Forces on horseback in Afghanistan struck a chord of frontier justice. Vice President Dick Cheney made the most relevant and chilling assessment of the coming war on terror, saying on *Meet the Press* that the U.S. would have to work "sort of the dark side, if you will. We're going to spend time in the shadows.... And so, it's going to be vital for us to use any means at our disposal, basically, to achieve our objectives."[1] This work in the shadows seemed to perfectly conjure the liminal space where both The Batman and James Bond dwelled. Both would be reinvented for the post-9/11 world in decidedly darker tones, embracing the dark impulses of Batman the vigilante and Bond the assassin.

Batman landed the first blow, bouncing off the ropes into Bond with the more realistic, hard-action approach of 2005's *Batman Begins*. Clearly inspired by the gritty tones of the *Batman: Year One* graphic novel, it features an alienated Detective James Gordon drowning in a sea of Gotham corruption as Batman is vilified as a vigilante. Borrowing sequences where Batman summons a swarm of bats and faces off against a SWAT team, David S. Goyer's script also blazes new geopolitical trails that find Bruce Wayne imprisoned in a Chinese labor camp before the idea of being Batman ever crosses his mind. This is a clear "reboot" of the Batman story, positioning us in a disorienting space so that we evolve with Wayne from orphaned rich boy to lost soul until he returns prodigal son-like to the Wayne corporation towering above the crumbling infrastructure of Gotham. Cheney's comments seem to prefigure the introduction of a literal "League of Shadows" as the overarching nemesis of the trilogy. The global reach of this organization brings to mind another enemy network found in the Bond cosmos, namely SPECTRE. Director Christopher Nolan, an admitted Bond fan, steers the Wayne Corporation's Lucius Fox straight into Q-branch territory with his DARPA-like R&D division filled with gadgets, weapons systems, and vehicles. This Wayne foundation is in the military business—and though Batman may not hold a state-issued license to kill, there are taxpayer dollars behind him.

Over in the Bond corner, a stroke of luck opened a new passageway for 007 to traverse. The movie rights to *Casino Royale*, the first Fleming novel and the only one not controlled by Bond's EON Productions, became available and the producers had themselves a new beginning. Here was a way to do a "first" adventure, introducing Bond as a new character played by a new actor: Daniel Craig. Almost a reboot (except for Judi Dench returning as M in the kind of off-continuity weirdness the series is famous for) the novel offered untapped elements imagined by Fleming: a non-state actor villain, a high-stakes poker game aided by a CIA ally, a brutally realistic torture scene, and the heartbreaking betrayal and death of Bond's first true love, Vesper Lynd. Set against the backdrop of global terrorism and manipulation of international financial markets, there would be no invisible car or tsunami surfing here. The essential nature of Bond as an assassin would be embraced like never before. In earlier installments, Bond usually killed as a last resort, sometimes even as an afterthought. But when this Bond is ordered to kill an enemy responsible for the death of a fellow agent, as in 2012's *Skyfall*, he accepts "with pleasure."

The Bond producers were surveilling The Batman as they prepared *Casino Royale*. In an interview with the Canadian website CJAD, co-screenwriter Paul Haggis confessed: "We're trying to do for Bond what *Batman Begins* did for Batman."[2] The fact that *Batman Begins* brought in more than $350 million had to give EON confidence that steering Bond into reality—and the shadows—was a good plan. Not only would *Casino Royale* begin with flashbacks to a pair of ugly assassinations that earn Bond his "double 0" designation, it would follow Batman's "trilogy" strategy and make the Daniel Craig films the most directly serialized run of films in the franchise. The ensuing *Quantum of Solace* in 2008 would pick up the action only moments after the conclusion of *Casino Royale,* opening with a high-octane car chase with rapid editing and furiously disorienting hand-held camera. Critics would compare it to the Euro-action Jason Bourne films, possibly valid given *Quantum* director Marc Forster's indie-art house pedigree. Also to blame was a writers' strike and an unfinished script that functions more like an epilogue-addendum to *Casino*'s open ending. With its title derived from one of Fleming's short stories, it feels like a novella, clocking in at well under two hours. But it also offers resonant themes on the nature of revenge, something Bond desires in the wake of Vesper's death, and is personified in Bond-girl Camille and her unwavering pursuit for family vengeance. By being bound so directly to *Casino Royale*, *Quantum* exists in the same visual world of modernist design, where ruling elites attend extravagant operas for secret meetings with an eco-terrorist villain seeking to monopolize water concessions. Although its box office surpassed *Casino Royale*, the critical consensus was mixed. What was more significant was that Bond was going head-to-head against The Batman that year, and *Quantum*'s riches paled in comparison to *The Dark Knight*'s nearly $1 billion haul. Bond must have considered the Joker's exuberant taunt in the wake of ticket sales: "If you're good at something, never do it for free!"

Into the Past

As the wrestlers twist and tangle, mid-match, in a blur of body armor and Barbour sportswear, Bond merges with The Batman. Following the phenomenal success of *The Dark Knight* a decidedly gothic sensibility takes root in 2012's *Skyfall*. Its title sequence departs from the illustrated graphics and sharp lines of its predecessor and embraces images of crumbling mansions, tombstones, and bat-like Rorschach patterns. Director Sam Mendes told Indiewire that he was reassured by audiences embracing the darkness of The Batman, giving him the confidence to "take this movie in directions that, without *The Dark Knight*, might not have been possible."[3] The gothic tones of *Skyfall* are not entirely Batman inspired. Fleming's novels are rife with gothic touches: physically and psychologically deformed villains, "Gypsies" and circus performers, rats and vermin, voodoo, pirates, and dragons (albeit mechanical). Before the Batman's influence, the films skewed toward modernist aesthetics, largely due to production design by Ken Adam and Syd Cain.

But even the modern cities of *Skyfall* are phantasmagorial, exploding with hyper-saturated blues and greens in Shanghai or bleeding red in Macao above a pit of hungry Komodo dragons. In both *The Dark Knight* and *Skyfall*, our heroes fight inside skyscrapers, crashing through plates of gleaming glass, and in a direct homage to 1965's *Thunderball*, The Batman is whisked away by a "skyhook" aircraft, like Bond and Domino's romantic liftoff four decades earlier. It is in this Shanghai office building that *Skyfall*'s most meta musical move plays out. As an elevator ascends, Bond leaps to grasp the undercarriage, hanging on as composer Thomas Newman seems to quote the Batman fanfare from the Danny Elfman-Shirley Walker scores of the Burton films and *Batman: The Animated Series*.

The past haunts *Skyfall*. Its villain is Silva, a former MI6 agent turned terrorist like The Joker, who lays waster to MI6 as part of a revenge plot against M. Believed dead, as is Bond after the disastrous opening mission, both men return to M, one as assailant, the other as protector, their similarities not lost on her. As she tells Tanner, "He comes from the same place as Bond: the shadows." Once Bond is on the run with M, they detour to a shadowy storage unit to acquire a getaway car unfettered by MI6 tracking devices. Bond whips off a dust cover to reveal the Aston Martin DB5 from 1964's *Goldfinger*, replete with a hidden switch in the gearshift. Even M knows the car and its special features, quipping "Go on, eject me, see if I care." Of course, there is no way to really understand how *this* Bond got *that* car and as the retro Vic Flick electric guitar twangs the Bond theme, it could just as easily be the tinkling guitar opening of *The Twilight Zone*. M wonders where are they going. Bond replies: "Back in time."

All superheroes need an origin story and until the 21st century, James Bond was not a superhero. But with the extended cinematic universes of DC, Marvel, *Star Wars*, and *Star Trek* populating the corporate movie-making galaxy, Bond finally succumbed to pop culture pressure. Even Ian Fleming avoided Bond's backstory, preferring him to be something of a blank slate with a "flat, quiet name."[4] It was the popularity of the films and the appeal of Sean Connery that provoked Fleming to include Bond's Scottish heritage in the penultimate novel *You Only Live Twice*. That backstory finds its way into *Goldeneye* when we learn Bond's parents died in a mountaineering accident and, four films later, Vesper reiterates Bond's orphan status in *Casino Royale*. Even M acknowledges that "orphans make the best agents" as they arrive at Skyfall, the decaying Bond family estate, a miniature Wayne Manor in the Scottish Highlands. Bond acknowledges that M knows his whole story, but we don't, and we'll have to wait, except for a few tantalizing morsels from Bond's own version of Alfred, the gamekeeper and sole inhabitant of the manor, Kincaid. For now, all we know is that Bond "always hated this place."

The Author of All Your Pain

The combatants return to their corners, exhausted and beaten to a draw. Both Bond and The Batman overestimated their abilities, were cautioned by their mentors, and suffered painful losses of those closest to them. Bond lost M at Skyfall. Batman lost Rachel in Gotham. Both will retire only to be recalled to duty, against their own better judgment. But it won't be for a rematch.

"You wanna know how I got these scars?" the Joker repeatedly asks those he terrorizes in *The Dark Knight*. The subsequent Bond films will ask the same question of 007, constructing a familial mythology that moves from Bond's traumatic past, through homicidal sibling rivalries and beyond him into a family he'll never know.

Just as the interlocked *Casino–Quantum* films formed part one of the Craig-era saga, its part three also spans two interconnected films: 2015's *SPECTRE* and 2021's *No Time to Die*. 2012's *The Dark Knight Rises* wraps things up neatly with three films, but it takes Bond five. The agenda is arguably more complicated in its transformation of Bond into superhero. It is certainly more convoluted. The Quantum organization is revealed to be SPECTRE, the brainchild of Bond's long lost stepbrother, now calling himself Ernst Stavro Blofeld. This preposterously baroque invention, far more comic book (or soap opera) than anything in a Fleming novel, is only one of many complicated family ties. The fallout of Blofeld's efforts give rise to Safin, the villain of *No Time to Die* who is determined to destroy Blofeld and the new love of Bond's life, Madeleine Swann, daughter of the man who killed Safin's family. Through the fallout of all these machinations, Bond discovers a daughter he never knew and suffers unexpected collateral damage. He'll even make breakfast for the little girl.

Bruce Wayne doesn't have it much easier. Almost as fascinating as the Bond and Batman mid-saga merging is the divergence that follows in their saga conclusions. After all the pressure for Bond to become Batman and Batman to be more like Bond, neither seems to need the other any longer. Both have acquired so much narrative fuel (and baggage) that their final installments proceed toward entropic, sometimes illogical, inevitable conclusions. Fate befalls both the final Bond films and *The Dark Knight Rises*. The League of Shadows returns to plague Batman just as the organization behind Vesper's death looms over Bond. And just as Al-Qaida splinters and morphs into new real-world threats, the League of Shadows spawns domestic terrorists for Gotham and a secret MI6 bio-chemical assassination program falls into the wrong hands creating a multitude of new threats. It's "Whac-A-Mole" in broad daylight now, with no time for the dark romance of the shadows. No wonder Bruce Wayne dreams of dropping off the grid and spending the rest of his days living with a wife and kids in Italy, where he is spotted by Alfred at the end of *The Dark Knight Rises*.

Permission to Die

In Philip Kauffman's 1983 epic mediation on heroism, *The Right Stuff*, a young woman asks Pancho Barnes what a pilot has to do to get their picture on her bar room wall. Pancho laconically replies, "You have to die, Sweetie." In comic books, Superheroes have been dying and coming back via restructured timelines since at least the 1950s when The Flash sped through "Earth Two." The Man of Steel perished in 1992's *Death of Superman* and The Joker and Batman went down together in 2014's *Batman: Endgame*. In the movies, Captain America disappeared into the mists of time and Tony Stark bought the farm in 2019's *Avengers: Endgame*. It's a wonder we didn't see this coming with 21st-century Bond. Whether or not Bond's death was Daniel Craig's deal-breaking position for his final outing, it makes a kind of cosmic sense. A fitting end in a world of corporate franchises and extended universes where timelines and continuities and multiverses all twist and turn like the wrestlers in the ring.

With Bond's abandonment of being Batman in *No Time to Die* the filmmakers embraced Bond's own cinematic legacy and a deep sense of nostalgia. Composer Hans Zimmer leans into the melancholy of John Barry's "We Have All the Time in The World," from 1969's *On Her Majesty's Secret Service*. For Bond fans, this song signals the tragic murder of Bond's beloved Tracy only moments after becoming Mrs. James Bond. It is a sudden, shattering event for Bond, played by George Lazenby, left alone on the side of the road, cradling his dead wife who has been gunned down by Blofeld. It is a hopeless moment and not the only time Fleming ended an adventure with Bond adrift. In one instance he collapses from poison. In another he suffers from amnesia. But *No Time to Die* leaves us with three far more comforting impressions after the shock of watching Bond consumed by an inescapable bomb blast. He is remembered in a toast by his team, his story is told to his daughter by her mother, and, most importantly, familiar letters appear on screen reassuring us that "James Bond Will Return." All the time in the world, indeed.

Notes

1   James Mann, "The World Dick Cheney Built," *The Atlantic*, January 2020. https://www.theatlantic.com/ideas/archive/2020/01/dick-cheney-cJamesharted-americas-future-september-11/603313/.
2   "A Makeover for 007?" News2, WFMY News, Greensboro, North Carolina, WFMY, October 13, 2005. https://www.wfmynews2.com/article/news/a-makeover-for-007/83-403649050.
3   Adam Chitwood, "Sam Mendes Says The Dark Knight Directly Influenced Skyfall," *Collider*, October 18, 2012. https://collider.com/sam-mendes-skyfall-the-dark-knight/.
4   Ian Fleming, "Fleming Villa History," *The Fleming Villa*, https://www.theflemingvilla.com/the-history/.

CHAPTER 22

Trick or Deceit

Deception Unleashed in the Superhero Multiverse

Erica Iverson

"Pay no attention to the man behind the curtain." Toto the dog unmasked the "Great and Powerful Oz," revealing not a wonderful, mighty wizard, but a mortal whose powers of illusion are created by a fog machine and microphone.[1] When Toto pulls back the curtain, there stands Oscar Zoroaster Phadrig Isaac Norman Henkle Emmannuel Ambroise Diggs, shortened from OZPINHEAD to OZ. He stands exposed as his true self—powerless and meek—the opposite of whom he was trying to portray.[2]

Similar tricks and deceptive tactics have been hoodwinking humans for thousands of years. In Greek mythology, Pandora—the first woman on Earth—is presented with a special box but directed never to open it. When temptation prevailed and Pandora opened her box, she unleashed illnesses and hardships that wreaked havoc upon the universe and, by extension, the Multiverse.[3] In that special mix was Apate, the Greek goddess and personification of fraud, trickery, and deceit, who operationalized her nefarious gifts, teaching both god and mortal beings alike the ways of deception. Like Apate in the Greek pantheon, the Romans had Mercury, the god of trickery and thievery. The Celtic pantheon had a unique twist in that Lugh was the god of justice who also practiced deception for his own self-serving purpose.

Yet the most famous of these mythological characters is Loki, the cunning Nordic god of deception and mischief. Marvel Comics' and the Marvel Cinematic Universe (MCU) deviate from Norse mythology, which highlights Loki's relationship as blood brother to Odin and thus uncle to Thor, not adopted brother. The one constant across all genres is Loki using his magical powers of self-serving deceit to punk anyone, especially those closest to him. Arguably, one of Loki's memorable deceptions in the MCU was faking his death (a second time) and then using his holographic projection powers to masquerade as Odin, King of Asgard, whom he had sent off to greener fjords in Norway.[4]

Grounded in culture and religion, the art of deception has been in practice for thousands of years. Deception is subjective and connotes various definitions and complex layers which permeate our lives every day, whether we are aware of it or not. By no means inclusive, deceit can be categorized by function (fabrication, trickery, deceit, manipulation, fraud), employment (tactical to strategic), application (cognitive, social sciences, economic, political, business, intelligence, military), intent (deliberate/disinformation or unintentional/misinformation), perception, validity (fact or fiction), ethics, legality, or effectiveness. Or in combination. This chapter's definition relies upon expert stage magician Barton Whaley's, as he encapsulates the complex nature of deception into the simple definition of "the intent to distort another person or group's perception of reality."[5] From Oz to Loki to even the Marvel villain Mysterio, the level of deception applied hinges on the level of desired effect. With technological advances, the increase in scope and scale of deceptive operations through illusionary magic, warfare, and artificial intelligence (AI) further blurs the line between what is real and what is not.

Mind Over Magic

Illusionary magic overwhelms our senses and holds hostage the rational part of our minds—even Houdini subscribed to the power of "seeing becomes believing" for his tradecraft. Illusion magic is a deception of the senses. The Black Panther's homeland of Wakanda and Wanda Maximoff's town of Westview, New Jersey, in the television miniseries *WandaVision* are illusions—disguised in one case to protect the Wakandans from the outside world and the other to protect the outside world from the Scarlet Witch. Wanda used chaos magic to manipulate and distort reality to her own ends while holding captive the minds of Westview citizens. Her illusion became their delusions. Illusion with a sprinkle of magic can deceive even those who have a built-in resistance to block mental manipulation. Illusion magic requires a more cognitive approach. Dr. Strange is a mentalist, even without the Time Stone. The Ancient One reminds him of the mysteries beyond his senses, the power of the unknown is where "mind and matter meet. Thoughts shape reality."[6] Along with his other mystical and magical powers, Dr. Strange splits versions of himself to distract Thanos by invoking the Images of Ikonn spells. What makes Dr. Stephen Strange so powerful is not something he read in the Book of Vishanti or gained from the Mind Stone; he knows true power comes from, and is controlled by, the mind.

Arthur C. Clarke once said that "magic is a science we don't understand yet;" there is both a science and art required to deceive the curious eye. American master illusionist John Mulholland knew this. Success in his line of work required foresight to know that "the appeal of magic is mental, not visual, and the magician must fool the minds, rather than the eyes of his audience."[7] An American stage performer with a unique skillset, Mulholland's expertise on deceptive tactics and sleight of hand magic was exactly what the Allied Forces needed during World War II, for both entertainment and education. Different than stage magic/stunts, sleight of hand translates to "tricking people in a clever way;" it is up close and personal, a minuscule sleight in hand position or posture.[8] Allied troops stationed overseas in World War II received copies of Mulholland's book: *The Art of Illusion: Magic for Men To Do*.[9] Intended not as instruction on cheating at card games but to provide tips that could help with intelligence collection using accessible items: wax to pick up papers off a desk, a button distinguished by size or color to signal messages, folded paper to fit in the palm of a hand.

A contemporary of Mulholland was Jasper Maskelyne, a British Royal Engineer who moonlighted as an illusionist in the famed British Magic Gang during World War II. Together, they created illusions of vehicles, armies, and battleships to misdirect enemy advances—but their piece de resistance was masking the Suez Canal and the city of Alexandria to misdirect Luftwaffe bombers.[10] An entire mock-up city, complete with a lighthouse, was built of cardboard and a revolving cone of mirrors accentuated by shadows, ground lights, and explosive charges that spanned nine miles wide. By design, this grand illusion masked the actual location of the Suez Canal and misdirected enemy pilots to drop bombs on the decoy, thus saving the Suez Canal. While magic—as a table trick or mind manipulation through chaos magic—uses deception as a tool for more utilitarian needs, when the stakes are higher, effects come at a more significant cost.

Know Thy Enemy

Deception permeates all layers of everyday life, from a little white lie to a nefarious scam to the conduct of warfare. At the strategic level, warfare and statecraft are linked, with deception playing a title role in how a state conducts war. In the 5th century BC, Chinese theorist Sun-Tzu wrote the *Art of War*, with the premise that deception is the foundation of all warfare and is the key to victory.[11] A century later, Hindu philosopher Kautilya emphasized the importance of deception in tactics, formations, and camouflage techniques to dodge and overcome the enemy. Russia's military operating concept is built upon a foundation of Maskirovka, or "little masquerade," fittingly coined on the conclusion that wars are won and lost in the information space rather than on the battlefield.[12] The Russian government uses information weapons as military, political, and psychological warfare, like "intellectual jiu-jitsu," by propagating false information or half-truths to achieve deception and mislead friendly, enemy, and neutral militaries, populations, and political entities.[13] Comparatively, the MCU's Kree Empire are notorious gaslighters as well.

Deception is one card in the deck of information operation capabilities the Kree employ in their war against the Skrulls. Within this great power competition between intergalactic empires, the technologically advanced and arrogant Kree use conventional warfare, psychological warfare, and even genocide to force Skrull submission.[14] Kree rulers execute a Russianesque disinformation campaign. They vilify the Skrulls as ruthless aggressors who use their shapeshifting abilities to deceive, infiltrate, and destroy civilizations from the inside while glorifying themselves as selfless and noble. After the Kree destroy their home world, the Skrulls scatter across the galaxy but continue to fight, and the next two movie phases of the MCU hint we have not seen the last of either race. Or flerkens, hopefully.

When deception is used in warfare, the ante is raised given there are additional capabilities and complexities that a military could bring to a conflict, especially with an adversary that is not always visible or known. Military deception (MILDEC) targets adversarial decision-makers by misleading them to make a decision that puts them at a disadvantage.[15] Much like the many layers of deception, MILDEC can be broken down further by functions, principles, levels of ambiguity, means, tactics, and techniques.[16] Ingenuity prevails on the battlefield, as history is ripe with examples of how deception has played out amongst the three levels of war. Unlike many of Loki's self-serving deceptive tactics, in warfare, even tactical deceptions can have strategic implications. MILDEC before World War II was mostly tactical, from the famous Greek gift of the Trojan Horse to the city of Troy during the Trojan War to the Quaker Guns used by the Confederate Army in the Civil War.[17] MILDEC is as complex as it is complicated, but when a deception campaign is flawlessly executed at the strategic level, the achieved effect can change the tides of the war.

World War II was a testbed for strategic deception, mastered by the Allies but also utilized at great length by the Axis Powers. Operations *Mincemeat*, *Bodyguard*, *Barclay*, and *Cockade* are a few notorious examples which required whole of government secrecy. Operation *Fortitude* was illustrative of effective MILDEC in exploiting Magruder's Principle, a maxim of deception that posits it is easier to induce a target to maintain a pre-existing belief than introduce a new idea. The elaborate plan devised by the Western Allies during World War II was to deceive Germany on where the invasion of France would occur. Presumably, Hitler and his band of generals believed Pas de Calais would be the invasion site, and the Allies both reinforced and exploited this fixed preconception to mask the actual landing in Normandy, 200 miles southeast. Et voila—success! Strategic-level MILDEC efforts continue to evolve, given that technological advances have made the element of surprise that much more challenging. The future battlefield, like the changing character of war, is already dominating the information battlespace, where deception plays a central role on the frontlines.

Mysterious Lies

> "A lie can be halfway around the world before the truth has got its boots on."
>
> —WINSTON CHURCHILL

Ironically, Winston Churchill never said these words, as accurate as they may be, nor did Mark Twain—another false attribution, which spread through the internet faster than a speeding bullet at 1,800 miles per hour. An MIT Sloan School of Management study reports that false news spreads six times faster than the truth and is 70% more likely to be retweeted on Twitter.[18] Actual attribution for this now-famous quotation was tracked back several versions to Jonathan Swift in 1710: "Falsehood flies and the truth comes limping after it."[19] Long gone are the days of "everything on the internet is true," which should now be replaced with "assume nothing is."

The Multiverse has caught up, knowing the vital role artificial intelligence and machine learning (AI/ML) have in shaping the environment. Advances in AI/ML make very real the emergence of a Supreme Intelligence (ruler of the Kree Empire) or a more villainous Ultron. The MCU's version of the robot villain from *Avengers: Age of Ultron* is a 21st-century Pinocchio, except as an advanced sentient AI, Ultron is a machine with a license to kill since "there are no strings on me."[20] If this is ever actualized, there is no best worst-case scenario.

As fiction can sometimes be a precursor to reality, the antics displayed by Mysterio may be strategic forecasting of where AI/ML advancements could take us. When Mysterio first debuted in *The Amazing Spider-Man* #13 in June 1964, his illusionary magic was just like the formidable Great and Powerful Oz.[21] To earn acclaim as the world's best superhero, Quentin Beck, as Mysterio, had to deceive not just Peter Parker but the entire Multiverse. The MCU upped his tech game.[22] A little technological illusion here, with a little natural disaster from an Elemental there. To Beck's credit, he ran a brilliant deception campaign of holographic illusions featuring flamethrowers, explosives, pyrotechnics, and weaponized battle drones with machine guns to heighten the level of destruction. Every attack on humanity was a projected illusion by the man behind the mask, with Mysterio saving humanity from the very attacks he designed and incited. Despite his success in creating chaos and weakening Peter Parker to give up his technology, Beck was bested by his own hubris to earn the superhero status as Mysterio. Ultimately, Mysterio's deception was about generating misperception by projecting capabilities he didn't possess, a one-dimensional ruse. This makes for great entertainment—until it is not just entertainment.

In 2022, the People's Republic of China set the Guinness World Record for the largest synchronized drone display in the world, using 3,051 unmanned aerial vehicle (UAVs) to make art in the sky, with images of China's global satellite navigation system and space station.[23] Marketed as "art," this synchronized drone production displays the same organized flight technology used by Mysterio, sans weaponized tech. State and non-state actors are already using enhanced AI/ML to manipulate information in a digital levée en masse, or virtual battlefield.[24] From clone wars to drone wars, even with kamikaze drones, it took pulling back the curtain during the 2022 Russo-Ukraine war to see Russia's military might at face value. To optimize the deception of both man and machine, the manipulation of information is now easier than ever.

Humans can no longer afford to just see to believe. With the swipe of a finger, images, audio, and video files can be created or manipulated over existing data by computer systems that "compete with themselves and self-improve."[25] If that isn't scary enough, adaptive advancements in AI through generative adversarial networks (GAN) are now weaponizing deepfakes as the ultimate deception tool.[26] Altered biometrics, written text, altered photographs, distorted video—deep fakes are the new magic trick, when everything you read, see or hear is circumspect. Counter-deception and deception detection advancements are trying to keep up, but the propagation of software and AI tools is accelerating faster. Chances are high that by the time you are reading this, some information here may already be dated. In the Information Age, the competitive advantage is relative as it is not how fast a soldier can load a weapon or call for air support, but how fast an adversary can type.

To the Multiverse and Beyond

Given the nature of the Multiverse's many alternate timelines and universes, there are endless possibilities and outcomes for fans to continue to be deceived. Deception at any level—through magic and illusion, warfare or technology—has the potential to rewrite history. When we see what is behind the curtain, the magical illusion is oftentimes a lot scarier. In a 2019 TED Talk, cyber illusionist Marco Tempest challenges the crowd by asking if we can still create illusions in a world where technology makes anything possible. He answers his own question by fusing technology and magic as he controls a small swarm of mini-drones using only the flick of a finger or hand wave.[27] For Tempest, this "art is a deception that creates real emotions—a lie that creates a truth … and when you give yourself over to that deception, it becomes magic." Deception will continue to show up in the everyday aspect of our lives—but it is up to each person how to deal with it. For the Greeks, after Apate's tricks and deceits and other evils are unleashed onto all mankind, Pandora desperately tries to close her box but it is too late. Yet she does find one thing that remains left in her box for humanity, which is something we all can still hold on to: hope.

Notes

1   *The Wizard of Oz*, directed by Victor Fleming, George Cukor, and Mervyn LeRoy (Los Angeles: Metro-Goldwyn-Mayer, 1939).
2   L. Frank Baum, *Dorothy and the Wizard of Oz* (Chicago: Reilly and Briton, 1908), 24.
3   N.S. Gill, "Understanding the Significance of Pandora's Box," *ThoughtCo*, June 27, 2019. https://www.thoughtco.com/what-was-pandoras-box-118577.
4   *Thor: The Dark World*, directed by Alan Taylor (Los Angeles: Marvel Studios, 2014).
5   Barton Whaley, "Toward a General Theory of Deception," *Journal of Strategic Studies* (London), Vol. 5, Issue 1 (March 1982), 180.
6   *Doctor Strange*, directed by Scott Derrickson (Los Angeles: Marvel Studios, 2017).
7   No author cited, obituary. "John Mulholland, Magician and Author, 71, Dies," *New York Times*, February 26, 1970. https://www.nytimes.com/1970/02/26/archives/john-mulholland-magician-and-author-71-dies-had-lectured-and.html.

8   *Oxford Learner Dictionary*, University of Oxford. Oxford University Press, 2022. https://www.oxfordlearnersdictionaries.com/.

9   In addition to this book, the Central Intelligence Agency commissioned Mulholland to write a pocket guide for intelligence agents called the CIA Manual of Trickery and Deception. In 1944, 100,000 pocket-size copies of his book, *The Art of Illusion*, were distributed to Allied soldiers in World War II. Mulholland, John. 1944. *The Art of Illusion: Magic for Men To Do (Armed Services Edition):* University of California Berkeley: Charles Scribner's Sons.

10 Website Wargaming.Net. n.d. "How A Magician Made A Harbor Vanish." Last modified 2022. https://wargaming.com/en/news/jasper_maskelyne/.

11 Sun Tzu. *The Art of War*, trans. Samuel Griffith (New York: Oxford UP, 1963), 3.

12 Frederick Kagan, Nataliya Bugayova, and Jennifer Cafarella, "The Russian War of War—Confronting the Russian Challenge: A New Approach for the U.S.," *Institute for the Study of War* (June 2019), 34.

13 Thomas Timothy, *Cyber Defense Review*, Vol 5, Issue 2 (Summer 2020): 2. https://cyberdefensereview.army.mil/Portals/6/Documents/CDR%20Journal%20Articles/Thomas_CDR%20V5N2%20Summer%202020.pdf.

14 Psychological warfare (PsyWar) is codified in military doctrine now as Military Information Support Operations. Joint Publication 3-13, *Information Operations*, (Washington, DC: Joint Staff, 2014), xi.

15 Definition of Military Deception (MILDEC): actions executed to deliberately mislead adversary military, paramilitary, or violent extremist organization decision makers, thereby causing the adversary to take specific actions (or inactions) that will contribute to the accomplishment of the friendly mission. Joint Publication 3-13.4. *Military Deception* (Washington, DC: Joint Staff, January 2012), vii.

16 Joint Doctrine 3-13-4. *Military Deception* (Washington, DC: Joint Staff, January 26, 2012), xii.

17 Quaker guns were logs that were painted black, positioned to appear like cannons in fortified positions, a ruse to exaggerate force strength and capabilities. George Barnard, "*Quaker Gun, Centreville Virginia*" (New York: MET Museum, March 1862). https://www.metmuseum.org/art/collection/search/285727.

18 Shuman Ghosemajumder, "Deepfakes, Deception, and Disinformation," *MIT Management Sloan School*, May 27, 2022. https://www.youtube.com/watch?v=d4jhATru47M.

19 Stephen Dubner, "Quotes Uncovered: How Lies Travel," *Freakonomics*, April 7, 2011. https://freakonomics.com/2011/04/quotes-uncovered-how-lies-travel/.

20 *Avengers: Age of Ultron*, directed by Joss Whedon (Los Angeles: Marvel Studios, 2015).

21 Marvel Comics, *The Amazing Spider-Man*, Issue #13 (New York: Marvel Comics, June 10, 1964).

22 *Spider-Man: Far from Home*, directed by Jon Watts (Los Angeles: Columbia Pictures / Pascal Pictures / Marvel Studios, 2019).

23 Echo Zhan, "3051 drones create a spectacular record-breaking light show in China." Guinness World Records, October 20, 2020. https://www.guinnessworldrecords.com/news/commercial/2020/10/3051-drones-create-spectacular-record-breaking-light-show-in-china.

24 Kate Kilgore, "Russia-Ukraine Conflict: Sign Post to the Future (Part 1)," *Mad Scientist Laboratory*, May 26, 2022. https://madsciblog.tradoc.army.mil/400-russia-ukraine-conflict-sign-post-to-the-future-part-1/.

25 Edward Geist and Marjory Blumenthal, "Military Deception: The Killer AI App," *War On the Rocks*, October 23, 2019. https://warontherocks.com/2019/10/military-deception-ais-killer-ap.

26 Matthew Fecteau, "The Deep Fakes Are Coming," *War Room Podcast* (U.S. Army War College), April 23, 2021. https://warroom.armywarcollege.edu/articles/deep-fakes/.

27 Marco Tempest, "TED Talk—A swarm of mini drones makes… magic," *TEDSummit*, Edinburgh, Scotland, July 2019. https://podcasts.apple.com/jm/podcast/a-swarm-of-minidrones-makes-magic-marco-tempest/id470616189.

CHAPTER 23

Unbeatable

Dan Ward

In 1991, Marvel Comics introduced a one-off joke character named Squirrel Girl. Her powers seemed of dubious value, and she was only 14 years old, but in her debut she managed to defeat a top-tier villain, Doctor Doom, and rescue Iron Man from his clutches.[1] Despite her impressive showing, it would be more than a decade before she made her next appearance. She eventually joined a short-lived B-list team known as the Great Lakes Avengers, later partnered up with a few other minor-league teams, and made an occasional cameo in a handful of titles, often achieving improbable victories over archvillains in unexplained off-panel fights.

Everything changed for Squirrel Girl in 2015, with the launch of her solo title. Now she had a whole new look, a full back story, a catchy slogan ("I eat nuts and kick butts!"), and an alter ego as a first-year computer science student at Empire State University. She quickly became one of the most interesting, engaging, and unusual characters in Marvel comics. She also joined the ranks of the Incredible Hulk, the Amazing Spiderman, and the Mighty Thor when she gained that classic superhero accessory, an adjective. Squirrel Girl was now … The Unbeatable.

This latest incarnation clarified her skill set and moved her previous off-panel victories to center stage. While earlier storylines focused on her ability to leap like a squirrel and talk to squirrels, now she frequently described herself as having "the powers of both squirrel and girl." Her girl-power message attracted lots of new fans and created opportunities for storylines that were quite different from other heroes.

In addition to her squirrel companion Tippy Toe (who took the mantle of the previously deceased squirrel Monkey Joe), she also assembled a small but constantly expanding crew of crime fighters, many of whom are fellow students at Empire State. Two even have matching animal-rhyming names: Koi Boi and Chipmunk Hunk. Her college roommate, Nancy, rounded out the team, despite not having any superpowers.

Squirrel Girl's approach to fighting crime is as unusual as it is effective. Although she can hold her own in a slugfest when the occasion calls for it, that is not her primary strategy. Instead, she brilliantly blends physical prowess with mighty social skills like listening and empathy. Her superhuman ability to see her opponents as something other than an enemy to be defeated contributes as much to her unbeatability as that killer left hook.

For example, in one early issue, a rampaging hippopotamus-man named Hippo the Hippo[2] delivers a classic villain monologue to Squirrel Girl and company. He describes the economic circumstances that led him to embark on a life on crime, at which point Squirrel Girl stops him in his tracks when she replies by saying, "That's fair ..." She expresses compassion and understanding for the would-be bank robber's situation, hardly a typical superhero response to crime, but it turns out to be highly effective.

While using her massive squirrel-strength to physically restrain Mr. Hippo, her other superpower kicks in. She hears his complaint, then offers him an alternative career path, suggesting he seek employment as part of a demolition crew where his ability to bust through walls would be put to good use ("as long as you only knock down the buildings you're supposed to") and could create the financial security he sought.

The other option she offers, of course, is to "kick your butt really hard. Like, *really* hard." He chooses the better option and heads off to make phone calls and fill out job applications.

Squirrel Girl's approach prevented the bank from being robbed and turned Hippo into a productive member of society. Plus, it was a funny and thought-provoking scene, with bad puns and energetic action. That's everything you want in a superhero.

Of course, you don't get to be called Unbeatable just by foiling a minor bank robber. To really earn that adjective, you've got to triumph over a mega villain. Galactus, for example. When Squirrel Girl and Tippy Toe shoot into space on their way to stop Galactus ("The God of Oblivion and Destroyer of Worlds") from his latest attempt to eat Earth, she quips that it doesn't seem fair ... "for him." Along the way, she explained her strategy to Tippy-Toe: "You don't defeat a Galactus by being *stronger*. You don't defeat a Galactus by being *smarter* either. The only way you'll *ever* defeat Galactus is by giving him what he wants: a source of life energy."

Having successfully determined Galactus' actual needs, she proceeds to beat the stuffing out of him. Just kidding—she actually takes Galactus to a planet full of acorns where he eats himself into a food coma and declares Squirrel Girl to be his friend. Bam—Earth is saved, thanks to the power of girl, the power of squirrel, and the power of friendship.[3]

This knack for redirecting negative behaviors into positive directions and converting adversaries into friends is a magnificent superpower. It makes Squirrel Girl not only Unbeatable, but also an outstanding example of how to build alliances and teams in the real world. Sure, it's cool to shout "Avengers assemble!" and have a cadre of costumed crimefighters strike dramatic poses for a group photo. But it's even cooler (and frankly, harder) to change hearts and minds of those who seek to cause chaos and destruction.

Squirrel Girl's approach has a direct parallel in modern military conflict. When I deployed to Afghanistan in 2011 as part of NATO's International Security Assistance Force, the team I led included officers from Croatia, Romania, and the Czech Republic. We all got along swimmingly, and partway through my tour it occurred to me that our parents had been on opposite sides of the Cold War. Countries that were once adversaries had become allies, standing shoulder-to-shoulder in support of a common mission. This did not happen overnight, but it happened, and it's a beautiful thing.

In addition to overseeing officers from former Eastern Bloc countries, I reported to officers from countries that were formerly Axis powers during World War II.[4] One level up the chain of command was an Italian general, and he reported to a German general. Our grandparents could never have imagined such a situation when they were young and facing off over the battlefields of Europe, but there we were. Continuing even higher up the chain, a British general or two rounded out the leadership team. Students of history and fans of musical theater alike will recall that once upon a time a ragtag volunteer army in need of a shower somehow defeated a global superpower.[5]

The American colonists going toe-to-toe with the mighty British Empire in the 1770s was the equivalent of Squirrel Girl fighting Galactus. The Americans kicked some British butt to be sure, but then we built a special relationship and established an alliance that was not only important for both countries, but for the world as a whole. That alliance is the equivalent of Galactus joining Squirrel Girl's team and fighting alongside her and Chipmunk Hunk.

If the pattern holds—and there is every reason to believe it will—then future generations of American troops will deploy alongside or even under the leadership of Iraqi, Afghan, Russian, and Chinese military personnel. As someone who has served alongside former adversaries, I'd say this would be a big win, and I look forward to these future partnerships.

You know who else would love that situation? The Unbeatable Squirrel Girl.

All this "turning enemies into friends" stuff may strike some as a touchy-feely daydream, particularly those who view the military's purpose as solely to "kill people and break things." But as Squirrel Girl might point out, "It's the Department of Defense, not the Department of Kill People and Break Things." Yes, like our bushy-tailed hero, we have the capacity to employ lethal force in pursuit of our objectives, but using force is not itself the objective. Figuring out a way to achieve our objectives without actually fighting is also a way to win. And no, that's not some hippy peacenik opinion. It's literally Sun Tzu's description of the supreme art of war: the best way to win. So maybe Squirrel Girl should adopt a new adjective: *Supreme* Squirrel Girl has a nice ring to it.[6]

Now, Squirrel Girl's teambuilding is not limited to former villains. As mentioned earlier, she also includes her non-superpowered roommate Nancy in her capers, to say nothing of the army of squirrels who regularly join in the fun. This is a stark contrast to Tony Stark's approach.

Heroes like Iron Man are notorious for their "get out of my way, kid" attitude[7] toward anyone they view as insufficiently super, and they often take a go-it-alone approach. Squirrel Girl does the opposite, welcoming and including Nancy, insisting that she has something meaningful to contribute, and encouraging her to see herself as a capable partner even though she can't talk to animals (she tried!). Squirrel Girl often sees Nancy's abilities better than Nancy herself does. Sure, she can't punch through a wall, but wall-punching alone is almost never the solution in Squirrel Girl's eyes.

This ability to build diverse partnerships has interesting and important implications for today's geopolitical situation, specifically the competition between the U.S. and China. Viewing the world through that lens, we see there are two phases to this competition. The first involves recognizing the threat and assembling a team to confront it. This is where Squirrel Girl calls Nancy, Koi Boi, and the rest, who—for instance—agree to work together to stop Ratotoskr, the Norse god-squirrel[8] recently arrived from Asgard. In the real world, this is where the U.S. engages with our allies and other affected parties to—for instance—build a consensus that China's intentions and actions are counter to the wider world's health and safety.

On that note, ever notice how supervillains like Galactus and Doctor Doom don't have many friends or allies? Sure, Doom has Doombots, and Galactus has a herald, but they are servants at best, not true partners. Rather than building collaborative alliances, these villains tend to operate as solo chaos-makers and as authoritarian dictators. Similarly, China currently has just one military ally—North Korea—and a small number of low-commitment/low-trust partnerships with other nations. Going alone like that is sort of sad, honestly, and it definitely reduces their effectiveness in the world.

In contrast, all the best heroes have friends, partners, and teams (e.g., the Avengers, X-Men, Justice League, etc.). The United States has 30 fellow NATO allies, soon to be 31, as well as friendly and committed partnerships with non-NATO countries like Japan, South Korea, Australia, etc.

A report titled *Six Lessons from a Decade of Asia Strategy Simulations*[9] makes a similar point when it observes that Chinese President Xi Jinping's recent actions have resulted in "heightened tensions with Australia, India, Japan, the Philippines, Taiwan, Vietnam, and South Korea, among others." Yikes, that's a lot of tension!

The authors go on to suggest that "Strong democratic powers in Asia are good for the United States and bad for China in the long term." Their scenarios indicate the U.S. security posture is improved when we work toward "a regional approach that is more accepting of the rise of new power centers." Countries that "remain free to make whatever choices best fit their interests and values" are likely to be good partners with the U.S. and important counterweights to a rising China. The authors describe this as "a regional order that is broadly supportive of [U.S.] interests yet less dependent on U.S. guarantees." Our nut-chomping, butt-stomping hero would certainly approve of this posture.

Building a team brings us to the start of the second phase of the competition, where Squirrel Girl and friends figure out how to redirect the villain's efforts into a positive direction. This often begins with a demonstration of butt-kicking power, and always includes consultation across the wider team to get their ideas and suggestions. As we've already seen, this phase inevitably involves a liberal application of *strategic empathy* based on genuine inquiry, attentive listening, and pursuit of deep understanding of what the villain-du-jour actually wants. If there's a way to give it to them without causing harm, Squirrel Girl will find it.

It may be tempting to dismiss these empathetic and teambuilding superpowers as somehow inferior to the more classically muscular and masculine strategies employed by other heroes. However, such a dim view of her powers misses the point of her story AND overlooks the whole "unbeatable" thing (to say nothing of her massive physical strength she uses whenever necessary). It also buys into a weird bias against collaboration, which is much more suitable for villains than heroes. On top of that, it diminishes the very real and very well-established historical record of how wars are actually won and how national objectives are actually achieved.

Ultimately, the thing that makes Squirrel Girl unbeatable is neither her power of girl nor her power of squirrel—it's the combination of the two, which expands the range of options she can draw from. As she explained to her squirrel companion, "That's the secret to being unbeatable, Tippy; always have a Plan B." So, when she confronts villains whose narrow perspectives present limited options ("I have to rob this bank because I have no job"), she presents a Plan B ("Have you considered working in demolition?") as a less punchy alternative. In response to Galactus' single-minded hunger for planets, she identifies a different source of life energy for him to consume. Eating nuts solves the problem, so she doesn't have to kick butts.

While China continues to antagonize countries around the world, and while global public opinion of China grows increasingly negative,[10] the U.S. would do well to take a page out of Squirrel Girl's playbook. Rather than trying to maintain the status quo or revert to some unavailable past, the U.S. could demonstrate leadership by fostering strong coalitions with a range of other countries—superpowered and non-superpowered alike—to build outcomes where all players can win and eventually even become friends. This is the secret to being Unbeatable.

This is the key to being Supreme.

Notes

1 With the help of a bunch of squirrels, naturally.
2 That's a real villain, look it up! He's actually got a super interesting backstory!
3 In the context of competition with China, one might wonder what might be the equivalent of the planet full of acorns.
4 Fun fact: Romania and Croatia were also part of that Axis. The more you know!
5 I apologize if that song will now be in your head for the rest of the day. Although it's a pretty great song, so maybe I'm not sorry after all!
6 Assuming Doctor Strange, the Sorcerer Supreme, doesn't mind sharing that particular title.
7 As we saw in Squirrel Girl's first appearance, and pretty much every interaction she has with her friend Iron Man.
8 Again, this is also a real villain with a pretty cool multi-issue storyline.
9 Authored by Zack Cooker and Aaron Friedberg, and published by the German Marshall Fund of the United States in June 2022.
10 https://www.pewresearch.org/global/2022/09/28/how-global-public-opinion-of-china-has-shifted-in-the-xi-era/.

CHAPTER 24

The Veidt Method

Why Ozymandias Was Right

Ian Boley

It's tough to talk about superheroes without talking about nuclear weapons. Superman, Green Lantern, Captain Atom, multiple Kryptonians, Thor, Magneto, Storm, various members of the Summers/Grey lineage—each has displayed destructive power capable of leveling a city in minutes, and these individuals are only on the lower-midrange end of superhuman capabilities. Unfortunately, the sheer scope of superhero powers tends to be forgotten unless the author and artist make a point of including it. One notable exception wherein a superhero's destructive power looms over everything is Alan Moore's Hugo-winning graphic novel *Watchmen*. Moore, along with artist Dave Gibbons, took on the problems of the Reagan era in a brilliant use of the comic medium's unique strengths. Together, they explored what the existence of these physical gods could mean for society as a whole, as well as for the troubles of a nuclear-armed world.

The cultural, political, and historical ramifications of nuclear weapons are many, but *Watchmen* attempts to explore them in a way that shows how superheroes might intersect with these issues. Through the lens of this graphic novel, we can examine a few of these ramifications, including deterrence, compellence, nuclear blackmail, and how everything we think we know about nuclear weapons might be called into question. Ozymandias' path to world peace is deeply instructive for those studying great power conflicts such as the Russian invasion of Ukraine and the NATO response. More generally, it serves as a thought experiment regarding the nature of the power that nuclear weapons convey. Had Ozymandias chosen a less violent means of getting the world's attention, he probably would not have achieved his goal—and the reason why lies in the way great powers see nuclear weapons.

First, though, a bit of background is in order. I'm told that the second person singular prompts all sorts of editorial anxieties, but if you (yes, you, the person reading this right now) haven't read *Watchmen*, you should. This essay will still be here when you're done. If you haven't read it in a while, you should re-read it, especially if you first read it, as I did, in your teenage years. The story is relatively simple in concept yet shockingly complex in its execution. (Turn back now to avoid spoilers.) The world of *Watchmen* is one in which a handful of Batman- and Punisher-style unpowered superheroes have existed since the late 1930s. Their exploits, while colorful, made little positive societal impact. In fact, their spiritual descendants made matters worse, consigning the idea of the masked adventurer to legal oblivion per the demands of a riotously enraged America. The one publicly acknowledged exception is the U.S. government's own walking, talking, blue-dong-dangling nuclear deterrent, Dr. Manhattan. Dr. Manhattan, AKA Jon Osterman, is the sole superhero in *Watchmen* with real superpowers, including the ability to warp reality as he pleases—sort of (again, spoilers abound). Osterman is in turn overwhelmed by his non-linear perception of time and his growing detachment from the human race. When he hares off to Mars to contemplate the transience and insignificance of human existence, his employers in the U.S. government are, understandably, dismayed.

One of the other active heroes, the mentally disturbed Rorschach, notices a trend. Superheroes, retired and otherwise, are being taken off the board in what appears to be a coordinated fashion. He begins getting the abysmally dysfunctional gang back together again in the hopes of stopping whoever is behind the trend. As part of this, Rorschach attempts to warn Ozymandias, AKA Adrian Veidt, the world's smartest man. Veidt seems unconcerned, even after a suicidal assassin kills his assistant. Eventually, Rorschach, along with Osterman and the second Nite Owl and Silk Spectre, uncover the truth (really, this is the last chance to avoid spoilers!): Veidt was behind everything. Veidt had foreseen a global societal collapse in the mid-1990s and had begun working in secret to stabilize the world through a metaphorical slap to the face.

When Osterman disappeared, Soviet tanks began moving into Afghanistan and Pakistan within days under the pretense of "securing the USSR's borders." By the end of the book, there are tanks in East Berlin. The U.S. in this scenario is apparently helpless to do anything to stop the USSR's conventional advance short of firing off a nuclear salvo. While unpacking the flaws with this scenario would take another (much longer) essay, the tension built is undeniable and reflective of left-leaning cultural attitudes in the 1980s. So what does Veidt do? He destroys half of New York City to get both superpowers' attention, setting up both the novel's final moral conundrum and its ambiguous ending.

Veidt, as befits the world's smartest man, chooses the simple and cost-effective solution of destroying NYC with an exploding giant psychic alien squid and a teleporter, naturally. Yes, it's weird, but it's also satirizing an entire medium. Moving on. The idea was to give the world a common enemy: extra-dimensional aliens that supposedly would follow up with an invasion threatening the entirety of humankind.

There you have it—the world's smartest man couldn't think up anything better than a psychic squid-bomb to bring the world back from the brink of nuclear apocalypse and eventual societal collapse. Even accounting for satire, this solution is, quite simply, weird in a way that only comic books can be, and fans have long debated its efficacy. But was there a better way? I argue that, within the parameters Veidt faced, there probably wasn't.

Obviously, a lot of the messiness on the national security side of the story stems from Moore being an anarchist comic-book writer and not a policymaker or scholar.[1] But let's take a few pages and imagine Veidt's thought process as he came to the decision to squid-whip the Big Apple. The first thing to determine is Veidt's goal. For our purposes, we will say that it was to compel a shift to peaceful behavior on the part of the superpowers via a method that ensures the new behavior will persist for several years at least.

Compellence, Deterrence, and Toasters

Compellence, as defined by Thomas Schelling, is a "threatening action that is intended not to forestall some adversarial action but to bring about some desired action, through [fear of consequences]."[2] For a visceral example, imagine two people, Alice and Bob, and a toaster. Alice wants Bob to change his behavior—say, to stop kicking her dog, Charlie. One morning, she sees Bob kicking Charlie at a breakfast buffet. Alice walks up to Bob, seizes his hand, and shoves it into a heated toaster. She says, "Stop kicking my dog and I'll turn off the toaster." Bob might struggle for a time, but Alice is able to keep his hand in the toaster for long enough that he eventually agrees to stop kicking Charlie. Alice then releases his hand and monitors Bob to ensure he complies with the terms of their agreement. A real-world example of this was Operation *Desert Storm*, where coalition forces shoved most of the Iraqi military into a toaster until Saddam Hussein departed Kuwait.

Ozymandias may have considered a more above-board form of compellence. It probably crossed his mind to build multiple decapodal kamikazes and drop them into cities after the world inevitably rejected his demands that the superpowers be at peace. In addition to destroying a great deal of the world he was nominally trying to save, this approach would have only provided a short-term solution, as the superpower response would likely have been to destroy Veidt's Antarctic fortress and eventually return to their previous behaviors. If things had gotten to that point, Veidt's logical counter-response in this scenario would have been to threaten retaliation against those who wished him harm—in other words, to establish a deterrent.

Deterrence, per Schelling, "posits a response to something unacceptable but is quiescent in the absence of provocation."[3] Let's return to Alice and Bob. Bob is feeling larcenous at breakfast, and Alice notices. Alice says to Bob, "I don't like the way you've been looking at my stuff. If you come over here, I'll stick your hand in this toaster." Bob then decides that Alice's possessions are not worth the char marks, and Alice would simply continue with breakfast until Bob decided the benefits of taking Alice's stuff outweighed the pain of toasted mitts. Alice could also choose to extend deterrence to Charlie—that is, she could promise Bob that any harm to Charlie would bring the toaster around. This example is, in broad terms, the essence of the nuclear standoff between America and the Soviet Union; the variation is what happened when America began to use nuclear weapons to guarantee the security of Western Europe.

There's a key element to deterrence that should be highlighted: It must be explicit. Alice cannot simply say to Bob, "Don't do things I don't like." Bob is, at least nominally, a rational actor. That means he weighs the costs and benefits of his actions. The cost of his hand being in the toaster is high. The benefit of stealing Alice's stuff may be lower, higher, or equivalent. But if Alice does not make clear what the cost will be, Bob is less likely to be deterred. Now, that doesn't mean that Alice must go into detail—she doesn't need to tell Bob what exact moves she will make to put his hand in the toaster—but she does need to convey certain essential facts of the situation for Bob to make an accurate and rational assessment. Similarly, while American nuclear targeting documents (known during the Cold War as the SIOP, or Single Integrated Operational Plan) were among the most sensitive elements of U.S. national security policy, the rough number and general disposition of American nuclear weapons was public.

Let's back up, though—isn't Alice assuming a lot here? Bob is just looking at her possessions. Is Alice actually the aggressor? Is she trying to maintain the status quo via deterrence, or is she really trying to change Bob's behavior via a compellent threat? For that, we'd need to dig into the history of their relationship a bit more deeply. If we were to do that, we might find all sorts of complicating factors that make deterrence and compellence difficult to distinguish. Ozymandias, as an intelligent, historically minded individual, might have done exactly that sort of digging to realize that nuclear deterrence doesn't necessarily work the way international relations scholars have discussed it for decades. In fact, it may be far more complicated and unstable than anyone would like to admit.

Under the Hood of Deterrence Theory

In the last twenty years, a few scholars have begun questioning the bases of nuclear theory. Historian Francis Gavin has found that several fundamental assumptions about American nuclear policy were incorrect or distorted by the gap between public rhetoric and classified reality. His research highlights some unanswered questions in the nuclear strategy literature. Gavin asks, "Is strategic nuclear arms control always stabilizing? Can we meaningfully distinguish between compellence and deterrence? ... What is a nuclear crisis, and what does it mean to 'win' such a contest? … Truth be told, we cannot conclusively demonstrate how nuclear deterrence works, however vehement our claims to the contrary."[4] Gavin, building on the work of others before him, is the latest historian to question the nature—if not the existence—of the so-called nuclear revolution, the idea that nuclear weapons by their very existence have fundamentally altered the way states behave in the international sphere.[5] But Gavin is a historian, examining the past through more knowledge than any one historical actor could have had. Would Ozymandias have had access to the same sort of perspective on the nuclear revolution? Would he have been able to reason the same way?

Let's assume for a moment that Veidt, as not only the world's smartest man, but also one of its richest, would have been able to gain access to behind-the-scenes information regarding national security crises. Through the same sort of inducements as the Soviets used in reality, he could have suborned American national security personnel—not easily, perhaps, but it could be done. Veidt probably would have seen some of what Gavin has seen, but work like Gavin's is based on extensive archival research and would have taken a great deal of time to duplicate. So what would the fashionable young hero with an empire to run do with his time instead?

Here we come to the work of Vipin Narang. Currently the Principal Deputy Assistant Secretary of Defense for Space Policy, Narang is also a professor of international relations at MIT. His first book offered a concept of nuclear weapons that addresses some of the questions that Gavin raised. In short, Narang proposes the idea that nuclear weapons have an element of strategy to them, and that not every state uses these destructive tools the same way.[6] Some, such as Israel, use them catalytically, to signal for conventional help from larger allies. In the case of the 1973 Yom Kippur War, Israeli officials began assembling their nuclear weapons in a way that the United States could see but their Arab opponents could not. The U.S. promptly intervened to keep the conflict from turning nuclear. Other states, such as India, use a direct deterrence posture based on the threat of assured retaliation. This posture of a certain second strike is intended to prevent existential losses in conventional conflict and ensure that such states will not be attacked with nuclear weapons. Still others, such as France, employ a posture of asymmetric escalation. They hold their nuclear forces in a relatively high state of readiness and vow that any attack on their soil will bring nuclear retaliation. Finally, the U.S. and USSR were able to accomplish any of these goals with nuclear weapons because they spent enormous resources on their respective arsenals. To Narang, the focus on these two superpowers has distorted the field of nuclear studies. Veidt may have seen the same and been privy to enough information to raise questions in his mind about the viability of a "nuclear" deterrent in his unique circumstances.

Surely, though, Veidt could have secretly—or openly—told the superpower governments what cards he was holding? Couldn't he have, in essence, blackmailed the world into sanity? Unfortunately, this too would be unlikely to succeed. In fact, it seems to be a rite of passage for nuclear-armed autocrats to discover that nuclear blackmail rarely prospers. Todd Sechser and Matthew Fuhrmann, both scholars of international relations, argue that this is because there are three main variables to consider when states try to compel others: "(1) the challenger's ability to impose its will militarily, (2) the stakes in a dispute, and (3) the costs of military conflict."[7] They argue that military weapons are, in essence, overly powerful for most disputes and difficult to use with impunity. It is far easier for a state to use conventional power to get what it wants in most cases. This is particularly true since very few things outside a state's control are worth a nuclear exchange and its attendant long-term consequences.

This doesn't mean Ozymandias couldn't try nuclear blackmail, though—Sechser and Fuhrmann lay out a few conditions that can help the would-be blackmailer seem more credible. The first of these, possessing weak conventional power that would be bolstered by nuclear coercion, Veidt probably clears by virtue of being just one man. The second support to credibility comes if the challenger, Veidt, is looking down the barrel of an extreme provocation. This is more debatable, as no one has appointed Ozymandias king of kings with responsibility for the world's population. Instead, he simply wants very badly to solve the problems he foresees. The final credibility booster is similar, and Veidt clearly fails to establish a claim to it: if the would-be compeller is truly desperate with nowhere left to run. Veidt could have created such a situation for himself, but it is vanishingly unlikely that he would have. Veidt's psychology dictates that being in such a situation would be anathema to him—he famously enacts his master plan a full 35 minutes before informing the heroes of its existence. So would nuclear blackmail per Sechser and Fuhrmann have worked for Veidt? Probably not. Just as Vladimir Putin appears to have discovered in Ukraine, nuclear blackmail sounds intimidating, but in reality it is a shockingly easy bluff for a serious competitor to call.

This Isn't the Movies

There's still one more variant to address: the Snyder ending. The 2009 *Watchmen* film, directed by Zack Snyder, brings up a new solution: Frame Dr. Manhattan. This approach is the riskiest of all. The problems are many: First, the entire world must be given a believable motive for Osterman's bolt-from-the-blue slaying of fifteen million people. When world leaders are asked how they could have trusted someone who in hindsight was so obviously untrustworthy, they would likely face renewed pressure to use an external foe to help them stay in office. Osterman himself is a massive wildcard—who knows what a human forced to expand his consciousness to encompass most of the universe would think of such a crime? In the film, Veidt bets Osterman will simply do the math and sacrifice his reputation, but what if Dr. Manhattan had more ego than Ozymandias gave him credit for? Far better to deal with the conservatism inherent in most policymakers and the institutions surrounding them. Finally, the global scale of Veidt's solution in the film makes the whole thing deeply problematic. The Soviet Union, which had spent decades in fear of Dr. Manhattan, is supposed to embrace the United States, his nominal masters, after his destruction of a major Soviet city? This seems unlikely in the extreme.

Ozymandias' options were bad from the start. Having set his course away from politics early in life, he was never going to be in a position to influence the superpowers at the levels needed to forge a true peace. When he saw the world on a course for doomsday, he acted in the way he thought most likely to succeed, and succeed he did for a time, despite methods that were, at best, reprehensible. Ultimately, the false peace Veidt built was unlikely to last, especially as evidence of his plot reached the media through Rorschach's actions. In the cold light of reality, Veidt's approach is primarily instructive for all the many ways in which it could just as easily have failed before launch—some of which would not necessarily be accounted for by conventional models of nuclear strategy. Thought experiments like those posed by *Watchmen* are useful reminders that even the most seemingly certain social scientific theories can fall apart on the rocks of human agency. Even vast social forces like nuclear weapons carry the potential for individual actors to radically alter the framework surrounding them. With that in mind, the question to ask shifts to the one proposed by Moore's original work: Who watches people like Adrian Veidt?

Notes

1 "A FOR ALAN, Pt. 1: The Alan Moore interview," Mile High Comics Presents The Beat at Comicon.com, November 1, 2005, https://web.archive.org/web/20060505034142/http://www.comicon.com/thebeat/2006/03/a_for_alan_pt_1_the_alan_moore.html.

2 Thomas C. Schelling, *Arms and Influence* (New Haven: Yale University Press, 2020), Location 211, Kindle.

3 Schelling, *Arms and Influence*, Location 193.

4 Francis Gavin, *Nuclear Weapons and American Grand Strategy* (Washington, D.C., Brookings Institution Press: 2020), Location 141, Kindle.

5 See for example, Marc Trachtenberg, *History and Strategy* (Princeton: Princeton University Press, 1991), especially chapter 1, "Strategic Thought in America, 1952–1966" and Bruce Kuklick, *Blind Oracles: Intellectuals and War from Kennan to Kissinger* (Princeton: Princeton University Press, 2006).

6 Vipin Narang, *Nuclear Strategy in the Modern Era* (Princeton: Princeton University Press, 2013), 14.

7 Todd S. Sechser and Matthew Fuhrmann, *Nuclear Weapons and Coercive Diplomacy* (Cambridge, UK: Cambridge University Press, 2017), 12–13.

PART V

TO THE BATCAVE!

"Come on, Robin, to the Batcave! We haven't one minute to lose!"
—BRUCE WAYNE IN *BATMAN* (1966)

CHAPTER 25

I've Come to Save the World

Why Human Heart Must Remain in AI

Kera Rolsen

"There is only one path to peace ... your extinction."

—ULTRON

Imagine if Vision had been birthed from the internet and not Tony Stark's personal Artificial Intelligence (AI). He would have been a meme-fluent, walking-talking-flying biased nightmare who screamed "Yeet!" as he threw Sokovia into the sun. Instead, the Marvel Cinematic Universe (MCU) expands on the pop culture understanding of AI with Vision coming from J.A.R.V.I.S. In the first MCU Phase One movie, *Iron Man* (2008), J.A.R.V.I.S. is Tony Stark's in-home AI, responsible for everything from telling the time and weather forecast to being a voice-activated home computing system with access to Tony's corporate systems and personal projects. Throughout the main MCU plot arc, J.A.R.V.I.S. evolves from a system-bound AI to something more. During *Avengers: Age of Ultron* (2015), Tony and Bruce Banner's tinkering causes J.A.R.V.I.S.'s personality and knowledge to be uploaded into a body powered by the Mind Stone. This creates an ethical quandary of whether the J.A.R.V.I.S. AI, thereafter called Vision, can be trusted to hold the Mind Stone, an incredibly powerful artifact. We, the viewers, are later reassured when Vision is able to pick up and wield Mjölnir Thor's magic hammer, which can only be wielded by the "worthy."

The movie treats viewers to a fabulous storytelling technique where we see our villain as the mirror of our hero. Ultron, who is also birthed from Tony and Bruce's experiment, becomes the unethical, misanthropic version of Vision. After one trip onto the internet, Ultron decides that humankind cannot be trusted, and he should destroy us all and start over. (To be fair, sometimes this author doesn't think Ultron is all that wrong, given the current state of discourse on the internet.)

This gives us two perfect examples of possibilities for the future of AI and a foundation from which to consider the ethics of AI in military applications. It also brings up three important questions: How does one design an "ethical AI," how does AI-driven warfighting impact ethics in war, and if the AI mistargets, who do we blame?

Age of Ultron is by no means the first science fiction story to cover AI and how to ensure it meets ethical standards. Isaac Asimov introduced the idea of the Three Laws of Robotics in the *I, Robot* story collection. Many of his subsequent stories hinged on human-robot interactions around these laws. Asimov's Three Laws stated:

1. A robot may not injure a human being or, through inaction, allow a human being to come to harm.
2. A robot must obey the orders given to it by human beings except where such orders would conflict with the First Law.
3. A robot must protect its own existence as long as such protection does not conflict with the First or Second Law.[1]

Despite their brevity, the laws are fairly comprehensive for an AI-driven robot interacting with humans in normal settings. But how would this alter when the purpose of the AI is to control weapons of war, automatically breaking Rule #1? What rules or ethical considerations must go into the programming of these machines?

A Machine Who Can Wield Mjölnir—Designing an Ethical AI

There could be days of arguments over which story holds the title of the best "worst sci-fi," but for this author, it's *Friday* by Robert Heinlein. Don't bother going to buy or read it; it is not worth the pulp for a paperback. However, while the plot lacks any discernable structure, the story brings up several interesting ethical quandaries. The main character, Friday, discusses with her friend and occasional polyamorous paramour, Ian Tormey, why humans are still allowed to be airline pilots. In this tale, technology has evolved to include ballistic travel that is still captained by human pilots. Even Ian admits that should a mishap happen, he would be unable to save the vessel. He notes that technology exceeded human reaction times long ago. So, they ask, why keep human captains? Why not switch to genetically modified life forms whose reflexes are fast enough? Or an AI-piloted ballistic vessel? Ian argues that humans are reassured by their own humanity. He proposes that humans trust that another human will try their best to save the vessel. In contrast, they couldn't trust a so-called Living Artifact which could hate humanity and crash the vessel on purpose. And no one would trust the AI which has no emotional ties to humanity. The fictional discussion touches on many of the questions asked during the Space Race about why the astronauts were still allowed control of their spaceships when leaving things to the technology of the day may have been more sound.

This argument can be evolved to fit modern times as well. We live in a world where we have the technology to create swarming drones capable of spacing themselves autonomously, remotely piloted aircraft (RPA) with lethal weapons strapped to them, and predictive analytics can tell maintenance professionals which jet engine fan blades to replace before it can fail. The world of conflict is still dominated by the most advanced technology. In this modern world, are there ways to build ethics into the AI that is the next step in modern kill chains? If one evolves RPAs into autonomous platforms, can ethics be built into the AI?

Quite simply, yes—but as the saying goes, garbage in, garbage out.

There are two primary ways in which we can view AI design ethics: ethics by design and pro-ethical design. Ethics by design is the more paternalistic of the two and seeks to constrain the options available. Like Asimov's Three Laws, it gives rules that must be obeyed, sometimes to the detriment of the AI or its mission. An easy way to conceptualize it is to consider speed bumps. The speed bump is placed in an area where residents wish for traffic to slow. The bump itself forces drivers to slow or risk damage to their vehicle. However, it constrains all drivers, including those with legitimate reasons to drive quickly through residential areas like fire, police, and EMS vehicles.[2] AI coders and designers would input Asimov's Three Laws or facsimile of such in place to ensure no AI-driven RPA fires across a country border when combatants know that simply stepping across a certain line of latitude or longitude will inhibit a munitions launch.

The other option for building ethics into an AI is pro-ethical design. This version of AI ethics is less of a rigid law and more of a nudge; the rule exists, but there is an option to ignore it and accept the consequences.[3] The pro-ethical design parallel to a speed bump would be a speed camera. Drivers are aware of both the camera and the speed limit; however, they are still physically able to speed and accept the ticket. In the same analogous vein, a fire truck or ambulance can exceed the speed limit with due regard for safety and the greater public good. AI algorithms designed under this model would have the ability to ignore certain rules. For example, an AI-driven RPA could follow a "hot pursuit" rule to override an inhibit on a country border and let the combatants decide the consequences of the infraction.

There is one final aspect of designing an ethical AI that is human, all too human.

Evidence shows that human bias bleeds into AI. As machine learning occurs, it is only as good as the databases to which the machine has access, and it is the humans designing the AI who are choosing what trains it. For instance, if a crime prediction AI has been trained by a majority white police force on a majority minority population, the AI will be biased to find crime only in these minority populations.[4] If a workplace that is predominately men trains an algorithm to find more "like" candidates based on their resumes, it will exclude characteristics of women, further biasing the population of the office, and the algorithm will show advertisements for that type of job to fewer women than men.[5] Following our Vision analogy, if the only knowledge J.A.R.V.I.S. had was information from the internet, then he would have appeared to the Avengers and deemed all the women lesser contributors and assumed that, since James "Rhodey" Rhodes was black, he may be a criminal. In the real world, this could translate into an AI-driven RPA firing into a non-hostile location because its historical data showed patterns of life consistent with enemy activity. There are groups researching ways to detect bias in AI,[6] and it will behoove all militaries considering the use of ethical AI to pursue this line of research as well.

The Soul of the Machine: What Do we Value in Our Warriors?

In February 2013, the United States military introduced a new medal, the Distinguished Warfare Medal (DWM). This medal was intended to honor the impact of personnel who fought within the cyber domain or through the use of RPAs. Then-Secretary of Defense Leon Panetta wrote a note that accompanied the announcement of the medal stating:

> The DWM provides an avenue to recognize appropriately extraordinary direct impacts on combat operations warranting recognition above the Bronze Star Medal. Since September 11, 2001, technological advancements have, in some cases, dramatically changed how we conduct and support combat and other military operations. Accordingly, the DWM award criteria intentionally do not include a geographic limitation on the award, as it is intended to recognize Service members who meet the criteria, regardless of the domain used or the member's physical location.[7]

The announcement of the medal and its awarding criteria sparked controversy among military members, veterans, and civilians who felt the medal's precedence over the Bronze Star was unwarranted.

Similarly, members of the United States Air Force's nuclear enterprise have questioned the precedence of the Nuclear Deterrence Operations Service Medal (NDOSM) below the Humanitarian Service Medal. This author knows the injustice of having fifteen years of honorable service in the nuclear enterprise outranked by her three days of moving sandbags during a flood. If medals are intended to honor what the military values, then the DWM indicates that the US military currently values personnel capable of executing strikes against an enemy far from the battlefield. It shows that the culture supports the concept of a warrior whose only "skin in the game" is the toll on their mental health.

While military medals reflect a military branch's values and culture, surely awards and medals don't mean anything to an AI? After all, Vision didn't strut around displaying an Infinity Stone as a badge of honor ... except for the Mind Stone embedded in his forehead. Perhaps the true test of AI sentience is not the machine asking, "What's in it for me?" but when AIs begin to fight on their own social media about whether the defense of the White House's cyberspaces is a "deployment" when compared to being the weapon firing AI in warfare. Perhaps the humorous idea of AIs fighting over DWMs, NDOSMs, and the now-ended National Defense Service Medal brings us to the heart of the second issue: When you don't have skin in the game, is warfare honorable?

Evolving technology has always been a hallmark of military advantage. From the stirrup to the longbow to machine guns, humans seek the technology that brings them an advantage on the battlefield. However, as we created larger and more destructive weapons, which created uneven effect-to-risk ratios, humankind had to reconsider what is honorable in warfare. The advent of machine guns in World War I demonstrated that a single soldier with a machine gun could destroy a cavalry charge. During World War II, the world understood that nuclear war meant the decision of one American or Russian president could end the world in a nuclear holocaust from the comfort of their office.

Now the ethics of warfare is reframed in the context of RPA pilots and technicians releasing weapons from an aerial vehicle thousands of miles from their seats. While those RPA personnel do not face bodily risk, there is "skin in the game" due to the risk to their mental health. But when the month of observation and five minutes of engagement is conducted by an AI, with no human in the loop other than in the learning phase, can we still claim to have "skin in the game?" And if not, do we still have the moral high ground?

The Court Martial Question: "Who's in Ruttin' Charge Here?"

One of the hardest parts of being a leader in the military is dissecting when things go wrong, especially when it means one of your subordinates will face nonjudicial punishment for their actions. The process is stressful for the subordinate, the leader, and the whole unit. But what happens when the root cause is the AI?

Envision yourself on the operations floor of the Combined Air Operations Center (CAOC) in the Middle East. Britney Spears is playing in the background because it's strike night, and she is heavily featured on the strike night playlist. An RPA squadron has been assigned to identify a particular target and has been dispatched to an area for months. The identification software has taken enough pictures to generate a valid identification and pipes its feed to massive screens over the CAOC operations floor. The mission commander validates action to be taken and that it meets the current rules of engagement. Dusk settles over the valley, and as lights from the local village twinkle out, a massive explosion rocks the target. Later that evening, ground forces reach the area and find the target is not there—the action should not have taken place and now there is collateral damage. Someone runs for the nightshift Judge Advocate General (or JAG, i.e., the lawyer) and the legal process begins.

In this vignette, it is relatively easy to assign blame and assure allies that the error has been fixed and will not occur again. But what happens when we begin to substitute AI for humans in this loop? Given the vignette above, substitute an AI validating the building for human verifying coordinates. This AI would have been trained to distinguish one building from another, its algorithms strengthened with every iteration. However, should the AI have a minor flaw in the algorithm, a bias that snuck in from its very human coders, who does the JAG prosecute? Clearly, one could not prosecute an algorithm. But then, who is to blame? The coders who wrote the original algorithms? Those who verified and validated the machine learning process?

In the MCU, after the events of *Age of Ultron*, the Avengers are asked to sign an accord stating they will only function under the supervision of the government. In the real world, the AIs would have been developed for and by their respective governments. However, machine learning does not occur at one single, massive software factory. It is completed by individual units, contractors, and subcontractors. As the algorithms are trained and grow to massive programs, finding individual lines of bad code becomes more difficult.[8] When paired with policies that have not kept pace with modern technology, as is often the case in the military, it has deadly results.[9] It doesn't take a Hollywood writer to create a story in which poor coding intersects outdated policy to create an event in which AI strikes the wrong target and takes innocent human lives. But in the same vein, it seems improbable that a horde of civilian coders would be, or even could be, brought to a court martial. The dispersion of blame across multiple companies and millions of lines of code would make justice and reassuring allies nearly impossible. The government would continue to use the contracted companies, a blood money of sorts would be exchanged, but no justice would be served.

Conclusion: Keeping the Human Heart in AI

The Vision from *Age of Ultron* came into existence already an ethical being able to wield Mjölnir while his counterpart, Ultron, was a clearly unethical AI bent on destroying humanity. Unfortunately, in the real world, creating ethical AI is not as magically easy, and it is not as clearly delineated into "good" and "evil" AI. Additionally, introducing AI to modern battlefields creates new ethical quandaries that must be resolved before AIs should be used in combat. Finally, the method by which machines learn and AIs are trained disperses the possibility for errors across hundreds of people who may or may not be punishable by the Uniformed Code of Military Justice, which makes providing justice difficult should the worst happen. So, how does the military ensure that AIs in combat are ethical and not headed down the Ultron path?

First, keep the human heart in AI. AI should be designed ethically from the ground up with pro-ethical designs. This will ensure that, unlike Asimov's Three Laws, a human can override certain AI choices for safety or allow an AI-driven asset to be destroyed rather than end lives. Humans should also keep their fingers on the pulse of the AI's training, checking for bias and validating ethical operations in several stages of development.

Second, in combat operations, the human should always be the lead. AI can support human interaction but should never be the lead operator. While humans are flawed creatures, our AI children, who have inherited our biases, are no better. With no heart of their own, it will always fall to the human in the loop to make the ethical choice.

Like all good sci-fi and fantasy, the MCU gives us the creative space to explore our own problems against a backdrop that causes no harm in the real world. It's easy to imagine Vision considering the CAOC's target and halting a strike, while Ultron would have hit the Big Red Button and launched nukes at it. We can use them as the framework for how we want AI to function and what we want to avoid. In the real world, we have to take steps to ensure machine learning drives us toward Vision and that we keep the very human heart in AI. Perhaps then it can be considered worthy.

The views expressed are those of the author and do not reflect the official guidance or position of the United States Government, the Department of Defense, the United States Air Force or the United States Space Force.

Notes

1   Isaac Asimov, "Runaround," in *I, Robot* (New York, NY: Doubleday, 1950), 40.
2   Morley, J., Floridi, L., Kinsey, L. et al, "What to How: An Initial Review of Publicly Available AI Ethics Tools, Methods and Research to Translate Principles into Practices," *Science and Engineering Ethics* 26, 2141–2168 (2020). https://doi.org/10.1007/s11948-019-00165-5
3   Ibid.
4   Jack Smith IV, "Crime-Prediction Tool May Be Reinforcing Discriminatory Policing," *Business Insider* (Business Insider, October 10, 2016, www.businessinsider.com/predictive-policing-discriminatory-police-crime-2016-10?r=US&IR=T.
5   Julia Carpenter, "Google's Algorithm Shows Prestigious Job Ads to Men, but Not to Women," *The Independent (Independent Digital News and Media*, July 7, 2015), www.independent.co.uk/tech/google-s-algorithm-shows-prestigious-job-ads-to-men-but-not-to-women-10372166.html.
6   Hanna Devlin, "Discrimination by Algorithm: Scientists Devise Test to Detect AI Bias," *The Guardian* (Guardian News and Media, December 19, 2016), www.theguardian.com/technology/2016/dec/19/discrimination-by-algorithm-scientists-devise-test-to-detect-ai-bias.
7   Leon Panetta, Secretary of Defense, memorandum, February 13, 2013.
8   Hanna Devlin, "Discrimination by Algorithm: Scientists Devise Test to Detect AI Bias," *The Guardian* (Guardian News and Media, December 19, 2016), www.theguardian.com/technology/2016/dec/19/discrimination-by-algorithm-scientists-devise-test-to-detect-ai-bias.
9   "Collision Between Vehicle Controlled by Developmental Automated Driving System and Pedestrian" (National Transportation and Safety Board, March 18, 2018), www.ntsb.gov/investigations/AccidentReports/Reports/HAR1903.pdf.

CHAPTER 26

Your Ancestors Called It Magic,
But You Call It Science

Jonathan Klug

My uncle had a copy of *Strange Tales* #111 that I used to read when I was a seven-year-old. The 12-cent comic's cover had the Human Torch battling the Asbestos Man, a long-forgotten villain for obvious reasons. The feature story of this 1963 comic centers around a fight between Johnny Storm and Dr. Orson Karloff, "the world's foremost analytical chemist." The next story—the second appearance of Dr. Strange that introduces his archenemy Baron Mordo—was much less straightforward for a young reader. This tale of the mystic arts featured Dr. Strange and Baron Mordo using astral projection and engaging in magical combat. You might ask: But what does an old comic with a short story about magic have to do with cyberwar today? Magic in the Marvel and DC universes provides a surprisingly apt metaphor for understating cyberwar. Here metaphor is not the instrument of poets; instead, "the essence of metaphor is understanding and experiencing one kind of thing in terms of another."[1] In other words, understanding the fictional magic of Marvel and DC can assist in understanding non-fictional cyberwar.

This chapter's title is from Thor, and it is important to understanding the nature of magic in Marvel. The quote is a tribute to Arthur C. Clarke, the author of *2001: A Space Odyssey*, and establishes the nature of magic in the Marvel Cinematic Universe (MCU). The head of Marvel Studios Kevin Feige explained this by recounting The Ancient One's early explanation of magic to novice Dr. Stephen Strange: "She goes, 'It's the same. It's the same thing, whether you're looking at an ancient study of acupuncture, pressure points or you're looking at an MRI.' She's trying to say we're talking about the same things here. If you're not comfortable with the word 'spells,' let's use the word 'program.' It's all the same thing."[2] As the Sorcerer Supreme in the comics, Dr. Strange once observed, "There is a distant relationship between the energies of science and those of sorcery, but my power over the former is limited." He added, "I can't make something out of nothing. Magic is basically a study of forces. Once one knows how to channel these forces, though, the results can be quite striking."[3] Like any aspect of storytelling, there must be "rules" to maintain the suspension of disbelief.

The "rules" or nature of Marvel magic are a bit complicated. There are three magical energies. Personal energies come from the spellcaster, which explains why using this kind of magic can exhaust anyone who employs too much for their skill level. Universal energies come from the spellcaster channeling magical energies from the environment around them. Dimensional energies, however, are a bit different in that spellcasters call upon extradimensional beings or objects. When Dr. Strange called upon "the Hosts of Hoggoth," he was using dimensional energies. Similarly, Dr. Strange's amulet is known as the Eye of Agamotto, as the "mysterious extradimensional entity Agamotto" empowered it. (As a side note, the comics treat this differently from the MCU, where the Time Stone powers Strange's amulet.) Additionally, there are challenges with using magic on intelligent machines, making a villain like Ultron a formidable foe for Dr. Strange.[4] Interestingly, this reveals a paradox between "science and magic as the same" and the two acting like proverbial oil and water.

Two other important aspects of the Marvel universe are dimensions and magical nexuses. Other dimensions can be very alien, as time, gravity, and any imaginable aspect may work differently. As an example, a Dr. Strange comic panel had villages on rock islands floating at crazy angles across a vast space with the written description: "Far across the dark dimension, in the very heart of the most populous region, tiny villages drift past one another in patterns which would surely drive an earth-born physicist mad."[5] In addition to other dimensions, Marvel has magical nexuses, such as Dr. Strange's Sanctum Sanctorum and sanctums in London and Hong Kong. What makes these places important is not the buildings but that they are on intersections of magical "ley lines" or "cosmic energy currents." These places are focal points of mystical energy that make using magic easier. In this way, these places add to the power of spellcasters and make opening interdimensional gates easier.

Astral projection is another aspect of magic that is useful to understand cyberwar. This ability allows the separation of the astral self—a person's spirit—from the physical body. The Ancient One demonstrated this when she introduced Dr. Strange to magic by knocking his astral self out of his body and sending him hurtling through a kaleidoscopic extradimensional tour. This ability was also on display when she drove Dr. Bruce Banner's astral self out of the body of Hulk in *Avengers: Endgame*. When someone is in astral form, they are invisible except to other magical beings. Similarly, combat between astral forms does not usually affect physical reality—only those in astral form normally know of the struggle.[6]

Like magic in the Marvel Universe, there is a relationship between magic and science in the DC Universe. For DC, "magic is a natural, primal force able to influence events and beings without recourse to the physical world. It consists of pieces of creations which can be harnessed from select practitioners."[7] Where Thor provided a nod to Arthur C. Clarke, Wonder Woman similarly said, "Magic is simply that which is not yet understood." Interestingly, she was replying to Cyborg's complaint, "And you wonder why I don't like magic?"[8] This exchange underscores the theme of the relationship between magic and science. It also raises the paradox of the challenge of magical characters and technological characters fighting due to the very different nature of their powers. The discussion occurs when Wonder Woman, Cyborg, and Superman are fighting the Enchantress, a magical villain, demonstrating that magic and supernatural foes challenge the "normal" members of the Justice League.

DC does have two well-known magical superheroes in Zatanna Zatara and the anti-hero John Constantine. Zatanna is both an accomplished stage magician and a real sorceress. Although not as powerful as Zatanna, John Constantine has similar magical skills. Constantine is an anti-hero who enjoys being anti-social and will do whatever is required to reach a goal. Both Zatanna and Constantine are among the most potent magicians on earth. In addition to having their own stories, Zatanna and Constantine are often part of DC's Justice League Dark (JLD), a branch whose primary role is to address magical and supernatural foes. The members of JLD often include Batman, Zatanna, Constantine, Jason Blood/Etrigan the Demon, Deadman, Black Orchid, and Swamp Thing. Each superhero has mystical powers except Batman, who is, well, Batman.[9] Not only did this team appear in the comics, but there was a 2017 *Justice League Dark* movie—one of the many superb DC Comics animated features. In this movie, an ancient sorcerer easily dealt with three "normal" members of the Justice League—Green Lantern, Wonder Woman, and Superman—but JLD won the day, underscoring the need for this branch of the Justice League.[10]

The JLD movie incorporates dimensions and magical nexuses. The House of Mystery, for example, has a long history in DC, and it most recently belonged to John Constantine. A powerful focal point for magic, the house simultaneously exists in Kentucky and another dimension. This dual existence allows the House of Mystery to appear and disappear at the whim of its owner, making it the perfect base. The house also created an avatar for itself called Black Orchid. Like the Sanctum Sanctorum, spellcasters in the House of Mystery often create gates to the many other dimensions in the DC Universe. As just one example of these dimensions, the "Other Place" is an ominous dimension described as "a Dark Multiverse realm that is the source of all dark magic" that was gifted "to the magicians of Earth in hopes that they would destroy themselves with it."[11]

The explanations of magic in the Marvel and DC universes lead back to the question of how they help build an understanding of cyberwar—and there is a need to understand cyberwar, as it is unlike other more familiar aspects of fighting on land, at sea, in the air, or even in space. A great place to start is with the late Professor Colin Gray, arguably the most important author on strategy for the last thirty years, who provided an excellent discussion on the topic in 2005.

Gray outlined eight features of cyber. Magic provides apt metaphor for Gray's first four features, aiding the understanding of cyber and cyberwarfare. Gray's first point was that "commerce rules," meaning that people primarily use cyber for business purposes and hardware and software are mainly civilian, not military. Magic is separated from other aspects of universes, yet it is ever-present in the background. Second, Gray argued that cyberwar was "bloodless warfare" when conducted in isolation in that cyberattacks can temporarily render animate objects inoperative. Magical attacks have had the same effect on things—and people—in the comics. Gray's third point was that "cyberwarfare is instant warfare" as it occurs at the speed of light—magic behaves similarly. Fourth, "cyberwarfare is global," as spatial location is meaningless. As long as the spellcaster and the affected area or person are in the same dimension, magic behaves the same way. Gray's fifth feature was "cyber power is accessible to all," as it is inexpensive compared to aerospace power, seapower, and landpower; thus, less wealthy nations and non-state actors can be significant players in cyberwar. In the comics, physically weak individuals are often the most powerful spellcasters; for example, The Ancient One is physically weak compared to the Hulk.[12]

Just as magic helps to understand Gray's first five features, magic assists with understanding his last three. His sixth feature is that "cyberwarfare is a joint team player or it is inconclusive." Gray's point is cyber has permeated every military service at every level, and an effective joint team must use all capabilities, including cyber, together to be successful. The comic magical corollary is that spellcasters are necessary and integral parts of superhero teams, such as Dr. Strange being a part of the Avengers, Defenders, and Illuminati. Gray's seventh feature is that "cyberspace and cyber power are lawless" as cyber is largely beyond regulation by international law, just as magical and supernatural entities are beyond any form of law, although there are generally observed norms. Finally, the eighth feature is that "cyberwarfare is warfare: Clausewitz rules!" Gray's point here is that cyber is changing the character of warfare—how wars are fought—not the nature of war, a violent extension of politics to coerce an adversary to act in a certain way that is a timeless and ugly part of the human condition. Entities like Dormammu or Destiny use magic to accumulate power, either directly or through coercion.[13]

Gray's features remain relevant, but cyber and cyberwarfare have evolved since 2005. Perhaps the most important event was the use of the first cyberweapon, which historians will likely point to as the 2010 Stuxnet cyberattack. Stuxnet was a highly complex malicious computer virus or worm whose use was the first known cyberattack to have produced a physical effect. This computer worm damaged Iranian nuclear centrifuges as a second-order effect, significantly setting back the Iranian nuclear enrichment program. Moreover, Stuxnet ushered in a new era of cyber conflict. For example, in 2012, two years after Stuxnet, non-state actors used the Shamoon virus in a destructive cyberattack on Saudi Aramco, the company that pumps ten percent of the global oil supply.[14] These two attacks are similar to magical attacks in both Marvel and DC—spells that attack suddenly from an anonymous source for unspecified reasons. In the fictional world of comics and the real world, someone or something may take responsibility, or the who and the why for the attack may remain unknown.

After Stuxnet and Shamoon, Peter Singer advanced the terminology and theoretical understanding of cyber in 2014. Singer defined cyberwar as having "parallels and connections in warfare in other domains … war always has a political goal and mode (which distinguishes it from crime) and always has an element of violence," adding, "the US government's position is that to meet this definition of the use of force, a cyberattack would to 'proximately result in death, injury or significant destruction.' That is, even if conducted through cyber means, the effect must be physical damage or destruction." Singer's definition clearly situated what cyberwarfare was and remains. However, here is an example where magic as metaphor is less clear. Spellcasters and non-magical characters cooperate to achieve objectives, such as the Avengers, especially Dr. Strange, cooperating to defeat Thanos. Yet, magic often directly causes death and destruction, unlike cyber, which can do so through second-order effects.

In addition to providing an excellent definition of cyberwar, Singer examined two other key points. First, he argued that one of the central problems is "whether cyberspace dominance is achievable and whether deterrence in cyberspace is workable in execution. Such posture requires knowing who your adversaries are, which is exceedingly difficult in cyberspace." Thus, cyber warfare is often waged instantly with no knowledge of where or from whom the attack originates. Singer's point underscored the still anonymous nature of cyberattacks, like the earlier Stuxnet and Shamoon attacks. Again, magical attacks can have the same lack of a known sender. Secondly, Singer reinforced Gray's point that many "believe that cyberspace is one of those strange places where the weak have an advantage over the strong," which is also true for magic, as The Ancient One demonstrated to Bruce Banner/The Hulk.[15]

In 2018 Singer added another work on cyber conflict. He updated his previous work and examined the weaponization of social media in *Like War*, which had become dramatically more influential after his 2014 book. One of the powerful examples of the weaponization of social media was Macedonian teenagers creating shoddy social media posts that generated advertising wealth through the number of clicks. To the authors, it mattered little if the stories were true, only that they got paid. Their stories resonated in "echo chambers" of like-minded people, who inadvertently built the momentum of falsehoods. The advent of bots—programs with repetitive tasks posing as people—further reinforced these untruths. Thus, the internet is a battlefield, and this battlefield changes how we think about information itself, as social media has intertwined war and politics to an unprecedented level. There are now countless invisible information battles happening all around us, altering our views.[16] In this, social media can be like an illusion performed by novice spellcasters and supported by the dimensional energies of Marvel's Loki or DC's

Destiny. Additionally, the invisible nature of these information battles is much like how astral magical combat is typically unknown to the physical world. Perhaps someday we will know if invisible cyber "battles" were occurring as part of the war in Ukraine, but for now, only the Shadow knows.

The cyber system itself provides a final metaphor for cyber and magic, as the system requires a global fiber-optic and satellite network to function, and any system has vulnerabilities. Today's cyber system is not unlike the nineteenth- and twentieth-century system of submarine telegraph cables. Users of the submarine cables feared other nations were using the system for intelligence or potentially creating false messages. For example, Great Britain enjoyed a near monopoly on the submarine cable network, and it exploited the system for intelligence and other purposes. Similarly, the cyber physical system is also vulnerable, as the fictional Chinese demonstrated in the recent novel *2034*. The Chinese attacked satellites and nexus points of fiber-optic undersea cables, like attacking magical nexuses such as Dr. Strange's Sanctum Sanctorum or John Constantine's House of Mystery.

Understanding cyberwarfare is challenging, and magic in the Marvel and DC universes provides metaphors to assist us wrestling with warfighting in the cyber domain. Perhaps the most valuable thing is that magic can help us understand the nature of cyberwarfare can be anonymous, instantaneous, intangible, and unrelated to physical position. In fact, not only is magic in comic books a good metaphor for cyberwar, but it is also the only helpful metaphor I have found. Other metaphors are welcome to help understand cyberwarfare, as this form of conflict is now a permanent part of warfare.

Notes

1   George Lakoff and Mark Johnson, *Metaphors We Live By* (Chicago: University of Chicago Press, 1980), 5.

2   Comicbook, "Doctor Strange: Kevin Feige Explains How Science & Magic Mesh," https://comicbook.com/marvel/news/doctor-strange-kevin-feige-explains-how-science-magic-mesh/; and *Discover: The Magazine*, "Thor Pays Tribute to Arthur C. Clarke's Rule About Magic and Technology," https://www.discovermagazine.com/mind/thor-pays-tribute-to-arthur-c-clarkes-rule-about-magic-and-technology.

3   Kim Eastland, *Realms of Magic, Book 2* (Lake Geneva, WI: TSR, Inc., 1986), 2 and 5.

4   Eastland, *Book 1*, 3; and *Book 2*, 5, 18, 25, and 31.

5   Eastland, *Book 2*, 6.

6   Eastland, *Book 1*, 16 and 34.

7   DC Database, "Magic," https://dc.fandom.com/wiki/Magic.

8   DC Database, "Enchantress," https://dc.fandom.com/wiki/Enchantress_(Prime_Earth)/Gallery?file=Pandora_Justice_League_Dark_001.jpg.

9   DC Database, "Zatanna Zatara," https://dc.fandom.com/wiki/Zatanna_Zatara_(New_Earth); "John Constantine," accessed April 9, 2022, https://dc.fandom.com/wiki/John_Constantine_(Prime_Earth); and "Justice League Dark," accessed April 3, 2022, https://dc.fandom.com/wiki/Justice_League_Dark_(Prime_Earth).

10   DC, "Justice League Dark—'Are You Talking About Magic?'" https://www.dccomics.com/videos/justice-league-dark-are-you-talking-about-magic; IMDb, "Justice League Dark," https://www.imdb.com/title/tt2494376/; and Rotten Tomatoes, "Justice League Dark," https://www.rottentomatoes.com/m/justice_league_dark.

11   DC Database, "The House of Mystery," https://en.wikipedia.org/wiki/House_of_Mystery#The_House; and "Other Place," https://dc.fandom.com/wiki/Other_Place.

12   Colin S. Gray, *Another Bloody Century: Future Warfare* (Weidenfeld & Nicolson: London, 2005), 291–294 and 322–330.

13   Ibid.

14   Fred Kaplan, *Dark Territory: The Secret History of Cyber War* (New York: Simon & Schuster, 2014), 203–220; and Peter W. Singer and Allan Friedman, *Cybersecurity and Cyberwar: What Everyone Needs to Know* (New York: Oxford University Press, 2014), 114–120.

15   Singer and Friedman, 121, 136, 151.

16   Peter W. Singer and Emerson T. Brooking, *Like War: The Weaponization of Social Media* (New York: Mariner Books, 2018), 118–147, 261–262.

CHAPTER 27

Where Does He Get All Those Wonderful Toys?

Technology, Innovation, and *The Hunger Games*

Candice E. Frost

Technology, often viewed in terms of an apocalyptic struggle through the lens of science fiction, can also provide glimpses into opportunities not readily available in the present. When seen through rose-colored glasses, even fiction demonstrating the darkest components of humanity can shed a ray of light toward brighter days. It creates chances for renewal and revelations through innovative leadership. The process of such transformation is addressed through the creation, testing, and refining of an innovation pipeline.[1] An example of such a development is presented in the science fiction trilogy of books by Suzanne Collins: *The Hunger Games* (2008), *Catching Fire* (2009), and *Mockingjay* (2010). In these books, there is a clear demonstration of how organizations' needs are met, and missions achieved. Approaching the process through problem definition, discovering opportunities, creating operational concepts, developing prototypes, and arriving to a solution exists throughout the entirety of the heroine's journey in the *Hunger Games* trilogy. The iterative and innovative approach are clearly presented to the reader. The narrative creates imaginative and innovative tactics to survival like how superheroes survive in their journeys.

Katniss is not a traditional superhero, but she shares many similarities with those characters. Like Batman, Black Widow, and Green Arrow, she possesses no superhuman abilities. She instead relies on her intelligence, experience and specialized training, including her immense skill with a bow and arrow, to navigate conflict. Like Iron Man and Falcon, she is also aided by advanced technologies at times. Her origin story thrusts her into scenarios that hone her skills and challenges her with difficult decisions. At the onset, the theme of the "Hunger Games" rests in its title. The dystopian work combines the problems of haves and have nots within the spectrum of technology, government, and economic imbalances. The problem with the organizational construct in the fictional country of Panem, in North America, demonstrates how hunger itself, in a modern society, exists. While some portions of the society rapidly innovate, others are left behind. The heroine of the story is sixteen-year-old Katniss Everdeen, who volunteers to take the place of her sister in the Hunger Games event, where one boy and one girl from each of the twelve districts is selected by lottery to compete in a televised battle royale to the death.[2]

The Capitol exercises political control over the rest of the nation comparable to Batman's Gotham City and Superman's Metropolis. The annual Hunger Games requires selected "tributes" to participate in a contest where they fight to the death in an outdoor arena until only one contestant remains alive. Their survival makes them the victor and a celebrated hero. Katniss becomes aware of the injustices and evils in her society where reluctantly she begins to fight against them, first on a personal scale and later for the benefit of all. As her journey continues, Katniss goes from an individual to a symbol in a larger movement. Like Captain America in the Marvel Cinematic Universe, she is forced to consider her willingness to serve as an exemplar or instrument for a cause greater than herself all while dealing with the unforeseen results of actions taken with the best of intentions.

Problem

From the onset of the games, an apocalyptic problem exists for survival. Understanding the source of the problem provides opportunities through innovation. As often seen in both superhero legends and science fiction, the Hunger Games is not different; survival is key to the entire story. This constructive design process allows viewers to travel along the path from the current, into the past, and on toward an unknown future. For instance, the Capitol in the plutocracy Panem is a technologically advanced metropolis. As it stands atop the other twelve poorer districts, there is a demonstrable difference in its citizens' way of life. There are clear differences in the well-being and lifestyle in the Capitol because access to advanced science and engineering is offered only to Capitol citizenry. The heroine understands and clearly sees the problem of the districts' lack of progress when compared to the Capitol. A simple example of the differences in technological progress comes when Katniss mentions that her home, in District 12, is lucky to get more than a few hours of electricity in the evening.[3] Akin to how Peter Parker, also known as Spider-Man, grew up poor being raised by his aunt and uncle.

Aside from a lack of distributed technology exists the problem with inequitable development. Each district is responsible for a different sector of Panem's economy. Combined, they keep their world habitable. The technologically dominant area, District 3, has citizens highly adept at engineering and has factories that manufacture computers and electronics. Outside of the capital city, District 13 exists as the most technologically advanced area but remains cut off from the remaining districts because of a non-aggression pact signed with the Capitol. Therefore, they are unable to share their technology with other districts.[4] Although solutions exist for distribution of technology there are impediments due to the construct and nature of the societal, economic, and governmental structure of Panem.

The heroine works within the societal constructs. She demonstrates a creative approach and clear mindset to develop technically advanced solutions. Within the game itself, Katniss understands that survival requires an innovative and rebellious approach. The awareness of the government's attempt to control the population is acknowledged by both those close to her in the Hunger Games and herself. Recognition of the problem is simply the first step. Katniss requires use of all her personal attributes to not only succeed but also to live. From the beginning, her selflessness—she volunteered to not only save her sister's life but also to represent her district—is one of her strengths. In the process of innovation, Katniss requires more than just personal attributes to create lasting change. Katniss also applies innovation to strategically solve the problem of survival. She solves immediate problems during the games through her foresight to best master and control the most promising approaches to survive. In this manner she uses her excellent skills as an archer, like Green Arrow, to survive.

Prioritization of Katniss' approaches in the context of her journey through the science fiction challenge and context of the Hunger Games demonstrates how innovation increasingly applies when set against the anticipatory, futuristic, and even prophetic dimensions of Panem.[5] The strategic discourse amongst the players and their overseers is outlined in the order and interaction between the heroine and her unique challenges, created by power brokers.[6] In the Hunger Games, Katniss, with her partner Peeta, stands up against the game's overseers. This leadership team dynamically works to place obstacles of increasing complexity in the way of Katniss and Peeta's success. Their adaptability to the evolving situations results in a type of entrapment for the power brokers who are positioned to choose between having both Katniss and Peeta survive together or watching them willingly commit suicide, possibly mirroring a Romeo and Juliet ending.

Katniss demonstrates activities indicative of psychologist Abraham Maslow's hierarchy of needs based on her own fulfillment and change through personal growth. She begins the hierarchy journey by satisfying biological and physiological needs exemplified by securing food and clothing. She moves next to personal safety as she creates protection from the elements and freedom from fear. Then she experiences love and belongingness through friendships and partnerships that are formed inside of the Hunger Games. She finds acceptances and value by others for her achievements. As she realizes her personal potential and self-actualizes, it becomes clear in the Hunger Games that her values transcend beyond the personal to help others.[7] As the narrative awakens the viewer's or reader's sense of clear lines of right and wrong, the heroine works to innovate.[8] Katniss champions the opposed citizens, while fighting with them against their own government. She covers villains and victims, while other superheroes only choose one.[9] From her position as a heroine she pushes others into action.

Operating Concepts

Moving from surviving to thriving occurs as the heroine finds solutions. New operating concepts, discovered during the determinative start of the Hunger Games, proved critical for survival. Solutions were developed due to the creativity, resolve, and innovativeness of Katniss and her group. For instance, the demonstration of tenacity, knowledge, and determination are evident through a group member's statement that, "we can manage without food for a while, but in this heat we really need water."[10] This clear movement along Maslow's hierarchy of needs also demonstrates, at the survival stage, that there remain key problems to solve. As the narrative develops further in *The Hunger Games*, Katniss cuts down a nest containing a lethal type of insect, Tracker Jackers, which allows her to depart her hiding spot atop a tree and again survive the game. This innovative use of knowledge creates a lethal weapon through tools available to the heroine. As Katniss moves up the hierarchy of needs, the group evidences greater innovative traits. For instance, Katniss's partner Peeta camouflaged himself into the environment by blending into the rocks for his survival.[11] Concepts of creative innovation allowed the heroine and her partner to use their minds and imagination to go from enduring to flourishing. Superheroes who similarly demonstrate this ability are those who lack superpowers. Examples, of Batman, Iron Man, and Black Widow make up for their lack of superpower with the aide of technology, cunningness, and developed skills.[12] Throughout the journey, Katniss, often unwillingly, is thrust into positions of leadership. She is placed into positions where she must extrapolate her concepts to innovate, amongst an ever changing and growing environment of conflict, to leading others. Her followers often place her into positions where she is required to sacrifice her ideals to meet the desires of others. Katniss dances around the operational concept of doing what is required at the time, while also staying true to herself. Katniss sticks to her guns and brings others, especially her followers, to where she stands as a leader.[13] Although she does not have a superhero secret identity, she does have some duality: she performs in front of cameras, and also keeps her true self hidden.[14]

As the innovation process moves forward and concepts are created to expand the vision of Katniss and her followers, she works to create change. At times, an almost forced leadership is a bitter pill for Katniss. The more others try to turn her into a figurehead, the less natural it becomes. In one notable event, her mentor asks followers to recall a time when Katniss inspired them. They admit that they were moved most when she existed as her authentic self, when no one was telling her what to do. This changed the concept of how Katniss used her vision and leadership to inspire others, resulting in the heroine filming videos amongst the wreckage of bombed districts, in an area of increased danger, rather than simulating them from their headquarters. The interplay of using an innovative approach through technology in her broadcasting of a strategic message and vision creates a genuineness in her leading, similar to the genuine nature of how Wonder Woman leads. As Katniss demonstrates her leadership, from a place of authenticity, it is a significantly more effective message because it was delivered directly from the heart.[15]

Prototypes

Throughout the science fiction narrative of *The Hunger Games*, solutions to the social, cultural, and economic problems of the strict hierarchy set forth by the social constructs of Panem are challenged with the incubation factory of solutions amongst the rebels. The initial flat structure—with weak boundaries—between organizations places a low emphasis on hierarchy.[16] As the organization grows with Katniss' leadership, additional contributors further the cause and innovate. Group collaboration incubates greater solutions, and by selecting appropriate allies to partner with Katniss, creates matches with people who have different strengths than she does. This team combines to build survival strategies. During the Hunger Games, Katniss chooses Rue, a tiny wisp of a girl, with non-strength-based talents: a perfect match for Katniss' own strengths.[17] Rue helps Katniss survive during the most challenging time during the first round she experiences in the Hunger Games. Later in the series, Katniss further grows this skill of capturing ideas and incubating them as a key feature of the rebel organization. Here she gathers with others to collectively promote creativity and collaborative thought.[18] The team bonding together through several crucible-type events generates greater support for their efforts.

Although the community behind Katniss demonstrably supports her, there is a larger community and culture Katniss must fight against to create lasting transformation of her environment. Despite the technological innovation in the capital city and one isolated district, citizens fail to pursue the struggle to challenge the norm. The culture itself existed in a quagmire of a power struggle that failed to encourage organizations to adapt to new ideas. The existing hierarchies and egos of the leaders created barriers for those with power to protect their grip on power. The lack of innovative approaches to economic, social, and political changes failed to adjust until a change agent steps forward. This prevention of the surfacing of ideas stagnates until the heroine steps forward. Katniss, as she is put through a "keyhole" experience, demonstrates her ability to adapt, overcome, and achieve success.[19] She is squeezed, pushed around, tested, denied access and, in the process, becomes tougher and more durable. Like prototyping, her ideas survive largely because of the resilience and passion of the innovator.[20] As her scope of leadership grew, so did her ability to innovate, encourage others, and inspire a desire in others to continue to work towards a larger goal. Due to her resilience and ability to motivate others, she survives against a culture unwilling to support change.

Katniss' impact takes time to grow, similar to the complication of solutions in any innovative space. As an immediate solution would make for a dull read, *The Hunger Games* series allows for readers to understand complications and see exemplified prototyping in action. Although Katniss serves as the literary focal point, she does not rapidly fix the entire environment akin to how the Avengers, led by Captain America, fight crime. As well, her enemies are not as fantastical as the villains encountered in comic books. Although, in *The Hunger Games*, some have modified their bodies for aesthetic or functional purposes, undergoing plastic surgery to resemble a cat or sharpening their teeth into lethal fangs. The storyline witnesses a maturity of prototyping solutions of the environment around her. This allows for collective action (with other key characters) requiring change. For instance, Katniss' partnered relationships vacillate between Gale and Peeta. Whereas this makes for a great romantic twist to the story, it also shows that the leaders working in an innovation pipeline come up with their best results when partnered with the right person. Throughout this process, the heroine grows in her own relationships, which seep into her actions as a leader. As evidenced in Katniss' actions, she moves away from leading as an angry rebel to that of a transformational leader.[21]

Solution

Throughout the heroine's journey there exist periods of trials, tribulations, and eventually a successful conclusion. Like the innovation process, a transition into the solution space exists. The evolution in Katniss's character moves her from an individual surviving to a team member, a small group leader, and finally an unwilling but accepting leader placed into the position of the face of the movement.[22] Collectively, she leads a revolution with a solution to overturn a tyrannical government successfully because of her ability to innovate. She reached this solution through leadership that understood the risk of remaining in an unchanged environment was untenable. Similar to how many superheroes protect those weaker than themselves, Katniss takes on the mantle of leadership.

From the beginning of the series, the creation of the Hunger Games came about to both provide entertainment for the Capitol and as a reminder to subordinate districts that the Capitol held all power. The games emphasized a clear message that their lack of remorse or forgiveness for the failed rebellion of the current competitors' ancestors would continue to occur for generations, randomly killing the offspring of the losers.[23] Throughout the trilogy, the themes of "haves" and "have nots" and their ruling by an elite class, backed by police forces, clearly speaks to why Katniss' revolutionary solution against the governing worked against the tyrannical rulers in Panem. The solution against the distrustful authoritative figures, through organized innovation and action by mass revolution, economic sabotage, and a populist fight against the oligarchy resulted in a victory for Katniss.[24] She is cast as a rebel: she struggles to navigate between this and not becoming a puppet of the Capitol, just as Batman uses the dark paths against the criminals of Gotham.[25] In the end, she worked to ensure the vicious Hunger Games never happened again.

The nexus of the solutions applied by Katniss and those of many superheroes comes in the moral decisions faced during the journey. In the good verse evil or right and wrong landscape set forward in both the science fiction world of Panem or that of Gotham City or Metropolis the heroine often achieves success but at a great personal cost. This is clearly witnessed during the entirety of Katniss' attempt to innovate throughout her journey. Solutions in *The Hunger Games* are reflective of so many similar lessons learned by superheroes; where bad deeds never go unpunished and that one person can make a difference. As Katniss represented the very essence of justice in her society, so too does an entire league of justice seekers like Batman, Superman, the Flash, the Atom, and other DC comic superheroes.

The Hunger Games provide a litany of examples as to why the innovative process for change creates opportunities. Throughout the battles against those in positions of power, Katniss creates opportunities for change through her movement across an innovation pipeline. She clearly understood defining the problems, discovered opportunities, created operational concepts, developed multiple prototypes, and arrived at a solution to meet the future structure of the newly created social, economic, and governmental landscape in Panem. *The Hunger Games* launched a science fiction trilogy that explores innovative approaches to both technological changes and to the leaders who implement this change. Glimpses into the opportunities that exist when individuals challenge the norm are clearly a part of the heroine's journey, where Katniss meets success through both her approaches to change and through her own leadership journey.

Notes

1   Sabre Horne, *The Innovation Pipeline* (Palo Alto: BMNT Inc., 2022), 28. This work outlines the innovation pipeline process.

2   The Hunger Games (novel) https://en.wikipedia.org/wiki/The_Hunger_Games_(novel).

3   The Hunger Games Wiki, "Technology," https://thehungergames.fandom.com/wiki/Technology.

4   Ibid.

5   Thomas Michaud, editor, *Science Fiction and Innovation Design* (Hoboken, New Jersey: ISTE Ltd and John Wiley & Sons, Inc., 2020), i.

6   Ibid.

7   Saul McLeod, "Maslow's Hierarchy of Needs," published 2007, updated April 04, 2022 https://www.simplypsychology.org/maslow.html.

8   Charley Locke, "The Real Reason Dystopian Fiction Is Roaring Back," *WIRED* (February 22, 2017). https://www.wired.com/2017/02/dystopian-fiction-why-we-read/.

9   Chris Gavaler, "Is Katniss Everdeen a Superhero?" https://www.hoodedutilitarian.com/2015/11/is-katniss-everdeen-a-superhero/.

10 Peter Dry, "Hunger Games and Ubuntu: Which is the Ultimate Innovation Culture?" (2017) http://simunyeprojectus.org/2018/01/23/hunger-games-and-ubuntu-which-is-the-ultimate-innovation-culture/, 68.

11 Peter Dry, "Hunger Games and Ubuntu: Which is the Ultimate Innovation Culture?" (2017) http://simunyeprojectus.org/2018/01/23/hunger-games-and-ubuntu-which-is-the-ultimate-innovation-culture/.

12 Gavaler.

13 Zoe Henry, "What You Can Learn from Katniss Everdeen's Fearless Leadership Style?" *Inc.* (November 24, 2014), https://www.inc.com/zoe-henry/leadership-lessons-from-katniss-everdeen.html.

14 Gavaler.

15 Henry.

16 Dry, 68.

17 Cristina Hartmann, "What, If Anything, Does The Hunger Games Series Teach Us About Strategy?" *Forbes* (Oct 21, 2011), https://www.forbes.com/sites/quora/2011/10/21/what-if-anything-does-the-hunger-games-series-teach-us-about-strategy/.

18 Dry, 68.

19 Keyhole experience is defined as one where the individual must pass through an exceptionally uncomfortable transformational experience to result in success on the other side. Similar to a chrysalis, this metamorphosis creates dramatic change after the experience.

20 Dry, 68.

21 Bloom.

22 Zoe Henry, "What You Can Learn from Katniss Everdeen's Fearless Leadership Style?" *Inc.* (November 24, 2014), https://www.inc.com/zoe-henry/leadership-lessons-from-katniss-everdeen.html.

23 The Hunger Games (novel) https://en.wikipedia.org/wiki/The_Hunger_Games_(novel).

24 Bloom.

25 Gavaler.

CHAPTER 28

To the Warrior, Their Arms

Mick Cook

Tony Stark's greatest quality is not that he is Iron Man, it is his remarkable ability to accelerate technology research and development (R&D). Unlike today's technology companies, Stark does not need a multidisciplinary team of university professors, engineers, military advisors, and business executives to create new technology. Instead, Stark does it all from his Malibu basement laboratory. He even conducts the field trials himself, though this tends to occur in public urban areas and is not generally considered a suitable environment for new capability testing. Humor aside, the *Iron Man* film trilogy provides audiences with a rare and somewhat informative glimpse into the sometimes-shadowy world of technology R&D and commercialization for military capabilities.

The trilogy uses the archetype of military capability R&D as a core plot device. All three films address the process of fundamental research, academia-industry collaboration, government requirements determination, and technology commercialization. Like other films in the Marvel Cinematic Universe (MCU), the *Iron Man* films use the relationship between the military and technology development as a central element of the story arc. Stark develops technology to protect humanity, whereas the villains develop technology to achieve profit, power, prestige, and—in most cases—payback. The result is a moral ambiguity about the sale and use of military technology that conflates technology development with the human flaws of greed and vanity while pointing to a brighter future through engagement with new technology.

The *Iron Man* trilogy portrays brilliant minds developing technology at speeds faster than Stark outpacing a pair of F-22s over Central Asia. After all, they are superhero movies, and viewers expect the filmmakers to take liberties with what is—and is not—possible. The trilogy presents a caricature of the technology R&D process, including the commercial elements. This caricature blends the possible and the impossible, including a brief glance into the realities of business development, market analysis, and strategic positioning of business priorities against customer requirements. Superhero films often show technology as a battlefield game-changer, but the trilogy offers a fictional exposé on the business of R&D, especially in relation to military technology.

There Was an Idea

When it comes to military technology, a company's commercial goal usually involves a government purchasing the technology and ordering large-scale production for its armed forces. However, businesses need to follow a set process to ensure R&D provides an operational capability that is commercially viable. As a result, technology is developed on a continuum defined by nine technology readiness levels (TRLs). The continuum is designed to track a technology from fundamental concept through the prototyping phase to commercial viability. Often the research organization, the industry partner, and the government collaborate during the earliest stages of the research to ensure R&D addresses end-user capability requirements.

Capability requirements, outlined by the government on behalf of their military forces, are vital to ensuring that the technology is commercially viable and will meet the needs of the end-user. Unfortunately, the importance of end-user inputs at the beginning of the R&D process is often missed in the *Iron Man* movies. In the first and third films, the brilliant researcher—typically a captain of industry such as Stark—develops a technology without consulting the end-user, yet somehow manages to create something perfectly suited to the military's needs.

These movies may have a few omissions that reduce the complexity of technology R&D, but they still provide a sound basis for exploring the fundamental elements of the process. Although the trilogy touches on the scientific method from fundamental concept to operational capability, it also provides—to a limited degree—insights into the commercial outputs and capability requirements at the heart of the military-industrial relationship.

Sometimes You Gotta Run Before You Can Walk

The first *Iron Man* film opens with Stark demonstrating a new weapons technology—the Jericho missile system—developed for the United States military. During his return from the demonstration site—conveniently located in an active combat zone—Stark's military convoy is ambushed and the "genius, billionaire, playboy, philanthropist" kidnapped. In a timely piece of foreshadowing, he is nearly killed by a Stark Industries mortar round, underscoring the significant market share Stark holds in the military technology sector—particularly in terms of its primary customer, the U.S. Department of Defense.

Real-world examples of companies such as Stark Industries, known as "defense primes," include industry heavyweights such as Lockheed Martin, Raytheon, and Boeing. Many defense primes grew from companies that benefited from the technology boom resulting from the Second World War. While some primes predate the war, their growth into global industrial superpowers was driven by the competition of the Cold War. The characterization of the family patriarch, Howard Stark, and the empire he founded is one way the *Iron Man* trilogy acknowledges the role of the Cold War and its subsequent impact on the military-industrial complex. Stark Industries is a modern prime dominating the military technology sector, with the elder Stark fulfilling the role of progenitor of the modern techno-industrialist.

At the beginning of *Iron Man*, Howard Stark's legacy—his company and son—fundamentally transforms during Tony Stark's imprisonment in the terrorist cave complex. During his internment, Stark's captors force him to develop a weapon salvaged from parts of other Stark Industry munitions. As he toils in his subterranean prison cell, he becomes increasingly aware of the proliferation of his company's weapons technology, and his conscience bears the burden of the consequences of that proliferation. Determined to escape so that he can make amends for his war profiteering, the suave savant deceives the terrorists and develops the prototype of the Iron Man armor with the help of a local physicist, Yinsen, who is also being held captive.

The development of the Mark I (MkI) armor by Stark and Yinsen is an ideal origin story for Iron Man, a technological feat that could only exist in a superhero film. The prototype development montage portrays complex schematics, remarkable feats of engineering, and the cannibalization of advanced military technology, providing just enough reality to make the viewer believe the arc reactor technology that powers the armor could be replicated in a remote desert cave infested with terrorists. Stark is successful in both developing the MkI armor and escaping his captors.

The R&D process from the cave sequence is echoed when Stark returns to his Malibu estate and creates the MkII armor. However, this time around Stark has cutting-edge equipment in the lab, including the Artificial Intelligence assistant J.A.R.V.I.S.—short for "Just A Rather Very Intelligent System"—replacing Yinsen, who was killed while helping Stark escape. The development of the second-generation armor in the Malibu lab is similar in many respects to the cave scene. This is crucial to the character development of the reformed Stark, who seeks to redeem himself as a former war profiteer. The cave and Malibu scenes are essential to the film's plot but miss the mark on how new technology is researched and developed. That's where Stark's former mentor, the megalomaniac Obadiah Stane, enters the picture.

Stane is the perfect villain, willing to go to any lengths in his quest for power and profit, including selling weapons to terrorists, attempting to have Stark killed—several times, in fact—and unleashing a new weapon on a city crowded with innocent civilians. Despite his obvious character flaws, Stane proves to be an excellent teacher on the subject of modern technology R&D. Brilliantly played by Jeff Bridges, Stane opens a window into how defense primes conduct the later stages of technology research development when he tasks a team of engineers to miniaturize the arc reactor technology used to power the Iron Man armor. Stane may have been motivated by greed, but his application of the development process was sound.

Viable military capabilities are developed by teams of researchers and engineers, not individual geniuses. The failure of the engineers to achieve the goal Stane assigned to them is a consequence of plot requirements rather than a flaw in his methods. Stane knew that a stable, replicable technology that would power his version of Iron Man armor would best be developed by a multidisciplinary team—a group of intelligent and diligent individuals exploring the possibilities at the bleeding edge of technology development.

This Is the Key to the Future

Such groups looking to change the world through the R&D of new technology are why events such as the Stark Expo from *Iron Man 2*—the superhero film version of the start-up incubator or military technology trade show—exist. Rather than promote military capability development, Stark's motivation for reinvigorating the Stark Expo is primarily to divert intellectual capital toward other applications for new technology. As explained by Stark himself at the start of the film, Stark Expo is supposed to be a beacon of hope for R&D of technology that ultimately improves people's lives. Enter Justin Hammer.

Hammer is a B-Grade Tony Stark. He lacks Stark's charm, intellect, and moral purpose. His desire to compete with Stark leads him to seek the support of the film's central villain, Ivan Vanko. After springing Vanko from a foreign prison, Hammer enlists his technological genius to overhaul the latest Hammer Industries product—a poor man's clone of the Iron Man armor—for an unveiling at Stark Expo. Although the presentation of the Hammer drones seems contradictory to Stark's intent for the exposition, the choice of the exposition for the showdown is important, both for the plot and the audience's understanding of the military technology industry. Technology expositions are exciting events that optimistically point toward a bright future. Military technology expositions, incubators, and conferences are critical events in the calendars of researchers, industry representatives, and government employees. These events are vital in providing insights on commercially available technology and opportunities for networking and relationship building with a mind toward collaboration on future technology development.

One of the misconceptions drawn from events such as the Stark Expo is the perceived maturity of the technology on display. It is not always clear whether a particular technology is being pitched as an operationally ready capability—commercial-off-the-shelf (COTS) or military-off-the-shelf (MOTS)—or whether it is an aspirational prototype needing further development and testing. Exposition floors are often replete with both. This range exists because events like the Stark Expo are designed to encourage investment in emerging technology development, create new opportunities for collaboration, and announce recent acquisition decisions and contract awards. Hammer's desperate push to field the immature drone technology in hopes of spurring military investment underscores the risk inherent in entering mass production before achieving fully operational capability.

In reality, defense primes do not begin mass production of a capability until a contract has been awarded and the system is approved for integration into the military. Defense primes need to stay in business. Therefore, they seek to avoid Hammer's error of mass production before a contract is awarded; however, this also creates a production shortage when demand increases. A balance between the pressures of the business world and the requirements of the military end-user must be found. Regular engagement between academia, industry, and government can help. One such meeting between Hammer and Stark's ally Lieutenant Colonel James Rhodes provides an insight into how this balance can be achieved.

Hammer and Rhodes are forced to collaborate when Rhodes gains possession of the MkII armor, which they reimagine as the War Machine. The United States Government, wary of Stark, directs Rhodes to work with Hammer to upgrade the weaponry in the MkII armor. In an early scene in *Iron Man 2*, Hammer provides Rhodes with a veritable shopping list of weapons technologies he could integrate into the armor. Rhodes listens to the available technologies and then directs which ones should be included in the upgrade. This short scene highlights a much deeper level of engagement between industry and government when developing military technology. From the industry perspective, it needs to design technology that is a viable market offering; therefore, engagement with the potential customer in the design process is critical.

On the other hand, the government, including the military, needs capabilities that enable it to conduct operations in a specific way, knowing that each new capability must be able to integrate with existing processes and technologies with minimal disruption. The definition of user requirements is vital; the defense industry and government engagement on the types of technology available to inform the user requirements must be based on knowledge of the latest advances in science and engineering. Academia, universities, and other research organizations are the institutions that house the intellectual capacity to address the most challenging aspects of technology R&D: turning a concept into a prototype.

Everybody Needs a Hobby

Iron Man 3 highlights how industry and academia collaborate to move technology from a fundamental concept to an operational capability. The collaboration between the film's principal antagonist, Aldrich Killian, and Stark's former flame, Maya Hansen, demonstrates how industry and academia work together to achieve technological maturity. After Stark rebuffs his business proposal, Killian—another villain of the rogue-genius trope—convinces Hansen to work with him to develop new human performance enhancement technology. The results of their collaboration, however, was not for the benefit of mankind: Killian operationalizes Hansen's research to realize his quest for power and revenge. Despite this plot turn, the characterization of the relationship between the industrialist and the academic researcher is instructive, demonstrating how technology moves from concept to capability to commercial availability.

As noted previously, the progress of the development of a particular technology is tracked through the TRL continuum, which maps a technology from fundamental concept through commercial availability. There are nine stages on the continuum, ranging from TRL 1 (representing where fundamental principles are initially formulated) to TRL 6 (system prototype) to TRL 9 (fully operational and commercially viable). Focusing on these three levels is instructive, as they each highlight a pivotal point in military capability development where the roles of academia, industry, and government are significant.

Academia is often at the forefront of technology development. The MCU is replete with characters with some form of science-based doctorate firmly attached to their intellectual utility belts. The premise of the terminal degree is an ability to infuse revolutionary new knowledge into a field of research. Academics, often driven by a curiosity for what is possible, will start with basic level research (TRL 1) and, depending on their field, move a technology through to the prototype stage (TRL 6) before engaging with a commercial partner to support further development. Often, multidisciplinary teams are involved in academic research, with individuals providing different levels of expertise in theoretical and applied research.

Defense primes have limited resources for fundamental R&D. By building relationships with individual academics, teams, or universities, an industry partner can reduce the cost of future technology development without limiting the opportunity for a new commercial product or service. Often, a workable prototype provides the industry with a clear indication of whether an investment in a particular technology will meet its commercial objectives. This does not mean that the industry does not engage with academia prior to the TRL 6 stage; in fact, industry will often engage with academia at different points along the TRL continuum, depending on the technology potential, commercial opportunities, and funding source.

However, activities between TRLs 6 and 9 are the primary domain of the industry partner and their technology development teams. The industry partner will often lead in developing the intellectual property created through the prototype into a commercially viable product or service. The industry partner will also lead in marketing the product or service to the potential customers; in a military technology context, this would be the government and its military. Finally, once TRL 9 is achieved and a contract is awarded, the industry partner will enter into systems integration for the customer and mass production.

Based on the portrayal of military technology acquisition in the *Iron Man* trilogy, it would be easy for the average person to believe that governments wait for industry to pitch a desired capability and then hands over buckets of cash. In practice, the "see-want-buy" process of military capability is quite rare and generally occurs only when a COTS or MOTS product has been proven elsewhere by other customers. Most military capability development is done in partnership, with the government entering the development phase early along the TRL continuum to advise on user requirements and provide funding to ensure that when a particular technology reaches TRL 9, it is fit for its intended purpose.

The House Party Protocol

The University Consortium on Advanced Hypersonics (UCAH) is an example of an academia, industry, and government collaboration to realize a technological capability. The UCAH is a United States-based initiative that involves researchers and industry partners from around the world, unifying them with the primary purpose of furthering innovation and workforce requirements for advanced hypersonic flight for application in the defense sector.[1] In terms of scope, its membership comprises over 100 universities, close to 150 industry partners, and 16 affiliated research centers. Research into advanced hypersonic flight has continued for decades, and the UCAH is only one example of the intellectual capital invested in this military technology development field. The consortium has over 260 institutions working toward realizing one of the most significant military technologies of the modern era—quite a contrast compared to the image of Stark and Yinsen working away in a cave.

The Australian Trailblazer Universities Program is the second example that highlights the scale of collaboration between academia, industry, and government in developing technology for the military. This program, designed by the Australian Department of Education, provided up to $50 million in funding for collaborative teams led by academic institutions with industry partners.[2] The competitive bidding process required academic institutions and industry partners to match the amount of funding sought from the government and demonstrate how the technology developed would benefit Australian society. The Department of Education was specific on the technological themes in which it sought to establish programs and urged all bids to clearly articulate the economic and social benefits of the proposed technology R&D programs. Bids that focused on the Defense theme were also required to demonstrate the dual-purpose potential of their R&D program.

A defense-focused bid led by the University of Adelaide and the University of New South Wales successfully brought together over 50 industry partners and secured significant government funding.[3] This bid, known as the "Defence Trailblazer— Concept to Sovereign Capability," is the most extensive academia/industry-led program of its type in Australia. Enabled by a government investment of AUD 250 million, the effort focuses on military technology development and workforce uplift and is expected to yield a return on investment four times that for the Australian economy. Defence Trailblazer is another example of the scale of funding and intellectual capital needed to realize the potential of military technology R&D. Something unachievable in a secluded basement or home garage, even if it is in Malibu.

The *Iron Man* trilogy provides a good caricature of real-world R&D. However, for narrative purposes, the films cannot offer a complete picture of the complexity of technology development, particularly as it relates to military capabilities. Nevertheless, the characterization of the relationships between academia, industry, and the military is close enough to reality to provide meaningful lessons for audiences on the realities of technological collaboration. The scale of such collaboration is, ironically, understated in terms of the amount of intellectual capital required to ensure the military has the best possible tools to achieve its mission. On screen (and in the comics) Tony Stark may be a sophisticated genius who can do it all, but in the real world, no single person—no matter how wealthy—can develop such advanced operational capabilities alone.

Notes

1   "University Consortium for Advanced Hypersonics," *Texas A&M*, https://hypersonics.tamu.edu/.
2   "Australian Trailblazer Universities Program," *Department of Education*, https://www.education. gov.au/trailblazer-universities-program.
3   "Defence Trailblazer—Concept to Sovereign Capability," *University of Adelaide*, https://www. adelaide.edu.au/icp/defence-trailblazer.

CHAPTER 29

We Need to Be Put in Check

Superheroes, Norms, and New Technology

Clara Engle

Imagine you are at a sporting event, say the Super Bowl. You paid hundreds of dollars to be there, and as the teams are lining up for kickoff, a becaped man flies down and goes section-to-section blocking your view until you listen to his pitch for a new political party, evading security's attempts to remove him. Alternatively, imagine you hear a strange buzzing. As you look up, the sky is full of drones of varying sizes, hovering just above the field. One swoops a few feet above your head, dropping a series of small objects. You and your family dive for cover, and the objects burst open as they hit the ground—plastic eggs full of coupons for a local shawarma restaurant. Meanwhile, you have missed a heroic 80-yard punt return.

Without regulation and norm setting, new technologies—real or imagined—go unchecked in daily life. The Federal Aviation Administration (FAA) prohibits drones from flying in specific areas—such as professional sports stadiums—during public events and establishes legal penalties for such behavior.[1] But these penalties are insufficient, as the norms surrounding drones have yet to be fully realized, and people persist in these behaviors. At sporting events, authorities can do little to stop drones from dropping by, save investing in expensive anti-drone technologies. Why? Quite simply, drones are small and often hard to track. As a result, the individual user must guard against the temptation to send a drone flying around something fascinating but off-limits. While regulations exist, this lack of norms can lead to severe problems. Anything a democratic system does to restrict the power of new and potentially dangerous technologies is inherently limited by the amount of power the system imparts to the entities charged with controlling it. Therefore, regulatory agencies and methods must use a two-part approach to controlling new technologies. The first is to establish regulations through a transparent and easily predictable process. The second is to encourage the development of norms among users, particularly those with massive resources, such as large corporations.

What does this have to do with superheroes? Superheroes provide a means for us to understand the potential pitfalls of regulation-heavy responses to new technologies. They also offer ideas for possible solutions. This chapter will treat superheroism like a technology and ask how we can be expected to regulate the users of this technology, and how their ability to self-regulate can manifest. It will reflect on how a government regulatory body can be expected to manage all the nuance that comes with bad (or good, or just plain clueless) actors using such technologies and how the government can respond to rapid technological change that outstrips the pace of regulation, including a real-world example that focuses on the relative success of norms and regulations in controlling new technologies.[2]

Managing Technological Revolutions at an Individual Scale

Superheroes are an excellent metaphor to highlight the problems new technology poses—much like science fiction technologies, they help authors explore technology's impact on humanity in an enjoyable and insightful way. Generally, though, the analogy of the hero-as-technology falls apart when confronted with human agency. In the best stories, superheroes are real people who choose to fight because of their origin stories. Even the most over-the-top villain is a person who can make choices—they just happen to choose evil. On the other hand, despite the fervent wishes of some actor-network theorists, technologies at present do not possess their own agency.[3] They are, however, developed, sold, and used by people who do have agency, which brings us back to the superhero again, but this time as an individual user—one who happens to be in sole possession of a revolutionary technology. These users can and should be managed through the active establishment of norms, and those who violate such norms should be condemned as the supervillains they are.

In most superhero stories, the heroes are portrayed as their own best regulators, usually because of some character element that is either innate or learned at high cost. For example, Steve Rogers is selected to become Captain America explicitly because of his personality and capacity for good. He is expected to make countless hard choices with an eye to the greater good, no matter the cost to his own happiness. This self-regulation is central to his story arc, but it also makes him an excellent example of how early movers can contribute—or fail to contribute, in Cap's case—to norm-building.

Since Steve Rogers self-regulates so well, he easily slides into a chain of command in an established agency, the Strategic Homeland Intervention, Enforcement and Logistics Division (S.H.I.E.L.D.). Far from prompting the creation of a new regulatory body, he just becomes part of the government, kicking the problem down the road. The regulatory body that evolves as more heroes appear on the scene learns the wrong lessons from Rogers. When superpowered bad actors like Loki appear, only Rogers and his peers are eventually able to resolve the situation; S.H.I.E.L.D., despite its massive scale, cannot. Nick Fury chooses to rely on the superheroes to police themselves—and other superpowered beings who operate outside established laws and norms—rather than intentionally building a norms-based framework to assist the heroes. The necessary norms develop slowly over time, as more and more superpowered individuals appear in the MCU.

A superhero in such a framework is effectively asked to choose between their instinct to do good and their willingness to trust a bureaucratic system when their conscience and S.H.I.E.L.D. conflict. Unless otherwise noted, superheroes in the MCU generally work in accord with a democratic government or agency. When they are portrayed as working against the government, it is often because there is a flaw in "the system" that makes it act in a non-democratic fashion, rather than because of a flaw with the heroes themselves. The social contract that bounds the heroes is tied not to one specific government but to the greater societal benefits that accrue from their autonomy. This is another arena in which intentionally created norms are important—helping good actors like Cap exert a greater influence on the system. Unfortunately, a real-life S.H.I.E.L.D. probably would not find itself dealing exclusively with individuals of strong moral fiber like Steve Rogers, Clint Barton, and assorted philosophy-spouting androids. We must look elsewhere, to another universe entirely, to explore what happens when individuals of poor character represent the vast majority of superheroes.

In *The Boys*, the supes are—more often than not—unhindered by a perceived social contract with anyone. The central conflict developed in Season 1 is between the supes who have returned to the Hobbesian state of nature, such as A-Train, and those who are bound by larger social contracts, such as Starlight. The lack of any but the loosest and most cynical means of control on supe behavior leaves the government and general populace struggling with how to manage their incredible power. Without a social contract or norms built around the safe and appropriate use of power, supes run amok, and the powerless are left dodging fallout. How can this new technology be regulated if the users will not self-regulate? Vought International, the superhero entertainment conglomerate, attempts to manage its supes through emotional manipulation, financial leverage, and appeals to public opinion. By the end of Season 3, however, it's clear that these levers no longer grant control over the supes—especially Homelander, a Superman-esque demigod—in the way they once did. Similarly, user self-regulation and regulation through base urges are unlikely to address new technologies effectively.

Much like in the MCU, in *The Boys* Season 2, international super-terrorists appear seemingly out of nowhere. Vought's response is to push for supes to work alongside the U.S. military to address the emergent problem of a more widely available technology posing a global threat. Since this is *The Boys*, Vought is revealed to be behind everything, but the main question remains. How do governments contain and manage technologies that are beyond their existing systems? How do they contain actors like Homelander, Vision, or Tony Stark, who have the power to destroy the existing system—and anything else on Earth, should they so choose? Superhero stories often present a one-two punch of realist and constructivist solutions, where the initial way out is based on the righteous use of force to dispose of a villain, but the ultimate way forward is dependent on norms and their expansion within the extant system, leading to greater buy-in from superheroes and the general public.

Norms, Normals and Supe Regulations

Season 3 of *The Boys* presents an interesting solution to these problems: the Federal Bureau of Superhuman Affairs (FBSA). This is *The Boys*, where nothing ever goes to plan—and usually causes more problems than it solves—but the idea of a bureau that contains rogue superheroes and tracks down people who are misusing their powers is worth consideration. In theory, such a dedicated agency under sub-cabinet level long-term leadership, ala the FBI, would nimbly respond to crises as they emerge. Such an organization could do the work of technology containment better than lumping yet another mission under the existing infrastructure of the Departments of Commerce or Defense. Marvel writers developed the idea of S.H.I.E.L.D. decades ago, and the point is well-taken: A focused agency is often needed to deal with rapid challenges as new technologies arise. There is, however, a difference between an organization set up to respond to crises and one intentionally building a framework to prevent future problems.

The Boys offers something tangible regarding how to begin building the first part of that framework: regulation. The FBSA is presented as a small, flexible bureau with extensive discretion in hiring and utilizing contractors. It is designed to manage rogue supes, much like the initial conception of S.H.I.E.L.D. Both the Bureau and S.H.I.E.L.D. are initially well-organized around a unifying principle. Ultimately, both create more significant problems, in S.H.I.E.L.D.'s case through the nature of the agency's initial short-term successes. As superhumans grow in response to and outstrip the functions of these agencies, both find themselves unable to resolve crises the way they had previously. The solution is not to remove superhumans from governmental control but to build on initial successes by developing norms within a broader system. More importantly, it also aids powerhouse users like Starlight who have already accepted these norms as they seek to model responsible behavior and demonstrate that following the system can lead to success.

At the same time, even as early in the MCU timeline as the first *Iron Man* film, we see that these agencies have only as much power and influence over superpowered individuals as the people who compose and direct them can personally bring to bear. In that film, Phil Coulson attempts to meet with Tony Stark after the billionaire displays a new technology that S.H.I.E.L.D. wants to understand and manage.

Stark responds by shuffling him off to his assistant and then is reluctant to engage with the organization in the next film. If private citizens and business entities do not want to interact with a governmental system or contribute their technology to that system—as Google and Microsoft employees have said regarding Department of Defense contracts—then there is not much any agency can do absent changing the law to compel compliance or developing its own version of a technology.[4] In a liberal government built on bureaucracy and the rule of law, how do we empower real-life Agent Coulsons to respond to new technologies without getting tangled in red tape? The answer is, once again, found in norms, but this time those restricting government behavior.

Managing New Technologies that are Actor-Dependent

The Battle of New York in *The Avengers* saw the titular team fighting the Chitauri and a rogue Asgardian, all of whom used weapons technology far beyond anything generally available on Earth. Much of this hardware was left scattered throughout the tri-state area, and the U.S. government did not have an immediate plan for cleanup. The Feds pushed this task to the state and local level, where it was farmed out to contractors, including Adrian Toomes and his company.

So far, this makes sense. Allowing bids for public works contracts is a standard operating procedure in a democracy. So long as everybody gets a fair shot and there is no favoritism or corruption at play, this typically leads to a quicker and more cost-effective solution than building a new capability within the government. *Spider-Man: Homecoming,* however, shows Toomes' lucrative contract falling apart when the government tasks a heretofore unknown agency to clean up the alien technology, replacing Toomes' crew and forcing them to turn to the black market as a revenue stream. *Homecoming* largely portrays Toomes' descent into villainy—becoming the Vulture—as a response to systemic change that happened seemingly out of the blue and in contrast to accepted norms of liberal government.

The tale of Toomes' travails points us to the ability of the government to create villains in a supremely mundane fashion. These villains do not manifest through the development of new technology like Iron Monger or the Winter Soldier but rather in response to everyday policy decisions. On an international scale, we see a liberal and nominally democratic system unsure how to address the problems posed by the existence of superheroes after *Avengers: Age of Ultron*. Similar to how the United States government dealt with the potential fallout from the Chitauri attack on New York, the United Nations decided against changing the system gradually or developing a new means of managing the threat. Instead, they attempted to use broad-brush legal tools and a series of shaky norms to bind the Avengers, leading to a costly and destructive internecine clash between the heroes that nearly wrecked a major European airport.

In the first case, we saw a liberal government attempting to affect a rapid response to a threat and causing a serious problem for itself. In the second, a more traditional attempt to use the rule of law led to an even worse failure. In both cases, the governments were moving to contain phenomena that were, if not revolutionary, certainly large evolutionary leaps, violating established norms to do so. In *Homecoming*, these were alien weapons literally dropped from the sky. In *Civil War*, the catalyst is the Sokovia Accords the team is asked to sign to allow government control of the new "technologies" they represent. Unfortunately for the world (and our heroes), the Accords do not fully or appropriately address the complexities of the new technologies introduced to the international system.

From Four Colors to Reality

Cleanup contracts for alien tech are all well and good in the fictional Marvel Universe; however, real-world technology needs regulation and norm development as a few "super" users push their limits. Drone technology has a remarkable way of pushing to the front of the pack. Despite their revolutionary potential, drones have entered the realm of the mundane. One signal of this change is that the term now encompasses everything from MQ-9 Reapers carrying air-to-ground missiles to 3D-printed hobby models that cost a few hundred dollars. The former benefit governments by keeping friendly troops out of direct physical danger, but this use is almost entirely predicated on the accuracy of target selection and the intelligence provided to make those selections—in short, on following established norms.

However, these norms do not cover every possible scenario. By law and norm, the international community has agreed not to intentionally target non-combatants. Nevertheless, U.S. military drone attacks have repeatedly struck non-combatants, even at events like weddings.[5] International and domestic condemnation was and is swift in such incidents—the U.S. government tries to set norms of behavior and should be called out for hypocrisy and failing to adhere to principles of due diligence. The agencies at fault fill the role of the superhero-user in these cases—they may not be the sole decision makers, but they wield enormous power and should be subject to regulation.

Unfortunately, not all governments have a citizenry that seeks regulation and accountability when norms are violated, nor are they as responsive to public backlash when norms are violated. Liberal democracies must regulate themselves and assist in norm development for the rest of the world. These efforts can be particularly challenging when illiberal and authoritarian states possess extensive resources and have benefitted from norm violations in the past. While international norm development paired with internal regulatory development is one of the best methods for managing new technologies, things still fall through the cracks, and overcorrection can be equally harmful to the system. Instead, norm setters must take a flexible approach to ensure technologies continue to be used primarily for the greater good.

By now, it should be clear from trends in Syria and Ukraine that drones pose a significant security threat anywhere if they carry explosives. What is less obvious is that they pose a threat to airplanes regardless of malicious intent. Regulation alone will not adequately stop the improper use of drone technology. There must be norms in place around their use that cause people to stop and wonder if their behavior is responsible and what the cost of violating known norms would be.

Commercial aircraft are at particular risk because a misplaced drone could cause significant loss of life. A drone, much like a bird, can get sucked into a jet engine and destroy a plane as it takes off or lands. Here, norms are further along in development. The most famous "drones at the airport" incident occurred over Christmas 2018 at Gatwick Airport in England.[6] During this incident, over 800 flights were canceled or diverted over the course of about a day and a half—despite regulatory barriers and severe penalties in the law. This incident thrust the potential for private-actor malicious drone use into the public eye.

The public response has been overwhelmingly aimed toward further control of drones. There have been more incidents since Gatwick Airport; however, the scale of the disruption is typically much smaller, and public sentiment has reflected, rather than terror or curiosity, a feeling that the norms around air travel and airport security have been violated. Public reactions of this sort are, ultimately, the most effective way to regulate new technologies. First, the technology is regulated by a government agency; then, norms develop around the use of the technology; and then, further regulatory frameworks are put into place as needed. In a liberal democratic system, this solution also proves to be the most effective in the long term. As new technologies continue to develop, this will best serve the interests of the state looking into the future.

Conclusion

Ultimately, superheroes are important because they allow us to explore fantastic and mundane topics in one concentrated space. The MCU and *The Boys* help us examine a future not too dissimilar to our own in terms of technology and compare that with an examination of how government can best respond to and manage said technology. While they do not provide all the solutions and do not fill all the gaps regarding successful norm creation, superhero stories show us how to conceptualize better responses to new technologies. Often, these stories explain how new technologies are good if the people who manage them are good and the behaviors with which they manage them propagate responsible decision-making. Reality is like fiction as real-world new technologies bring tremendous potential for positive change if managed by regulatory agencies that focus on not just the law, but also on how to think about a technology as a whole and what norms can be built around it to lead to the best outcomes for the greatest good.

Notes

1 "Stadiums and Sporting Events," *Stadiums and Sporting Events | Federal Aviation Administration*. https://www.faa.gov/uas/getting_started/where_can_i_fly/airspace_restrictions/sports_stadiums.

2 These themes show up across the spectrum of superhero media, so it makes sense to examine them in both the generally optimistic Marvel Cinematic Universe (MCU) and in the much darker world of *The Boys*. There's a lot to cover in the Marvel comics universe, so it's more practical to keep things limited to the MCU in a short essay. As to *The Boys*, the TV series does a better job of focusing on what I want to discuss, without quite as many events added purely for shock value.

3 Bruno Latour, *Science in Action: How to Follow Scientists and Engineers Through Society* (Milton Keynes: England: Open University Press, 1987).
   For a more down-to-Earth understanding of the social elements of technology, see: Wiebe E. Bijker, Thomas P. Hughes, and Trevor Pinch, eds. *The Social Construction of Technological Systems: New Directions in the Sociology and History of Technology*, anniv. ed. (Cambridge: MIT Press, 2012).

4 Avie Schneider and Laura Sydell, "Microsoft Workers Protest Army Contract with Tech 'Designed to Help People Kill'," *NPR*, February 22, 2019. https://www.npr.org/2019/02/22/697110641/microsoft-workers-protest-army-contract-with-tech-designed-to-help-people-kill.
   Scott Shane and Daisuke Wakabayashi, "'The Business of War': Google Employees Protest Work for the Pentagon," *The New York Times*, April 4, 2018. https://www.nytimes.com/2018/04/04/technology/google-letter-ceo-pentagon-project.html.

5 Dave Philipps, Eric Schmitt, and Mark Mazzetti, "Civilian Deaths Mounted as Secret Unit Pounded Isis," *The New York Times*, December 12, 2021. https://www.nytimes.com/2021/12/12/us/civilian-deaths-war-isis.html.
   "Yemenis: Drone Strike 'Turned Wedding into Funeral'," *NBC News,* NBCUniversal News Group. https://www.nbcnews.com/news/investigations/yemenis-drone-strike-turned-wedding-funeral-n5781.

6 Kelsey Atherton, "Anti-Drone Tech's Tangled Regulatory Landscape," *Brookings*, October 2, 2020. https://www.brookings.edu/techstream/anti-drone-techs-tangled-regulatory-landscape/.
   Ilaria Grasso Macola, "The Airport Drone Threat: A Storm in a Teacup?" *Airport Technology*, May 14, 2021. https://www.airport-technology.com/analysis/airport-drone-threat-storm-teacup/.
   Benjamin Mueller and Amie Tsang, "Gatwick Airport Shut down by 'Deliberate' Drone Incursions," *The New York Times*, December 20, 2018. https://www.nytimes.com/2018/12/20/world/europe/gatwick-airport-drones.html.

PART VI

KNEEL BEFORE ZOD!

"Kneel before Zod! You are not the President. No one who leads so many could possibly kneel so quickly."

—GENERAL ZOD IN *SUPERMAN II* (1980)

CHAPTER 30

The Caped Crusader and the Road to Radicalism

Max Brooks

"It begins here—an army—to bring sense to a world plagued by worse than thieves and murderers." These are some of the last lines in Frank Miller's *The Dark Knight Returns*, and it is, possibly, the most important Batman story ever told.

In this limited comic series, Bruce Wayne is an old man, long retired and retreated into seclusion. Around him, Gotham crumbles. Crime is rampant. A new gang of rootless, violent youths called "The Mutants" rules the streets. Aging super-criminals like the Joker and Two-Face are about to be paroled by a soft, deluded, criminal justice system. The citizens are terrified, they're desperate, but no one is doing anything to protect them. The mayor is a joke. The police chief is inept. The media has devolved into insipid, ratings hungry jackals. And the greatest of all heroes, Superman, serves a war-mongering federal government headed by a demented Ronald Reagan.

Something has to be done. Someone has to step into the void. That is when Bruce Wayne comes out of retirement, dons his cape, and crusades across Gotham City. He vanquishes his old enemies, defeats the leader of the Mutants, then recruits their rank and file into a vigilante force known as "The Sons of Batman." Finally, during his duel with the Man of Steel, he fakes his own death and retreats into the caves below Wayne Manor to train his "army."

The Dark Knight Returns single-handedly resurrected a flagging franchise and turned it into what is today, a billion-dollar bonanza. Miller accomplished this feat by banishing the tongue-in-cheek campiness of Adam West's 1960s TV character and returned Batman to his original hard-boiled noir roots. No more "Batusi" dancing, no more "Holy Joker got away, Batman." This Dark Knight is a bone breaker, with battle banter like, "You don't get it, boy, this isn't a mudhole, it's an operating table and I'm the surgeon."

But behind the gritty aesthetic was a much deeper, darker theme. *The Dark Knight Returns* and, it could be argued, the entire story of Batman is a call for radical extremism.

Yes, there's always the gray area of government cooperation. In most Batman stories, he works behind the scenes with the police (hence the iconic Bat Signal), But that gray area gets very black and white in Miller's tale. As the action unfolds, we see the Dark Knight defeat the Mutant leader in single combat, thereby attracting the gang to his side. Donning bat tattoos across their faces, the young street fighters swear blind allegiance by declaring, "Gotham City belongs to the Batman."

The point is rammed home at the beginning of the last act. The electromagnetic pulse of a distant nuke knocks the power out of Gotham. The city goes dark, fires rage, and normal citizens lose their minds. They loot. They kill. The "Sons of Batman" are about to "purge" the city, when, suddenly, the Dark Knight shows up, on a horse (in a dead-ringer for Jacques Louis David's "Napoleon Crossing the Alps") to announce, "I am the law."

Frank Miller has officially denied any totalitarian themes in his story. In an interview with *The Hollywood Reporter* he stated, "Anybody who thinks Batman was a fascist should study their politics…. Fascists tell people how to live. Batman just tells criminals to stop." That may be true, but if the definition of a criminal is someone who breaks the law, and, as Batman said, "I am the law," then isn't a criminal anyone who crosses Batman? By that simple logic, how is he any different from Hitler, Stalin, Kim Jong Un, or even Louis XIV, who famously proclaimed, "I am the state?" Isn't one person dictating the law the literal definition of a dictator? And anyone who thinks that Miller's savior will stop at just stopping street crime really needs to "read their politics." Plenty of bloody tyrants began their rise as idealistic crusaders, just ask the ghosts of Fidel Castro, Robert Mugabe, and Muammar Khadafi. There's a reason the "Final Solution" was final and not first. Hitler didn't exactly run for Chancellor on the platform of world war and genocide.

If the Dark Knight's words aren't enough, the actions of the citizens speak for themselves. During the EMP riot, a normally law-abiding citizen shoots a priest because, "It was the end of the world, and I had a gun." That gun was taken from a solitary wounded (or dead) cop. But where were the other cops? The State Police? The National Guard? As "Crazy Eyes" once shouted during the prison riot scene in *Orange is the New Black*, "Where are the grownups!?"

There aren't any. The system has collapsed. The message is clear. The people cannot be trusted to govern themselves, and a system of, by, and for the people is therefore doomed to fail.

Miller might have given us a fascist fantasy, but he also (possibly, unwittingly) gave us a blueprint on how to prevent it. When viewed as a cautionary tale, *The Dark Knight Returns* carries a powerful warning for the times we're living in. Radicalism flourishes when moderates fail to meet the needs of the people.

Extremist movements never simply poof into existence. They build on legitimate grievances such as poverty, corruption, and crime. There's always something. And when those in charge can't or won't address those grievances, the people will turn to whomever shouts, "I will!" We see it in Miller's fictional Gotham, just like we've seen in it in the very real Russia, China, Iran, Afghanistan, and, of course, Germany.

It's not hard to imagine an alternate Batman story taking place in the Fatherland. Bruce Wayne could have lost his parents in the post-WWI chaos, donned the cowl sometime in the late 1920s, and took to the streets to protect the common volk from a horde of Germanized villains. Two-Face could easily be a battle-scarred war veteran turned communist rabble rouser. Penguin fits the exploitative, internationalist businessman. Riddler could be the *Lügenpresse* yellow journalist seeking to paint the Caped Crusader as a villain. And who can't see the Joker as a psychotic murdering version of Joel Grey in *Cabaret* singing "Everything is funny!" When confronting these arch fiends, as well as a host of "thieves and murderers," why wouldn't Batman abandon the incompetent apathy of the Weimar Republic for a new movement centered around a man who promised "law and order."

He might strike a devil's bargain with the new Leader. He might even dismiss the rhetoric of *Mein Kampf* as political theater. So many others did. Too many of Germany's elite thought, hoped, that once this fiery soap box shouter became Chancellor, he could eventually be controlled, tempered, and used. Would Bruce Wayne, obsessed with his "Holy War" (a line from Miller's Superman), have been any different?

The Devil's bargain might even have appeared to pay off at first. No more crime, no more street violence. How vindicated would Wayne have felt to see all his old enemies carted off to a new special prison near a Bavarian town called Dachau? Remember, this was 1933, the ovens and gas chambers were still a long way off.

Wayne might have come to his senses sooner, maybe when he actually read the new "Jewish Laws" or after *Kristallnacht*, or after they came for the "thieves and murderers," or perhaps, when they started coming for his friends like Gordon, Alfred, Dick, and Selena. By then, of course it would be too late. As Lex Luther once said to another Batman, "The bell's already been rung."

Fortunately for the fictional DC universe, Bruce Wayne was born in the United States of America. And, fortunately for the real USA, the same circumstances that spawned Adolf Hitler also elected FDR. Just like Der Fuhrer, America's 32nd President saw the link between public discontent and radicalization. He was so aware of the stakes that when an advisor warned that failure would leave him the "worst" president in American history, FDR responded that he wouldn't just be the worst, he'd be the last.

That is why the New Deal turned out to be the greatest counter-extremist campaign in the history of the human race. By giving Americans jobs, shelter, services, and, most importantly, hope, he ensured that they wouldn't swing too far to the right or the left. Sadly, this winning strategy was diluted with each subsequent generation, until we finally found ourselves facing FDR's nightmare.

Donald Trump didn't just happen overnight. His revolution was decades in the making. Globalization tore the economic heart out of America's heartland and replaced it with poverty, despair, and opioids. No one did anything about it. None of the powerful educated class seemed to care anymore about the "flyover states." Some even seemed to take pleasure in lampooning the "herds of hillbillies" (thanks, Fran Leibowitz). It seemed like no one was listening to the cries of forgotten America, except Trump. Like all radicals, he perverted their pain and twisted fear into hate. And when the establishment had one last chance to turn the tide, they not only failed to address the growing extremists within their own ranks but arrogantly lumped anyone on the other side into "a basket of deplorables." The stage was set for Trump, whose lies and venom stoked a fire that lit the path the White House.

None of these facts are up for debate. What could be, though, is which side Frank Miller's Dark Knight would be on. He might have been disgusted with the exploding crime in America's "blue" cities; from the gun violence in Chicago, to the "police free zones" in Minneapolis and Seattle, to the homeless encampments just a few doors down from where I write this, where supposedly compassionate politicians pay lip service to human beings who are forced to live on the streets and die like animals. Batman might even see a kindred spirit in a man who declared, "I am the law-and-order candidate."

Hopefully, the moral compass we've come to expect from Bruce Wayne would steer him away from kids in cages, neo-Nazis in Charlottesville, and the traitorous insurrection of January 6th. He might have seen that final, feces-smeared rebellion as a wakeup call to save the American system. Then again, he might have felt that a system that couldn't save itself wasn't worth saving. Like the EMP chaos in *The Dark Knight Returns*, he might have seen January 6th as an opportunity to recruit a gang of disaffected, violent youth, and train them into "an Army—to bring sense to a world plagued by worse than thieves and murderers."

The lesson of *The Dark Knight Returns* must be learned if we hope to avoid a real-world version of Gotham. The only way to deradicalize our population is to get at the root causes of their discontent. It won't be easy. It won't be fast. And it won't happen if we don't all participate in a system that still allows us to do so.

Imagine another alternate Miller story, where, instead of prowling the streets as Batman, Bruce Wayne hit the streets in a campaign for public office. It's not like he doesn't have the money or the connections to run for mayor, governor, or even president. There would still be plenty of enemies to fight. Instead of the Joker, he'd face a corporate America whose outsourcing of jobs and refusal to pay its fair share of taxes created the poverty that turned so many to crime. Instead of the Mutants, he'd tangle with cloistered academics and fringe, spotlight-seeking politicians who want to defund the police. Punches and batarangs can't win those battles. He'd have to convince and (gulp) compromise, in order to get anything done. Throw in the complications of race, class, gender, religion, and political tribalism, on top of the social media empires that profit from our division, the former superhero might find himself wishing for the good old days of a knife between the ribs. But the hard truth for him (and us) is that tackling issues instead of bad guys will end up saving a lot more innocent lives.

This kind of story might not be the kind that sells a lot of comic books for DC, but it's the only one that will save us. We need to be the grownups missing from Gotham. We need to save ourselves. And we don't have a lot of time. Trump is planning a big comeback, and there's an army of Trump wannabes behind him. All of them can't wait to lead an army that will bring "sense" to our world. All of them can't wait to declare, "I am the law."

CHAPTER 31

Where Monsters Dwell

Steven Leonard

"To save his adoptive father's life, a young cyclist sold his soul to the Devil. But Satan deceived him, and now each night brings an awful transformation. His face bursts into a flaming skull, his strength grows, and his soul is as one with the fiery regions of Hell. The mortal Johnny Blaze becomes … THE GHOST RIDER!"

—*GHOST RIDER* # 9 (1974)

Somewhere in the volumes of faded family photos, there is a picture of a bespectacled nine-year-old boy sitting on a tree stump next to a campground firepit. In one hand the boy is holding a half-eaten Pop-Tart; in the other, he is holding a well-worn copy of *Astonishing Tales* #12. It was July 1972. The Watergate break-in was barely two weeks old. Bill Withers was singing "Lean on Me" on the radio. And America was still excited about the prospect of the Space Shuttle Program, which President Nixon had announced earlier in the year.

But on that day, none of that mattered. I was thoroughly engrossed in the latest adventures of Ka-Zar and his sabretooth tiger, Zabu. I had stumbled upon Ka-Zar earlier that year after reading Andre Norton's science fiction classic, *Daybreak 2250 A.D.*, which featured a very similar set of characters in a darkly post-apocalyptic future. In that particular issue of *Astonishing Tales*, entitled "Terror Stalks the Everglades," Ka-Zar and Zabu travel to Citrusville, Florida, to help two scientists search for their missing colleague, Ted Sallis, with whom they have been working on Project Gladiator, a S.H.I.E.L.D.[1] research program intended to recreate the super-soldier serum that transformed Steve Rogers into Captain America. But, like so often occurs in comics, a nefarious antagonist is involved—in this case, A.I.M.[2]—that has their own designs for the serum. After being shot several times by his lonely, bitter wife, Ellen Brandt—who A.I.M. had surreptitiously recruited as an agent—Sallis escapes into the swamp with the untested serum. With Ellen hell bent on murder, the formula committed to memory, and his records destroyed, Sallis does what any self-respecting Marvel character would do when faced with a life-or-death dilemma: He injects himself with the only remaining vial of the serum.

As a character, Sallis is as fascinating as he is intertwined within the intricate and often convoluted web of Marvel canon. A biochemistry professor at Empire State University, Sallis was recruited by the United States Army for Project Sulfur, a program designed to develop a vaccine to help soldiers survive the horrors of biological and chemical warfare. His SO-2 serum offered immunity to all known biochemical agents but had the unintended and somewhat inconvenient side effect of transforming its users into monsters. When he later joined Project Gladiator, he continued—unsuccessfully, as it were—to refine the SO-2 serum, working closely with Dr. Curt Connors and even combing some of the regenerative elements of Connors's research into a new serum.[3]

The events that followed captivated me then, and the memory is as vivid today as it was more than 50 years ago on that tree stump. The super soldier serum transformed Sallis. It healed his injuries. It gave him superhuman strength. It gave him the power to burn whoever feared him. But along the way it interacted with the "magical energies" of the swamp. When the transformation was complete, Sallis was the massive, hideous swamp creature that would come to be known as the Man-Thing. Instead of a super soldier, Sallis was a monster. With his memory largely gone and without the ability to communicate, whatever little was left of Ted Sallis escaped deeper into the Everglades.

The Man-Thing represented something unique in the annals of Marvel Comics. He was a monster, that much was unequivocally clear. But the Man-Thing was also more than a monster. Somewhere within the mindless, lumbering mass of a swamp creature, a sense of morality remained. On some level, the Man-Thing knew right from wrong. It could sense evil. It understood when an innocent was being hurt. And it possessed the strength, size, and presence to provoke fear. And whatever knows fear, burns at the touch of the Man-Thing.

The Man-Thing was a superhero.

My nine-year-old self read and re-read that issue of *Astonishing Tales* until the pages separated from the cover. Two months later—*Astonishing Tales* was published bi-monthly, a common fate for less popular comics—I scraped up the twenty cents to buy the next issue. In December, when *Adventure into Fear* featured the Man-Thing as its lead character, I began reading that series. And when the Man-Thing premiered in his own eponymous comic in January 1974—an issue which I keep framed in my office today—I was hooked.

But that was only the beginning. My fascination with Marvel's monsters was unleased with abandon. Monsters were nothing new to Marvel, in fact, series such as *Journey into Mystery*, *Strange Tales*, and *Tales of Suspense*—which would later introduce the superheroes Thor, Dr. Strange, and Iron Man—were early horror titles that featured creatures ranging from giant aliens to kaiju. But the monsters that so enthralled me were different. Like the Man-Thing, they were a different breed of monster, ones that conveyed all the fear associated with a more traditional monster, but who used their powers for good. Most of the time. They were still monsters, after all.

With the help of my friendly neighborhood used bookstore—where my unspent lunch money[4] could be used to buy old comics for a penny or two—I surrounded myself with monster superheroes. There was Morbius the Living Vampire, whose failed experiment—failed experiments are a common theme in Marvel origin stories—to cure a rare blood disease imbued him with the power of a vampire. And the thirst, unfortunately. Johnny Blaze, who sold his soul to the Devil in a failed quest to save his adoptive father's life, was cursed with the powers—flaming skull and all—of the Ghost Rider. Eric Brooks, the vampire hunter known as Blade, was himself a human-vampire hybrid. Even Daimon Hellstrom, the son of Satan, joined the superhero ranks.

Those monsters were soon joined by others: Werewolf by Night, Man-Wolf, Frankenstein's monster, and the Manphibian. N'Kantu the Living Mummy debuted in *Supernatural Thrillers* #5 and, as a member of the Legion of Monsters, fought alongside Morbius, Werewolf by Night, the Manphibian, and the Man-Thing. In the early 1990s, when Marvel debuted the limited crossover series *Rise of the Midnight Sons*—with Dr. Stephen Strange uniting Ghost Rider, Morbius, and Blade as The Sprits of Vengeance to do battle with Lilith, the Mother of Demons—the 30-year-old version of the boy on the tree stump was the first in line at the local comic shop to buy each issue.

Mine was a curious fascination. Monsters were generally not something to which I was attracted. The appearance of the horned ape-carnivore, the mugato, on the *Star Trek* episode, "A Private Little War," haunted my dreams for months. The sight of Norman Bates's dead mother in *Psycho* had me sleeping with a light on for years (and taking baths instead of showers). And I have a hard rule about watching films that feature ghosts. So, what was it about these particular monsters that intrigued me so?

Our fascination with monsters in nothing new. At one point or another in our lives, we have all gathered around a campfire to regale each other with scary stories: the man with the hook hand scratching at the car door, the ghost of La Llorona searching for her missing children, or even the vanishing hitchhiker. Terrifying monsters have a way of making a story more memorable. There is a relatively simple formula to creating an especially memorable monster: one, take something normal and twist it in such a way that it inspires fear and repulsion and two, use your monster to play on existing fears. Then use the monster to do horrible things. But if you want the monster to connect with an audience, it takes a little more than fear. For that, the monster must show us something about ourselves.

Leo Braudy, the author of *Haunted: On Ghosts, Witches, Vampires, Zombies and Other Monsters of the Natural and Supernatural Worlds*, explains our fascination with monsters: "We all love frightening stories—because they allow us a kind of mastery.

They're comforting, but also titillating."[5] In *Haunted*, Braudy separates monsters into four broad categories. Monsters from nature, such as Sasquatch, the Yeti, or the Loch Ness Monster, embody our fear that nature seeks revenge for perceived transgressions against her. Monsters from science, such as Frankenstein's monster, represent the hubris of scientists who believe they can create and control life (and science). Monsters from within, such as Mr. Hyde, represent a Freudian exploration of the repressed creatures that lurk within our minds. Finally, monsters from the past, such as Count Dracula, seek revenge against what they see as a morally bankrupt modern cult of progress, improvement, and change.[6]

Braudy offers that our love of monsters is revealing, reflecting our preoccupation with death and mortality. Those monsters, according to Braudy, help to "keep our mortality squarely in front of us."[7] When we explore those monsters in literature or film—or in comics—we are allowed to indulge our fears without penalty. The pleasure we derive from that indulgence is quite simple: We escaped. As a result, according to Braudy, "Our fascination with monsters is perpetual."[8]

Of the four types of monsters described by Braudy, most of the creatures that cross the line from villain to hero in the comics come from either science or within, or a combination of both—Bruce Banner, the Incredible Hulk, is a prime example of science unleashing the creature within. There were times when a comic might feature a monster from one of the other categories, but those tended to be short lived and not as well received. Godzilla and King Kong, both examples of monsters from nature, were interesting enough, but it was King Kong's relatability—his almost human characteristics—that connected him to audiences. And that connection is what matters most.

Marvel's horror comics from the late 1940s through the early 1960s were standard fare, intended to scare audiences into reading more. From a purely psychological perspective, they succeeded at just that. The superhero genre was a thing of the past; *Captain America Comics*, a mainstay of Atlas Comics (the predecessor to Marvel), became *Captain America's Weird Tales* two issues before its cancellation in 1949. By 1959, Marvel's flagship titles were pushing out three to four horror stories with each issue, but the monsters—although certainly frightening in their own right—weren't all that relatable to readers.

Monsters that frighten us—vampires, swamp creatures, and even the spawn of Satan—help us to cope with what we fear most in life. "Vampires and monsters—they're just us," according to John Edgar Browning, a professor of Liberal Arts at the Savannah College of Art and Design. "They're what we aspire to be, what we're told to hate most about ourselves, what we secretly yearn for, but shouldn't."[9] Browning, who has written extensively on the depiction of vampires in our culture, emphasized the importance of relatability to our monsters. "The vampire of today's popular culture ... may provoke empathy or pathos, forcing us to recognize its monstrosity as our own, to embrace what we were taught to loathe."[10]

This relatability—creating creatures that connected to readers on a human level—was the seed that spawned Marvel's monstrous transformation in the 1960s. In the same way Stan Lee and Steve Ditko created Spider-Man—a superpowered young man with the same problems suffered by every other teenager—the team at Marvel re-envisioned their monsters. The standard horror comics just were not selling like they once had; readers were not connecting with the creatures and people stopped reading. With a wave of the pen, monsters like Sporr ("The Thing That Could Not Die") and Rommbu ("His Very Name Made Mankind Tremble") were gone. By early 1962, Marvel's monsters began to evolve into more than antagonists.[11] They started to become more human.

Through the 1960s, creating relatable characters was an emphasis for Marvel's creative team of Stan Lee, Steve Ditko, and Jack Kirby. Though their characters were endowed with extraordinary abilities, readers saw in them a reflection of themselves. Peter Parker (Spider-Man) was just another nerdy teenager who couldn't get a date. Reed Richards (Mr. Fantastic) was a brilliant scientist who never seemed to be able to pay his bills. Wanda Maximoff (Scarlet Witch) was a gifted young woman who yearned for social acceptance. They were superheroes with everyday issues. Just like the rest of us.

But could Marvel do the same with monsters? How do you take something utterly horrifying and make it relatable? How do you make a monster resonate with an audience? The answer is empathy—recast the monsters in an empathetic light. Empathy tends to draw in readers and engage them on a personal level. It hooks them. It makes them care. It compels them to keep coming back for more. And, it turns out, building empathy for a character is not all that difficult.

First, imbue the character with a valued trait, such as loyalty, faith, or love. The Man-Thing might have appeared to be a mindless brute, but some vestige of Ted Sallis remained and possessed a clear sense of morality. Second, show that the character cares about something deeply, especially at great cost to themselves. Love drove Johnny Blaze to sell his own soul in a vain attempt to save his adoptive father's life. Third, reveal their wounds. Morbius is a tortured soul who is deeply tormented by what he has become, and the pain of that emotion tends to be a driving force behind the good that he does. Fourth, show how they are treated unjustly. In almost every case, monsters are misunderstood in the public eye and largely despised. They are subjected to some form on injustice at every turn. Fifth, expose their grief. In some form, loss haunts many of the creatures—a true love, a valued family member, or just their former lives.[12]

Once a reader begins to empathize with a monster, one final step remains to cement the connection. Redemption. One of the hallmarks of Marvel's narrative storytelling is that "villains are rarely beyond redemption, and as likely as not to become its heroes or even its saviors."[13] The same holds true for its monsters.

Everyone loves a good villain-redemption story. We all cheered when Darth Vader sacrificed himself to save Luke Skywalker. Tony Stark's sacrificial character arc across a decade of films left us all with a lump in our throats when the final credits rolled in *Avengers: Endgame*. The moment we realized that Severus Snape was actually one of the bravest characters in *Harry Potter* left us all with a tear in our eye. One of the main reasons why *Spider-Man: No Way Home* is so uniquely satisfying to watch is not that the film brings closure to three separate movie franchises—which is no small feat, even for Marvel Studios president Kevin Feige—but because literally every villain in the film is redeemed. Every last one. Even Norman Osborn, whose psychotic turn as the Green Goblin makes him a largely despicable monster in every respect.

People crave redemption. We need redemption to see the potential in others and in ourselves. We need redemption to learn, to grow, to move beyond our mistakes. The redemption journey offers a very relatable human story because it allows us to see ourselves through a different lens, to question ourselves and our decisions in life, and to have faith that we can become better versions of ourselves. The redemption of a monster is no different. We see in the monster a part of ourselves, and we empathize, making their redemption all the more enjoyable an experience.

None of this was apparent to that nine-year-old boy on the tree stump. I simply knew that I felt a connection to the Man-Thing, and I read every issue cover-to-cover in hopes that one day his redemption would come. I was captivated by his adventures, intrigued by the cultural and societal undercurrents weaved into the narrative, and enthralled by the seemingly endless array of cameos from other superheroes in the Marvel universe. The Man-Thing teamed up with Spider-Man, fought alongside the Thing, and engaged Dr. Strange in battle. Daredevil, Captain America, and Shang-Chi made noteworthy appearances. But redemption was an elusive silver bullet.

The years passed, and eventually my monsters found their way into storage boxes along with a few thousand other comic books. By my teenage years, my money went to other pursuits, other interests. In time, the Man-Thing became a distant memory. Then, one day, shortly after graduating from high school in the spring of 1981, I saw a copy of *Man-Thing*—"Tear-Stained Last Issue"—on the shelf at the neighborhood grocery store and picked it up. I thumbed through the issue, skimming the pages with a bit of nostalgic sentimentality. Then something caught my eye. As the issue came to a close, Thog the Nether-Spawn, a demon and frequent antagonist of the Man-Thing, restored Ted Sallis to his human form. Redemption. Finally.

But that's not how things work in the comics. After restoring Sallis, Thog cursed a character named Chris Claremont[14] to be the Man-Thing, who then battles and defeats the demon. Dr. Strange subsequently restores Claremont to human form, at which point Sallis transforms back into the Man-Thing and the issue comes to an end.

For a brief moment, I had considered buying the issue, but for someone who had never paid more than a quarter for a comic book, 50 cents seemed like an awful lot of money. I carefully replaced the comic on the shelf, so as not to crease the cover or scuff the spine. Old habits die hard.

Notes

1   In the Marvel Comics universe, the Strategic Homeland Intervention, Enforcement, and Logistics Division, or S.H.I.E.L.D., is an international peacekeeping, law enforcement, and counter-terrorism agency founded by Howard Stark and sanctioned by the United Nations.

2   Advanced Idea Mechanics, or A.I.M., is a privately funded think tank established to acquire and develop advanced technologies with the intent of overthrowing the governments of the world. A.I.M. is a consistent antagonist in Marvel's comics and was referenced directly in the film, *Iron Man III*, as the malevolent force behind the terrorist attacks of the Mandarin.

3   Curt Connors is a character well known to readers (and viewers) of the Spider-Man franchise. Connors, one of Peter Parker's professors at Empire State University, was missing his right arm, which had been lost to an explosion in combat. His research to develop a regenerative compound led him to create a serum using reptilian DNA, as those creatures possessed the ability regenerate lost limbs. Using himself as the first test subject of his serum, Connors is transformed into the villain known as the Lizard.

4   My own superpower as a young boy was using a yardstick and masking tape to retrieve dropped lunch tokens from below the grates outside our school room doors. An average Saturday fishing expedition could yield two weeks' worth of lunch tokens and a handful of quarters, which allowed me to use my weekly three dollars of lunch money to buy comics, baseball cards, and, of course, candy.

5   Susan Bell, "Monsters on our minds: What our fascination with frightful creatures says about us," *USC News*, October 30, 2017. https://news.usc.edu/130364/monsters-on-our-minds-what-our-fascination-with-frightful-creatures-says-about-us/.

6   Leo Braudy, "Why we'll always be obsessed with—and afraid of—monsters," *The Conversation*, October 28, 2016. https://theconversation.com/why-well-always-be-obsessed-with-and-afraid-of-monsters-65080.

7   Bell, "Monsters on our minds."

8   Ibid.

9   Patricia Donovan, "Why we create monsters," *UB Reporter*, October 27, 2011. https://www.buffalo.edu/ubreporter/archive/2011_10_27/monster_culture.html.

10   Ibid.

11   Douglas Wolk, *All of the Marvels* (New York: Penguin Press, 2021), 69–76.

12   Creating character empathy is a common theme in most writing workshops. Although the approach might change slightly between writers, the formula remains largely consistent.

13   Wolk, 8.

14   Chris Claremont is one of the most celebrated writers in the history of Marvel Comics, and he also took a turn writing *Man-Thing*, including this issue, #11 (Vol. 2). Claremont was the long-time writer of the *X-Men* comics and is credited with revitalizing that franchise with his remarkably crafted stories.

CHAPTER 32

Marvel Zombies

When Heroes and Villains Confront Ever-Shifting Morality

Jon Niccum

No two subjects have dominated the pop culture landscape of the last 20 years more than superheroes and zombies.

Marvel created a way to capitalize on both.

First appearing in 2005, Marvel's zombie metaseries pioneers an excuse to pit the valiant costumed protectors of comic books against the flesh-eating monsters from film and television. But it also provides an environment in which the roles of heroes and villains fluctuate. Someone so rooted in Boy Scout-respectability as Captain America can instantly transform into a ravenous, amoral fiend. A foe as inherently ruthless as Kingpin can become the lone voice of reason in a dystopian battle zone.

As the 2006 standalone debut issue trumpets: "This is no world of Marvel Heroes. This is the world of *MARVEL ZOMBIES*."

Not surprisingly, the higher-ups at the publishing empire originally hated the idea.

Scottish writer Mark Millar was attending one of Marvel's quarterly retreats when he pitched the concept of a zombie superhero from another dimension infecting the Avengers.

"I remember it was so universally loathed, and everyone thought I was kidding when I suggested it. I just smiled and took it on the chin," he says.[1]

Fortunately, then-editor-in-chief Joe Quesada found merit in the kooky notion and allowed Millar to incorporate it into his first effort for *Ultimate Fantastic Four*. The story revolves around a young Reed Richards, leader of the fledgling FF, being invited to "gather the smartest minds in the multiverse" by a version of himself from a parallel dimension. But … it is actually just a ploy for a zombified Richards to open a portal to an alternate world for a fresh source of meat.

"Ever get the feeling you've been had?" Richards's bloodthirsty counterpart greets him.

The book proved a success, and a *Marvel Zombies* miniseries was greenlit. This time zombie connoisseur Robert Kirkman, creator of *The Walking Dead*, took the helm alongside artist Sean Phillips.

"I didn't even really want to do this book," Kirkman reveals.[2] "I love zombies—zombie movies, zombie comics, zombie lunch boxes—I love it all. But the thing is, *The Walking Dead* pretty much scratches that itch."

Kirkman initially fumbled with a hook, admitting that ideas such as Hawkeye or Luke Cage being pursued by the undead did not exactly thrill him. But when an editor suggested he make the zombies the lead characters, his interest piqued, as did the notion of incorporating "severed arms and swollen legs and chewed intestines and all kinds of gross gore stuff that every zombie story should be chock-full of."[3]

Yet what makes the series so compelling is the nature of this particular infection. The virus (officially called either the Hunger or the Hunger Gospel in Marveldom) seems so much worse than those found in *Night of the Living Dead*, *28 Days Later*, *World War Z*, *Train to Busan*, or even Kirkman's own *The Walking Dead*. This is undoubtedly the most aggressively evil contagion yet conceived.

The horror community often debates the virtues of "slow zombies vs. fast zombies." This introduces a third option. Not only do these creatures move quickly—and in the case of turned superheroes, someone as swift as Quicksilver can infect thousands in seconds—the virus itself spreads exponentially. Zombie Richards claims, "Within 24 hours, we'd consumed the entire planet."

Worse, no organic individual appears immune. Wolverine's healing factor does not cure him. Luke Cage's bulletproof skin provides no protection. Morbius, the Living Vampire's cursed blood disease is overwhelmed by this even nastier affliction. (By comparison, how could the *Night of the Living Dead*-style shuffling, intellect-free cadavers hope to surmount the radar-heightened reflexes of Daredevil, for example?)

It also proves challenging for the uninfected who are attempting to combat these virtually immortal enemies because the zombies can survive most anything except complete destruction of the brain. Thus, one can pulverize an adversary into near nothingness and still not "kill" it. Deadpool's most annoying feature—his mouthiness—continues in the form of a disembodied head that is hauled around. Captain America's brain even survives on its own for decades before placed in another host body.

The virus seems similar to what Kyle Reese (Michael Biehn) memorably describes in *The Terminator*: "It can't be reasoned with. It doesn't feel pity, or remorse, or fear. And it absolutely will not stop ... ever, until you are dead!"[4]

Or undead in this case.

But unlike mankind's deadliest viruses such as Ebola or smallpox, this one is sentient. Sorceress Jennifer Kale of the Midnight Sons identifies it as "some kind of collective super-consciousness" in Fred Van Lente's *Marvel Zombies #3*.

The Hunger can communicate with its brethren, make long-term plans, and execute complicated deceptions. The only goal is to multiply. It can jump to different planets, universes, dimensions, or timelines. And it does it with almost religious fervor.

As Zombie Kingpin exclaims, "The Gospel will be spread."

In Van Lente's *Marvel Zombies* #4, Morbius theorizes how the Hunger nestles within bone marrow and distributes a "secondary nervous system" which animates the infected host, and that is what ultimately controls the victim—even though memories and personalities remain intact. Here is one more reason why this viral concept is more thematically provocative than "everyone becomes braindead" as in most zombie shows. For instance, a good many jokes are had at the expense of Zombie Spider-Man that he continues to beat himself up over the fact he ate his beloved Mary Jane and Aunt May. Giant Man and the Wasp's marital spats take on new meanings when they entail whether to consume a fellow Avenger. (Wasp temporarily loses the argument when Giant Man bites off her head to preserve the secret he has kept a drugged Black Panther alive in order to devour him piecemeal.)

What are its limitations?

For Earth's superheroes, it may bolster their durability but often diminishes their innate powers.

Hulk is still the strongest but also the hungriest, making him unbelievably reckless around his infected colleagues. Black Bolt endures necrosis of the vocal cords, so his vaunted sonic scream becomes useless (and like Deadpool, he now will not shut up). Dr. Strange can only perform two spells.

"One (spell) causes manna to fall from the Heavens. Quite inedible to our kind, I'm afraid. But the other casts windows to interdimensional crossroads with our world," Zombie Kingpin says.

Yet another way for superheroes to spread the Gospel.

"The Rules have Changed"

Millar's modest first pitch became canon. Zombie Richards recounts how another world's superhero (who is probably a version of Sentry, based on the visible bits of his costume, but could easily be construed as Superman) intentionally materializes as a threat to Manhattan. The Avengers are dispatched. Things do not go as planned.

"What they didn't know is that the infection had targeted the superheroes of this dimension and a thousand realities before us," he explains. "This was how it consumed, you see, by infecting superheroes just like him and sending them out to infect the others."

Part of the appeal of this scenario is seeing characters who have weathered any number of death-defying contests become suddenly slain or converted into malevolent expediters of a devastating plague. As showcased so vividly in Amazon Prime's adaptation of *Invincible* (also written by Kirkman), few images are more intrinsically shocking than the graphic murder of a superhero. In *Marvel Zombies*, it happens perpetually.

While that admittedly can get numbing, what persists are the ethical issues presented. This is where the metaseries becomes more interesting than the typical Secret Wars, Secret Invasion, or JLA/Avengers setups—the so-called "everybody in the pool" plot—used to procure a whole legion of characters interacting with others not typically part of their neighborhood. In this chthonic setting, the definition of hero or villain is nebulous because it can change instantaneously.

It is what makes Kirkman's opening image from the first issue of *Marvel Zombies* so arresting: Uber-villain Magneto is sprawled on an urban hellscape, proclaiming, "It worked—the machine has been destroyed. It ends here. Those monsters—they're trapped in this dimension."

An ensuing splash page reveals what he is looking at: zombie versions of Thor, Spider-Man, Moon Knight, Daredevil, Captain America, Luke Cage, Giant Man, Angel, and Wolverine (with silhouettes of even more turned-heroes in the background).

Daredevil responds, "Yeah, we're trapped here, all right. With you."

This leads to a battle where Magneto, the master of magnetism—who is surrounded by all kinds of metal found on a city block—takes on these famished adversaries. The reader's sympathy immediately shifts to the notoriously anti-humanistic mutant as he slays and maims a batch of Marvel headliners … and uses Cap's shield as a key projectile.

Kirkman's implication is evident straightaway: The normal rules do not apply. Moral integrity becomes a sliding scale when an external factor upends the natural balance.

For some—like Magneto—it offers a chance for unlikely redemption. The leader of the Brotherhood of Evil Mutants finds himself the improbable protector of non-mutant civilians. Constructing a refuge in a railway tunnel, he harbors a small band that includes a police officer, insurance salesman, and diabetic teen.

"The end of the world is a great leveler—beggars can't be choosers when you're down to the last few people alive," he says.

Magneto even stays behind to destroy the teleporter after these civilians escape to a safe dimension where zombies cannot follow, leaving him at the mercy of an army of hostiles—a selfless act to save homo sapiens by the one who spent his life advocating they should be supplanted by homo superior.

For others, it exposes the true nature of their commitment to dogma at all costs. In John Layman's *Marvel Zombies vs. Army of Darkness*, loudmouth and human pincushion Ash Williams (cheekily played by Bruce Campbell in the Evil Dead flicks) finds himself in a world dominated by infected super folks along with the parasitic demons he customarily combats. Encountering various luminaries throughout his ordeal, he gets teamed with the Punisher at one point. Despite the zombie plague ravaging New York, the skull-adorned vigilante busts in on a meeting of crime lords that includes Kingpin, Hammerhead, and the Owl.

Kingpin parlays, "You see what's happening outside? The rules have changed now. We're on the same team…. Us versus them. Human versus zombie."

The machine gun-toting antihero responds by firing bullets through their heads. The Punisher says, "As far as I'm concerned, you were never human."

For a lethal, mission-oriented sentinel such as the Punisher, optics do not matter. A villain is a villain, regardless of the context. Had Kingpin's cronies been the last humans left on Earth, they still would have been executed.

Similarly, in *Marvel Zombies*, a group of infected heroes vie with a group of infected villains for the right to eat the massive, downed conqueror Galactus. This frenzy pits Captain America against his arch nemesis Red Skull. Irrespective of the fact Cap is missing the top of his cranium, he boasts, "You never could hope to best me in a physical fight—what makes you even try? Has the Hunger consumed you that much?"

The Red Skull replies that his foe has never displayed such a glaring weakness, prior to reaching in and pulling out Cap's brain. Upon himself getting decapitated, the Nazi's head continues gloating: "So worth it—all of it. Just for this."

Even though both men are equally afflicted and experiencing the same overwhelming craving, their nearly 100-year antagonism continues to the bitter end.

Exploring New Realms

In an episode of the first season of the Disney+ series *What if … ?*, Marvel finally brought the storyline to television. *What if … Zombies?!* emerges as the most memorable entry of the Emmy-winning streaming show, albeit one diverging considerably from the groundwork laid by Millar and Kirkman. Matthew Chauncey (a veteran of TV's *Ms. Marvel*) pens a genuinely harrowing tale that begins when Hank Pym enters the Quantum Realm searching for his wife, only to find her infected with the virus.

Meanwhile, the events of *Avengers: Infinity War* are playing out, but when Thanos' Black Order arrives to announce their impending conquest, they are converted into living dead by Iron Man, Dr. Strange, and sorcerer Wong. A band of superhero survivors seek out Vision, hoping his Mind Stone can halt the epidemic, eventually discovering he has been luring others to feed a Zombie Scarlet Witch.

Once again, Marvel finds a way to thwart expectations of good and evil. Thanos and his crew represent the ultimate threat in the MCU. Yet in this zombie-overrun Earth, they could be its best hope. The Infinity Gauntlet-wearing Titan might advocate wiping out "half the universe," but at least his surviving members would retain their uninfected humanity.

This rather bleak installment of the animated series features an equally downbeat ending. Spider-Man, Black Panther, and Ant-Man fly to Wakanda, oblivious to the fact the country has already been overthrown by a Zombie Thanos brandishing a near-completed Infinity Gauntlet.

Following the release of this episode, Marvel Studios announced a *Marvel Zombies* series that will reportedly pick up where the cliffhanger left off.[5]

Viral Messaging

But … what does it all really *mean*?

Such a collision of pop-culture tropes could have been mere exploitation. A simple cash grab. Yet there is something deeper at play here.

Any number of socio-historical analyses involving George Romero's iconic *Night of the Living Dead* and *Dawn of the Dead* bring up the notion that "the zombies are us."[6] As such, their plight remains fundamentally comparable to human flaws and misfortunes.

Among the interpretations of this zombie tale, the Hunger can be seen as a metaphor for addiction. Sure, this one is a bit obvious. With oxycodone-like efficiency, the virus can instantly transform "you into one of them." As William S. Burrough wrote in *Junkie*, "You don't decide to be an addict. One morning you wake up sick and you're an addict."[7]

True addiction can make individuals turn on anyone to secure their high. Logic, decency, integrity, self-destruction—none of these costs matter more than the next fix when someone is overcome by such dependence.

What is ironic about the zombie sickness is that those corrupted by it do not even need a stomach or digestive system in order to suffer unrelenting hunger pangs. There is no true purpose to feeding their habit, just a purpose in spreading the *addiction* to the habit.

The Hunger can also be seen as a metaphor for propaganda—or perhaps the more buzzworthy term "fake news."

Intensifying during the 2016 American presidential election cycle, fake news has now burrowed itself as an unavoidable part of everyday life. Identified as the purposeful dissemination of information, rumor, or lies with the intent of injuring a cause, individual, or institution, modern propaganda carries with it a kind of cult-like ability to proliferate thanks to advances in communication technology. (Gone are the old days when military aircraft dropped flyers from the sky as a way of manipulating allies and enemies.)

More alarming is that not only has the sheer amount of it increased, but research shows the confidence in it is amplified upon repeated exposure. As evidenced by Gordon Pennycook and David G. Rand's "Who Falls for Fake News?," familiarity plays "an important role in belief about fake news despite the fact that fake news content is often quite implausible."[8]

The logline: "A tainted hero first recruits other heroes to foster an epidemic" could easily describe how congressional election deniers got recruited to promote "the Big Lie." Or, playing devil's advocate, it could also be argued how the so-called "woke agenda" gets circulated through Hollywood.

The zombie plague itself is even introduced through such informational deceit. A young Reed Richards is originally enticed with the promise of sharing knowledge that might benefit others, yet he is really just a pawn to further an agenda explicitly harmful to himself. (If that isn't the definition of U.S. politics in the 2020s, then what is?)

Finally, the Hunger can double as a metaphor for religion.

The famously "anti-theist" author Christopher Hitchens often posed what has become known as "Hitchens's Challenge" when debating religious leaders: Name at least one moral action that a person without a faith could not perform, and name one immoral action that only a person with a faith could perform.[9]

When applied to the Hunger, the challenge becomes: Name at least one moral action that an uninfected person could not perform, and name one immoral action that only an infected person could perform.

That is a pretty easy solve. (A: Any of them. B: Infecting someone with the virus.)

If treating religion like an unnecessary spreadable disease—or more accurately treating a religious cult or doctrine as such—the comparison matches up. Zombies retain all the memories of their previous selves but give the entirety of their focus toward indoctrinating others, even when those targets do not want to be indoctrinated.

Attending worship services or accomplishing good deeds might seem like the primary facet of most religions. However, many emphasize that the most significant service a member of the faith can perform is to proselytize. Recruit. Convert. Repeat.

No wonder Zombie Kingpin affirms, "We exist *only* to spread the Hunger Gospel."

And yet there may be hope.

As with any compulsion—whether involving opiates, fake news, or cult-like religions—the initial step toward freeing oneself is removing the source. Wasp is among the first of the former heroes who realize the Hunger subsides once she stops ingesting flesh for a few weeks. She notes her "recovery" is not a fluke. Not an "isolated case."

Zombie Spider-Man confesses, "The longer we go without eating, I could be imagining this but ... it seems like the pain—the Hunger is ... starting to fade."

For *Marvel Zombies* fans, however, there will be little pause from feasting on this fascinating overlap of action and horror. A four-episode series is set to appear on Disney+ in 2024, which also represents the first animated Marvel property to earn a TV-MA rating for its mature content.

The Gospel is indeed spreading ...

Notes

1   Henry Varona, "Mark Millar Reveals the Never-Told Secret Origin of Marvel Zombies," *Comic Book Resources*, September 15, 2021. https://www.cbr.com/marvel-zombies-mark-millar-secret-origin/.

2   Robert Kirkman, *Marvel Zombies* (Marvel Comics, 2006), foreword.

3   Ibid.

4   James Cameron, director. 1984. *The Terminator*. Orion Pictures.

5   Ben Hurley, "Marvel announces new Marvel Zombies series for Disney+," The Cultured Nerd, November 12, 2021. https://theculturednerd.org/2021/11/marvel-announces-new-marvel-zombies-series-for-disney/.

6   Nick Muntean, "'The zombies are us': a socio-historical analysis of George Romero's 'Night of the Living Dead,'" (University of Texas Libraries, 2007), 1–2.

7   William S. Burroughs, *Junkie: Confessions of an Unredeemed Drug Addict* (New York: Ace Books, 1953), prologue.

8   Gordon Pennycook and David G. Rand, *Who falls for fake news? The roles of analytic thinking, motivated reasoning, political ideology, and bullshit receptivity* (New Haven, Connecticut: Yale University Press, 2017), 4.

9   Christopher Hitchens, *"Hitchens Challenge," 2007*, https://www.youtube.com/watch?v=4TnA3b8MhD0v.

CHAPTER 33

Strip Mining the Superhero Archetype

Janeen Webb

Humans are hard-wired for stories. And since narrative forms the basis for all our social interactions, from family anecdotes to national identities, it follows that narrative control confers great power. Such control is an essential part of any effective strategy, whether civilian or military. "Reality," like "history" (and unlike the physical laws of the universe), is socially constructed through culturally significant narratives. It is a fable upon which we have agreed to agree—an amalgam of shared values, shared experiences, shared cultural history, and shared beliefs, all of which feed into our concept of ourselves in time and space.[1] In this context, it is arguable that the overarching narrative of the Marvel Universe, with its multitudinous variations on the archetypal theme of the superhero, can be seen as emblematic of our current battle to maintain social cohesion in the face of concerted attack.

What we understand as reality changes over time: Galileo, for example, was persecuted for supporting Copernican heliocentrism—the idea that the earth orbits the sun—a position now widely accepted as a basic truth of our existence in the universe. But not all truths are so readily demonstrable. The explanatory narratives we create are often biased, distorted, conjectural, simplistic, politicized, and so on, but for all that they remain a powerful force that impinges directly upon our collective world view. We now live in a post-truth age of competing narratives, where media-savvy politicians and corporate entities employ strategies like "fake news" and "deep fake technology" in a battle to control not just the social narrative of a given situation, but the idea of reality itself. The recent advent of social media—and in the midst of all the hurly-burly it is easy to forget that it *is* a recent phenomenon—has brought us, with incredible speed, to a point where the philosophical concepts of "truth" and "reality" have been reduced to a question of which unexamined assumptions people will believe, and which unmediated sources they will trust—and, as a result, our social narrative is fragmenting. Ironically, this process of "like" speaking only to "like"—where certain groups take their "news" only from their own sources—is an inherently medieval structure, isolating self-interested groups in echo chambers of their own making.

Available media always drive popular perceptions. Narrative archetypes were, of course, already ancient and thoroughly culturally embedded by the time medieval religious groups used them to create pictorial representations of their codified truths—showing the triumph of good over evil, depicting the Devil and the tortures of Hell as the consequence of stepping out of line. It is a huge technological step from early Church iconography to the secular wide-screen cinema of the MCU, and from cinema to online streaming, but the didactic impulse remains the same. And the story structures have not changed a bit.

Archetypal hero paradigms are traditional narrative image patterns that recur often enough in our cultural stories to be immediately recognizable—they are so familiar that we respond almost viscerally to their symbols of power and conquest, supremacy, and subjugation. These structures function as a universal narrative shorthand, and audiences automatically settle back to watch the drama unfold as heroic quests play out. When transferred to the big screen, this is cinematic comfort food. The interest is in *how* the heroes will triumph—there is, generally, no doubt about the end result. In these paradigmatic narrative sequences, the heroes occupy the central position. These stories are dialectic in form, focused on the conflict between the heroes and their opposing forces and the tension between the partisan groups they generate and represent. And because the superhero dominates the action, the dramatic events are largely portrayed in terms of significance to that hero—everything else is secondary.

Superheroes themselves also adhere to the archetypal narrative patterns of epic tales, beginning with a mysterious or traumatic childhood: The hero may, for example, have hidden lineage and be raised by foster parents for the sake of safety, only to emerge when their inherited or acquired powers become apparent and concealment is no longer possible or necessary. Many gods and heroes also have a secret flaw: Greek hero Achilles, for example, had an unprotected spot on his heel and died when a god-directed arrow found its mark; Norse god Balder could only be killed by mistletoe, and died when mischievous Loki threw a mistletoe twig at him; Superman is vulnerable to kryptonite, and so on. Conversely, superheroes depend on superior skills and often have magical and talismanic weapons: King Arthur has the sword Excalibur; Thor, Norse god of thunder and protagonist of several MCU movies, has his hammer, Mjölnir. Such weapons of power tend to be hero specific—only Arthur can wield Excalibur, only Thor can truly wield Mjölnir. However, some superhero scenarios include transferable objects—for example, the recent Netflix series *Warrior Nun* (2020) features an "angel halo" which confers superpowers upon whoever currently has it embedded in their flesh. Heroes also often have mentors and are advised by wizards or wise elders: Arthur has Merlin, Frodo has Gandalf, the X-Men have Charles Xavier, and so on. And when an enemy tests them, superheroes most often resolve the challenges in single combat.

The elements of this archetypal superhero pattern can be laid as a palimpsest over any hero of your choice: It works across mythologies and religions, and it works from the earliest Saxon superhero, Beowulf, to modern heroes Luke Skywalker and Harry Potter. It works. If we look, for example, at Marvel's Spider-Man, we learn that Spider-Man is the alias of Peter Parker, who was raised by his foster parents Aunt May and Uncle Ben after Peter's parents were killed. He acquires his superhuman powers (superhuman strength, agility, and speed; ability to cling to surfaces; danger warning spider-sense; and so on) from being bitten by a radioactive spider. He is supported through a difficult adolescence by mentors such as J. Jonah Jameson and Harry Osborn. In the MCU, he fights crime with the aid of his talismanic objects, which are web-shooter devices attached to his wrists.[2] There is no mistaking the archetypal patterning.

Superheroes often defend humanity against destruction by elemental forces. Superman regularly saves the earth from imminent disasters—most recently, in Infinite Frontier #3, from a meteorite. Superheroes also fight elemental adversaries— dragons, ogres, monsters of all kinds—inherently destructive creatures that simply act according to their natures and for whom the concepts of "good" and "evil" have no meaning. We cannot, for example, ascribe moral intention to monsters such as Grendel in *Beowulf*, or Tolkien's giant spider Shelob: "... she served none but herself, drinking the blood of Elves and Men, bloated and grown fat with endless brooding on her feasts, weaving webs of shadow; for all living things were her food, and her vomit darkness."[3]

But where superheroes face antagonists of equal and opposite stature or ability, the archetypal pattern may apply, in equal measure, to the villains of these narra-tives—MCU characters such as Loki have their own childhood traumas (abandoned as a baby, fostered by Odin), wield their own talismanic weapons (special knives and a Chitauri Scepter), are aided by their own mentors (the goddess Frigga teaches him astral projection and sorcery) and so on. Such characters are often charismatic and attractive, but for them the darker path is a matter of personal inclination, of deliberate choice.

It is also worth noting that it is a simple imperative of serial fiction that protag-onists—villains as well as heroes—must evolve to maintain audience interest. So, where popular MCU villains recur, they acquire increasingly complex motivations. For example, the mutant villain Magneto (appearing mostly in X-Men movies) is a holocaust survivor who changes gradually from supervillain to anti-hero to hero; in turn, he hates Red Skull, the Nazi archenemy of Captain America. Additionally, some recent MCU villains, like black ops U.S. Navy SEAL Erik "Killmonger" Stevens in *Black Panther* (2018), do have a point to make.

For the heroes on the side of the angels, the idea that "with great power comes great responsibility" is taken seriously in the MCU. Superheroes who champion what they believe to be "right" are powerful enough to do whatever they please, but they place limits upon themselves (or society does) for the continued wellbeing of the less powerful humanity. On the other hand, the villains do not care for such niceties—they generally have no compunction about the consequences of their self-indulgent actions. The balance between the forces subjectively termed "good" and "evil" must be maintained; otherwise, there would be no contest, no story. In the end, the overarching narrative determines that despite occasional setbacks the hero wins out, unleashing superpowers on the side of "right" despite the personal ethical dilemmas this may occasion or the collateral damage it may cause. But this, in itself, creates a dilemma for strategists: after all, if force is the solution to every problem, there is no incentive for leaders to invest time and resources in creative problem-solving—it is much easier, if much more destructive, to let the opposing sides just fight it out.

So, what happens when these universal archetypes of gods and heroes, of myth, epic, and romance, are deliberately co-opted into the Marvel Multiverse, a spectrum of stories that smashes together elements of multiple, competing mythologies? Do we get something greater than the sum of the parts? Or are we merely trapped in the pattern, celebrating endlessly replicating memes? Is this construct capable of offering divergent, innovative strategic thinking, or does it simply enlarge the tropes of "might is right" in on-screen battles where the biggest weapons win?

The constantly evolving MCU has created an overarching narrative that functions like polytheistic religions: It is a huge, sprawling, dysfunctional family group of gods and heroes, each with their own superpowers, each competing in one way or another with other members of the group, generating useful plot tensions and endless possible story variations. The result is a complex surrealist tapestry where we follow a single thread for each movie, or cluster of movies, making our own connections where we can and stepping back to try to understand the bigger picture. The creation of The Avengers—a team of "earth's mightiest heroes" who come together to fight planetary threats—is generally seen as pivotal in the expansion of the MCU. This new team was the crossover point where technology-based heroes like Iron Man (with his mechanized, weaponized suit of armor) and Captain America (whose powers stem from his being injected with a super soldier serum) were combined with supernatural, myth-based characters like Thor.

This founding group of core Avengers forms the basis for a fluid superhero team where others are co-opted as needed—some, like *Guardians of the Galaxy* (2014) characters Rocket and Nebula, have very temporary Avengers status. Others who appear more often also include, at various junctures and in no particular order, Hulk, Black Widow, Hawkeye, Spider-Man, Ant-Man, Captain Marvel, Falcon, and Vision. As Owen Gleiberman commented in his *Entertainment Weekly* article on *The Avengers*, these team members are often at odds: "Simply put: These freaks of goodness may be a team, but they don't like each other very much."[4] There is significant tension within the core group—there is, for example, a shield-versus-hammer fight when Captain America first encounters Thor. More significantly, Iron Man and Captain America don't get along a lot of the time. Their antagonism is explicit in their reactions to the Sokovia Accords, which arise from events in *The Age of Ultron* (2015) and at the opening of *Captain America: Civil War* (2016), where collateral damage to humanity prompts the UN to create legislation to bring superhumans under its authority—Iron Man supports the Accords, Captain America is opposed. The resolution of issues such as these indicates just one of the many ways in which the MCU allows its superheroes to act and interact in different ways according to the various versions of the multiverse in which they find themselves, thus expanding and extending their narrative reach.

One of the ways in which this multiverse works best for modern audiences is that it makes the mysteries of the old gods literal, keeping their traditional backstories but replacing their more enigmatic aspects with careful explanations of their intrinsic powers and limitations. The lists are exhaustive. And they still point squarely to their origins in archetypal hero structures. For example, the well-known Norse mythological characters Thor and Loki have long been co-opted into the Marvel universe, and a quick check of the official Marvel website reveals that Thor Odinson, God of Thunder, Defender of Asgard and Midgard, is renowned for his strength, endurance, and stamina.[5] He commands the elemental forces of nature, especially thunder and lightning, and his talismanic weapon is his hammer, Mjölnir, said to have been forged by his father, Odin, from the heart of a dying star. He is at odds with the mischievous Loki, his half-brother. Loki is an intelligent, tactical thinker with the typical Asgardian powers of strength, durability, and longevity. He also has magical abilities such as astral projection, shape-shifting, hypnosis, molecular rearrangement, energy blasts, levitating, conjuration, cytokinesis, telekinesis, teleportation, telepathy, and the ability to create rifts between dimensions. His physical weapons of choice are throwing knives and small blades.

In a process that provides a literal demonstration of Joseph Campbell's influential characterization of the archetypal hero as *The Hero with a Thousand Faces*,[6] the MCU creators are strip mining these archetypes to produce superpower lists for every one of the multiplicity of their characters. These detailed lists support on-screen roles and attempt to differentiate each character through minor variations on the heroic tropes. It is a very successful strategy that taps into deep-seated audience acceptance of what stories should be. It privileges entertainment above all else. After so many of these movies, MCU consumers applaud spectacle, not depth: As Mysterio (a villain whose *modus operandi* is to create the illusion of threats in order to appear to save humanity from them) explains to Spider-Man, "You can be the smartest guy in the room, the most qualified, and no one cares—unless you're flying around with a cape and shooting lasers from your hands no one will even listen."[7] This comment is, of course, recursive, directed as much at the cinematic audience as the internal audience of the movie.

The title of Michael Roman's impressive online site, *Everything Always*, summarizes how the MCU actually works—giving consumers a bit of everything all the time.[8]

It is also an accurate analogy for how social media works. It is addictive. Users are always hungry for more. The release strategies for successive MCU films are a calculated trail of breadcrumbs, drawing the audience inexorably toward the next iteration. We know, for example, that there will be further Spider-Man movies in 2023 and 2024 and Avengers movies in 2025 and 2026. The advertising is already with us. The narrative hooks precede the new stories, and the faithful audience dares not look away for fear of missing out—one of the many ways the MCU uses social media mechanisms to guarantee commercial success.

Social media is already changing the way we think and what we will accept: We are taught to want endless previews, immediate answers, and reports. While this is not inherently dangerous in the realms of fiction, when transposed into the 'real' world of news stories and political debate, the distortions of unconsidered information have already begun to disrupt our social fabric. The disjuncture between information and knowledge has widened to a gaping chasm: The very nature of social media is that it presents as a surrealist construct, where everything has the same surface value and observers must decide for themselves how the pieces fit together—if they do fit together at all. This situation encourages half-truths and the magpie collections of bits and pieces that fit so very easily into conspiracy theories of all sorts, leaving an unsuspecting population vulnerable to the garbled pseudo-scientific babble of conspiracist groups. As informed readers, we have emerged from a background where editorial processes ensured a modicum of scrutiny, or at least a sense of the relative knowledge bases of contributors. Now, online research into any given topic (even the MCU) will offer up everything from a high school student essay to a research paper by a Harvard professor, without comment—it is up to the individual to undertake additional research into the source of every article. Serious researchers have learned to find ways to circumvent search engines, which push inexorably toward the information biases of the corporate cultures which create them. It takes time and focus to keep re-framing the question until the engine is derailed enough to permit access to different sources to find an alternate route through the maze. This challenge is not just a case of the medium controlling the message—it is a matter of the medium blocking certain messages, determining what is expressible.

The superheroes of the Marvel Universe offer us an updated cinematic window into archetypal thinking and narrative patterning. The real lesson for strategists lies in understanding how traditional archetypes operate in the construction of political and military narratives and in accepting that the ancient paradigms of heroic behavior are not susceptible to logic—the intended audience is likely to give credence to stories that fit established narrative tropes in the face of any amount of factual evidence. And the particular archetypes adopted by combatants reveal a great deal about how they are positioning themselves in the ongoing global media battle for hearts and minds. Archetypal narratives shape not just the thinking, but also the strategy and tactics of contemporary warfare. Post-WWII commentary and debates taking place in fora such as the United Nations were largely focused on logic, with an emphasis on uncovering hidden truths. But in the late twentieth century, some world leaders successfully reversed that debate, turning the dialogue back from demonstrable knowledge to belief—a position more susceptible to narrative manipulation.

In every conflict there is evidence of propaganda, disinformation, and deliberate political appropriation and manipulation of heroic tropes. The current war in Ukraine, playing out in the ruins of the USSR, allows us to see that process in action. The countries have diverged: Russia has held to old beliefs and economic systems; Ukraine has adopted a more modern, western-style democratic economy. Both sides are using the archetypes of leader and hero, but they have chosen different variations. In Russia, the ageing Putin styles himself as the great general, immaculately dressed, controlling military operations from the safety of his fortress. He presents as an absolute ruler surrounded by a praetorian guard—a repressive dark overlord who is as dangerous to his own people as he is to his enemies.

On the other hand, in Ukraine, the much younger, media-adept Zelensky appears for the cameras wearing a T-shirt and combat pants. He is shown standing alone in a bombed-out landscape of ruined streets in his besieged cities, ready to defend his people against overwhelming odds, overtly embracing the archetypal symbolism of David against Goliath, of Frodo defying Sauron, of Luke Skywalker challenging Darth Vader. Both narratives have their roots in myth, epic, and romance—the very archetypes upon which the Marvel Universe is based. The process has come full circle—now politicians are strip mining the tropes of the MCU. And in a world where newsworthy events are all "stories," entertainment to be consumed by mass media audiences, scenes such as the explosive battle between Spider-Man and Mysterio in London offer a hyperreal visual representation of destruction which appears every bit as authentic as the recorded footage of a drone strike in Kyiv. And there's the rub … as the boundaries between fact and fiction become increasingly and deliberately blurred, as we give archetypal narrative patterns precedence over objective analyses, we risk the magical thinking that comes along with that. As Mysterio puts it, "It's easy to fool people when they're already fooling themselves."[9]

Notes

1   See Peter Burger and Thomas Luckmann, *The Social Construction of Reality* (New York: Anchor Books, 1966), for extensive discussion.
2   The official website, marvel.com, provides exhaustive notes on all MCU characters.
3   J.R.R. Tolkien, *The Lord of the Rings: The Two Towers* (London: George Allen & Unwin, 1966) 296.
4   Owen Gleiberman, "The Avengers," *Entertainment Weekly*, August 14, 2012. Cited in "Avengers (Marvel Cinematic Universe)," en.Wikipedia.org archived from original August 1, 2020; retrieved May 12, 2021.
5   See marvel.com

6   Joseph Campbell, *The Hero with a Thousand Faces* (London: Abacus, 1975).
7   *Spider-Man: Far from Home*, directed by John Watts (Columbia Pictures / Pascal Pictures / Marvel Studios, 2019), DVD.
8   Michael Roman, "Everything Always," *YouTube*. https://www.youtube.com/c/EverythingAlways.
9   *Spider-Man: Far from Home*.

CHAPTER 34

The New Gods

The Leadership Lessons of Jack "King" Kirby

Patrick Sullivan

If there was a Mount Rushmore of comic artists, then Jack Kirby would be its George Washington. Many of the heroes in this book are his creations, a fact lost perhaps on readers, especially given the well-known association between Stan Lee and Marvel. Several of the characters or teams most associated with Lee from Marvel's Silver Age—The Fantastic Four, The Incredible Hulk, Thor, Black Panther, the X-Men, and The Avengers—were actually collaborations between him as writer and Kirby as artist. These achievements built upon earlier success that Kirby—along with writer Joe Simon—in creating Captain America in the early 1940s for a pre-Marvel publisher called Timely Comics.[1]

Kirby's character creations were sufficient to secure his legacy reputation as "The King" among hardcore comic fans, but his enduring influence over the medium extends much further. His character motifs, creative use of frame space, collage-like layouts, and natural depictions of cosmic and futuristic elements (i.e., the "Kirby Krackle") defined the modern "Marvel Look" that revolutionized the comics industry and proved so profitable in translation to film and television.[2] Additionally, Kirby is credited with developing the now-standard trade paperback format, which was a natural extension of the more expansive storytelling that he and Lee had ushered in with "The Galactus Trilogy" in *The Fantastic Four* #48-50 (March—May 1966).[3] According to his biographer and one-time production assistant, Mark Evanier, Kirby believed that comics deserved better than the "cheap, disposable format" of the newsstand, with bookstores (and its young adult fantasy novel consumers) being a logical next step as well as important untapped market.[4]

Notwithstanding the career-defining achievements that Kirby had at Marvel, he departed the company for DC Comics in 1970 after a contract dispute.[5] Although his work at DC is not as popularly known, it reflects the height of his creative genius and artistic integrity. Colloquially described as "The Fourth World," Kirby's

DC work represented the "first true comic book epic," wherein he brought a career's worth of unrealized characters and ambition into an uncompromising and interconnected mythology that showed the world what the comics medium could and should be.[6] Kirby envisioned The Fourth World as encompassing a story arc with cosmic stakes—literally the fate of its Universe hanging in the balance—that spanned multiple titles over multiple years, culminating in a decisive ending where good triumphs over evil. This seems almost pedestrian given the structure of multiple "cinematic universes" in the current popular entertainment milieu. Moreover, like many innovators, Kirby's vision was not fully appreciated (or understood) at the time and ran up against a corresponding lack-of-vision within DC Comics' corporate leadership. Such disregard does not detract from The Fourth World's significance, however, as a landmark achievement in comics history that categorically influenced multiple mediums moving forward.

The signature title of The Fourth World was *The New Gods*, which established said cosmic stakes and the underlying mythology. Evanier suggests that Kirby was highly self-aware in selecting this title. New gods imply the existence of old ones. In resurrecting unrealized characters and ideas for The Fourth World, Kirby looked back to Thor and his original plan to start a series with the events of Ragnarök, the great battle from Norse mythology that promised to kill off old gods to make way for new ones, thereby ushering in the world's renewal. In this context, Kirby's introduction of The Fourth World under DC Comics is possibly a meta-commentary on his move from Marvel and the attendant separation from his past work, as well as his view of the creative opportunity that the move provided him.[7]

The New Gods centers on a conflict between two sister planets, the pastoral New Genesis and the dystopian, mechanistic Apokolips. New Genesis and Apokolips were once a single planet that was the home world of the old gods. With the planet's destruction, New Genesis formed from the positive residual "living atoms" and Apokolips formed from their negative counterparts. As such, the conflict between the two planets represents a good versus evil dynamic, and the planet's leaders—Highfather for New Genesis and Darkseid for Apokolips—are the archetypes of the heroic and evil New Gods, respectively.

A conflict between god planets is expectedly destructive, so much so in the case of New Genesis and Apokolips that the cosmos themselves were imperiled (which was possibly another Kirby dual meta-commentary on the nuclear age and the Cold War). Accordingly, Highfather and Darkseid entered a truce that was sealed by an exchange of sons. Neither planet dared attack the other with their progenies in the line of fire, with Highfather seeking a lasting peace through the arrangement whereas Darkseid played for time to develop surreptitious, less cosmically risky means to achieve ultimate victory. These means came to center on Earth, where the Anti-Life Equation supposedly lay waiting for discovery. With the Anti-Life

Equation, Darkseid could manipulate the free will of all sentient beings throughout the cosmos, Highfather and the gods of New Genesis included.

The main character of *The New Gods* is Darkseid's biological son and New Genesis' greatest hero, Orion. Trained and socialized by his surrogate father, Highfather, Orion wields a metaphysical projection of the divinity-like Source as a force for good and righteousness. Over the course of the original 11-issue Kirby run plus a culminating chapter in the six-issue reprint, Orion fights a rogues gallery of Darkseid's minions on Earth to prevent discovery of the Anti-Life Equation, and then returns to Apokolips for a battle with his birth father.[8] He is often accompanied in battle by the youthful warrior Lightray, occasionally receives assistance from the neutral knowledge-seeker Metron, and regularly enlists the help of four human allies (quasi-eponymously known as O'Ryan's Mob). Orion flies via the Astro-Harness, has a suit and helmet that allow him the focus the Astro-Force (the metaphysical Source projection described above), and utilizes a living computer called a "Mother Box" to travel inter-dimensionally. Orion also uses his Mother Box to change his appearance from its normal Apokolips-ian monstrosity to a form more palatable to New Genesis and its humanistic sensibilities. In an excellent character analysis published on the Cinema Debate website, writer Aaron Johnson suggests that Orion's use of the Mother Box and helmet reflects his self-loathing.[9] Kirby illustrates this to a degree in *The New Gods* #3 (June–July 1971) with two panels that show Orion's transition back to his original face, presented around Orion's self-commentary that his normal "mask of peace … stem[s] the pain of one who must live forever a riddle!"[10]

Orion's formidability as a warrior reflects the riddle associated with him being the son of two worlds. The deep bonds of trust and respect that marked his relationship with Highfather allowed him to focus the rage and raw power that he inherited from Darkseid. That rage and power were necessary for Orion to defeat the Apokolips-ian gods that he fought on Earth, however, especially his half-brother Kalibak (who is basically what Orion would have been with Highfather). In keeping with his nature, Orion relished battle and had no qualms about fighting without restraint, which did not always serve him well. On the occasions that Orion's discipline waned, and he began to lose focus or drift towards impulsivity, the ebullient Lightray or calculating Metron were there to serve as an anchoring influence.

Internal tension aside, Orion's love for and loyalty towards New Genesis never wavered, and that characteristic alone made him the antithesis of Darkseid's "creed of total violence."[11] Knowing that Orion was incorruptible in this regard, Darkseid did not attempt to bring him back to Apokolips' side, rejecting Orion in their battle by saying, "Don't call me father, you were never like me …—you don't plot, you don't scheme! You leap at life like a beast of prey!"[12] Accordingly, Orion is a powerful character vehicle through which to analyze the nurture versus nature debate. Kirby is practically explicit about this in *The New Gods* #6 (December 1971), asking,

"What is man in the last analysis—his philosophy or himself?"[13] The reason that Orion is New Genesis' champion is because only in the combination of his nature and the nurturing he received—the "power and purpose" of New Genesis as he describes it, a fierce warrior of the Apokolips disposition but ultimately just—can Highfather marshal the capability to defeat the forces of Darkseid. Ironic, and possibly another Kirby meta-commentary, that the exchange of sons contained the seeds of Darkseid's defeat in his play for time.

Although Orion relies on the bequests of both of his fathers, the fact that he consistently applies them towards heroism suggests that Kirby falls squarely on the side of nurture. The other side of the exchange of sons affirms this suggestion. Highfather's biological son, Scott Free, grew up in a "terror orphanage" on Apokolips where he was subjected to unrelenting horror and abuse. His subsequent escape and own heroic character development would seem to support the nature argument. On the contrary, and as explained in the longest running of The Fourth World titles, *Mister Miracle,* Scott Free's escape and follow-on development were actually abetted by three key nurturing agents: the aforementioned Metron, an Apokolips Resistance leader named Himon, and the woman who would eventually become his wife, the gentle giant Big Barda. In later treatments of the character, particularly the incredible 12-issue limited series by Tom King in 2017, Big Barda's nurturing proved instrumental in Scott Free overcoming various psychological issues related to his childhood trauma.

Even Highfather becomes fully formed through nurturing. Notwithstanding his narrative role as the character archetype for the heroic New Gods, Highfather's participation in the interplanetary war that led to the exchange of sons resulted from his "infection" by Darkseid and his evil ways.[14] The increasingly dangerous tapping into cosmic power to develop ever-more destructive weapons spawned a proliferation cycle that Highfather got swept up in. Prompted by Metron's intercession, Highfather re-found himself and committed to the cause of peace, and in so doing gained access to the Source as an oracle of sorts. The religious overtones here are obvious and further reinforce the nurture piece. In fact, the only New Gods in the original Kirby run who seem to act entirely according to their nature are Lightray (as an idealization of morality), Metron (as an idealization of logic), and Darkseid and his cartoonishly evil minions.

There have been subsequent volumes to Kirby's original run that add depth to Orion's character development and introduce new elements of Fourth World lore. Kirby wanted to end the entire Fourth World saga with the death of the New Gods—again, his original vision was a decisive ending where good triumphs over evil, a fitting epilogue to the death of the old gods in Ragnarök—but DC had a different vision and shifted the property to other writers and artists. Jim Starlin and Mike Mignola had a 28-issue run of *The New Gods* from 1989 to 1991, followed by *Jack Kirby's Fourth World* under a different creative team from 1995 to 1997. Concurrent with this volume, Walt Simonson produced a 25-issue series eponymously titled *Orion*, which just focused on the character. More recently, Jim Starlin produced an eight-issue limited series called *Death of the New Gods* as a lead-in to Grant Morrison's seminal *Final Crisis,* and most of Kirby's original Fourth World characters survived into DC's *The New 52* continuity and beyond. Focusing just on Kirby's treatment of the character, however, and if you side with nurture as Kirby does, then there are several powerful leadership lessons that come from Orion as a case study:

Build diverse teams. Everyone has experiential bias, and the "trust what you" know instinct can prompt leaders to populate their teams with members who are exactly like them (i.e., "mirroring"). This team-building approach is short-sighted and self-limiting, as it will rob the team of the variety of experiences (and associated points of view) that a diverse team composition offers. To wit, if New Genesis had mirrored in its selection of warriors, then it would not have been able to compete with Apokolips. A diverse team brings together a rich panoply of individual natures, and the more diversity you have the more complete the team's collective experience will be—a necessary condition for effective problem-solving and crisis response.

This lesson extends past the individual to the group level; your team of teams should be equally diverse. Although diversity can induce the leadership challenge of internal competition borne of team members "fighting" their interests to the limits of their respective natures, the potential benefits outweigh the leadership costs. Good teams thrive on internal competition, as it draws out the most provocative ideas and creative solutions in a dialectical, market-like fashion. Keep in mind that "team of teams" encompasses coalitions as well. Although humans are weak in comparison to the immortal New Gods, and thus could have easily been dismissed by Orion as useless in a fight, he would have not been victorious against Darkseid's minions without the small but utterly necessary contributions of O'Ryan's Mob.

Trust that institutionalization can work ... but be careful. The "forming and norming" of a team is analogous to nurturing at the group level and produces the team's collective character within a leadership environment that expresses the organization's climate and culture. Like how nurturing formed Orion into the "power and purpose" of New Genesis and normed him to a heroic ethos, you can trust that nurturing a team will produce the desired collective. Be aware, however, that what you institutionalize will not be inherently good or bad. Rather, it will reflect the ethic of your organization and leadership environment. Focus on making that good (normatively speaking). Had Highfather approached the exchange of sons in bad faith or was himself flawed such that he could not train Orion towards being New Genesis' "purpose," then Darkseid's play for time would have been all too easy.

Promote self-awareness. Leaders lead examined lives, and the most important examination that they should be subject to is the one they perform on themselves. Done with rigor and circumspection at important transition points in one's chosen profession, self-examination can be a pathway to self-awareness. Individuals have positive qualities and negative qualities consistent with their nature, measured against utility towards the team's goals and supporting objectives. Through self-examination … a personal process of nurturing, if you will—one can identify what these qualities are and then self-consciously amplify the positive and minimize the negative, thereby optimizing one's contributions within the team dynamic.

One's degree of self-awareness is reflected in their choice of advisors, who should buttress your weaknesses and guard your blind spots. If you have an incisive and complete understanding of these pursuant to rigorous and routine self-examination, then you can select an advisor cohort that best enhances your prospects for success. This is the essence of humility. Notwithstanding any manifestation as self-loathing, Orion knew his dark nature and under what circumstances it could betray New Genesis' purpose. He was humble enough to accept Lightray's friendship and Metron's counsel when reliance on his natural power alone was counterproductive for the fight at hand.

Seek empathy and think critically. Empathy follows naturally from self-awareness in a diverse and properly nurtured team. Attunement to and understanding of oneself begets the same towards others. The power of empathy is that, once you validate another's point of view—even if you do not agree—it expands your cognitive and emotional horizons towards seeing the world critically. Not contrarily (which is what all-too-often passes for critical thought these days), but rather approaching problems with the humble recognition that you need to understand before you solve, and that proper understanding necessarily involves the cooption of as many points of view as possible. In this context, empathy and critical thinking are natural extensions of diversity within your teams.

If you have proper understanding of a problem—if you have framed it properly in terms of facts, assumptions, desired outcome, system tension, and residual risk—your solution is much more likely to be the "right" one than if you had proceeded unilaterally. Good problem framing also ensures that you are dealing in fact instead of emotion (a la Metron), avoiding antagonistic relationships, and not short-circuiting good planning (a drumbeat within Lightray's counsel to Orion).

Problem solving can be a messy, chaotic business. Orion, through his counselors and as a product of Highfather's nurturing, brings order to chaos when he is at his best. Good leaders do this. Bad leaders, like Darkseid, are agents of chaos.

Deliver on core competencies. As a product of proper institutionalization, achievement of self-awareness, an empathetic worldview, and the ability to think critically, every team member should know and deliver on their core competencies—the things that only they can do by virtue of position and authority. Good teams are composed of members who do their jobs well, full stop. Bad teams are composed of members who do not, either because they lack ability (which includes meddling in others' work) or lack understanding of their core competency (which may indicate a lack of guidance in kind from the leader).

New Genesis was successful in its conflict with Darkseid because Orion did the fighting that only he could do, Lightray reinforced Orion in a way that only a best friend and moral conscience could, Metron interceded at times and locations that only he could foresee, and O'Ryan's Mob provided Earth-awareness and material support that could only come from human allies. Take away any of these—if any team member failed to deliver on their core competency—then the outcome would have been different.

Leading through and delivering on core competencies is important for another reason: It guards against micromanagement. Micromanaged organizations can appear to be effective, but they tend not to do new things well, and the whole enterprise breaks down at a certain level of complexity or task variety. Moreover, micromanagement seems antithetical to a nurturing leadership environment.

There is a final lesson, and one that comes from Jack Kirby himself: Know your worth and demand that it be paid. His departure from Marvel was an act of courage and a matter of personal integrity, as the contract he was offered did not reflect the value of his contributions over the Silver Age. No team or organization, no matter how positive the leadership environment or well-considered the ethic, will value you as much as you should value yourself. Do not have so much of your identity defined by your employment or team membership that you lose yourself, as Highfather did, when the employment or membership inevitably end. As a wise mentor once told me, good judgement is knowing the right answer when it is presented to you. If you are not valued by a team—if options have closed for you in it—then accept the necessity of the situation and find the environment where you will be valued. Stated simply, follow the example that King Kirby set for all of us.

Notes

1   Kirby brought the modern version of the Captain America character with him to Marvel Comics.

2   The Kirby Krackle is an illustration technique that uses clusters of black dots on colored fields to depict various modes of cosmic and other exotic energies. See Harry Mendryk, "Evolution of Kirby Krackle," Jack Kirby Museum, https://kirbymuseum.org/blogs/simonandkirby/archives/3997.

3   "The indisputable pinnacle of the… Silver Age." See David Sims, "Stan Lee Was Synonymous with American Superhero Comics," *The Atlantic*, November 12, 2018, https://www.theatlantic.com/entertainment/archive/2018/11/stan-lee-marvel-comics-dies/575638/.

4   Jack Kirby, *The Fourth World Omnibus* (Burbank, CA: DC Comics, 2021), 8.

5   The circumstances of Kirby's departure from Marvel are chronicled in numerous sources. For a comprehensive explanation (and primary account), see Mark Evanier, *Kirby: King of Comics* (New York: Abrams, 2008).

6   Kirby, *The Fourth World Omnibus*, 9–12.

7   *Ibid.*, 8–12. See also Aaron Johnson, "Orion: The Son of Two Worlds," Cinema Debate, November 26, 2019, https://cinemadebate.com/2019/11/26/orion-the-son-of-two-worlds/.

8   Jack Kirby, "Even Gods Must Die!" from *New Gods* (Reprint Series) #6 (November 1984), published in *The Fourth World Omnibus* (Burbank, CA: DC Comics), 1371–1418.

9   Johnson, "Orion: The Son of Two Worlds."

10   Jack Kirby, "Death is the Black Racer!" from *The New Gods* #3 (June–July 1971), published in *The Fourth World Omnibus* (Burbank, CA: DC Comics), 322–345.

11   Jack Kirby, "Darkseid and Sons," from *The New Gods* #11 (October–November 1972), published in *The Fourth World Omnibus* (Burbank, CA: DC Comics), 1184.

12   Kirby, "Even Gods Must Die!" 1414.

13   Jack Kirby, "The Glory Boat," from *The New Gods* #6 (December 1971), published in *The Fourth World Omnibus* (Burbank, CA: DC Comics), 672.

14   Jack Kirby, "The Pact!" from *The New Gods* #7 (February 1972), published in *The Fourth World Omnibus* (Burbank, CA: DC Comics), 822.

CHAPTER 35

ХАЙЛЬ ГИДРА!

Marvel's Hydra and Russian Intelligence

Joshua C. Huminski

"Желание, Ржавый, Семнадцать, Рассвет, Печь, Девять, Добросердечный, Возвращение на Родину, Один, Товарный вагон." (Longing, rusted, furnace, daybreak, seventeen, benign, nine, homecoming, one, freight car.) With that string of seemingly unconnected words, the Winter Soldier was activated. Awoken from cryogenic sleep, the Winter Soldier—formerly Bucky Barnes, Captain America's best friend—received his orders: find and eliminate Tony Stark's parents and retrieve, for his Russian handlers, the super-soldier serum. With a ruthlessness of purpose and a relentless focus, the Winter Soldier descended upon the unsuspecting Starks, causing a car accident, murdering Iron Man's parents, and completing his mission. His mission complete, his memory was wiped, and he was consigned to deep sleep until he was needed again.

Fast forward nearly two decades and return to the real world. The Cold War is a distant memory; the Soviet Union is no more. The United States is ten years into the Global War on Terrorism, yet the fine arts of skullduggery and espionage are alive and well. In a New York City coffee, a Russian intelligence officer meets with her handler.[1] One imagines that when they met a coded phrase shared between the two, something simple and easily remembered, but distinct enough to be recognizable. Anna Chapman was not a modern-day Winter Soldier (despite the Kremlin's best efforts to make her more than she was, and her post-espionage career exploits). Her work was anything but exciting, mostly collecting publicly available information. Yet, she represented something far more insidious and concerning—an "illegal" or an intelligence officer without official cover, meant to hide in plain sight. In the end, she and nine other spies were arrested as part of Operation Ghost Stories—a more than ten-year investigation into a Russian Foreign Intelligence Service (SVR) spy ring.

The reality behind Marvel's HYDRA and Russia's political warfare and intelligence efforts is far more interesting than fiction. Yet, looking at the latter through the lens of the former is instructive. It shows us that the real risks are not the Alexander Pierces of the world—the Secretary of the World Security Council and HYDRA agent-in-place—the Machiavellian figures sitting at the apex of power, orchestrating elaborate plots. Rather, the most dangerous threats are the most insidious and most hidden ones: the long-term penetration of institutions and subversion from within.

Russia, Hydra, Myth and Reality

In the Marvel Universe—both the cinematic and comic book versions—HYDRA is an expansive, regenerative, multi-headed organization, dedicated to achieving world domination and establishing a fascist global government. Its means are eerily familiar—subversion, propaganda, assassination, and even cyber warfare. It's hard not to look at HYDRA and see parallels with the Soviet Union's KGB and Russia's successor organizations—the FSB (domestic security and intelligence), the SVR (foreign intelligence), and the GRU (military intelligence). Russia's spies, assassins, propagandists, and hackers all sought and seek to undermine Western alliances, undercut democracy, and advance Moscow's interests around the world. While certainly more circumscribed than HYDRA's goal of global governance, Russia sought to create a world more favorable for the Kremlin, and until the February 2022 expanded invasion of Ukraine, Moscow, arguably, largely succeeded.

HYDRA makes for a brilliant villain, particularly in the Captain America story arc of the Marvel Cinematic Universe (MCU). It's seemingly everywhere, behind every bit of instability and crisis. It managed to outlive the Red Skull, survive the closing days of the Second World War, and infiltrate S.H.I.E.L.D. It used the Winter Soldier to kill Tony Stark's parents and steal the super-soldier serum. It penetrated the highest ranks of the World Security Council, which oversaw S.H.I.E.L.D. operations, even turning on Captain America when he wouldn't comply with Pierce's directions. It almost succeeded in eliminating all those who stood in its way, using Arnim Zola's algorithm and S.H.I.E.L.D.'s Helicarriers to target HYDRA's opponents. Were it not for the intervention of Captain America, Natasha Romanoff (AKA Black Widow), Sam Wilson (AKA the Falcon), and Maria Hill, over 200,000 people would have been killed.

Creating a Hydra of Our Own

In many ways, the West did much of Moscow's work for it, building a hydra-like myth from Moscow's political warfare and active measures in its own conception. There was a Russian intelligence officer behind every nefarious development, responsible for mayhem, death, and destruction. encourages a highly risk-tolerant approach to operations as evidenced by Salisbury and others.[2] The aim was, in the main, pursuing national interests and weakening adversary unity by introducing doubt and political paralysis to prevent responses to Russia's pursuit of those interests. Even when an operation is unsuccessful or exposed, it contributed to the perception of Russia as a strong actor, willing to act in pursuit of its interests and hunt down any threat wherever it may be found (however overblown that perception may well be, and indeed is). Just as Howard Stark wasn't beyond the reach of HYDRA, Russia's opponents are not beyond the Kremlin's long arm, or so it would like the West to believe. The Red Skull or Baron Zemo couldn't have asked for a better outcome than that which the West provided for Putin. Russia's leadership, just as assuredly as HYDRA,

Success is just that, but a failure is, counterintuitively, also a signal. Russia's failed efforts to kill Sergei Skripal and Alexei Navalny are not as catastrophic as they perhaps would be for a Western agency—it is worth noting that America's Intelligence Community is prohibited from undertaking assassinations by executive order.[3] Failure or not, the fact that Moscow sought to eliminate one of its own spies on foreign soil—a NATO ally no less—sends a signal to any would-be defector, spy, or opposition figure that they are not beyond the Kremlin's reach. In the West's view, if one operation was uncovered, how many more might have evaded detection?

What if the Winter Soldier failed? What if Stark's father survived? Tony Stark's character arc in the MCU would have been decidedly different (and likely with fewer father-figure issues), but for HYDRA—just like Russia—the attempt itself still would have sent a signal to the Starks, to the United States, and to S.H.I.E.L.D.

Hydra's Prime Movers and Russia's Intelligence Officers

In many ways, Marvel's HYDRA fits what most people think of when they think of the global intelligence operations and covert action—the far-reaching plots with agents everywhere serving as a constant *deus ex machina* for the absurdly complex schemes. The world of intelligence is sadly, for Marvel fans, far more sedate. Despite Russia's best hopes (so far as we know), Moscow never achieved the level of penetration that HYDRA did of the World Security Council and S.H.I.E.L.D. From his position as the Secretary of the World Security Council, Pierce was able to advance HYDRA's agenda, declare Captain America and Nick Fury *personae non grata*, and send STRIKE after both.

During the Cold War, the Soviet Union did, however, get very close. The infamous Cambridge Five, ideologically driven recruits in the 1930s found themselves rising to high ranks within the British intelligence and political establishments.[4] Donald Maclean and Guy Burgess were both senior diplomats in the Foreign Office at the time of their defection. Anthony Blunt became a Surveyor of the King's Pictures and later the Queen's Pictures, as well as an MI5 officer. John Cairncross was a member of the Foreign Office but also worked for Bletchley Park, the codebreaking predecessor to GCHQ.

Perhaps most damaging and potentially most significant of the Five was Kim Philby. He rose to become a senior officer in the United Kingdom's Secret Intelligence Service (SIS, or MI6) and ultimately served the KGB for over 50 years. At one point he was seen as on track to become the head of SIS—"C" or Chief of Service. As a liaison officer during the Second World War in Washington, D.C., he was party to the most intimate secrets of the burgeoning "special relationship," all while indulging his love of drink and social habits. His charm and wit would likely have seen him in good, if nefarious, company with Tom Hiddleston's Loki—though who would have gotten the Tesseract in the end is up for debate.

His relationship with James "Jesus" Angleton, the counterintelligence chief of the Central Intelligence Agency, may have resulted in some of the most damaging effects for the Agency during the Cold War. After Philby's betrayal, Angleton saw the hidden hand of Moscow behind every Soviet defector and potential agent, undoubtedly turning away legitimate spies. As a result of Philby's betrayal, he feared some master plot by the Kremlin, potentially undermining much of the Agency's efforts at the time.[5]

George Blake may not be as well-known as the Cambridge Five, but his case is illustrative of the value of a long-term penetration. An officer with SIS, Blake was captured in North Korea, subject to communist indoctrination, and later became a double-agent for the KGB.[6] Blake most infamously compromised an allied effort to tunnel into the Soviet sector of Berlin to tap into Soviet communications lines (Operation *Gold*).[7] Despite knowing the Allies were listening to their messages, the KGB allowed the tapping to continue as exposing their knowledge of the tunnel would have risked compromising Blake—the KGB found him to be too valuable as an agent-in-place.

The Soviet Union and later Russia ran two of the most damaging spies in modern history in Aldrich Ames and Richard Hanssen.[8] Ames was a CIA case officer who volunteered to spy for the Soviet Union, meeting repeatedly with his KGB handlers and receiving money for the intelligence he passed on. Ames was arrested in 1994, but the Intelligence Community found that information was still finding its way into Russian hands. Richard Hanssen, an FBI special agent, also volunteered for the Soviet Union in 1985, ultimately receiving some $1.4 million for the intelligence he sold to Moscow. He was arrested in 2001 and sentenced to life in prison without parole.

The end of the Cold War did not bring about an end to these intelligence operations. Operation *Ghost Stories*, referenced at the opening of this chapter, was a long-term intelligence gathering operation run by Moscow.[9] While the media focused on the glamorous, but hapless, Anna Chapman, the real threat posed by Russia's spies was not immediately apparent. These SVR "illegals" were part of a long-term penetration operation, one that could have seen their sons and daughters (natural-born citizens) receive security clearances and enter into U.S. government service. Were it not for the FBI's interdiction, Russia could well have achieved a long-term intelligence coup, seeing their own Pierces reach sensitive positions within the federal government.

Russia's invasion of Ukraine significantly compounded the difficulties Moscow's intelligence officers, and the agents they run, face.[10] In response to the expanded invasion, the West accelerated and increased its counterintelligence efforts. Innumerable official cover spies—spies operating under diplomatic cover—were evicted from across Europe. This left the agents these officers served in the lurch, cut off from their handlers and risking identification and arrest to communicate with their Moscow masters. In response to these new pressures Russia, according to Finland's Security and Intelligence Service, may increase its reliance on cyber-espionage, targeting foreigners within Russia for recruitment, or rely on the very expensive deep-cover illegals … illegals like Anna Chapman, to meet their intelligence needs.[11]

Yet in all of these cases, and the countless not referenced in this chapter, the influence and importance was not found in grand conspiracy. It was less "Hail HYDRA!" and more the quiet collection of intelligence and passing of information. The impact of this dynamic cannot be underestimated. Ames and Hanssen are believed to be responsible for the deaths of countless Soviet and Russian agents—agents who risked their lives to spy for the United States.

The Winter Soldiers and Assassinations

At least in the MCU, assassinations are relatively rare. Rare, but not unheard of—in 1991, HYDRA activated the Winter Soldier to kill Stark's parents and capture the super-soldier serum. Later, in *Captain America: Civil War*, Zemo framed Bucky Barnes for the murder of King T'Chaka of Wakanda in Vienna as part of his plan to avenge the events of *Avengers: Age of Ultron* and the destruction of Sokovia.

For the Soviet Union and certainly Russia under Putin, assassination was and likely remains a tool of statecraft. From poisoning dissidents, murdering opposition figures, and targeting former spies, the Kremlin sees assassination as a means of advancing national and personal interests. It is important to note that Russia is not the monolithic actor that many in the West assume it to be. Its security and intelligence services exist in a power structure that incentivizes competition, operational entrepreneurship, and independence of action to a degree not seen in other states.[12] Beyond the arms of the state, there are those political entrepreneurs who act in a manner to curry favor with Putin. While all roads may lead to Moscow, not all murders lead directly to the hands of Putin himself.

Moscow, nevertheless, has historically used political murder to target opponents in a manner that would certainly be at home in the pages of Marvel (though perhaps less so on the now-Disney-fied screen). From the murder of Georgi Markov, a

Bulgarian dissident who was poisoned by a pellet-dispensing umbrella (no less) on a London bridge in 1978 through to perhaps the first case of nuclear terrorism (one that could have easily been ripped from the pages of Marvel).[13] In 2003, Russia targeted Alexander Litvinenko, a former FSB officer, with polonium-210 delivered via tea (how fitting for London), resulting in his agonizing and slow death.[14] The assassins left a radioactive trail across London and Europe and sent a clear warning not to cross the Kremlin. In 2015, opposition leader Boris Nemtsov was gunned down allegedly on the orders of Ramzan Kadyrov, the leader of the republic of Chechnya (a one-time breakaway province).[15] That same year, Russian intelligence officers are believed to have tried to poison and kill, not once, but twice (seeing as the first attempt failed), a Bulgarian arms dealer.[16]

More recently, in 2018 the Kremlin used Novichok—a nerve agent unique to Russia—to poison Sergei Skripal, a former Russian intelligence officer who defected to the United Kingdom.[17] The attempt, carried out by Ruslan Boshirov and Alexander Petrov, who later claimed to be hapless tourists interested in Salisbury Cathedral, merely poisoned Skripal and his daughter, but later resulted in the death of a woman who thought the Novichok container she found in the trash was perfume.[18]

One failed attempt was not enough. Just two years later, Russia used Novichok again to attempt to kill Alexei Navalny, an opposition figure in Russia. Navalny fell ill on a flight to Moscow after FSB officers placed the nerve agent in his underwear. He was, however, lucky to receive care from a doctor who identified the symptoms of the nerve agent and was later evacuated to Germany for treatment. In a turn of events worthy of Marvel's often strange sense of humor, Navalny managed to not only identify the FSB officers tasked with his murder but also to convince one of them to disclose how they attempted to do so.[19]

Slaying the Hydra and Countering Russian Political Warfare

HYDRA's defeat came at the hands of members of the Avengers: Captain America, Black Widow, Falcon, and Maria Hill in a climactic battle over D.C. While other HYDRA cells lived on in the series *Agents of S.H.I.E.L.D.* and through the use of the Tesseract to create Quicksilver and Scarlet Witch, the group was quickly eclipsed by Thanos as the villain du jour.

The downfall of Russia's political warfare efforts, at least in the near-term, may have come at Putin's own hands. His February 2022 expanded invasion of Ukraine undermined the success the Kremlin achieved by its HYDRA-like methods. Prior to this, the West was distracted abroad and divided at home, mounting only half-hearted efforts to stop Russia's propaganda campaigns, hacking efforts, and espionage programs. Yet with his decision to invade, Putin managed to achieve the very thing he feared and worked so assiduously to prevent: an allied and reinvigorated West that belatedly responded to his campaign of political warfare and intelligence operations.

While it lacked the climactic battle between the Winter Soldier and Captain America on the Helicarriers over the Potomac River in Washington, D.C., the West's response to Russia's actions was just as impactful, at least thus far.

A fractured European Union found surprising agreement—though not total political unanimity—in opposing Moscow's invasion. The United States and Europe moved swiftly to close off avenues for Russian propaganda, shutting down RT and Sputnik media outlets. Countries in Europe belatedly, though not definitively, took steps to sharply limit Russian financial influence. Intelligence officers of the SVR and GRU were expelled from a number of European countries, weakening Moscow's reach. Russia's future ability to field both official and illegal intelligence officers will be increasingly challenged with the increased use of biometrics, paired with artificial intelligence (the real-world equivalents of J.A.R.V.I.S.). While a boon for counterintelligence and law enforcement, these technologies will make it much harder for intelligence officers to forge new identities and maintain cover—harder, but not impossible.

Ultimately, there will not be a climactic battle in the streets of New York or in the skies of Washington, D.C., to defeat Russia's political warfare and intelligence campaign. It is a long-term fight against an adversary that is constantly regenerative. Just like HYDRA, Russia's political warfare campaign will reemerge in the wake of Ukraine. Its core DNA will remain unchanged, even after Ukraine. It is constantly evolving; Moscow will adapt its toolset to new environments and avenues. This fight won't be fought by Captain America and the Falcon. It will be waged by their real-world equivalents: the quiet, unsung heroes of the Marvel Universe—the Nick Furys, Maria Hills, Agent Coulsons of the world. The men and women of the West's intelligence and law enforcement agencies like the CIA and FBI who work tirelessly to recruit America's own spies and find and arrest Russia's agents. The spy-versus-spy game will never go away (it is possibly the world's second oldest profession), but these real heroes will work to limit Moscow's success and counter the Kremlin's efforts.

Notes

1   The FBI, "Operation Ghost Stories: Video 1," *Federal Bureau of Investigation*, June 26, 2010. https://vault.fbi.gov/ghost-stories-russian-foreign-intelligence-service-illegals/videos/video-1/view.

2   Mark Galeotti, *Russian Political War: Moving beyond the Hybrid* (New York: Routledge, 2020).

3   Elizabeth Bazan, "Assassination Ban and E.O. 12333: A Brief Summary," *U.S. Library of Congress. Congressional Research Service*, January 4, 2002. https://irp.fas.org/crs/RS21037.pdf.

4   The BBC, "BBC—History—Historic Figures: The Cambridge Spies," *BBC Website*, n.d. https://www.bbc.co.uk/history/historic_figures/spies_cambridge.shtml.

5   "James J. Angleton, Anatoliy Golitsyn, and the 'Monster Plot': Their Impact on CIA Personnel and Operations," *Studies in Intelligence* 55, no. 4 (December 2011): 39–55. https://nsarchive2.gwu.edu/NSAEBB/NSAEBB431/docs/intell_ebb_019.PDF.

6   Robert D. McFadden, "George Blake, British Spy Who Betrayed the West, Dies at 98," *The New York Times*, December 26, 2020. https://www.nytimes.com/2020/12/26/obituaries/george-blake-british-spy-dead.html.

7   Steven Roberts, "Review | in Cold War Berlin, the Americans Had a Tunnel, but the Soviets Had a Mole," *Washington Post*, November 9, 2019. https://www.washingtonpost.com/outlook/in-cold-war-berlin-the-americans-had-a-tunnel-but-the-soviets-had-a-mole/2019/11/08/d7fa0328-b714-11e9-a091-6a96e67d9cce_story.html.

8   The FBI, "Aldrich Ames | Federal Bureau of Investigation," *Federal Bureau of Investigation*, 2016. https://www.fbi.gov/history/famous-cases/aldrich-ames.; "Robert Hanssen | Federal Bureau of Investigation," *Federal Bureau of Investigation*, 2016. https://www.fbi.gov/history/famous-cases/robert-hanssen.

9   Gordon Corera, *Russians Among Us: Sleeper Cells, Ghost Stories, and the Hunt for Putin's Spies* (New York: William Morrow, 2020).

10   Joshi Shashank, "The War in Ukraine Has Battered the Reputation of Russian Spies," *The Economist*, October 19, 2022. https://www.economist.com/europe/2022/10/09/the-war-in-ukraine-has-battered-the-reputation-of-russian-spies.

11   Finnish Security & Intelligence Service, "National Security Overview: Russian Intelligence Changes Approach," *Supo*, September 22, 2022. https://supo.fi/en/-/national-security-overview-russian-intelligence-changes-approach.

12   Andrew Bowen, "Russian Military Intelligence: Background and Issues for Congress," *U.S. Library of Congress. Congressional Research Service*, November 15, 2021. https://crsreports.congress.gov/product/pdf/R/R46616/7.

13   Lindsay Mackie and John Andrews, "The Poison-Tipped Umbrella: The Death of Georgi Markov in 1978—Archive," *The Guardian*, September 12, 1978. https://www.theguardian.com/world/from-the-archive-blog/2020/sep/09/georgi-markov-killed-poisoned-umbrella-london-1978.

14   BBC News, "Alexander Litvinenko: Profile of Murdered Russian Spy," *BBC News*, January 21, 2016. https://www.bbc.com/news/uk-19647226.

15   Shaun Walker, "Boris Nemtsov Murder: Chechen Chief Kadyrov Confirms Link to Prime Suspect," *The Guardian*, March 8, 2015. https://www.theguardian.com/world/2015/mar/08/boris-nemtsov-five-suspects-appear-in-court-over-opposition-leaders-killing.

16   Michael Schwirtz, "The Arms Merchant in the Sights of Russia's Elite Assassination Squad (Published 2021)," *The New York Times*, 2022. https://www.nytimes.com/2021/04/24/world/europe/arms-merchant-russia-assassination-squad.html.

17   Luke Harding, "The Skripal Poisonings: The Bungled Assassination with the Kremlin's Fingerprints All over It," *The Guardian*, December 26, 2018. https://www.theguardian.com/news/2018/dec/26/skripal-poisonings-bungled-assassination-kremlin-putin-salisbury.

18   "Salisbury Novichok Suspects Say They Were Only Visiting Cathedral," 2018. *The Guardian*. September 13, 2018. https://www.theguardian.com/uk-news/2018/sep/13/russian-television-channel-rt-says-it-is-to-air-interview-with-skripal-salisbury-attack-suspects.

19   Tim Lister, Clarissa Ward, and Sebastian Shukla, "Russian Opposition Leader Alexey Navalny Dupes Spy into Revealing How He Was Poisoned," *CNN*, December 21, 2020. https://www.cnn.com/2020/12/21/europe/russia-navalny-poisoning-underpants-ward/index.html.

Contributors

Ian Boley is a doctoral candidate in military history at Texas A&M University. His dissertation is on the nuclear strategy debates surrounding the Strategic Defense Initiative. He is a co-host of *The Joint Geeks of Staff*, a podcast featuring national security professionals who explore military, international law, and diplomatic lessons through the lens of science fiction. Ian has worked at United States Space Command, and he also holds an MA in Chinese Philosophy from Fudan University in Shanghai, China. He mostly lives overseas with his wife, a U.S. diplomat.

Mitch Brian is a filmmaker and educator. He co-created and wrote episodes for *Batman: The Animated Series* and co-hosts the podcasts *Alien Minute* and *007 x 7*. He teaches screenwriting and film studies at the University of Missouri–Kansas City.

Jo Brick is a legal officer in the Royal Australian Air Force. She holds a Master of Laws, and a Master of Military and Defence Studies (Advanced) from the Australian National University. A graduate of the Australian Command and Staff College, her primary interests are strategy and civil-military relations, the ethical aspects of the laws of war, and command decision making. Jo is a member of the Military Writers Guild, and you can follow her on Twitter at @clausewitzrocks.

Max Brooks is an author, public speaker, senior fellow at the Modern War Institute at West Point, and senior resident fellow at the Atlantic Council's Art of Future Warfare Project. He is the New York Times bestselling author of *World War Z* (Three Rivers Press, 2006), *The Harlem Hellfighters* (Broadway Books, 2014), and *Devolution* (Del Rey, 2020).

Mike Burke is a retired Command Sergeant Major who served in the United States Army for 25 years, where he primarily focused on special operations. Presently, he serves as a chief of staff in the private equity industry. Mike has established himself as a reputable podcaster and blogger, being the founder and host of two podcasts, *Always in Pursuit* and *Legends of the 75th*. His unwavering commitment to leadership is demonstrated through his desire to encourage and

274 • POWER UP

inspire other leaders to chronicle their experiences in writing, enabling others to benefit from their wisdom and facilitating their own personal growth.

Kelsey Cipolla is a writer, editor, and digital marketing specialist who has covered everything from nonprofits making a global impact to the best place to find tacos in Kansas City. An accomplished author and self-admitted comic book geek, she also contributed to *Winning Westeros: How Game of Thrones Explains Modern Military Strategy* and *To Boldly Go: Leadership, Strategy and Conflict in the 21st Century and Beyond.* Kelsey lives in Denver, Colorado, with her husband, dog, cat, and collection of *Lord of the Rings* Pez dispensers.

Amelia Cohen-Levy is currently a presidential appointee serving as speechwriter to the GSA Administrator and Deputy Administrator. Prior to that, she served as a speechwriter, public affairs officer, and change management specialist across the Department of Defense and Intelligence Community. She earned her Masters of Fine Arts in Poetry from American University and her Bachelor's in English from Mills College. She lives in Virginia with her two children and two cats, Catullus Archimedes Thor and Isadora.

Mick Cook is an Australian writer, digital content producer, and war veteran. Mick writes and produces digital content on war, warfare, and professional development of military personnel. He is passionate about strategic communications and enabling discourse on public issues. Mick has held positions at the University of New South Wales, the Modern War Institute at West Point, and University of Canberra. Mick spent 18 years as regular officer in the Australian Defence Force before transferring to reserve service.

Jeff Drake has written for *McSweeney's*, the *Bob's Burgers* comic book, *Nick Offerman & Megan Mullally: The Summer of 69: No Apostrophe, I'm Sorry* on TruTV, and *Central Park* on Apple TV+. Originally from Kansas City, he and his wife live in Burbank with their four sons, two cats, and a dog.

Clara Engle got her start in science fiction back in middle school when her teacher assigned her to read the *Foundation* Trilogy. From then she was hooked. Clara received her MA in International Relations from the University of Chicago and her bachelor's degree in Asian Studies and Political Science from Pomona College. Her research interests range from the role of protests in authoritarian states to the use of media in shaping narratives. Clara has worked for start-ups, the Census Bureau, and the Department of State. She is one of the co-hosts of *The Joint Geeks of Staff* podcast, where she discusses topics in national security through a science-fiction lens. Whenever possible, she attempts to relate everything to *Babylon 5*.

Candice Frost is a national security and cybersecurity expert. Her service to the nation for 25 years, as a U.S. Army officer, concluded with her serving in a command position in the United States Cyber Command. In her quarter of a decade in leadership positions across the military and intelligence community she focused on innovation combining strategy and policy with emerging technology. A tireless advocate for diversity in national security and the intelligence community, she most recently contributed to, *Unlocked—How Empowered Women Empower Women* (2021). A graduate of the United States Military Academy, Central Michigan University, and the United States Army School of Advanced Military Studies; currently, she is an adjunct professor at Georgetown University.

Ronald Granieri, PhD is Professor of History in the Department of National Security and Strategy at the United States Army War College, as well as Director of the Center for the Study of America and the West at the Foreign Policy Research Institute. A graduate of Harvard and the University of Chicago, he studies German History, European-American Relations, the Cold War, and contemporary politics and co-editor of *The Bondian Cold War: Global Connections of a Cold War Icon*.

Heather S. Gregg, PhD is Professor of Irregular Warfare at the George C. Marshall European Center for Security Studies, Garmisch, Germany. Prior to joining the Marshall Center, Dr. Gregg was a professor at the U.S. Army War College and the Naval Postgraduate School, where she worked primarily with Special Operations Forces. She holds a PhD in Political Science from MIT and is the author of *Religious Terrorism* (Cambridge University Press, 2020); *Building the Nation: Missed Opportunities in Iraq and Afghanistan* (University of Nebraska 2018); *The Path to Salvation: Religious Violence from the Crusades to Jihad* (University of Nebraska 2014); and co-editor of *The Three Circles of War: Understanding the Dynamics of Modern War in Iraq* (Potomac, 2010).

James Groves is an Artillery Officer in the Australian Army. He holds a Bachelor of Arts from the University of New South Wales, a Master of Military and Defence Studies from the Australian National University and is a graduate of the Australian Command and Staff College. His love of ancient history and science fiction frame his fascination with military and social matters. James has been active as a founding member of the Defence Entrepreneur's Forum Australia; a board member of the Royal Australian Artillery Historical Company; president of the Royal Australian Artillery Rugby Club; and most recently the commanding officer of the 1st Regiment, Royal Australian Artillery. He frequents the shadows of Twitter as @jmxgroves.

Geoff Harkness, PhD is an associate professor of sociology at Rhode Island College. He has been widely published in academic and popular mediums. His first book, *Chicago Hustle and Flow: Gangs, Gangsta Rap and Social Class* (University of Minnesota Press, 2014) was awarded the Distinguished Book Award from the Midwest Sociological Society. His second monograph, *Changing Qatar: Culture, Citizenship, and Rapid Modernization* (New York University Press, 2020) was based upon three years of immersive fieldwork in the Middle East. His third book, *DVS Mindz: The Twenty-Year Saga of the Greatest Rap Group to Almost Make it Outta Kansas* will be published by Columbia University Press in 2023. Harkness holds a PhD in sociology from Northwestern University and an MBA from the University of Rhode Island.

Theresa Hitchens is a former editor of *Defense News* and currently practicing her first career love, journalism, as the Senior Space Reporter for the online news magazine, *Breaking Defense*. She spent the two decades prior practicing punditry: working as a researcher, writer and opinion-leader on space and cyber security, multilateral governance, arms control and international security issues—including six years in Geneva, Switzerland as director of the United Nations Institute for Disarmament Research (UNIDIR). She's a self-described sci-fi geek, a voracious reader, an enthusiastic cook, a dabbler in poetry and the proud mom of a wonderful young man by the name of Nicholas.

Kayla Hodges is an adventure traveler, conservationist, and former U.S. Army officer. After concluding her final chapter in the Army as a military police company commander, she moved into her 4x4 Mitsubishi Delica van and traveled extensively across the United States. Her focus is producing written content aimed at educating and empowering others to navigate personal, professional, and institutional challenges related to leadership, the Army, and veteran transition resources. Now, she is documenting her work on different conservation and community development projects around the world. When Kayla isn't busy hacking a trail through the jungle or tracking elephants, you can find her road-tripping in her van, writing, or shuffle dancing.

Cory Hollon, PhD is an active-duty Air Force officer and instructor at the U.S. Air Force Air War College. He is an F-15E Weapon Systems Officer and graduate of the Air Force Weapons Instructor Course and the U.S. Army School of Advanced Military Studies. He has over two thousand flight hours and over one thousand combat hours. He has been a flight commander, fighter wing inspector general, director of operations, squadron commander, and airpower strategist at the Pentagon. He recently earned his doctorate from Temple University in early American military history. His interests include strategy, civil-military relations, all things *Star Wars*, and the Marvel Cinematic Universe.

Joshua Huminski is the Director of the Mike Rogers Center for Intelligence & Global Affairs at the Center for the Study of the Presidency & Congress. He helms the Center's national security and intelligence research programs and is the co-chair of the Center's Strategic Competition program, where he runs the Russia Policy Program. A thought-leader and policy commentator, he has been published in *Defense One, Breaking Defense, Space News, The Hill* and others, and has a regular book review column for the *Diplomatic Courier*. He received his graduate degree in War Studies from King's College London, where he focused on contemporary warfare and counterinsurgency, and is an honors graduate from the University of Connecticut undergraduate program. In addition to being a prolific reader, he is both a policy wonk and sci-fi/comic nerd.

Erica Iverson is a United States Army officer with a diverse range of strategic career assignments spanning the globe in Asia, Europe and the Middle East. A South Dakota native, she holds three graduate degrees in Strategic Studies, Legislative Affairs, and Business Administration. She is proud to be included amongst the distinguished collaborators on *Strategy Strikes Back* (Potomac Books, 2018), *Winning Westeros* (Potomac Books, 2019), and *To Boldly Go* (Casemate, 2021). She is currently serving as the Army Marketing Liaison at the Pentagon.

Alyssa Jones is the youngest member of the *Power Up* writing team and an MBA candidate at the University of Kansas, where she also received her BA in Industrial Design and BS in Marketing. She has a background in writing, designing and marketing and currently works as a Marketing Manager in Kansas City. Alyssa spends her free time with Ranger, her 75-pound poodle, and is busy planning for her next travel adventure when she is not doing DIY projects around her house.

Mathew Klickstein is a longtime writer, producer, and instructor whose work has appeared in such outlets as *WIRED*, the *NY Daily News*, and Vulture, and whose twenty books predominantly focus on pop culture histories including those of *The Simpsons*, Comic-Con, and the Nickelodeon network. He is also the screenwriter of Sony Pictures' *Against the Dark*, creator of AfterShock's highly acclaimed comic book series *You Are Obsolete*, and creator of the SiriusXM/Stitcher documentary podcast series *Comic-Con Begins* available free on all audio platforms.

Jon Klug is a U.S. Army Strategist serving as an Assistant Professor in the Department of Strategy, Planning, and Operations at the U.S. Army War College. Commissioned as an armor officer, he served in Haiti, Bosnia, South Korea, Egypt, and Iraq. His strategy assignments included writing U.S. Army, U.S. Joint, and NATO Joint counterinsurgency doctrine; teaching at the U.S. Air Force Academy and U.S. Naval

Academy; serving as the V Corps Deputy Plans and Strategy Officer; and strategic planning in NATO Training Mission-Afghanistan, International Security Assistance Force Joint Command, and Operation Resolute Support Headquarters. Jon holds degrees from the United States Military Academy, Louisiana State University, and United States Army School of Advanced Military Studies. He is a PhD candidate in Military and Naval History at the University of New Brunswick.

Matt Lancaster is an award-winning educator and school administrator and currently leads the co-curricular professional development program at the University of Kansas School of Business. He holds graduate degrees in Curriculum and Instruction from the University of Kansas and Educational Leadership from Kansas State University, and his passion and focus has been on equity and access in education. Matt lives in Lawrence, Kansas, with his wife, son, and animals, and enjoys tabletop wargaming, role-playing games, music, and reading.

Steve Leonard is an award-winning faculty member at the University of Kansas School of Business, where he serves as Senior Assistant Dean and a Professor of the Practice. A former senior military strategist and the creative force behind the defense microblog, *Doctrine Man!!,* he is a career writer and speaker with a passion for developing and mentoring the next generation of thought leaders. He is a senior fellow at the Modern War Institute at West Point; the co-founder of the national security blog, Divergent Options; co-founder of the Military Writers Guild; and a member of the editorial review board of the Arthur D. Simons Center's *Interagency Journal.* He is the author, co-author, or editor of several books, including *To Boldly Go* (Casemate, 2021), *Why We Write* (Middle West Press, 2019), *Winning Westeros* (Potomac Books, 2019), and *Strategy Strikes Back* (Potomac Books, 2018).

Karolyn McEwen is a former United States Army officer and public affairs advisor to our nation's military, having served commanders at every level of command and in every branch of service for more than 20 years. Her military service took her all over the world, including the Indo-Asia-Pacific, Europe, the Middle East, and the Arctic Circle. A graduate of the United States Military Academy at West Point, Kari received a master's degree in Public Relations and Corporate Communications from Georgetown University.

Eric Muirhead is an Armor Officer in the United States Army and an Assistant Professor of History at the United States Military Academy at West Point. He has operational deployments to both Afghanistan and the Republic of Korea. He has taught undergraduate courses in Asian Warfare and Politics, East Asian History, and the History of the United States Army. His research interests focus on German and

Japanese military culture in the 20th century with an emphasis on World War II. He holds a Master of Arts in History from the University of Tennessee in Knoxville, a Master of Operational Studies from the U.S. Army Command and General Staff College at Fort Leavenworth, and a Bachelor of Arts in Psychology from the College of William & Mary in Virginia. Eric is passionate about finding new ways to inspire and educate the next generation of leaders.

Jon Niccum is an award-winning journalist, author and screenwriter. He is a longtime entertainment writer and critic for the Kansas City Star. He is the author of *The Worst Gig: From Psycho Fans to Stage Riots, Famous Musicians Tell All* (Sourcebooks, 2013). Additionally, he has written and/or produced numerous independent features and documentaries, including *Big Fur, The Sublime and Beautiful, Jayhawkers,* and *Rhino.* He earned a degree in Film and Media Studies and a Master's in Journalism from the University of Kansas, where he currently teaches screenwriting.

Kera Rolsen is a United States Air Force officer, strategist, and B-52 aviator. She has a broad range of experience from the tactical to strategic levels of planning across multiple regions of the world. She holds graduate degrees in Intelligence, Military Operational Art and Science, and Military Strategy. Her professional writing has been featured on the *Over the Horizon* journal, Angry Staff Officer blog, and *Business Insider.* She is also a fiction novelist under a pen name that is possibly the worst kept secret in the Department of Defense.

Mick Ryan is a strategist and retired Australian Army officer. A combat engineer officer, he commanded tactical units at the troop, squadron, regiment, task force and brigade levels. He is a veteran of East Timor, Iraq, and Afghanistan, and served on the Pakistan-Afghanistan Coordination Cell on the US Joint Staff. A distinguished graduate of Johns Hopkins University and the USMC Staff College, and graduate of the USMC School of Advanced Warfare, he is an enthusiastic writer, reader and a passionate advocate of professional education and lifelong learning. He is the co-author of several books, including *To Boldly Go* (Casemate, 2021), *Winning Westeros* (Potomac Books, 2019), and *Strategy Strikes Back* (Potomac Books, 2018), and the author of *War Transformed: The Future of Twenty-First-Century Great Power Competition and Conflict* (Naval Institute Press, 2022), and *White Sun War* (Casemate, 2023).

Julie Still is on the faculty at the Paul Robeson Library on the Camden campus of Rutgers University. She co-edited *Buffy to Batgirl: Essays on Women and Gender in Science Fiction and Fantasy.* The journal articles she has written include a comparison between the Fair Witnesses in Robert Heinlein's *Stranger in a Strange Land* and librarians, and an exploration of Fantomette, a French literary crimefighter. Still has an BA in History and an MA in Library Science from the University of Missouri, an MA in History from the University of Richmond, and is currently completing her dissertation for a doctorate in American Studies from Penn State University.

Patrick Sullivan is closing out his third decade as an officer in the U.S. Army, having commanded units at company, battalion, and brigade levels, as well as served nine operational tours in the Middle East, South Asia, and the Republic of Korea. He studied civil engineering as an undergraduate, mathematics in graduate school, and is finishing a PhD in War Studies through the Royal Military College of Canada. He is currently the Director of the Modern War Institute at West Point, a position that allows him to ruminate on important questions such as whether *Batman Returns* is the best portrayal of both the character and Gotham (hot take: it is).

Aaron Rahsaan Thomas grew up in Kansas City, Kansas, developing a love for storytelling after completing a fifth-grade assignment to create an original Greek myth from scratch. Aaron eventually attended Morehouse College and the University of Kansas, earning honors in English literature, before attending graduate school at the University of Southern California School of Cinematic Arts. Aaron has written for such TV series as *Soul Food: The Series* and NBC's *Friday Night Lights*, as well as CBS procedurals such as *Numb3rs* and *CSI:NY*. Aaron served as a Co-Executive Producer on TNT's *SouthLAnd*, Fox's *Sleepy Hollow*, and Netflix's *The Get Down*. Aaron has had two screenplays produced as feature films: *Cover*, directed by Bill Duke, and *Assassination Games*, starring Jean Claude Van Damme. He has also directed an ESPN *30 for 30* film about the USC football team during the Pete Carroll era titled *Trojan War*. Aaron currently is the co-creator of *S.W.A.T.* on CBS and a partner in the new BET Studios, in which he develops content for Viacom networks. He is also an adjunct professor in the USC School of Cinematic Arts.

Dan Ward is an engineer and innovation catalyst at the MITRE Corporation. He previously served for more than 20 years as an officer in the United States Air Force, where he specialized in leading small, high-speed, low-cost technology development programs. Dan is the author of three books: *LIFT: Innovation Lessons from Flying Machines That Almost Worked and The People Who Nearly Flew Them* (2019), *The Simplicity Cycle: A Field Guide to Making Things Better Without Making Them Worse* (Harper, 2015), and *F.I.R.E.: How Fast, Inexpensive, Restrained, and Elegant Methods Ignite innovation* (Harper, 2014). He is also a contributing author for *Strategy Strikes Back* (Potomac, 2018) and *To Boldly Go* (Casemate, 2021). He holds a bachelor's degree in electrical engineering, a master's degree in engineering management and a master's degree in systems engineering.

Janeen Webb, PhD is a multiple award-winning author, editor, critic and academic who has written or edited a dozen books and over a hundred essays and stories. Her most recent books are *The Gold-Jade Dragon* (PS Publishing, 2020), and *The Five Star Republic* (co-authored with Andrew Enstice, IFWG Publications, 2021). Janeen has taught at various universities, is internationally recognized for her critical work in speculative fiction and has contributed to most of the standard reference texts in the field. She holds a PhD from the University of Newcastle.

Index

Adebayo, Leota, 23–24
Agents of S.H.I.E.L.D., 270
AI/machine learning, xiii, 89, 115, 166, 169–70, 189–95
Amazing (Adult) Fantasy, x–xi, xiv, 27
Ant-Man (Giant Man), x, 155, 243–45, 252
Aquaman, 93–94
Army Doctrine Publication (ADP) 6–0, 12, 14
Asbestos Man, 196
Asgard, 11, 12, 116, 165, 176, 223, 253
Atlas Comics, 237
Avengers Assemble!, xii, 47
Avengers: Age of Ultron, 115, 138, 169, 189–90, 194, 223, 253, 269
Avengers: Endgame, 138, 141, 164, 197, 239
Avengers: Infinity War, 86, 138, 245

Barrett, Ashley, 5–7
Batman, xi, 29–32, 44, 51–52, 68, 70, 74–75, 88–94, 121–27, 130–31, 133, 158–64, 180, 198, 203–04, 206, 209, 229–232
    detective skills, 91–92
    humanity, 88–89, 91
    in Nazi Germany, 231
    intelligence, 92–93
    leadership skills, 90–91
    people skills, 93–94
    reluctant leader, 90–91
    role of trauma, 89–90
    solitude, 90
Batman Begins, 29, 89, 121–22, 124, 160–61
Batman, xi–xii, 159
Batman: Endgame, 164
Batman: The Animated Series, 88, 94, 162
Batman: Year One, 159–60
Battle of New York, 11–12, 15–16, 223
Black Panther (T'Challa), xi, 145–47, 144166, 243, 245, 257

Black Panther, 146, 251
Black Panther: Wakanda Forever, 146
Black Widow (Natasha Romanoff), 12, 16–17, 74, 136, 138–40, 203, 206, 252, 266, 270
Black Widow, 138–41
Blade, 236
Bond, James, 158–60, 162, 164
Butcher, Billy, 8, 10

Cage, Luke, xi, 242, 244
Captain America (Steve Rogers), xi, 3, 11–16, 41–44, 100–02, 104–05, 115, 147, 164, 204, 208, 220–21, 234, 239, 241–42, 244–45, 251–53, 157, 265–67, 270–71
Captain America: Civil War, xii, 39, 99–101, 104, 115–16, 119, 139, 224, 253, 269
Captain America: The Winter Soldier, 138–39, 141
Chitauri Leviathans, 12–13, 15–17, 223, 251
Churchill, Sir Winston, xii, 32, 168
ComicCon, xii
Constantine, John, 198, 201
Coulson, Agent Phil, 13, 222
cyberspace, 192, 199–200
cyberwar, xiii, 196–201
Cyborg, 93–94, 198

Daily Planet, 35, 111–12
Daredevil, 239, 242, 244
Dark Horse Comics, viii, 54, 70
Dawes, Rachel, 123, 125–26, 163
DC Comics, 122, 129–30, 133–35, 198, 257–58, 270
Deadpool (Wade Wilson), xii, 67, 72, 242–43
Deadpool 2, 67
Death of Superman, 164
Death of the New Gods, 261
Destiny, 44–45, 199, 201

Disney, Walt, 32–33
Ditko, Steve, x, 52, 151, 238
Doctor Strange, ix, 39, 166, 196–97, 199–201, 235, 239, 243, 245, 252
Dormammu, 199
Dr. Doom, 49, 53, 155–56
Dr. Octopus, 38

Edgar, Stan, 4, 6, 9
Ethical AI, 189–92, 194

Falcone, Carmine, 122–24
Fantastic Four, x, xi, 49, 52–53, 144
Federal Bureau of Superhuman Affairs (FBSA), 222
Feige, Kevin, 196, 239
Final Crisis, 261
Fortress of Solitude, 110, 113
Frankenstein, 66, 69, 71, 236–37
Fury, Nick, 17, 83, 221, 267, 271

Galactus, 151–52, 155, 174–77, 245, 257
General Zod, xiii, 112, 227
Ghost Rider (Johnny Blaze), 234, 236, 238
Gigantos, 152, 154
Godzilla, 237
Gotham, xii, 29, 88–90, 92, 94, 121–27, 158–60, 163, 204, 209, 229–33
Great Lakes Avengers, 155, 173
Green Arrow, 203
Green Goblin (Norman Osborne), 239
Green Lantern, 179, 198
Green Lantern: Light!, xii, 97
Grimm, Ben (The Thing), 149
Guardians of the Galaxy, 252
Guardians of the Galaxy, 39, 84–86

Hammer Industries, 12, 214
Hammerhead, 245
Harcourt, Emelia, 19–20, 23–25
Hawkeye (Clint Barton), 12–17, 74, 139, 221, 242, 252
Hellstrom, Daimon (Son of Satan), 236
Hill, Maria, 266, 270–71
Homelander, 4, 7, 9, 221–22
Howard the Duck, 50, 52
Human Torch, 104, 196

HYDRA, xiv, 12, 138–39, 265–67, 269–70, 271
    Comparison with Soviet Union, 266–71
    Pierce, Alexander, 266
    Zola, Arnim, 266

Iceman, xi
Illuminati, 199
Image Comics, viii, 54
Injustice: Gods Amongst Us, 129–135
Iron Man (Tony Stark), viii, x–xi, 11–17, 28, 31, 38–39, 74, 81, 99, 101, 115, 138, 155, 164, 173, 176, 189, 206, 211–12, 213–15, 217–18, 222–23, 235, 238, 245, 252–53, 265, 267, 269
    creation of protypes with academia, 215–218
    Hammer, Justin, 214–15
    Hansen, Maya, 215–16
    Jericho missile system, 212
    Killian, Aldrich, 215–16
    Mark I (MkI) and Mark II (MkII) armor, 213
    military capability R&D/technology, 211–15
    Rhodes, Lieutenant Colonel James, 119, 191, 215
    Stark Expo, 214
    technology readiness level (TRL) continuum, 212, 216–17
    Vanko, Ivan, 12, 214
    Yinsen, 213, 217
Iron Man, xiii, 38, 189, 211–13, 217–18, 222
Iron Man 2, 140–41, 214–15
Iron Man 3, 215
Iron Monger (Obadiah Stane), xiii, 12, 28, 213–14, 228
Iwerks, Ub, 32–33

J.A.R.V.I.S. (Vision), x, 189, 191–92, 194–95, 213, 222, 245, 252, 271
Jor-El, 41–42, 109–110
Justice League Dark (JLD), 198
Justice League of America, 92

Ka-Zar, 234
    A.I.M., 234
    Man-Thing, xiii, 235–36, 238–39

Project Gladiator, 234–35
Sallis, Ted, 234–35, 238–39
Zabu, 234
Kal-El, 35–37, 39, 42, 107, 110
Karloff, Dr. Orson, 196
Kent, Clark, 35–36, 38, 94, 110–112
Kent, Jonathan, 41, 110
Kent, Martha, 110
Kick-Ass, 68–69, 72
King Arthur and Excalibur, 250
King Kong, 237
King T'Chaka, 269
Kingpin, 241, 243, 245, 247
Kirby, "King" Jack, x, xiv, 42, 144–45, 238,
    257–61, 263
    contributions to industry, 257
    Fourth World, 257–58
    Timely Comics, 257
    work at DC Comics, 257–58
Kirkman, Robert, 242–45
KISS and Stan Lee, 50–51
KISS, 49–54
Kraven the Hunter, 152
Krypton, 35, 41, 93, 109–10, 113, 130, 179,
Kryptonite, 67–68, 71
Kurtzberg, Jacob, 144

Lane, Lois, 36, 111–12, 130, 133
Lara (wife of Jor-El), 110
League of Shadows, 94, 122, 160, 163
Lee, Stan, x–xi, xiv, 49–51, 144–45, 238, 257
Legion of Monsters, 236
Lex Luthor, 111, 113
Loki, 11–14, 17, 138, 165–66, 168, 200, 220,
    250–51, 253, 268
Lumberjanes, The, xii, 73–75, 77–79

Maeve, 6, 9
Magneto, 69, 179, 244, 251
Major Bummer (Lou Martin), 70–72
Manphibian, 236
Marvel Cinematic Universe (MCU), 42, 74,
    100, 115–16, 136, 140, 165, 167–69,
    189, 194–97, 204, 211, 216, 221–22,
    224–25, 245, 249–55, 254–55, 266, 267,
    269, 271
Marvel Comics, x, 49–50, 52, 100, 116, 145,
    152, 165, 173, 235

Marvel Zombies, xiv, 241–47
    The Hunger as addiction, 246
    The Hunger as religion, 247
    The Hunger Gospel, 242–43, 245
Metropolis, 111, 113, 130, 132, 134, 204, 209
Miller, Frank, xiii, 44, 70, 159, 229–30, 232
Mind Stone, 166, 189, 192, 245
Miss Teschmacher, 111
Mjölnir, 12, 138, 189–90, 194, 250, 253
Morbius the Living Vampire, 236, 238,
    242–43
Mr. Fantastic (Reed Richards), 238, 241, 247
Ms. Marvel, xi, 245
Multiverse, iii, 165, 169–70, 198, 252
Mysterio (Quentin Beck), 166, 169, 253–255

New Avengers, 155
Nite Owl, 180, 245
Nkrumah, Kwame, 143–44
Nolanverse, 121–22, 127
Non-Proliferation Treaties (NPT), 117–18

Odin, 165, 251, 253
Orion, 259–263
Oz, Wizard of, 165–66, 169
Parker, Aunt May, 30, 243, 251
Parker, Uncle Ben, 27, 30–31, 33, 251
Pennyworth, Alfred, 27, 29–33, 88, 127
Professor X, 69
Punisher, 101, 180, 244–45
Pym, Hank, 245

Quicksilver, ix, 242, 270
Quill, 85–86

Ra's al Ghul, 92, 122–24
    radicalization of America, 232–33
Red Room, xiii, 139–40
Red Skull, 245, 251, 266–67
Rescue (Pepper Potts), 27–28, 31–33
Robin, 74–75, 187
Rocket Racoon, 81, 85–86, 252
Romanoff, Yelena, 139–40
Rommbu, 238
Ronan, 85–86

S.H.I.E.L.D., xiii, 17, 101, 138–39, 141,
    220–22, 234, 266–67, 270

Scarlet Witch (Wanda Maximoff), x, 166, 238, 245, 270

Secret Avengers, 101

Sentry, 243

Shuster, Joe, 67, 111

Siegel, Jerry, 67, 111

similarities of cyber and magic, 196–201

Simon, Joe, 42, 257

Skyfall, 161–63

Sons of Batman, 229

Soul Stone, 138

Sovokia Accords, xii, 115–16, 118–19, 139, 224, 253

Spawn, xi

Spider-Man, 30

Spider-Man (Peter Parker), ix–xi, 27, 30–31, 35, 37–38, 49–50, 52–54, 99–100, 152, 204, 238–39, 243–47, 251–55

Spider-Man 2, 37

Spider-Man: Homecoming, 223

Spider-Man: No Way Home, 239

Sporr, 238

Star Trek, ix, 162, 236

Stark, Howard, 213, 267

Starlight, 5–6, 8–9, 221–22

Stilwell, Madelyn, 4–6

Storm, 179

Superheroes,

    archetypal narrative pattern epic tales, 249–54

    charisma, xiii, 32, 71, 100, 103–05, 108, 112, 251

    common goal, 39, 86

    compassion, 86, 91, 130, 141, 151, 174

    competence, 11–12, 14, 85–86, 109

    conflict and conflict resolution, xi, xiii–xiv, 3, 9, 70, 85, 93, 100–02, 116–18, 123, 130–31, 151, 153–56, 168, 175, 179, 183–84, 190–91, 199–201, 203, 206, 221, 250, 255, 258, 263

    containment, 14, 16, 87, 222

    deception, xiii, 165–70, 243

    decision-making, xii, 3, 5, 7, 16–17, 19, 21–22, 28, 31, 44, 60, 81–82, 85, 93, 108, 110, 116–18, 122, 125, 144, 146–47, 155

    diplomacy, 144, 153

empathy, 19–20, 24, 27, 94, 151, 156, 174, 177, 237–38, 262

ethical fading, 4–5, 7, 10

ethics, ix, xi–xii, 19, 41–42, 45, 115–16, 127, 130, 133, 145, 166, 189–95, 244, 252, 261, 263

fear of failure, 21–23

fear, honor and interest, 131–32, 134

inspirational leadership, xi–xiii, 40, 60, 70, 108–09, 112, 143

intellectual stimulation, 108–09, 112–13

intelligence gathering, xiv, 13, 15, 17, 36, 126, 166–67, 201, 224, 265–71

leadership intent v. reality, 101–04

leadership, xi, xii, xiv, 7, 9, 1, 13, 17, 20–25, 27, 31, 39, 58, 72, 87, 90–91, 100, 102–05, 107–10, 112–13, 129, 131, 143, 175, 177, 203, 205–09, 222, 258, 261, 263, 267

leave no one behind, 85

misfits, 19–20, 24, 65, 73, 75–76, 78, 81–85

mission command, 11, 17

native intelligence, xii, 69, 70, 74, 89, 92–93, 108, 144, 174, 180–81, 183, 203, 241, 253

origins, 43, 65, 253

Permission to Die, 164–65

radicalization, 229–233

redemption, xiii, 136–38, 140–41, 238–239, 244

registration, 101, 105

relatability, xii, 6, 88–89, 237–38

reliability, 85–86

retribution/revenge, 62, 69, 123, 125–27, 130, 161–62, 216, 237

risk assumption, 5, 9, 11, 15–17, 20–22, 71, 81–85, 92, 126, 140, 145, 184, 191, 193, 208, 215, 225, 255, 258, 262, 266

role of narrative, xii, 17, 29, 56, 58–60, 62–63, 67–68, 70, 78, 139, 140, 145, 147, 163, 203, 205–07, 218, 238–39, 249–55, 260

role of regulations, 130, 199, 219–22, 224

role of the sidekick, 31–33

role of trauma, 6, 8, 44, 90–91, 93–94, 111, 137, 158–59, 163, 250–51, 260

rule of law, xii, 8, 9, 101, 117, 121–27, 199, 223–26, 230–33
secrets, xii, 12, 17, 19, 23, 35–39, 52, 61, 92–93, 138, 140–41, 161, 163, 177, 180, 183, 206, 243, 250
sense of community, 38–39, 73, 78, 81–82, 84, 127, 151, 154–56, 207
sincerity, 85–86
social media, 4, 6, 101, 103, 136, 192, 200, 233, 249, 254
teambuilding, 73, 76, 78–79, 176–77
teamwork, 67, 73–74, 76–79
The Challenge of Belonging, 83–84
The Reluctant Leader, 19–25
transactional leadership, 108–09
transformational leadership, 107–08
trust, 11, 13, 14, 23, 29, 31–33, 37–38, 76–79, 84–87, 94, 116, 121–22, 131, 155, 189–90, 221, 230, 249, 259, 261
unity of purpose, 81
Swamp Thing, 198
Syndrome (Buddy Pine), 69

Taskmaster, 140
Tesseract, 11–12, 14, 268, 270
Thanos, 4, 28, 86, 138, 151, 166, 200, 245–46, 270
The Amazing Spider-Man, 30, 53, 169
The Ancient One, 166, 196–97, 199–200
The Avengers, x, xii, 4, 12–17, 42, 47, 49, 53, 66, 73–75, 77, 83–84, 86, 115–16, 118–19, 138–41, 151, 174, 176, 191, 194, 200, 208, 223, 241, 243–44, 252, 257, 270
The Avengers, x–xii, 11, 13, 39, 138, 223, 254
The Boys, 221
The Dark Knight, 29, 88, 125–26, 161–63
The Dark Knight Rises, 121, 163
The Falcon (Sam Wilson), 203, 25, 266, 270–71
The Flash, ix, 91, 93–94, 164, 209
The Hunger Games, xii–xiii, 56–62, 76, 203–09
building a resistance movement, xii, 56–60, 62
Catching Fire, 203
Coin, President Alma, 61–62
Everdeen, Katniss, 59–61, 204

mockingjay as symbol of resistance, 51, 59–62
Mockingjay, 203
operating concepts, 206–07
Panem, 56, 59, 61, 204–05, 207–09
Peeta, 59–60, 205–06, 208
resistance narrative, 56, 58, 60, 62–63
solutions, 209–10
The Incredible Hulk (Bruce Banner), x, 12, 15–17, 51, 74, 116, 173, 189, 197, 199–200, 237, 243, 252, 257
The Mutants, 229
The New 52, 261
The New Gods, xiv, 257–60
Anti-Life Equation, 258–59
Big Barda, 260
Darkseid, 258–63
Free, Scott, 260
Highfather, 258–63
Metron, 259–60, 262–63
nature v. nurture, 259–60
New Genesis, 258–63
The Seven, 3–9
The Snap, 138
The Specials, 65–66, 68, 72
The Suicide Squad, 19–20, 23
The Tick, xii, 41–45
The Vigilante, 24, 159
The Wasp, 243, 247
Thog the Nether-Spawn, 239
Thor Odinson, 253
Thor, ix–xi, 12, 14–16, 39, 86, 116, 138, 155, 165, 173, 179, 189, 196, 198, 235, 244, 250, 252–53, 257–58
Time Stone, 166, 197
Toomes, Adrian, 223
Two-Face (Harvey Dent), 125–26, 229, 231

Ultimate Fantastic Four, 241
Ultron, xiii, 115, 169, 189, 194–95, 197
Unbeatable Squirrel Girl (Doreen Green), xiii, 151–56, 173–77
Brain Drain, 152, 155
Chipmunk Hunk, 155, 173, 175
Hippo the Hippo, 152, 174
Koi Boi, 155, 173, 176
Tippy-Toe, 152–54, 156, 173–74

Vanko, Ivan, 12, 214
Vibranium, xiii, 143, 147
Vought International, 3–10, 221

Wakanda, 115, 144–47
WandaVision, 166
Warrior Nun, 250
Watchmen, xiii, 179–80, 184–85
    Dr. Manhattan (Jon Osterman), 180,
        184–85
    Ozymandias (Adrian Veidt), xiii, 179–85
    Rorschach, 180, 185

Watson, Mary Jane, 37
Werewolf by Night, 236
Winter Soldier (Bucky Barnes), xiv, 223,
    265–67, 269, 271
Wolverine, 74, 147, 242, 244
Wonder Woman, ix, xii, 3, 39, 93–94, 132–34,
    198, 207

X-Men, x, 38, 49, 67, 69, 74–75, 77, 176,
    250–51, 257

Zatanna Zatara, 198